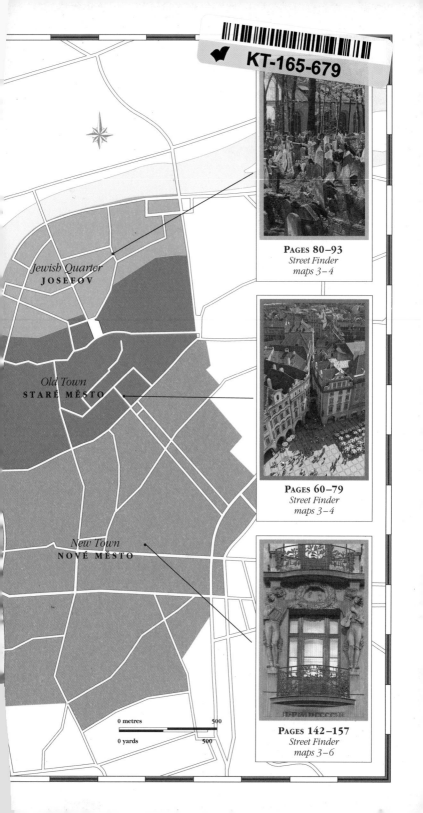

KT-165-679

Jewish Quarter
JOSEFOV

Old Town
STARÉ MĚSTO

New Town
NOVÉ MĚSTO

PAGES 80–93
*Street Finder
maps 3–4*

PAGES 60–79
*Street Finder
maps 3–4*

PAGES 142–157
*Street Finder
maps 3–6*

0 metres   500

0 yards   500

EYEWITNESS *TRAVEL GUIDES*

PRAGUE

EYEWITNESS *TRAVEL GUIDES*

PRAGUE

Main Contributor: VLADIMÍR SOUKUP

DK

DORLING KINDERSLEY
LONDON • NEW YORK • STUTTGART

A DORLING KINDERSLEY BOOK

PROJECT EDITOR Heather Jones
ART EDITOR Lisa Kosky
EDITORS Ferdie McDonald, Carey Combe
DESIGNERS Louise Parsons, Nicki Rawson
CONSULTANT Helena Svojsikova
LANGUAGE CONSULTANT Jake Reimann

MANAGING EDITOR Carolyn Ryden
MANAGING ART EDITOR Steve Knowlden
SENIOR EDITOR Georgina Matthews
SENIOR ART EDITOR Vanessa Courtier
EDITORIAL DIRECTOR David Lamb
ART DIRECTOR Anne-Marie Bulat

PRODUCTION CONTROLLER Hilary Stephens
PICTURE RESEARCH Ellen Root
DTP DESIGNER Salim Qurashi

CONTRIBUTORS
Petr David, Vladimír Dobrovodský, Nicholas Lowry,
Polly Phillimore, Joy Turner-Kadečková

MAPS
Caroline Bowie, Simon Farbrother, James Mills-Hicks, David Pugh
(Dorling Kindersley Cartography)

PHOTOGRAPHERS
Jiří Doležal, Jiří Kopřiva, Vladimír Kozlík, František Přeučil,
Milan Posselt, Stanislav Tereba, Peter Wilson

ILLUSTRATORS
Gillie Newman, Chris Orr, Otakar Pok, Jaroslav Staněk

•

This book was produced with the assistance of
Olympia Publishing House, Prague.

Film outputting bureau PLS, London
Reproduced by Colourscan, Singapore
Printed and bound by G. Canale & C. (Italy)

First published in Great Britain in 1994
by Dorling Kindersley Limited
9 Henrietta Street, London WC2E 8PS
Reprinted with revisions 1994, 1995

Copyright 1994, 1995 © Dorling Kindersley Limited, London

•

Every effort has been made to ensure that the information in this book is as
up-to-date as possible at the time of going to press. However, details such
as telephone numbers, opening hours, prices, gallery hanging arrangements
and travel information are liable to change. The publishers cannot accept
responsibility for any consequences arising from the use of this book.

We would be delighted to receive any corrections and suggestions for
incorporation in the next edition. Please write to the Managing Editor,
Eyewitness Travel Guides, Dorling Kindersley,
9 Henrietta Street, London WC2E 8PS.

CONTENTS

Rudolph II (1576–1612)

INTRODUCING
PRAGUE

Outdoor café tables

Wallenstein Palace and Garden in the Little Quarter

Church of Our Lady before Týn

Fiacre, Old Town Square

Czech beer-bottle top

Baroque façades of houses at the eastern end of Old Town Square

HOW TO USE THIS GUIDE

THIS EYEWITNESS Travel Guide helps you get the most from your stay in Prague with the minimum of difficulty. The opening section, *Introducing Prague*, locates the city geographically, sets modern Prague in its historical context and describes events through the entire year. *Prague at a Glance* is an overview of the city's main attractions, including a feature on the River Vltava. Section two, *Prague Area by Area*, starts on page 58. This is

Planning the day's itinerary in Prague

the main sightseeing section, which covers all the important sights, with photographs, maps and drawings. It also includes day trips from Prague and four guided walks around the city.

Carefully researched tips for hotels, restaurants, shops and markets, cafés and bars, entertainment and sports are found in *Travellers' Needs*. The last section, the *Survival Guide*, contains useful practical advice on all you need to know, from making a telephone call to using the public transport system.

FINDING YOUR WAY AROUND THE SIGHTSEEING SECTION

Each of the five sightseeing areas in the city is colour-coded for easy reference. Every chapter opens with an introduction to the part of Prague it covers, describing its history and character, followed by a Street-by-Street map illustrating the heart of the area. Finding your way around each chapter is made simple by the numbering system used throughout. The most important sights are covered in detail in two or more full pages.

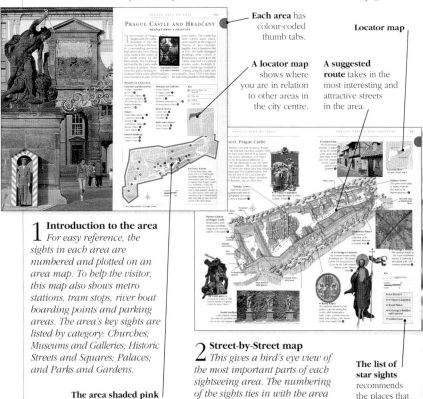

Each area has colour-coded thumb tabs.

A locator map shows where you are in relation to other areas in the city centre.

A suggested route takes in the most interesting and attractive streets in the area.

Locator map

1 **Introduction to the area**
For easy reference, the sights in each area are numbered and plotted on an area map. To help the visitor, this map also shows metro stations, tram stops, river boat boarding points and parking areas. The area's key sights are listed by category: Churches; Museums and Galleries; Historic Streets and Squares; Palaces; and Parks and Gardens.

The area shaded pink is shown in greater detail on the Street-by-Street map on the following pages.

2 **Street-by-Street map**
This gives a bird's eye view of the most important parts of each sightseeing area. The numbering of the sights ties in with the area map and the fuller descriptions on the pages that follow.

The list of star sights recommends the places that no visitor should miss.

PRAGUE AREA MAP

THE COLOURED AREAS shown in
this map *(see inside front
cover)* are the five main sightseeing
areas – each covered in a full
chapter in *Prague Area by Area
(pp58–157)*. They are highlighted
on other maps throughout the
book. In *Prague at a Glance
(pp36–57)*, for example, they
help locate the top sights. They
are also used to show some of
the top restaurants in *Travellers'
Needs (pp192–3)* and to plot the
routes of the river trip *(p54)* and
the four guided walks *(p170)*.

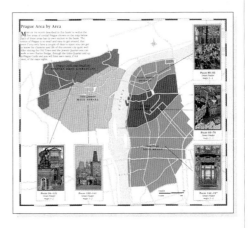

Numbers refer to each
sight's position on the
area map and its place
in the chapter.

Practical information lists all the information
you need to visit every sight, including a map
reference to the *Street Finder (pp244–9)*.

Façades of important
buildings are often
shown to help you
recognize them quickly.

The visitors' checklist
provides all the practical
information needed
to plan your visit.

3 Detailed information on each sight

*All the important sights in Prague are
described individually. They are listed
in order, following the numbering on
the area map. Practical information on
opening hours, telephone numbers,
admission charges and facilities
available is given for each sight. The
key to the symbols used can be found
on the back flap.*

A timeline
charts the key
events in the
history of the
building.

4 Prague's major sights

*Historic buildings are
dissected to reveal their
interiors; and museums and
galleries have colour-coded
floorplans to help you find
important exhibits.*

Stars indicate
the features
no visitor
should miss.

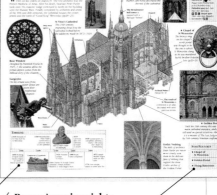

INTRODUCING
PRAGUE

Putting Prague on the Map

Prague has a population of just over 1 million and covers 500 sq km (200 sq miles) at its outer limits. It is the capital of the newly-formed Czech Republic and head of the region of Bohemia. Prague's geographical position at the centre of Europe makes it a convenient base from which to visit both the Bohemian countryside and many other major cities, such as Nuremberg, Vienna, Bratislava and Budapest.

View looking southwest over the Vltava

Europe
The Czech Republic, right at the heart of continental Europe, is completely landlocked. Prague, the capital, has one airport and road and rail links to neighbouring countries.

PRAGUE AND ENVIRONS

Veltrusy

Neratovice

Lysá n. Labem

Slaný

Kralupy n. Vltavou

Brandýs n. Labem-Stará Boleslav

Švermov

Roztoky

Čakovice

Čelákovice

Kladno

See next page

Horní Počernice

Ruzyně

Unhošť

Úvaly

Český Brod

Rudná

Říčany

Beroun

Zbraslav

Karlštejn

Jílové u Prahy

0 km   10

0 miles   5

POLAND

Oder

Warsaw

Breslau

Elbe

Prague and Environs

Most sights are in the central, historic area of Prague. These are covered in detail on pages 58–157. Important sights outside the centre and day trips can be found on pages 160–69. For road and rail networks, see pages 230–31.

CZECH REPUBLIC

Cracow

Ostrava

Brno

Morava

Aerial view of Greater Prague

VIENNA

SLOVAKIA

BRATISLAVA

Váh

BUDAPEST

HUNGARY

Rába

Lake Balaton

0 kilometres   50

0 miles   30

Zagreb

KEY

☐ Greater Prague

✈ Airport

═ Motorway

═ Major road

── Railway line

-·- Country boundary

Greater Prague

THE CITY OF PRAGUE IS MADE UP of five ancient towns (see pp54–169) with the Vltava, a tributary of the Elbe, running through the centre. In 1922 the greater Prague conurbation was formed. It incorporated 37 other districts and suburbs of central Bohemia. The greater Prague area is well served by public transport systems.

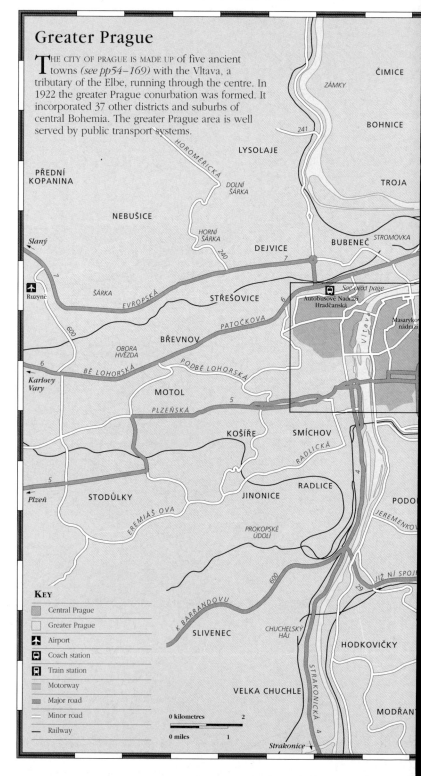

ČIMICE

ZÁMKY

BOHNICE

LYSOLAJE

PŘEDNÍ
KOPANINA

DOLNÍ
ŠÁRKA

TROJA

NEBUŠICE

HORNÍ
ŠÁRKA

Slaný

DEJVICE

BUBENEČ STROMOVKA

Ruzyně

ŠÁRKA

EVROPSKÁ

STŘEŠOVICE

See next page

Autobusové Nádraží
Hradčanská

PATOČKOVA

Masarykovo
nádraží

OBORA
HVĚZDA

BŘEVNOV

BĚ LOHORSKÁ

PODBĚ LOHORSKÁ

Karlovy
Vary

MOTOL

PLZEŇSKÁ

KOŠÍŘE

SMÍCHOV

RADLICKÁ

Plzeň

STODŮLKY

JINONICE

RADLICE

PODO

JEREMENKOV

JEREMIÁŠOVA

PROKOPSKÉ
ÚDOLÍ

JIŽ NÍ SPOJ

K BARRANDOVU

KEY

▨	Central Prague
▢	Greater Prague
✈	Airport
🚌	Coach station
🚆	Train station
▬	Motorway
▬	Major road
—	Minor road
—	Railway

CHUCHELSKÝ
HÁJ

SLIVENEC

HODKOVIČKY

VELKA CHUCHLE

MODŘAN

STRAKONICKÁ

0 kilometres 2

0 miles 1

Strakonice

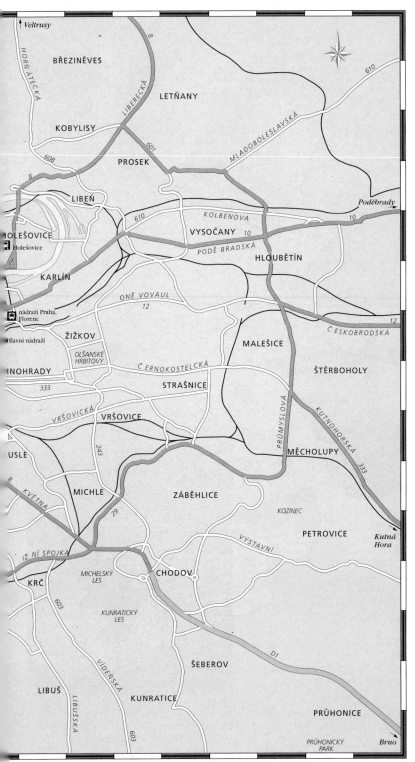

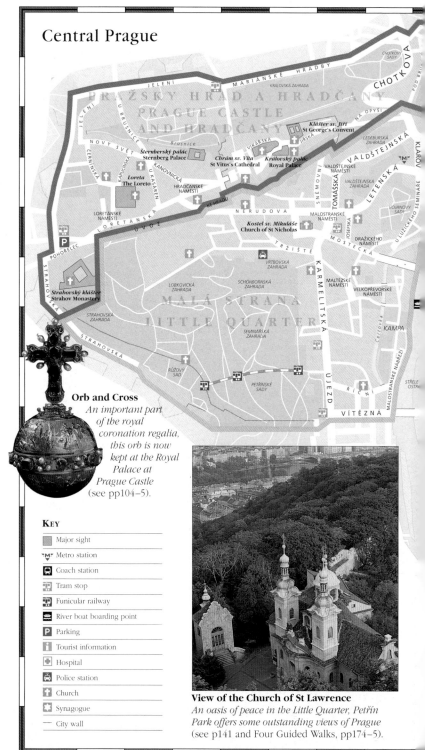

Central Prague

Orb and Cross
*An important part
of the royal
coronation regalia,
this orb is now
kept at the Royal
Palace at
Prague Castle*
(see pp104–5).

KEY

	Major sight
M	Metro station
	Coach station
	Tram stop
	Funicular railway
	River boat boarding point
P	Parking
	Tourist information
	Hospital
	Police station
	Church
	Synagogue
—	City wall

View of the Church of St Lawrence
*An oasis of peace in the Little Quarter, Petřín
Park offers some outstanding views of Prague*
(see p141 and Four Guided Walks, pp174–5).

Painted House Façade
The Old Town has many Gothic and Baroque houses. Some have colourful mural paintings like this one in Old Town Square (see pp66–9).

Art Nouveau Statue
The New Town has many examples of Art Nouveau architecture (see pp148–9).

0 metres   200
0 yards   200

THE HISTORY OF PRAGUE

Prague coat of arms

PRAGUE'S POSITION at the crossroads of Europe has made it a magnet for foreign traders since pre-recorded times. By the early 10th century it had developed into a thriving town with a large market place (the Old Town Square) and two citadels (Prague Castle and Vyšehrad), from where its first rulers, the Přemyslids, conducted their many family feuds. These were often bloody: in 935, Prince Wenceslas was savagely murdered by his brother Boleslav. Wenceslas was later canonized and became Bohemia's best-known patron saint.

During the Middle Ages Prague enjoyed a golden age, especially during the reign of the Holy Roman Emperor, Charles IV. Under the auspices of this wise and cultured king, Prague grew into a magnificent city, larger than Paris or London. Charles instigated the founding and building of many institutions, including the first University of Central Europe in Prague. The University's first Czech rector was Jan Hus, the reforming preacher whose execution for alleged heresy in 1415 led to the Hussite wars. The radical wing of the Hussites, the Taborites, were finally defeated at the Battle of Lipany in 1434. During the 16th century, after a succession of weak kings, the Austrian Habsburgs took over, beginning a rule that would last for almost 400 years. One of the more enlightened of all the Habsburg Emperors was Rudolph II. He brought the spirit of the Renaissance to Prague through his love of the arts and sciences. Soon after his death, in 1618, Prague was the setting for the Protestant revolt which led to the 30 Years' War. Its aftermath brought a serious decline in the fortunes of a city that would revive only in the 18th century. Prague's many fine Baroque churches and palaces date from this time.

The 19th century saw a period of national revival and the burgeoning of civic pride. The great public monuments – the National Museum, the National Theatre and Rudolfinum – were built. But a foreign power still ruled the city, and it was not until 1918 that Prague became the capital of an independent Republic. World War II brought occupation by the German army, followed by four decades of Communism. After the "Velvet Revolution" of 1989, Prague is today on the threshold of a new era.

View of Prague Castle and Little Quarter, 1493

◁ *St Wenceslas and St Vitus*, by Bartholomaeus Spränger, about 1600

Rulers of Prague

Three great dynasties have shaped the history of Prague: the Přemyslids, the Luxemburgs and the Habsburgs. According to Slav legend, the Přemyslids were founded by Princess Libuše *(see p21)*. Her line included St Wenceslas and Přemysl Otakar II, whose death on the battlefield at Marchfeld paved the way for the Luxemburgs. This family produced one of Prague's greatest rulers, Charles IV, who was King of Bohemia and Holy Roman Emperor *(see pp24–5)*. In 1526, the city came under the control of the Austrian House of Habsburg whose rule lasted 400 years, until 28 October 1918, when Czechoslovakia gained its independence. Since then there has been a succession of presidents.

The mythical Princess Libuše

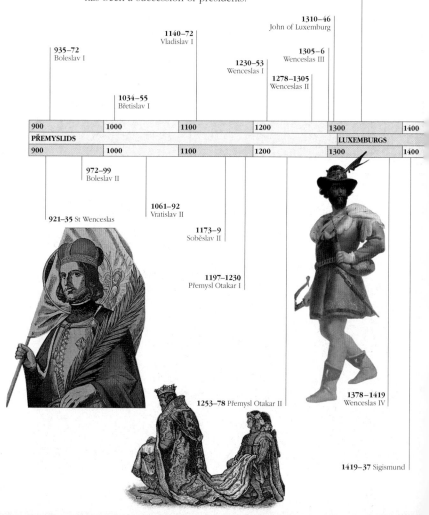

| **1346–78** Charles IV |
| **1453–** Ladisla Posthumu |
| **1310–46** John of Luxemburg |
| **1140–72** Vladislav I |
| **1305–6** Wenceslas III |
| **935–72** Boleslav I |
| **1230–53** Wenceslas I |
| **1278–1305** Wenceslas II |
| **1034–55** Břetislav I |

900	1000	1100	1200	1300	1400
PŘEMYSLIDS				**LUXEMBURGS**	
900	1000	1100	1200	1300	1400

972–99 Boleslav II

1061–92 Vratislav II

921–35 St Wenceslas

1173–9 Soběslav II

1197–1230 Přemysl Otakar I

1253–78 Přemysl Otakar II

1378–1419 Wenceslas IV

1419–37 Sigismund

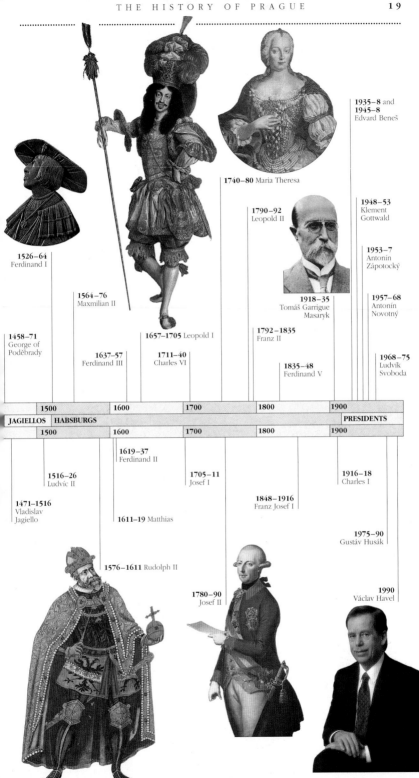

1935–8 and **1945–8** Edvard Beneš

1740–80 Maria Theresa

1948–53 Klement Gottwald

1790–92 Leopold II

1953–7 Antonín Zápotocký

1526–64 Ferdinand I

1918–35 Tomáš Garrigue Masaryk

1957–68 Antonín Novotný

1564–76 Maxmilian II

1657–1705 Leopold I

1792–1835 Franz II

1458–71 George of Poděbrady

1637–57 Ferdinand III

1711–40 Charles VI

1835–48 Ferdinand V

1968–75 Ludvík Svoboda

1500	1600	1700	1800	1900	
JAGIELLOS	HABSBURGS				PRESIDENTS
1500	1600	1700	1800	1900	

1619–37 Ferdinand II

1516–26 Ludvík II

1705–11 Josef I

1916–18 Charles I

1471–1516 Vladislav Jagiello

1848–1916 Franz Josef I

1611–19 Matthias

1975–90 Gustáv Husák

1576–1611 Rudolph II

1780–90 Josef II

1990 Václav Havel

Prague under the Přemyslids

EARLY CELTIC TRIBES, from 500 BC, were the first inhabitants of the area around the Vltava valley. The Germanic Marcomans arrived in 9–6 BC, and gradually the Celts left. The first Slavic tribes came to Bohemia in about 500 AD. Struggles for supremacy led to the emergence of a ruling dynasty, the Přemyslids, around 800 AD.

9th-century earring

They built two fortified settlements: the first at Prague Castle *(see pp94–110)*, the second at Vyšehrad, a rocky headland on the right bank of the Vltava *(see pp178–9)*. These remained the seats of Czech princes for hundreds of years. One prince crucial to the emerging Czech State was the pious Wenceslas. He enjoyed only a brief reign but left an important legacy in the founding of St Vitus's rotunda *(see p102)*.

EXTENT OF THE CITY
▨ *1000 AD*   ☐ *Today*

St Cyril and St Methodius
Originally Greeks from Salonica, these two brothers brought Christianity to Moravia in about 863. They baptized early Přemyslid, Bořivoj, and his wife Ludmilla, grandmother of St Wenceslas.

Boleslav's henchman raises his sword to strike the fatal blow.

Second assassin grapples with the Prince's companion.

Early Coin
Silver coins like this denar were minted in the royal mint of Vyšehrad during Boleslav II's reign from 967–99.

Wild Boar Figurine
Celtic tribes made small talismans of the wild animals that they hunted for food in the forested areas around Prague.

TIMELINE

Bronze head of a Celtic goddess

623–658 Bohemia is part of an empire formed by Frankish merchant, Samo

	600 AD		700

500 BC
Celts in Bohemia. Joined by Germanic Marcomans in 1st century AD

6th century
Slavs settle alongside Germanic tribes in Bohemia

8th century
Tribe of Czechs settle in central Bohemia

Vyšehrad acropolis – first Czech settlement on the right bank of the Vltava

Sword and Helmet
St Wenceslas was buried in the southern apse of the rotunda of St Vitus. His sword and helmet were preserved as relics and today form part of the Cathedral's treasure.

Wenceslas seeks sanctuary.

A monk opens the door for Wenceslas.

PRINCESS LIBUŠE

The legendary founder of the Přemyslids was Princess Libuše, head of a West Slavic tribe. She took notice of the discord among her clansmen, who were tired of being ruled traditionally by women. Choosing a humble plough-man (*přemysl*) as consort and ruler, she began a dynasty that was to last 400 years.

Princess Libuše foresaw the glory of Prague in a vision

Rotunda of St Vitus
Founded by Wenceslas in the early 10th century, the rotunda became a place of pilgrimage after the saint's death in 935. It stood where St Wenceslas Chapel is today.

Roman-arched windows

Curving stone walls

ASSASSINATION OF PRINCE WENCESLAS

In 935, the young Wenceslas was murdered on the orders of his brother, Boleslav. This manuscript illustration of 1006 shows the moment when the assassins caught up with the prince as he was about to enter the church for the morning mass.

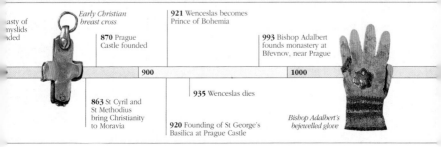

Early Christian breast cross

asty of nyslids ded

870 Prague Castle founded

921 Wenceslas becomes Prince of Bohemia

993 Bishop Adalbert founds monastery at Břevnov, near Prague

900　　1000

863 St Cyril and St Methodius bring Christianity to Moravia

935 Wenceslas dies

920 Founding of St George's Basilica at Prague Castle

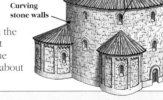

Bishop Adalbert's bejewelled glove

Early Medieval Prague

Prague Castle steadily grew in importance from the beginning of the 12th century onwards. Prone to frequent fires, its wooden buildings were gradually replaced by stone and the area developed into a sturdy Romanesque fortress with a palace and religious buildings. Clustered around the original outer bailey was an area inhabited by skilled craftsmen and German merchants, encouraged to come and stay in Prague by Vladislav II and, later, Přemysl Otakar II. This came to be known as the "Little Quarter" and achieved town status in 1257. It was joined to the Old Town by a bridge, known as the Judith Bridge.

Initial letter D from the Vyšehrad Codex

EXTENT OF THE CITY

▨ 1230   ☐ Today

St George's Convent and Basilica *(see pp106–9 and p98)*

PRAGUE CASTLE IN 1230

Sited on a high ridge, the Romanesque fortress had protective stone walls and easily-guarded gates.

The Prince's Palace grew into the Royal Palace *(see pp104–5).*

The White Tower gave access from the west.

Entrance from Old Town

Decorative Comb
This ornate, bone, fine-toothed comb was one of the relics of St Adalbert.

Site of Hradčany Square

External staircase

Living room

Vaulted ceiling

Ground floor

Romanesque Stone House
These three-storeyed houses were based around a very simple floor plan.

St Vitus's Basilica and Chapter House *(see pp100–3)*

Stone houses were built on what is now Nerudova Street in the Little Quarter *(see p130).*

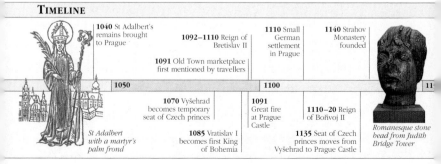

TIMELINE

1040 St Adalbert's remains brought to Prague	**1092–1110** Reign of Bretislav II	**1110** Small German settlement in Prague	**1140** Strahov Monastery founded
	1091 Old Town marketplace first mentioned by travellers		

1050 ... **1100** ... **11**

St Adalbert with a martyr's palm frond	**1070** Vyšehrad becomes temporary seat of Czech princes	**1091** Great fire at Prague Castle	**1110–20** Reign of Bořivoj II
	1085 Vratislav I becomes first King of Bohemia	**1135** Seat of Czech princes moves from Vyšehrad to Prague Castle	*Romanesque stone head from Judith Bridge Tower*

St Agnes
Sister of Wenceslas I, this devout woman built a convent for the order of the Poor Clares (the female counterparts of the Franciscans) (see pp92–3). She was not canonized until 1989.

WHERE TO SEE ROMANESQUE PRAGUE

Remains can be seen in the crypt of St Vitus's *(pp100–3)*, the basements of the Palace of the Lords of Kunštát *(p78)* and the Royal Palace *(pp104–5)*.

St George's Basilica
The vaulting in the crypt dates from the 12th century (p98).

The Black Tower was the exit to Bohemia's second town, Kutná Hora *(see p168)*.

Vratislav II
The Vyšehrad Codex, an illuminated selection from the gospels, was made to mark Vratislav's coronation in 1061.

Little Quarter Square

St Martin's Rotunda
This well-preserved building is in Vyšehrad (p179).

Přemysl Otakar II
The last great Přemyslid king was killed in battle after trying to carve out a huge empire.

Little Quarter Coat of Arms
Vladislav II's portrait was incorporated into this 12th-century miniature painting.

1233 Founding of St Agnes's Convent

1182 Romanesque construction of Prague Castle completed

1257 Little Quarter receives town status

1258–68 Strahov Monastery rebuilt in Gothic style after fire

1200　　　　　　　**1250**　　　　　　　**1290**

1212 Přemysl Otakar I receives the Sicilian Golden Bull, confirming the sovereignty of Bohemian kings

Sicilian Golden Bull

1278 Přemysl Otakar II dies at Marchfeld

1158 Judith Bridge built *(see pp136–9)*

Prague's Golden Age

IN THE LATE MIDDLE AGES, Prague attained the height of its glory. The Holy Roman Emperor, Charles IV, chose Prague as his Imperial residence and set out to make the city the most magnificent in Europe. He founded a university (the Carolinum) and built many fine churches and monasteries in the Gothic style. Of major importance were his town-planning schemes, such as the

Gift from Pope Urban V in 1368

reconstruction of Prague Castle, the building of a new stone bridge to replace the Judith Bridge, and the foundation of a new quarter, the New Town. A devout Catholic, he owned a large collection of relics which were kept, along with the Crown Jewels, at Karlstein Castle *(see pp166–7).*

EXTENT OF THE CITY

☐ 1350   ☐ Today

Charles IV wears the Imperial crown, set with sapphires, rubies and pearls.

St Wenceslas Chapel
Proud of his direct descent from the Přemyslids, Charles had this shrine to St Wenceslas built in St Vitus's Cathedral (see pp100–3).

The Emperor places the piece of the cross in its reliquary.

St Wenceslas Crown
Worn by Charles at his coronation in 1347, the Bohemian crown was based on early Přemyslid insignia.

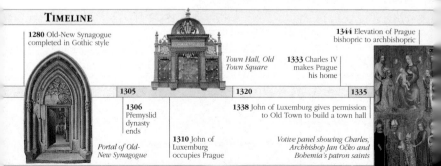

TIMELINE

1280 Old-New Synagogue completed in Gothic style

Town Hall, Old Town Square

1333 Charles IV makes Prague his home

1344 Elevation of Prague bishopric to archbishopric

1305	1320	1335

1306 Přemyslid dynasty ends

1310 John of Luxemburg occupies Prague

Portal of Old-New Synagogue

1338 John of Luxemburg gives permission to Old Town to build a town hall

Votive panel showing Charles, Archbishop Jan Očko and Bohemia's patron saints

St Vitus by Master Theodoric
This is one of a series of paintings of saints by the great Bohemian artist for the Holy Rood Chapel at Karlstein Castle (c1365).

A jewelled reliquary cross was made to house the new relic.

University Seal, 1348
The seal depicts the Emperor offering the foundation documents to St Wenceslas.

Building the New Town
This manuscript records Charles IV supervising the building of the New Town during the 14th century.

CHARLES IV AND HIS RELICS

Charles collected holy relics from all over the Empire. In about 1357 he received a part of Christ's cross from the Dauphin. This mural in Karlstein Castle is thought to be the best likeness of the Emperor.

WHERE TO SEE GOTHIC PRAGUE

Prague's rich Gothic legacy includes three of its best-known sights – St Vitus's Cathedral (pp100–3), Charles Bridge (pp136–9) and the Old-New Synagogue (pp88–9). Another very important building from Charles IV's reign is the Carolinum (p65). Churches that have retained most of their original Gothic features include the Church of Our Lady before Týn (p70).

Carolinum
This fine oriel window was part of the university (p65).

Old Town Bridge Tower
The sculptural decoration is by Peter Parler (p139).

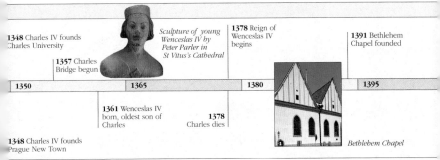

1348 Charles IV founds Charles University

1357 Charles Bridge begun

Sculpture of young Wenceslas IV by Peter Parler in St Vitus's Cathedral

1378 Reign of Wenceslas IV begins

1391 Bethlehem Chapel founded

1350	1365	1380	1395

1348 Charles IV founds Prague New Town

1361 Wenceslas IV born, oldest son of Charles

1378 Charles dies

Bethlehem Chapel

Hussite Prague

IN THE EARLY 15TH CENTURY, Europe shook in fear of an incredible fighting force -- the Hussites, followers of the reformist cleric, Jan Hus. Despite simple weapons, they achieved legendary military successes against the Emperor's Catholic crusades, due largely to their religious fervour and to the discipline of their brilliant leader, Jan Žižka, who

George of Poděbrady

invented mobile artillery. The Hussites split into two camps, the moderate "Utraquists" *(see p75)* and the radical "Taborites" who were finally defeated at the Battle of Lipany in 1434, paving the way for the moderate Hussite king, George of Poděbrady.

EXTENT OF THE CITY

☐ 1500   ☐ Today

Nobles' Letter of Protest
Several hundred seals of the Bohemian nobility were affixed to a letter protesting about the execution of Jan Hus.

GOD'S WARRIORS
The early-16th-century Codex of Jena illustrated the Hussite successes. Here the Hussites, who included artisans and barons, are shown singing their hymn, with their blind leader, Jan Žižka.

Jan Žižka

The priest held a gilded monstrance.

War Machine
For maximum effect, farm waggons were tied together to form a shield. A chilling array of weapons were unleashed including crossbows, flails and an early form of howitzer.

Satan Dressed as a Priest
Lurid images satirizing the corruption of the church were painted on placards and carried through the streets.

The banner was decorated with the Hussite chalice.

A variety of farm implements were used as makeshift weapons by the peasants.

Hussite Shield
Wooden shields like this one that bears the arms of the city of Prague, were used to fill any gaps in the waggon fortress's tight formation.

The peasant army marched behind Jan Žižka.

REFORMER, JAN HUS

Born to poor parents in a small Bohemian town, Jan Hus became one of the most important religious thinkers of his day. His objections to the Catholic Church's corrupt practices, opulent style and wealth were shared by many Czechs – nobles and peasants alike. His reformist preaching in Prague's Bethlehem Chapel earned him a huge following, noticed by the Roman Papacy, and Hus was excommunicated. In 1412 Wenceslas IV, brother of the Emperor Sigismund, asked him to leave Prague. In October 1414, Hus decided to defend his teaching at the Council of Constance. Even though he had the Emperor's safe conduct, he was put in prison. The following year he was declared a heretic and burned at the stake.

Jan Hus at the Stake in 1415
After suffering death at the hands of the Church on 6 July 1415, Jan Hus became a revered martyr of the Czech people.

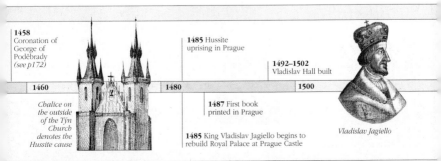

1458 Coronation of George of Poděbrady *(see p172)*

Chalice on the outside of the Týn Church denotes the Hussite cause

1485 Hussite uprising in Prague

1492–1502 Vladislav Hall built

1487 First book printed in Prague

1485 King Vladislav Jagiello begins to rebuild Royal Palace at Prague Castle

1460	1480	1500

Vladislav Jagiello

The Renaissance and Rudolph II

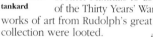

WITH THE ACCESSION of the Habsburgs, the Renaissance reached Prague. Art and architecture were dominated by the Italians who enjoyed the patronage of the Imperial court, especially that of Rudolph II. The eccentric Rudolph often neglected politics, preferring to indulge his passions for collecting and science. His court was a haven for artists, astrologers, astronomers and alchemists, but his erratic rule led to revolts and an attempt by his brother Matthias to usurp him. In the course of the Thirty Years' War *(see pp30 –31)* many works of art from Rudolph's great collection were looted.

Renaissance tankard

EXTENT OF THE CITY
- [ ] 1550
- [ ] *Today*

Fish pond

Dalibor Tower

Belvedere

Pergola

Rudolph II
A connoisseur of the bizarre, Rudolph was delighted by this vegetable portrait by Giuseppe Arcimboldo (1590).

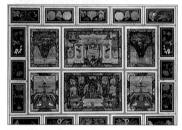

Orchard

Formal flower beds

Lion House

Mosaic Desk Top
Renaissance table tops with Florentine themes of fountains and gardens were made at Rudolph's court in semi-precious stones.

Rabbi Löw
A revered Jewish sage, he was said to have invented an artificial man (see pp88–9).

TIMELINE

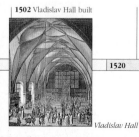

1502 Vladislav Hall built

1526 Habsburg rule begins with Ferdinand I

1541 Great fire in Little Quarter, the Castle and Hradčany

1556 Ferdinand I invites Jesuits to Prague

1520   1540   1560

Ferdinand I

1538–63 Belvedere built

1547 Unsuccessful uprising of towns of Prague against Ferdinand I

Vladislav Hall

Charter for manglers and dyers

Sense of Sight
Jan Brueghel's allegorical painting shows the extent of Rudolph II's huge collection – from globes to paintings, jewels and scientific instruments.

Ball Game Hall

Tycho Brahe
The Danish astronomer spent his last years living in Prague.

A covered bridge connected the Palace to the garden.

ROYAL PALACE GARDENS
No longer a medieval fortress, Prague Castle and its gardens were given over to the pleasure of the King. Here Rudolph enjoyed ball games, exotic plants and his menagerie.

WHERE TO SEE RENAISSANCE PRAGUE
The Royal Garden *(p111)* preserves much of the spirit of Renaissance Prague. Paintings and objects from Rudolph's collections can be seen in the Sternberg Palace *(pp112–15)*, the Picture Gallery of Prague Castle *(p98)* and the Museum of Decorative Arts *(p84)*.

At the Two Golden Bears
Built in 1590, the house is famous for its symmetrical, carved doorway, one of the most graceful in Prague (p71).

Belvedere
The palace is decorated with stone reliefs by Italian architect, Paolo della Stella (p110).

Ball Game Hall
Beautiful Renaissance sgraffito covers the façade of this building in the Royal Garden, but it has been heavily restored (p111).

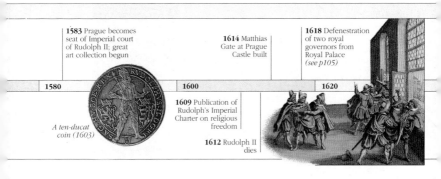

1583 Prague becomes seat of Imperial court of Rudolph II; great art collection begun

1614 Matthias Gate at Prague Castle built

1618 Defenestration of two royal governors from Royal Palace *(see p105)*

1580

1600

1620

A ten-ducat coin (1603)

1609 Publication of Rudolph's Imperial Charter on religious freedom

1612 Rudolph II dies

Baroque Prague

I N 1619 THE CZECH NOBLES deposed Habsburg Emperor
Ferdinand II as King of Bohemia and elected instead
Frederick of the Palatinate. The following year they paid
for their defiance at the Battle of the White Mountain,
the beginning of the Thirty Years' War. There followed
a period of persecution of all non-Catholics, accompanied
by the systematic Germanization of the country's
institutions. The leaders in the fight against Protestantism
were the Jesuits and one of their most powerful
weapons was the restoration of Prague's churches in
the new architecture of
the Baroque, coupled
with the building of
many new churches.

EXTENT OF THE CITY

▨ *1750*   ☐ *Today*

A sculpture of Atlas
(1722) adorns the
top of the tower.

Mirror Chapel

Church of St Nicholas
*This outstanding High
Baroque church in the
Little Quarter was the
work of the great
Dientzenhofers
(see pp128–9).*

**Grape
Courtyard**

Measuring
the World
*Some monasteries were
seats of learning. Strahov (see
pp120–21) had two libraries built,
decorated with Baroque painting. This
fresco detail is in the Philosophical Hall.*

**Holy Saviour
Church**

TIMELINE

1620 Battle of the
White Mountain

1627 Beginning of
Counter-Reformation
committee in Prague

*Old Town coat of arms –
embellished with the Imperial
eagle and 12 flags in
recognition of the defence of
the city against the Swedes*

1706–14
Decoration of
Charles Bridge
with statues

1625	1645	1665	1685	1705

1621
Execution in
Old Town
Square of 27
Protestant
leaders

1634
Wallenstein
killed by Irish
mercenaries

1631 Saxon
occupation of Prague

1648 Swedes occupy Prague
Castle. Treaty of Westphalia
and end of Thirty Years' War

1676–8
New bastions
built to fortify
Vyšehrad

1704–53
Building of
Church of
St Nicholas
in the Little
Quarter

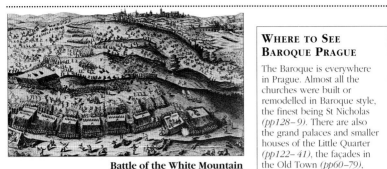

Battle of the White Mountain
In 1620 the Czech army was defeated by Habsburg troops at Bílá Hora (White Mountain), a hill northwest of Prague (see p163). After the battle, Bohemia became a de facto province of Austria.

Observatory
Tower

St Clement's Church
gave its name to the whole complex.

Italian Chapel

Monstrance
Baroque monstrances – used to display the communion host – became increasingly elaborate and ornate (see pp116–17).

CLEMENTINUM
The Jesuits exercised enormous power over education. Between 1653 and 1723 they built this College. It was the largest complex of buildings after Prague Castle and included three churches, smaller chapels, libraries, lecture halls and an observatory.

WHERE TO SEE BAROQUE PRAGUE
The Baroque is everywhere in Prague. Almost all the churches were built or remodelled in Baroque style, the finest being St Nicholas *(pp128–9)*. There are also the grand palaces and smaller houses of the Little Quarter *(pp122–41)*, the façades in the Old Town *(pp60–79)*, and statues on churches, street corners and along the parapets of Charles Bridge.

Nerudova Street
At the Golden Cup, No. 16, has preserved its typical Baroque house sign (p130).

Charles Bridge
This statue of St Francis Borgia by Ferdinand Brokof was added in 1710 (pp136–9).

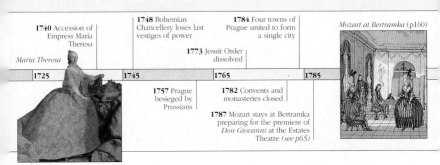

1740 Accession of Empress Maria Theresa

Maria Theresa

1748 Bohemian Chancellery loses last vestiges of power

1773 Jesuit Order dissolved

1784 Four towns of Prague united to form a single city

Mozart at Bertramka (p160)

1725   1745   1765   1785

1757 Prague besieged by Prussians

1782 Convents and monasteries closed

1787 Mozart stays at Bertramka preparing for the premiere of *Don Giovanni* at the Estates Theatre *(see p65)*

The National Revival in Prague

Emperor Franz Josef

THE 19TH CENTURY was one of the most glorious periods in the history of Prague. Austrian rule relaxed, allowing the Czech nation to rediscover its own history and culture. Silent for so long, the Czech language was eventually re-established as an official language. Civic pride was rekindled with the building of the capital's great showpieces, such as the National Theatre which utilized the talents of Czech architects and artists. The Jewish Quarter and New Town underwent extensive redevelopment and, with the introduction of public transport, Prague grew beyond its ancient limits.

EXTENT OF THE CITY
1890   Today

Days of the year

Smetana's Libuše
Written for the scheduled opening of the National Theatre in 1881, the opera drew on early Czech legend (see pp20–21).

Months and zodiac signs revolve around the centre.

Old Town coat of arms

Rudolfinum
A major concert venue beside the Vltava, the building (see p84) is richly decorated with symbols of the art of music.

OLD TOWN CLOCK TOWER CALENDAR
In 1866, the revolving dial on Prague's most enduring landmark was replaced by a new one by celebrated artist, Josef Mánes. His studies of Bohemian peasant life are incorporated into pictures symbolizing the months of the year.

TIMELINE

1805 Czechs, Austrians and Russians defeated by Napoleon at Battle of Slavkov (Austerlitz)

1833 Englishman Edward Thomas begins production of steam engines

1818 National Museum founded

Restored clock from the east face of the Town Hall Tower

1848 Uprising of people of Prague against Austrian troops

| 1800 | 1820 | 1840 | 18 |

1815 First public demonstration of a vehicle driven by a steam engine

The battle of Slavkov

1838–45 Old Town Hall undergoes reconstruction

1845 First train arrives in Prague

Expo 95 Poster
Vojtěch Hynais designed this poster for the ethnographic exhibition of folk culture in 1895. In the Art Nouveau style, it reflected the new appreciation of regional traditions.

WHERE TO SEE THE NATIONAL REVIVAL

Many of Prague's remarkable monuments, the National Museum for example, were built around this period. One fine example of Art Nouveau architecture is the Municipal House (p64), where the Mayor's Room has murals by Mucha. The Rudolfinum (p84) and the National Theatre (pp156–7) have gloriously-decorated interiors by great artists of the day. The Prague Museum has many objects from the late 19th and early 20th centuries as well as the original painting for Mánes' Old Town Clock.

December — **Sagittarius**

Municipal House
Allegories of civic virtues painted by Alfons Mucha adorn this Art Nouveau interior.

Jewish Quarter
From 1897 onwards, the slum housing of the ghetto was replaced with new apartment blocks.

National Museum
The Neo-Renaissance façade dominates the skyline (p147).

National Theatre
The décor has murals by Czech artists, including Aleš (pp156–7).

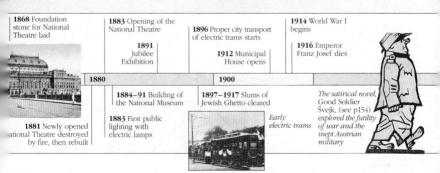

1868 Foundation stone for National Theatre laid

1883 Opening of the National Theatre

1896 Proper city transport of electric trams starts

1914 World War I begins

1891 Jubilee Exhibition

1912 Municipal House opens

1916 Emperor Franz Josef dies

1880

1900

1884–91 Building of the National Museum

1897–1917 Slums of Jewish Ghetto cleared

The satirical novel, Good Soldier Švejk, (see p154) explored the futility of war and the inept Austrian military

1881 Newly opened National Theatre destroyed by fire, then rebuilt

1883 First public lighting with electric lamps

Early electric trams

Prague after Independence

Metronome in Letná Park

JUST 20 YEARS AFTER its foundation, the Czechoslovak Republic was helplessly caught up in the political manoeuvring that preceded Nazi domination of Europe. Prague emerged from World War II almost unscathed by bombings, no longer part of a Nazi protectorate but of a Socialist republic. Any resistance was brutally suppressed. Ultimately, the intellectuals spoke out, demanding observance of civil rights. Denial of such rights led these dissidents to unite and prepare for the "Velvet Revolution". In the end, it was a playwright, Václav Havel, who stepped onto the balcony of Prague Castle to lead the country at the start of a long and often difficult return to independence.

1945 Soviet Red Army enter Prague on 9 May to rapturous welcome, following four days of uprisings. In October, provisional National Assembly set up under Beneš

1935 Edvard Beneš succeeds Masaryk as President. Nazi-funded Sudeten German Party, led by Konrad Henlein, makes election gains

1920 Avant-garde left-wing artists form Devětsil movement in Prague's Union Café

1938 Munich Agreement hands over parts of Republic to Hitler. Beneš flees country

1952 Most famous of many show trials under Gottwald, Slánský Trial sends 11 senior politicians to gallows as Trotskyites and traitors

Edvard Beneš

1918	1930	1940	1950

1918	1930	1940	1950

1924 Death of Franz Kafka, author of *The Trial*

1932 Traditional gymnastic rally or *slet* takes place at Strahov stadium

1942 Tyrannical "Protector" for only eight months, Reinhard Heydrich assassinated by Czech resistance

1955 Largest statue of Stalin in the world unveiled in Letná Park, overlooking city

1948 Communist Party assumes power under Klement Gottwald; announces 89% support in May elections

1958 Premiere of innovative animated film, *The Invention of Destruction* directed by Karel Zeman

1918 Foundation of Czechoslovak Republic. Tomáš Masaryk first democratically-elected President

1939 German troops march into Prague; city declared capital of Nazi Protectorate of Bohemia and Moravia

Welcome Home poster, to mark the president's return on 21 December 1918

1966 Jiří Menzel's *Closely Observed Trains* wins Oscar for Best Foreign Film, drawing the world's attention to Czech cinema

1989 Year of the "Velvet Revolution": growing civil discontent prompts demonstrations and strikes. Havel unites opposition groups to form Civic Forum. Temporary Government of National Understanding promises free elections; President Husák resigns and Václav Havel sworn in by popular demand

1968 Alexander Dubček elected to post of First Secretary

1990 First democratic elections for 60 years held in June, producing 99% turnout, with 60% of vote going to alliance of Civic Forum and People Against Violence

1962 Statue of Stalin in Letná Park demolished (replaced in 1991 by giant metronome)

1979 Playwright Václav Havel founds Committee for the Defence of the Unjustly Persecuted and is sent to prison

1992 Plastic People band perform at celebratory concert, 15 years after ban which resulted in Charter 77

60	1970	1980	1990

60	1970	1980	1990

60 Czechoslovak cialist Republic SSR) proclaimed

1969 Jan Palach burns to death in protest at Soviet occupation

1967 First Secretary and President, Antonín Novotný, imprisons dissident writers

1977 Human rights manifesto Charter 77 drawn up after arrest of band, Plastic People

1993 Prague is once again declared capital of Czech Republic

1984 Jaroslav Seifert, signatory of Charter 77, wins Nobel Prize for Literature but cannot collect prize in person

1989 Canonization of St Agnes *(see pp92–3)* takes place on 4 November. Vatican commissions painting by dissident Prague-born artist Gustav Makarius Tauc for the occasion. Czech legend that miraculous events will accompany her elevation to sainthood prove correct when "Velvet Revolution" begins on 17 November

The coat of arms of the Czech Republic has the inscription "truth victorious" and the arms for Bohemia (top left, bottom right), Moravia (top right) and Silesia (bottom left)

1968 Moderate Alexander Dubček adopts the programme of liberal reforms known as "Prague Spring". On 21 August, Warsaw Pact occupies Czechoslovakia and over 100 protesters are killed as troops enter Prague

PRAGUE AT A GLANCE

THERE ARE ALMOST 150 places of interest described in the *Area by Area* section of this book. A broad range of sights is covered: from the ancient Royal Palace, which was the site of the Defenestration of 1618 *(see p105)*, to cubist houses built in the Jewish Quarter in the 1920s *(see p91)*; from the peaceful oasis of Petřín Park *(see p141)*, to the bustle of Wenceslas Square *(see pp144–5)*. To help you make the most of your stay, the following 12 pages are a time-saving guide to the best Prague has to offer visitors. Museums and galleries, churches and synagogues, palaces and gardens all have their own sections. Each sight has a cross reference to its own full entry. Below are the attractions that no visitor should miss.

PRAGUE'S TOP TEN SIGHTS

Old Town Square
See pp66–9

National Theatre
See pp156–7.

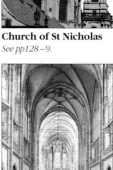

Church of St Nicholas
See pp128–9.

Charles Bridge
See pp136–9.

Old Town Hall
See pp72–4.

St Vitus's Cathedral
See pp100–3.

Wallenstein Palace and Garden *See p126.*

Old Jewish Cemetery
See pp86–7.

Prague Castle
See p96–7.

St George's Convent
See pp106–9.

◁ Mucha's allegory of Vigilance in the Mayor's Room in the Municipal House *(see p64)*

Prague's Best: Museums and Galleries

WITH MORE THAN 20 museums and almost 100 galleries and exhibition halls, Prague is a city of unexpected and rare delights. Here, religious masterpieces of the Middle Ages vie with the more recent opulence of Art Nouveau and the giants of modern art. New galleries have opened since 1989 with many more temporary exhibitions. There are museums devoted to the history of the state, the city and its people, many of them housed in buildings that are historical landmarks and works of art in themselves. This map gives some highlights, with a detailed overview on pages 40–41.

St George's Convent
Among the fine Bohemian art is
St Jerome *by Master Theodoric.*

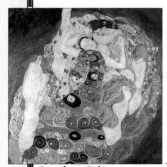

Sternberg Palace
The collection of European art here is outstanding. Modern art is well represented in works such as The Virgin *by Gustav Klimt (1912–13).*

**Prague Castle
and Hradčany**

The Loreto
The offerings of devout local aristocrats form the basis of this collection of religious decorative art. In 1721 this jewel-encrusted, tree-shaped monstrance was given to the treasury by Countess Wallenstein.

*Little
Quarter*

V L T A V A

Smetana Museum
The life and work of this 19th-century Czech composer are remembered beside the river that inspired one of his most famous pieces – the Vltava.

Schwarzenberg Palace
The ornate Renaissance palace forms a handsome backdrop to the Museum of Military History's displays of weaponry and memorabilia.

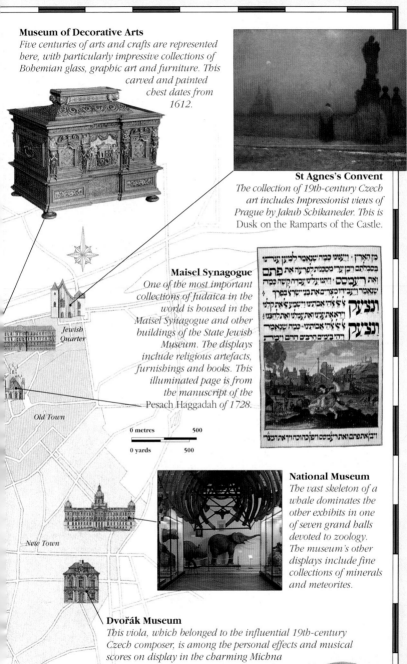

Museum of Decorative Arts
Five centuries of arts and crafts are represented here, with particularly impressive collections of Bohemian glass, graphic art and furniture. This carved and painted chest dates from 1612.

St Agnes's Convent
The collection of 19th-century Czech art includes Impressionist views of Prague by Jakub Schikaneder. This is Dusk on the Ramparts of the Castle.

Maisel Synagogue
One of the most important collections of Judaica in the world is housed in the Maisel Synagogue and other buildings of the State Jewish Museum. The displays include religious artefacts, furnishings and books. This illuminated page is from the manuscript of the Pesach Haggadah of 1728.

Jewish Quarter

Old Town

0 metres 500

0 yards 500

New Town

National Museum
The vast skeleton of a whale dominates the other exhibits in one of seven grand halls devoted to zoology. The museum's other displays include fine collections of minerals and meteorites.

Dvořák Museum
This viola, which belonged to the influential 19th-century Czech composer, is among the personal effects and musical scores on display in the charming Michna Summer Palace.

Exploring the Museums and Galleries

T HE CITY'S MUSEUMS give a fascinating insight into the history of the Czechs and of Prague's Jewish population. Also a revelation to visitors unfamiliar with the culture is the art of the Gothic and Baroque periods and of the 19th-century Czech National Revival. The major museums and galleries are cramped for space, but plans are under way to put more of their collections on show in the near future.

Carved figure on façade of the Museum of Decorative Arts

CZECH PAINTING AND SCULPTURE

T HE MOST IMPORTANT and wide-ranging collection in Prague is that of the National Gallery. Its holdings of Czech art are shown at three venues: works dating from the 12th to 18th centuries at **St George's Convent**; 19th-century art at **St Agnes's Convent**; 19th- and 20th-century sculpture at **Zbraslav Monastery**.

The **Picture Gallery of Prague Castle** is a reminder of Emperor Rudolph II's once-great collection. Alongside the paintings are documents and other evidence of just how splendid the original collection must have been.

For the best of the Castle's Bohemian art, you must visit the Gothic and Baroque works at St George's Convent. These include panels painted for Charles IV by Master Theodoric, and examples by Baroque masters Karel Škréta and Petr Brandl. Also within the Castle but currently without a permanent display space is the St Vitus Treasure, a collection of religious pieces including a Madonna from the School of Master Theodoric.

Centuries of Czech sculpture are housed in the Lapidarium at the **Exhibition Ground**. Among its exhibits is statuary formerly found on the Charles Bridge, and the Marian pillar that used to stand in the Old Town Square.

The collection at **St Agnes's Convent** includes works by Josef Mánes, the leading Czech 19th-century painter and ardent patriot. Works by 19th- and 20th-century Prague artists can be seen at the Prague Gallery. Its branches include the Baroque **Troja Palace**, where the architecture makes a marvellous backdrop. Exhibitions are drawn from the gallery's 3,000 paintings, 1,000 statues and 4,000 prints. At Zbraslav Monastery, Romanticism and Art Nouveau are both well represented, as is the work of Otto Gutfreund, whose gentle 1920s figures are understandably popular. What promises to be the best collection of modern Czech art is still being assembled

14th-century *Madonna Aracoeli,* St Vitus Treasure, Prague Castle

in the former Trade Fair Palace. Works by artists such as Václav Špála and Jan Zrzavý will represent almost every 20th-century artistic movement.

EUROPEAN PAINTING AND SCULPTURE

P RAGUE ALSO OFFERS visitors an opportunity to view an exceptional range of master-pieces by Europe's finest artists from antiquity to modern times, at **Sternberg Palace**.

The most treasured works in the collection are the *Feast of the Rosary* by Albrecht Dürer and *Haymaking* by Pieter Brueghel the Elder, but other equally delightful works include many by 17th-century Dutch masters such as Rubens and Rembrandt; Rodin bronzes; an outstanding collection of Picassos; and examples from almost every Impressionist, Post-Impressionist and Fauvist. Three notable self-portraits are those of Paul Gauguin (*Bonjour Monsieur Gauguin,* 1889), Henri Rousseau (1890) and Pablo Picasso (1907). The latter comes from the collect-ion of influential Czech art historian Vincenc Kramář, an early champion of Cubism. Modern German and Austrian painting is also on show, with works by Gustav Klimt and Egon Schiele. The *Dance of Life,* by Norwegian Edvard Munch, is considered greatly

Commerce by Otto Gutfreund (1923), Zbraslav Monastery

influential upon the Czech avant-garde art movement.

The other main venue for European art is the **Picture Gallery of Prague Castle**, which focuses on painters of the 16th to 18th centuries. As well as Titian's *The Toilet of a Young Lady*, there are works by Rubens and Tintoretto.

MUSIC

TWO CZECH composers merit their own museums, as does Prague's much-loved visitor, Mozart. The **Smetana Museum**, **Dvořák Museum** and **Mozart Museum** all contain personal memorabilia, musical scores and correspondence. In the summer, concerts are held on the terrace of the Mozart Museum.

The Museum of Musical Instruments is in the process of finding new quarters. Seek it out if you can; it has many rare and historic instruments, and scores by composers such as Josef Haydn.

HISTORY

THE HISTORICAL collections of the **National Museum** are held at the main Wenceslas Square building, and at Prague Castle. Of special interest in the former are displays which trace the development of Czech theatre. The artefacts at Prague Castle are housed in **Lobkowicz Palace** and focus on Czech life and culture.

Bohemian Baroque glass goblet (1730), Museum of Decorative Arts

The **Prague Museum** centres on the history of the city, with period rooms, historical prints and a model of Prague in the 19th century, made of paper and wood by the lithographer Antonín Langweil.

A branch of the museum at Výtoň, on the banks of the Vltava, depicts the way of life of a former settlement. Another at Vyšehrad records the history of this royal seat.

The exquisite Renaissance building of **Schwarzenberg Palace** is a fine setting for the battle charts, weaponry, uniforms and regalia of the Museum of Military History.

The State Jewish Museum is made up of various sites in the Jewish Quarter, including the **High Synagogue**, **Maisel Synagogue** and the **Old Jewish Cemetery**. Among its collections are holy artefacts taken from other Jewish communities and brought to Prague by the Nazis as part of a chilling plan for a museum of "an extinct race". Another moving display is of drawings by children imprisoned in the Terezín concentration camp.

DECORATIVE ARTS

WITH GLASSWARE spanning centuries, from medieval to modern, porcelain and pewterware, furniture and textiles, books and posters, the **Museum of Decorative Arts** in the Jewish Quarter is one of Prague's best, but only a small selection of its holdings is on show. Look out for specialized temporary exhibitions mounted either at the museum itself or at other venues in Prague.

Many other museums have examples of the decorative arts, ranging from grandiose monstrances – including one with 6,222 diamonds – in the treasury of **The Loreto** to simple everyday furnishings in the **Prague Museum**. There is also a fascinating collection of pre-Columbian artefacts from Central America in the **Náprstek Museum**.

16th-century astrolabe from the National Technical Museum

SCIENCE AND TECHNOLOGY

A VAST EXHIBITION hall holds the transport section of the **National Technical Museum**. Ranks of vintage cars, motorcycles and steam engines fill the space, and over them hang examples of early flying machines. Other sections trace the progress of sciences such as electronics. Visitors can even tour a reconstruction of a coal mine. As befits the city where Tycho Brahe and Johannes Kepler studied the stars, there is a fascinating astronomy exhibition.

Prague's Best: Churches and Synagogues

THE RELIGIOUS BUILDINGS of Prague vividly record the city's changing architectural styles, and many are treasure houses of religious art. But they also reflect Prague's times of religious and political strife, the lives of its people, its setbacks and growth as a city. This map features highlights of their architecture and art, with a more detailed overview on pages 44–5.

St George's Basilica
St George, sword raised to slay the dragon, is portrayed in this late-Gothic relief, set above the doorway of the magnificent early Renaissance south portal.

St Vitus's Cathedral
The jewel of the cathedral is the Chapel of St Wenceslas. Its walls are decorated with semi-precious stones, gilding and frescoes. Elizabeth of Pomerania, the fourth and last wife of Charles IV, is shown at prayer in the fresco above the Gothic altar.

Prague Castle and Hradčany

The Loreto
This shrine to the Virgin Mary has been a place of pilgrimage since 1626. Each hour, its Baroque clock tower chimes a hymn on the carillon of 27 bells.

Little Quarter

Church of St Thomas
The skeleton of the martyr St Just rests in a glass coffin below a Crucifixion by Antonín Stevens, one of several superb works of religious art in this church.

Church of St Nicholas
In the heart of the Little Quarter, this is Prague's finest example of High Baroque. The dome over the high altar is so lofty that early worshippers feared it would collapse.

V L T A V A

Church of Our Lady before Týn

Set back behind a row of arcaded buildings, the many-spired twin towers of the church dominate the eastern end of Old Town Square. The Gothic, Renaissance and Baroque features of the interior create striking contrasts.

Old-New Synagogue
Prague's oldest synagogue dates from the 13th century. Its Gothic main portal is carved with a vine which bears twelve bunches of grapes symbolizing the tribes of Israel.

Jewish Quarter

Old Town

Church of St James

Consecrated in 1374, this church was restored to new Baroque glory after a fire in 1689. Typical of its grandeur is this 18th-century monument to chancellor Jan Vratislav of Mitrovice. Fine acoustics and a superb organ make the church a popular venue for concerts.

Slavonic Monastery
These cloisters hold a series of precious frescoes from three Gothic masters depicting scenes from the Old and New Testaments.

New Town

| 0 metres | 500 |
| 0 yards | 500 |

Church of St Peter and St Paul

Remodelled many times since the 11th century, the design of this church is now 1890s Neo-Gothic. This striking relief of the Last Judgment marks the main entrance.

Exploring Churches and Synagogues

Reeligious building began in Prague in the 9th century, reaching its zenith during the reign of Charles IV *(see pp24–5)*. The remains of an 11th-century synagogue have been found, but during the 19th-century clearance of the overcrowded Jewish ghetto three synagogues were lost. Many churches were damaged during the Hussite rebellions *(see pp26–7)*. The political regime of the 20th century also took its toll, but now churches and synagogues are slowly being reclaimed and restored, with many open to visitors.

Altar, Capuchin Monastery

ROMANESQUE

Three reasonably well-preserved Romanesque rotundas, dating from the 11th and 12th centuries, still exist in Prague. The oldest is the **St Martin's Rotunda**; the others are the rotundas of the Holy Rood and of St Longinus. All three are tiny, with naves only 6 m (20 ft) in diameter.

By far the best-preserved and most important Romanesque church is **St George's Basilica**, founded in 920 by

11th-century Romanesque Rotunda of St Martin in Vyšehrad

Prince Vratislav I. Extensive reconstruction was carried out after a fire in 1142, but its chancel, with some exquisite frescoes on its vaulting, is a Late-Romanesque gem.

The **Strahov Monastery**, founded in 1142 by Prince Vladislav II *(see pp22–3)*, has retained its Romanesque core in spite of fire, wars and extensive renovation.

GOTHIC

Gothic architecture, with its ribbed vaulting, flying buttresses and pointed arches, reached Bohemia in about 1230 and was soon adopted into religious architecture.

The first religious building in Gothic style was **St Agnes's Convent**, founded in 1233 by Wenceslas I's sister, Agnes. Prague's oldest synagogue, the **Old-New Synagogue**, built in 1270, is rather different in style to the churches but nevertheless is still a superb example of Early-Gothic.

The best example of Prague Gothic is **St Vitus's Cathedral**. Its fine tracery and towering

High, Gothic windows at the east end of St Vitus's Cathedral

nave epitomize the style. Other notable Gothic churches are **Our Lady before Týn** and **Our Lady of the Snows**.

Important for its historical significance is the reconstructed Gothic **Bethlehem Chapel** where Jan Hus *(see p27)* preached for 10 years.

The superb Gothic frescoes found in abundance at the **Slavonic Monastery**, were badly damaged in World War II, but have been restored.

RENAISSANCE

In the 1530s the influence of Italian artists living in Prague sparked the city's Renaissance movement. The style is more clearly seen in secular than religious building. The Late-Renaissance period, under Rudolph II (1576–1611), offers the best remaining examples.

DOMES AND SPIRES

The domes and spires of Prague's churches are the city's main landmarks, as the view from the many vantage points will confirm. You will see a variety of spires, towers and domes: Gothic and Neo-Gothic soar skywards, while Baroque often have rounded cupolas and onion domes. The modern top of the 14th-century Slavonic Monastery, added after the church was struck in a World War II air raid, is a rare example of modernist religious architecture in Prague. Its sweeping, intersecting twin spires are a bold reinterpretation of Gothic themes, and a striking addition to the city's skyline.

Gothic   *Baroque*

Church of Our Lady before Týn (1350–1511)   **Church of St Nicholas in Little Quarter (1761)**

The **High Synagogue** and the **Pinkas Synagogue** retain strong elements of the style: the former in its 1586 exterior, the latter in the reworking of an original Gothic building.

The Church of St Roch in the **Strahov Monastery** is probably the best example of Late-Renaissance "Mannerism".

Renaissance-influenced vaulting, Pinkas Synagogue (1535)

BAROQUE

THE COUNTER-REFORMATION *(see pp30–31)* inspired the building of new churches and the revamping of existing ones for a period of 150 years. Prague's first Baroque church

was **Our Lady Victorious**, built in 1611–13. **St Nicholas** in the Little Quarter took almost 60 years to build. Its lush interior and frescoed vault make it Prague's most important Baroque building, followed by **The Loreto** (1626–1750), adjoining the **Capuchin Monastery**. The father-and-son team, Christoph and Kilian Ignaz Dientzenhofer designed both buildings, and **St John on the Rock** and **St Nicholas** in the Old Town.

A special place in Prague's history was occupied by the Jesuit **Clementinum**. This influential university's church was the **Holy Saviour**. The Baroque style is closely linked with Jesuit teachings: Kilian Ignaz Dientzenhofer was educated here.

Klausen Synagogue (now the State Jewish Museum) was built in 1689 with Baroque stuccoed barrel vaults.

Many early buildings were given Baroque facelifts. The Gothic nave of **St Thomas** has Baroque vaulting, and the once-Gothic **St James** went Baroque after a fire in 1689.

19th-century Neo-Gothic portal, Church of St Peter and St Paul

NEO-GOTHIC

DURING THE HEIGHT of the 19th-century Gothic Revival *(see pp32–3)*, **St Vitus's Cathedral** was completed, in accordance with the original Gothic plan. Work by Josef Mocker, the movement's leader, aroused controversy but his **St Peter and St Paul** at Vyšehrad is a well-loved landmark. The triple-naved basilica of **St Ludmilla** in Náměstí Míru was also designed by Mocker.

Nave ceiling of the Church of St Nicholas in the Little Quarter

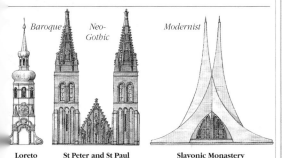

Baroque | Neo-Gothic | Modernist

Loreto (1661) | **St Peter and St Paul (1903)** | **Slavonic Monastery (1967)**

Prague's Best: Palaces and Gardens

PRAGUE'S PALACES and gardens are among the most important historical and architectural monuments in the city. Many palaces house museums or galleries *(see pp38–41)*, and some are concert venues.

The gardens range from formal, walled oases with fountains and grand statuary, to open spaces beyond the city centre. This map features some of the best palaces and gardens, with a detailed overview on pages 48–9.

Royal Garden
Though redesigned in the 19th century, the Renaissance garden preserves much of its original character. Historic statues still in place include a pair of Baroque lions (1730) guarding the entrance.

Belvedere
The Singing Fountain (1568) stands in front of the exquisite Renaissance summer palace.

Prague Castle and Hradčany

0 metres   500
0 yards   500

Little Quarter

South Gardens
Starting life as the Castle's defensive bastions, these gardens afford a wonderful view of Prague. First laid out as a park in 1891, their present design was landscaped by Josip Plečnik 40 years later.

Wallenstein Palace
Built in 1624–30 for Count Albrecht of Wallenstein, this vast Baroque palace was intended to outshine Prague Castle. Over 20 houses and a town gate were demolished to make room for the palace and garden. This Fountain of Venus (1599), stands in front of the arches of the sala terrena.

Wallenstein Garden
The garden statues are copies of 17th-century bronzes. The originals were plundered by the Swedes in 1648.

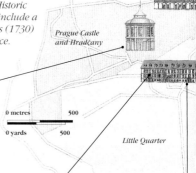

Kolowrat-Černín Garden
In the Baroque period, several palace gardens with spectacular terraces were laid out on the hillside below Prague Castle.

Golz-Kinský Palace
The Kinský coat of arms adorns the pink and white stuccoed façade designed by Kilian Ignaz Dientzenhofer. The Rococo palace is now part of the National Gallery.

Jewish Quarter

Old Town

Clam-Gallas Palace
Four giant statues of Hercules (c1715) by Matthias Bernard Braun show the hero straining to support the weight of the massive Baroque front portals of the palace.

Michna Summer Palace
This charming villa was designed by Kilian Ignaz Dientzenhofer in 1712. It now houses the Dvořák Museum. The garden's sculptural decorations are from the workshop of Antonín Braun.

New Town

Kampa Island
A tranquil waterside park was created on the island in 1941 by tearing down a number of garden walls.

Exploring the Palaces and Gardens

PRAGUE BOASTS an amazing number of palaces and gardens, spanning centuries. Comparatively few palaces were lost to the ravages of war. Instead, they tended to evolve in style during restoration or enlargement. Palace gardens became fashionable in the 17th century, but could only be laid out where there was space, such as below Prague Castle. More vulnerable to change, most have been relandscaped several times. In the 19th century, and again after 1989, many of the larger parks and private gardens were opened up to the public.

Statue on Kampa Island

MEDIEVAL PALACES

THE OLDEST PALACE in Prague is the **Royal Palace** at Prague Castle. In the basement is the Romanesque ground floor, started in about 1135. It has been rebuilt many times, particularly between the 14th and 16th centuries. The heart of the Palace, Vladislav Hall, dates from the 1490s and is late Gothic in structure. Less well known is the **Palace of the Lords of Kunštát**. Here, the vaulted ground floor of the 13th-century building survives as the basement of a later Gothic structure.

RENAISSANCE PALACES

ONE OF THE most beautiful Renaissance buildings in Prague is the 16th-century **Schwarzenberg Palace**. The work of Italian architects, its façade is entirely covered with geometric, two-tone *sgraffito* designs. Italians also

Bronze Singing Fountain in the Royal Garden by the Belvedere

worked on the **Belvedere**. Its graceful arcades and columns, all covered with rich reliefs, make this one of the finest Renaissance buildings north of the Alps. The **Martinic Palace**, built in 1563, was the first example of late-Renaissance building in Prague. Soon after came the **Lobkowicz Palace**. Its terracotta relief-decorated windows and plaster *sgraffito* have survived later Baroque modifications. The huge **Archbishop's Palace** was given a later Rococo façade over its Renaissance structure.

BAROQUE PALACES

MANY PALACES were built in the Baroque style, and examples of all its phases still exist in Prague. A handsome, if ostentatious, early Baroque

Southern façade of Troja Palace and its formal gardens

DECORATIVE PORTALS AND GATES

The elaborate gates and portals of Prague's palaces are among the most beautiful and impressive architectural features in the city. Gothic and Renaissance portals have often survived, even where the buildings themselves have been destroyed or modified by renovations in a later architectural style. The period of most prolific building was the Baroque, and distinctive portals from this time can be seen framing many a grand entrance around the city. Statues of giants, heroes and mythological figures are often depicted holding up the doorways. These were not merely decorative but acted as an integral element of support.

Gateway to Court of Honour of Prague Castle (1768)

example is the **Wallenstein Palace**. Similar ostentation is evident in the **Černín Palace**, one of Prague's most monumental buildings. The mid-Baroque had two strands, one opulent and Italianate, the other formal and French or Viennese in influence. **Troja Palace** and **Michna Summer Palace** are in Italian villa style while the **Sternberg Palace** on Hradčanské náměstí is more Viennese in style. Troja was designed in 1679 by Jean-Baptiste Mathey, who, like the Dientzenhofers (see p129), was a master of the Baroque. The pairs of giants on the portals of the **Clam-Gallas Palace**, and the **Morzin Palace** in Nerudova Street, are a popular Baroque motif. The **Golz-Kinský Palace** is a superb Rococo design by Kilian Ignaz Dientzenhofer.

GARDENS

T HE FINEST of Prague's palace gardens, such as the **Wallenstein Garden**, are in the Little Quarter. Though the style of Wallenstein Palace is Early Baroque, the garden still displays the geometric formality of the Renaissance, also preserved in the **Royal Garden** behind Prague Castle. The **South Gardens** on the Castle's old ramparts were redesigned in the 1920s.

Many more gardens were laid out in the 17th and 18th centuries, when noble families vied with each other to have fine winter residences in the Little Quarter below the Castle. Many are now the grounds of embassies, but others have been opened to the public. The **Ledebour Garden** has been combined with two neighbouring gardens. Laid out on a steep hillside, the **Kolowrat-Černín Garden**, in particular, makes ingenious use of pavilions, stairs and terraces from which there are wonderful views of the city. The **Vrtba Garden**, landscaped on the site of former vineyards, is a similar Baroque creation with statues and splendid views. Former palace gardens were also used to create a park on **Kampa Island**.

The many old gardens and orchards on Petřín Hill have

Ancient trees in Stromovka

been transformed into the large public area of **Petřín Park**. Another former orchard is **Vojan Park**, laid out by Carmelite monks in the 13th century. The **Botanical Gardens** are one of the few areas of green open to the public in the New Town.

Generally, the larger parks are situated further out of the city. **Stromovka** was a royal deer park, while **Letná Park** was developed in 1858 on the open space of Letná Plain.

The Royal Garden of Prague Castle, planted with spring flowers

Troja Palace (c1703)

Clam-Gallas Palace (c1714)

PRAGUE THROUGH THE YEAR

Painted Easter egg

PRINGTIME in Prague sees the city burst into colour as its gardens start to bloom. Celebrations begin with the Prague Spring Music Festival. In summer, visitors are entertained by street performers and the city's glorious gardens come into their own. When the weather begins to turn cooler, Prague hosts the International Jazz Festival.

The year often draws to a close with snow on the streets. The ball season starts in December, and in the coldest months, most events are held indoors. At Prague Castle, an all-year-round attraction is the changing of the guard around midday. For details of activities, check the listings magazines *(see p219)* or the Prague Information Service *(see p218)*.

Concert in Old Town Square during the Prague Spring Music Festival

SPRING

AS PRAGUE SEES its first rays of spring sunshine, the city comes alive. A mass of colours, blooms and cultural events makes this one of the most exciting times of the year to visit. The city's blossoming parks and gardens open their gates again, after the colder months of winter. During April the temperatures rise and an entertainment programme begins – dominated by the Prague Spring Music Festival.

EASTER

Easter Monday *(dates vary)* is a public holiday. Easter is observed as a religious holiday but it is also associated with a bizarre pagan ritual in which Czech men beat their women with willow sticks in order to keep them fertile during the coming year. The women retaliate by throwing water over their male tormentors. Peace is finally restored when the women present the men with a painted egg. Church services are held during the entire Easter period *(see p227)*.

MARCH

The Prague-Prčice March *(third Saturday of March)*. Thousands of people set out to walk from the city centre to the small town of Prčice, to the southwest of the city, in celebration of spring.

APRIL

Boat trips *(1 April)*. A number of boats begin trips up and down the Vltava.
Witch-burning *(30 April)*, at the Exhibition Ground *(see p176)*. Concerts accompany this 500-year-old tradition where old brooms are burnt on bonfires, in a symbolic act to rid nature of evil spirits.

MAY

Labour Day *(1 May)*. Public holiday celebrated with numerous cultural events.
Opening day of Prague's gardens *(1 May)*. Regular summer concerts are held in many parks and gardens.
Anniversary of Prague Uprising *(5 May)*. At noon sirens are sounded for one minute. Flowers are laid at the commemorative plaques of those who died *(see p34)*.
Day of Liberation from Fascism *(8 May)*. Public holiday for VE day. Wreaths are laid on the graves of soldiers at Olšany cemeteries.
Prague International Book Fair *(second week in May)*, Palace of Culture *(see p176)*. The best of Czech and international authors.

THE PRAGUE SPRING MUSIC FESTIVAL

This international festival presents a busy programme of concerts, ballet and opera from 12 May to 1 June. Music lovers can hear a huge selection of music played by some of the best musicians in the world. The main venue is the Rudolfinum *(see p84)* but others include churches and palaces – some of which are only open to the public on these occasions. The festival begins on the anniversary of Bedřich Smetana's death *(see p79)*. A service is held at his grave in Vyšehrad *(see p178)*, and in the evening there is a concert at the Municipal House *(see p64)* where musicians perform his most famous work, *Má Vlast* (My Country). The festival also ends here, with Beethoven's Ninth Symphony.

Bedřich Smetana

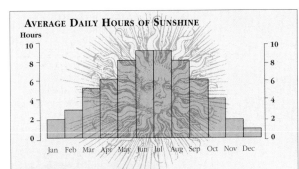

AVERAGE DAILY HOURS OF SUNSHINE

Sunshine Chart
Prague's longest and hottest days fall between May and August. At the height of summer, daylight starts at 5am. The snow-covered city looks stunning on a sunny winter's day. But sunny days can be spoiled by thick smog (see p53).

Czechs and tourists enjoying the beauty of Vyšehrad Park on a sunny afternoon

SUMMER

Summer arrives with high temperatures, frequent, sometimes heavy, showers and thousands of visitors. This is a beautiful, if busy, time to visit. Every weekend, Czechs set out for the country to go hiking in the surrounding hills or stay in country cottages. Those remaining in Prague visit the reservoirs and lakes (see p213), just outside the city to try and escape the heat. There is a wealth of entertainment on offer as culture moves into the open air taking over the squares, streets and gardens. Street performers, buskers and classical orchestras all help to keep visitors entertained. Many cafés have tables outside allowing you to quench your thirst while watching the fun.

JUNE

Mayoral Boat Race *(first weekend in June)*. Rowing races are held on the river Vltava, just below Vyšehrad.

Summer Concerts *(throughout the summer)*. Prague's gardens *(see pp46–9)* are the attractive and popular setting for a large number of free classical and brass-band concerts. One of the most famous, and spectacular, outdoor classical concerts is held by Křižík Fountain at the Exhibition Ground *(see p176)*. Full orchestras play to the stunning backdrop of coloured lights and water, synchronized to the music by computer.
Anniversary of the Murder of Reinhard Heydrich's Assassins *(18 June)*. A mass is held in remembrance at the Church of St Cyril and St Methodius *(see p152)* for those who died there.
Golden Prague *(first week of June)*, Kaiserstein Palace. International TV festival of prize-winning programmes.

Battle Re-enactments *(throughout summer)*, held in Prague's palaces and gardens.
Mozart's Prague *(mid-June to first week in July)*. Celebration of Mozart. International orchestras perform his works at Bertramka *(see p160)* and Lichtenstein Palace.
Dance Prague *(last week in June)*. An international festival of contemporary dance at the National Theatre *(see p156)*.

JULY

Remembrance of the Slavonic Missionaries *(5 July)*. Public holiday in honour of St Cyril and St Methodius *(see p152)*.
Anniversary of Jan Hus's Death *(6 July)*. A public holiday when flowers are laid on his memorial *(see pp26–7)*.

AUGUST

Theatre Island *(all of August)*, Střelecký Island. Czech theatre and puppet festival.

Changing of the Guard at Prague Castle

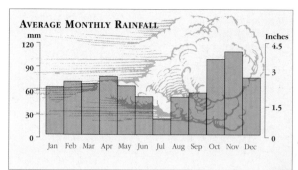

AVERAGE MONTHLY RAINFALL

	mm												Inches
	120												4.5
	90												3
	60												1.5
	30												
	0	Jan	Feb	Mar	Apr	May	Jun	Jul	Aug	Sep	Oct	Nov Dec	0

Rainfall Chart
*Prague has plenty
of rain throughout
the year. The wettest
months are October
and November, but
there are frequent
light showers in the
summer months as
well. Winter snow-
falls can be quite
heavy, but they are
rarely severe.*

AUTUMN

WHEN THE GARDENS below
Prague Castle take on
the shades of red and gold,
and visitors start to leave, the
city gets ready for the cold
winter months. This is also the
traditional mushroom-gathering
season when you encounter
people with baskets full of
freshly-picked mushrooms.
Market places are flooded
with fruit and vegetables. The
tree-lined slopes above the
Vltava take on the beautiful
colours of autumn. September
and October still have a fair
number of warm and sunny
days, although November
often sees the first snowfalls.
Football fans fill the stadiums
and the popular steeplechase
course at Pardubice reverber-
ates to the cheers of fans.

SEPTEMBER

Prague Autumn *(early
September)*, at the Rudolfinum
(see p84). An international
classical music festival.
The Autumn Fair *(dates vary)*,
at the Exhibition Ground
(see p176). Fairground, stalls,
food and drink, theatrical and
puppet shows and musical
performances of all kinds.
Kite competitions *(third
Sunday in September)*, on
Letná Plain in front of Sparta
Stadium. Very popular
competition for children but
open to anyone with a kite.
Bohemia Championship
(last Sunday in September). A
10-km (6-mile) road race
which has been run since
1887. Starts from Běchovice, a
suburb of Prague and ends in
Žižkov. Open to people of all
ages and levels of experience.

**Jazz musicians playing at the
International Jazz Festival**

OCTOBER

**The Great Pardubice
Steeplechase** *(second Sunday
in October)*, held at Pardubice,
east of Prague. This horse
race has been run since 1874
and is considered to be the
most difficult in Europe.
Velká Kunratická *(second
Sunday in October)*. Popular,
but gruelling, cross-country
race in Kunratice forest.
Anyone can enter.
The Locking of the Vltava
(early October). Symbolic
conclusion of the water sports
season, during which the
Vltava is locked with a key
until the arrival of spring.
International Jazz Festival
(date varies), Lucerna Palace.
A famous jazz festival, held
since 1964, attracts musicians
from around the world.
The Day of the Republic
(28 October). Despite the
splitting up of Czechoslovakia
into two separate republics,
the founding of the country in
1918 is still a public holiday.

NOVEMBER

**Celebration of the Velvet
Revolution** *(17 November)*.
Peaceful demonstrations take
place around Wenceslas
Square *(see pp144–5)*.

A view of St Vitus's Cathedral through autumn trees

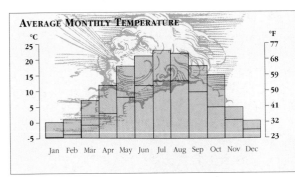

AVERAGE MONTHLY TEMPERATURE

Temperature Chart
The chart shows the average minimum and maximum temperatures for each month in Prague. The summer usually remains comfortably warm, while the winter months can get bitterly cold and temperatures often drop below freezing.

WINTER

IF YOU ARE lucky enough to catch Prague the morning after a snowfall with the sun shining, the effect is magical. The view over the Little Quarter rooftops with their pristine white covering is a memorable sight. Unfortunately Prague is rarely at its best during the winter months. The weather is changeable. Foggy days with temperatures just above freezing can quickly go down to -5° C (23° F). Pollution and Prague's geographical position in the Vltava basin, lead to smog being trapped just above the city.

As if to try and make up for the winter weather's shortcomings, the theatre season reaches its climax and there are a number of premieres. Balls and dances are held in these cold months. Just before Christmas Eve large barrels containing live carp – which is the traditional Czech Christmas delicacy – appear on the streets. Christmas trees adorn the city, and carol singers can be heard on street

View of the Little Quarter rooftops covered in snow

corners. Christmas mass is held in most churches and New Year's Eve is celebrated, in time-honoured style, throughout the entire city.

DECEMBER

Christmas markets *(throughout December)*, Můstek metro station, 28. října, Na příkopě, Old Town Square. Stalls sell Christmas decorations, gifts, hot wine, punch and the traditional Czech carp *(see p207)*.
Christmas Eve, Christmas Day and Boxing Day *(24, 25 and 26 December)*. Public holidays. Mass is held in churches throughout the city.
Swimming competitions in the Vltava *(26 December)*. Hundreds of hardened and determined swimmers gather together at the Vltava to swim in temperatures of around 3° C (37° F).
New Year celebrations *(31 December)*. Thousands of people congregate around Wenceslas Square.

Barrels of the traditional Christmas delicacy, carp, on sale in Prague

JANUARY

New Year's Day *(1 January)*. Public holiday.

FEBRUARY

Dances and Balls *(early February)*.
Matthew Fair *(end of February to beginning of April)*, the Exhibition Ground *(see p176)*. Fairground, stalls and various entertainments.

PUBLIC HOLIDAYS

New Year's Day (1 January); **Easter Monday**; **Labour Day** (1 May); **Day of Liberation from Fascism** (8 May); **Remembrance of the Slavonic Missionaries** (5 July); **Anniversary of Jan Hus's death** (6 July); **Day of the Republic** (28 October); **Christmas Eve, Christmas Day and Boxing Day** (24–26 December).

A RIVER VIEW OF PRAGUE

THE VLTAVA RIVER has played a vital part in the city's history *(see pp20–21)* and has provided inspiration for artists, poets and musicians throughout the centuries.

Up until the 19th century, parts of the city were exposed to the danger of heavy flooding. To try and alleviate the problem, the river's embankments have been strengthened and raised many times, in order to try to prevent the water penetrating too far (the foundations of today's embankments are made of stone or concrete). During the Middle Ages, year after year of disastrous flooding led to the decision to bury the areas affected under 2 m (6 ft) of earth to try to minimize the damage. Although this strategy was only partially effective, it meant that the ground floors of many Romanesque and Gothic buildings were preserved and can still be seen today *(see pp78–9)*. Despite

Statues on the wrought-iron Čechův Bridge

its destructive side, the Vltava has provided a vital method of transport for the city, as well as a source of income. As technology improved, the river became increasingly important; water mills, weirs and water towers were built. In 1912 a large hydro-electric power plant was built on Štvanice Island, supplying almost a third of Prague's electricity. To make the river navigable, eight dams, a large canal and weirs were constructed along the Slapy-Prague-Mělník stretch, where the Vltava flows into the river Elbe. For the visitor, an excursion on one of the many boats, paddle steamers and even a Chinese junk that travel up and down the river, is well worth it. River trips run daily in the summer months. There are trips to Troja *(see pp164–5)* and as far as Slapy Lake. Catching a boat from one of the piers on the river is one of the best ways of seeing the city and its surrounding countryside.

A view of the steamboat landing stage (přístaviště parníků) on Rašínovo nábřeží

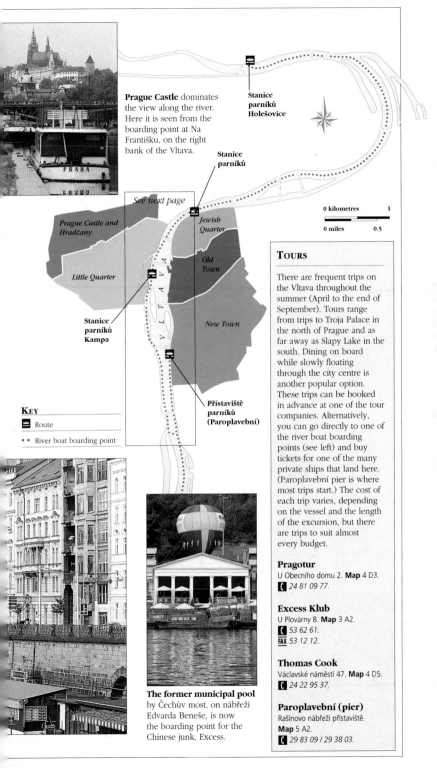

Prague Castle dominates the view along the river. Here it is seen from the boarding point at Na Františku, on the right bank of the Vltava.

Stanice parníků Holešovice

Stanice parníků

See next page

Prague Castle and Hradčany

Little Quarter

Jewish Quarter

Old Town

New Town

V L T A V A

Stanice parníků Kampa

0 kilometres 1

0 miles 0.5

Přístaviště parníků (Paroplavební)

KEY

Route

•• River boat boarding point

TOURS

There are frequent trips on the Vltava throughout the summer (April to the end of September). Tours range from trips to Troja Palace in the north of Prague and as far away as Slapy Lake in the south. Dining on board while slowly floating through the city centre is another popular option. These trips can be booked in advance at one of the tour companies. Alternatively, you can go directly to one of the river boat boarding points (see left) and buy tickets for one of the many private ships that land here. (Paroplavební pier is where most trips start.) The cost of each trip varies, depending on the vessel and the length of the excursion, but there are trips to suit almost every budget.

Pragotur
U Obecního domu 2. **Map** 4 D3.
24 81 09 77.

Excess Klub
U Plovárny 8. **Map** 3 A2.
53 62 61.
FAX 53 12 12.

Thomas Cook
Václavské náměstí 47. **Map** 4 D5.
24 22 95 37.

Paroplavební (pier)
Rašínovo nábřeží přístaviště.
Map 5 A2.
29 83 09 / 29 38 03.

The former municipal pool by Čechův most, on nábřeží Edvarda Beneše, is now the boarding point for the Chinese junk, Excess.

Prague River Trip

T AKING A TRIP on the Vltava gives you
a unique view of many of the city's
historic monuments. Although the left
bank was the site of the first Slavic
settlement in the 9th century, it was
the right bank, heavily populated by
merchants and traders, that developed
into a thriving and bustling commercial
centre, and the tradition continues today.
The left bank was never developed as
intensively and much of it is still an
oasis of parks and gardens. The river's
beauty is enhanced by the numbers of
swans which have made it their home.

Hanavský Pavilion
*This flamboyant
cast iron stair-
case is part of a
pavilion built
by Zdeněk Fiala
for the Jubilee
Exhibition
of 1891.*

Karlův most

Kampa

stanice parníků Kampa

Little Quarter Bridge Towers
*The smaller tower was
built in 1158 to guard the
entrance to the original
Judith Bridge, while the
larger one was built on
the site of an old
Romanesque tower in
1464 (see p136).*

Grand Priory Mill

most Legii

Střelecký ostrov

Plavební Kanál

Vltava Weir
*The thickly-wooded
slopes of Petřín Hill
tower above one of
several weirs on the
Vltava. During the
19th century this
weir, along with
others on this
stretch, were built
to make the river
navigable to ships.*

**The Vltava
Statue** on the
northern tip of
Children's Island
is where, every
year, wreaths
are placed in
memory of
the drowned.

Jiráskův most

Palackého most

Apartment buildings of Art Nouveau design

Little Quarter Water Tower
*Built in 1560, the tower
supplied river water to 57
fountains throughout the
Little Quarter.*

| 0 metres | 500 |
| 0 yards | 500 |

KEY

🚋 Tram

⬛ River boat boarding point

•• Boat trip

Železniční most

Rudolfinum
This allegorical statue of music by Antonín Wagner is one of two which decorate the imposing entrance to the Neo-Renaissance concert hall (see p84).

To Troja

stanice parníků

něšův st

The Clementinum, a former Jesuit college, is one of the largest buildings in the city *(see p79).*

The Old Town Bridge Tower was built as part of the city's 14th-century fortifications *(see p139).*

Weir

Smetana Museum
Sited on the edge of the river, this was originally the head office of the 19th-century municipal waterworks (see p79).

National Theatre
This symbol of the Czech revival, with its brightly-decorated roof, dominates the skyline of the right bank (see pp156–7).

Slovanský ostrov

The Šítka Tower, with its late-18th-century Baroque roof, was originally built in 1495 and pumped water to the New Town.

přístaviště parníků

The Memorial to František Palacký commemorates the life of this eminent 19th-century Czech historian and was built in 1905.

The Na Slovanech Monastery was built in 1347 by Charles IV. Its two modern steeples are easily recognizable from the river.

Výtoň Excise House
The coat of arms on this 16th-century house – built to collect duty on timber transported along the river – is of the New Town from 1671.

Church of St Peter and St Paul
The Neo-Gothic steeples on this much-rebuilt church were designed by František Mikeš and erected in 1903. They are the dominant feature of Vyšehrad rock (see pp178–9).

PRAGUE AREA
BY AREA

OLD TOWN
STARÉ MĚSTO

THE HEART OF the city is the Old Town and its central square. In the 11th century the settlements around the Castle spread to the right bank of the Vltava. A marketplace in what is now Old Town Square (Staroměstské náměstí) was mentioned for the first time in 1091. Houses and churches quickly sprang

Physician, Jan Marek (1595–1667)

up around the square, determining the random network of streets, many of which survive to this day. The area gained the privileges of a town in the 13th century, and, in 1338, a Town Hall. This and other great buildings, such as Clam-Gallas Palace and the importance of the Old Town.

SIGHTS AT A GLANCE

Churches
Church of St James ❹
Church of Our Lady before Týn ❽
Church of St Nicholas ⓫
Church of St Gall ⓮
Church of St Martin in the Wall ⓯
Church of St Giles ⓱
Bethlehem Chapel ⓲

Museums and Galleries
Náprstek Museum ⓰
Smetana Museum ㉔

Historic Streets and Squares
Celetná Street ❸
Old Town Square pp66–9 ❼
Mariánské Square ⓴
Charles Street ㉑
Knights of the Cross Square ㉕

Historic Monuments and Buildings
Powder Gate ❶
Municipal House ❷
Carolinum ❻
Jan Hus Monument ❿
Old Town Hall pp72–4 ⓬
House at the Two Golden Bears ⓭
Clementinum ㉓

Theatres
Estates Theatre ❺

Palaces
Golz-Kinský Palace ❾
Clam-Gallas Palace ⓳
Palace of the Lords of Kunštát ㉒

GETTING THERE
Můstek on metro lines A and B and Staroměstská on line A are both handy for the area. Trams do not cross the Old Town, but from Charles Bridge or Náměstí Republiky it is only a short walk to Old Town Square and the other sights.

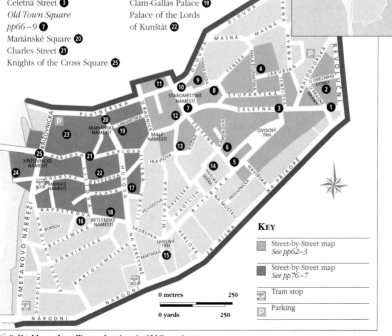

KEY

▨	Street-by-Street map *See pp62–3*
▨	Street-by-Street map *See pp76–7*
🚊	Tram stop
P	Parking

0 metres 250
0 yards 250

◁ **Café tables and strolling pedestrians in Old Town Square**

Street-by-Street: Old Town (East)

FREE OF TRAFFIC (except for a few horse-drawn carriages) and ringed with historic buildings, Prague's Old Town Square (Staroměstské náměstí) ranks among the finest public spaces in any city. Streets like Celetná and Ovocný trh are also pedestrianized. In summer, café tables spill out onto the cobbles, and though the area draws tourists by the thousands, the unique atmosphere has not yet been destroyed.

Golz-Kinský Palace
This stunning Rococo palace now serves as an art gallery ⑨

Church of St Nicholas
The imposing façade of this Baroque church dominates one corner of Old Town Square ⑪

★ **Old Town Square**
This late-19th-century watercolour by Václav Jansa shows how little the Square has changed in 100 years ⑦

S T A R O M Ě S T S K É
N Á M Ě S T Í

M A L É
N Á M Ě S T Í

Ž E L E Z N Á

Jan Hus Monument
Religious reformer Hus is a symbol of integrity, and the monument brings together the highest and lowest points in Czech history ⑩

U Rotta in Malé náměstí (Small Square) is an ironmonger's shop decorated with colourful paintings by the great 19th-century artist Mikuláš Aleš.

House at the Two Golden Bears
The carved Renaissance portal is the finest of its kind in Prague ⑬

★ **Old Town Hall**
The famous astronomical clock draws a crowd of visitors every hour ⑫

The Štorch house has painted decoration based on designs by Mikuláš Aleš showing St Wenceslas on horseback.

0 metres	100
0 yards	100

KEY

‒ ‒ ‒ Suggested route

Church of Our Lady before Týn
The church's Gothic steeples are the Old Town's most distinctive landmark **8**

LOCATOR MAP
See Street Finder, maps 3–4

Church of St James
This wooden Pietà, on the main altar, was made in the 15th century **4**

★ Municipal House
This Art Nouveau building is a popular concert venue **2**

J A K U B S K Á

U P R A S N É B R Á N Y

S T U P A R T S K Á

C E L E T N Á

Powder Gate
This much-restored Gothic gate is a relic of when there was a royal palace here at the entrance to the Old Town **1**

House at the Black Madonna

O V O C N Ý T R H

Ovocný trh *was Prague's fruit market.*

Estates Theatre
The 18th-century theatre featured in director Miloš Forman's film Amadeus **5**

Celetná Street
This ornamental Baroque plaque is the sign of the House at the Black Sun **3**

Carolinum
A magnificently carved Oriel window projects from the oldest surviving part of the Carolinum university – founded by Charles IV in the 14th century **6**

STAR SIGHTS

★ Old Town Square

★ Old Town Hall

★ Municipal House

Powder Gate ❶
PRAŠNÁ BRÁNA

Náměstí Republiky. **Map** 4 D3.
Náměstí Republiky. 5, 14,
26. **Open** 7am–7pm daily.

THERE HAS BEEN a gate here
since the 11th century,
when it formed one of the 13
entrances to the Old Town. In
1475, King Vladislav II laid
the foundation stone of the
New Tower, as it was to be
known. A coronation gift
from the city council, the gate
was modelled on Peter Parler's
Old Town bridge tower built
a century earlier. The gate had
little defensive value; its rich
sculptural decoration was
intended to add prestige to the
adjacent palace of the Royal
Court. Building was halted
eight years later when the
king had to flee the city
because of riots. On his
return in 1485 he opted for
the greater safety of the
Castle. Kings never again
occupied the Royal Court.

The gate acquired its
present name when it was
used to store gunpowder in
the 17th century. The
sculptural decoration, badly
damaged during the Prussian
occupation in 1757 and mostly
removed soon afterwards,
was replaced in 1876 when
the gate was restored.

**The Powder Gate viewed from
outside the Old Town**

Karel Špillar's mosaic *Homage to Prague* on Municipal House's façade

Municipal House ❷
OBECNÍ DŮM

Náměstí Republiky 5. **Map** 4 D3.
231 41 96. Náměstí
Republiky. 5, 14, 26.
(See **Restaurants, Cafés and Pubs**
pp 190–205). **Closed** for renovation
until May 1997.

PRAGUE'S MOST prominent
Art Nouveau building
stands on the site of the
former Royal Court palace,
the King's residence between
1383 and 1485. Abandoned
for centuries, what remained
was used as a seminary and
later as a military college. It
was finally demolished in the
early 1900s to be replaced by
the present cultural centre
(1905–11) with its exhibition
halls and large auditorium,
designed by Antonín Balšánek
assisted by Osvald Polívka.

The exterior is embellished
with stucco and allegorical
statuary. Above the main
entrance there is a huge semicircular mosaic entitled
Homage to Prague by Karel
Špillar. Inside, topped by an
impressive glass dome, is
Prague's principal concert
venue and the core of the
entire building, the

Smetana Hall, sometimes also
used as a ballroom. The
interior of the building is
decorated with works by leading Czech artists of the first
decade of the century, including Alfons Mucha *(see p149)*.

There are numerous smaller
halls, conference rooms and
offices, as well as cafés and
restaurants where visitors can
relax and enjoy the centre's
flamboyant Art Nouveau
decoration at
their leisure.
On 28 October,
1918, Prague's
Municipal
House was the
scene of the
momentous
proclamation
of the new
independent
state of
Czechoslovakia.

**Decorative deta
by Alfons Much**

Mayor's Salon
with paintings by
Alfons Mucha

Entrance hall

Entrance to Art
Nouveau café

Nightclubs

Hollar
Hall

Foyer

Celetná Street ❸
CELETNÁ ULICE

Map 3 C3. Náměstí Republiky, Můstek.

ONE OF THE oldest streets in Prague, Celetná follows an old trading route from eastern Bohemia. Its name comes from the plaited bread rolls that were first baked here in the Middle Ages. It gained prestige in the 14th century as a section of the Royal Route *(see p172)* used for coronation processions. Foundations of Romanesque and Gothic buildings can be seen in some of the cellars, but most of the houses with their picturesque house signs are Baroque remodellings.

On dark, windy nights, Celetná has more than its share of Prague's legendary ghosts. These include a butcher with a fiery axe and a prostitute who bared her breasts to a chaplain, who was so incensed that he hit her on the head with his cross and killed her.

Church of St James ❹
KOSTEL SV. JAKUBA

Malá Štupartská. **Map** 3 C3. Můstek, Náměstí Republiky. **Open** in the season, daily.

THIS ATTRACTIVE Baroque church was originally the Gothic presbytery of a Minorite monastery. The order (a branch of the Franciscans) was invited to Prague by King Wenceslas I in 1232. It was

Baroque organ loft in the Church of St James

rebuilt in the Baroque style after a fire in 1689, allegedly started by agents of Louis XIV. Over 20 side altars were added, decorated with works by painters such as Jan Jiří Heinsch, Petr Brandl and Václav Vavřinec Reiner. The tomb of Count Vratislav of Mitrovice (1714–16), designed by Johann Bernhard Fischer von Erlach and executed by sculptor Ferdinand Brokof, is the most beautiful Baroque tomb in Bohemia. The count is said to have been accidentally buried alive – his corpse was later found sitting up in the tomb. Hanging on the right of the entrance is a mummified forearm. It has been there for over 400 years, ever since a thief tried to steal the jewels from the Madonna on the high altar. But the Virgin grabbed his arm and held on so tightly it had to be cut off.

Because of its long nave, the church's acoustics are excellent and many concerts and recitals are given here. There is also a magnificent organ built in 1702.

Estates Theatre ❺
STAVOVSKÉ DIVADLO

Železná 11. **Map** 3 C4. 24 21 50 01. Můstek. **Foyer open** for guided tours only.

BUILT BY COUNT NOSTITZ in 1783, the theatre is one of the finest examples of Neo-Classical elegance in Prague. It is a mecca for Mozart fans *(see p212)*. On 29 October 1787, Mozart's opera, *Don Giovanni* had its debut here with Mozart at the piano conducting the orchestra. In 1834 a musical comedy called *Fidlovačka* had its premiere here. One of the songs, *Kde domov můj?* (Where is my Home?), became the Czech national anthem.

Carolinum ❻
KAROLINUM

Železná 9. **Map** 3 C4. 26 42 21/ 24 22 86 00. Můstek. **Closed** to the public.

AT THE CORE of the university founded by Charles IV in 1348 is the Carolinum. Little of the original building survives, except a fine oriel window, but in 1945 the courtyard was reconstructed in Gothic style. In the 15th and 16th centuries the university played a leading role in the movement to reform the church. After the Battle of the White Mountain *(see pp30–31)*, the university was taken over by the Jesuits.

Old Town Square ❼
STAROMĚSTSKÉ NÁMĚSTÍ

See pp66–9.

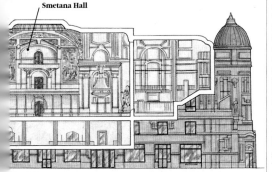

Smetana Hall

Old Town Square: North and East Sides ❼

STAROMĚSTSKÉ NÁMĚSTÍ

SOME OF PRAGUE'S colourful history is preserved around the Old Town Square in the form of its buildings. The north side of the Square is dominated by the white façade of the Baroque church of St Nicholas. The east side boasts two superb examples of the architecture of their times: the House at the Stone Bell, restored to its former appearance as a Gothic town palace, and the Rococo Golz-Kinský Palace. An array of pastel-coloured buildings completes the Square.

★ **House at the Stone Bell**
At the corner of the building, the bell is the sign of this medieval town palace.

Statues by Ignaz Platzer from 1760–65

Golz-Kinský Palace
C G Bossi created the elaborate stucco decoration on the façade of this Rococo palace (see p70).

EAST SIDE

Rococo stucco work

NORTH SIDE

★ **Church of St Nicholas**
Besides its original purpose as a parish church and, later, a Benedictine monastery church, this has served as a garrison church and a concert hall (see p70).

STAR SIGHTS

★ **Church of Our Lady before Týn**

★ **House at the Stone Bell**

★ **Church of St Nicholas**

East and north side

Jan Hus Monument

A solid gold effigy of the Virgin Mary

★ Church of Our Lady before Týn
Astronomer and astrologer Tycho Brahe is buried in Týn Church (see p70).

Entrance to Týn Church

Romanesque arcaded house with 18th-century façade

Týn School
Gothic rib vaulting is a primary feature of this building, which was a school from the 14th to the mid-19th century.

Restaurant U Sv. Salvatora façade dates from 1696

Ministerstvo Hospodářství
Architect Osvald Polívka designed this Art Nouveau building for the Prague City Insurance Company in 1898, with figures of firefighters on the upper façade. It now houses the Ministry of Commerce.

Staroměstské náměstí, 1793
The engraving by Filip and František Heger shows the Old Town Square teeming with people and carriages. The Old Town Hall is on the left.

Old Town Square: South Side ❼

STAROMĚSTSKÉ NÁMĚSTÍ

A COLOURFUL ARRAY of houses of Romanesque or Gothic origin, with fascinating house signs, graces the south side of the Old Town Square. The block between Celetná Street and Železná Street is especially attractive. The Square has always been a busy focal point, and today offers visitors a tourist information centre, as well as a number of restaurants, cafés, shops, and galleries.

U Lazara (At the Poor Wretch's)
Romanesque barrel vaulting testifies to the house's early origins, though it was rebuilt during the Renaissance. The ground floor houses the Staroměstská restaurace.

FRANZ KAFKA (1883–1924)

The author of two of the most influential novels of the 20th century, *The Trial* and *The Castle*, Kafka spent most of his short life in the Old Town. From 1893 to 1901 he studied in the Golz-Kinský Palace *(see p70)*, where his father later had a shop. He worked as an insurance clerk, but frequented a literary salon in At the Golden Unicorn on Old Town Square, along with others who wrote in German. Hardly any of his work was published in his lifetime.

At the Stone Table

At the Golden Unicorn

Železná Street

SOUTH SIDE

★ **At the Stone Ram**
The early-16th-century house sign shows a young maiden with a ram. The house has been referred to as At the Unicorn due to the similarity between the one-horned ram and a unicorn.

★ **Štorch House**
The late-19th-century painting of St Wenceslas on horseback by Mikuláš Aleš appears on this ornate Neo-Renaissance building, also known as At the Stone Madonna.

STAR SIGHTS

★ Štorch House

★ At the Stone Ram

Melantrichova Passage
*Václav Jansa's painting (1898)
shows the narrow passageway
leading to the Old Town Square.*

🔲 South side

⊛ Jan Hus Monument

At the Red Fox
*A golden Madonna and Child
look down from the Baroque
façade of an originally
Romanesque building.*

At The Ox
*Named after its
15th-century owner,
the burgher Ochs,
this house features an
early-18th-century
stone statue of
St Anthony of Padua.*

At the
Blue Star

At the Storks

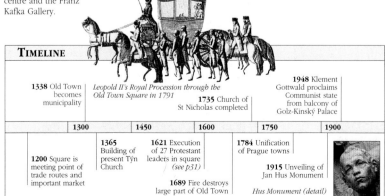

The arcade houses a
tourist information
centre and the Franz
Kafka Gallery.

U Bindrů
restaurant

Melantrichova
Passage

TIMELINE

	1300	1450	1600	1750	1900

1338 Old Town becomes municipality

Leopold II's Royal Procession through the Old Town Square in 1791

1735 Church of St Nicholas completed

1948 Klement Gottwald proclaims Communist state from balcony of Golz-Kinský Palace

1200 Square is meeting point of trade routes and important market

1365 Building of present Týn Church

1621 Execution of 27 Protestant leaders in square *(see p31)*

1689 Fire destroys large part of Old Town

1784 Unification of Prague towns

1915 Unveiling of Jan Hus Monument

Hus Monument (detail)

Statue of the Madonna on Our Lady before Týn

Church of Our Lady before Týn ❽
KOSTEL PANNY MARIE PŘED TÝNEM

Týnská, Štupartská. **Map** 3 C3.
📞 231 81 86. 🚇 Staroměstská,
Můstek. **Open** only for services.
✝ 5:30pm Mon–Fri, 1pm Sat,
11:30am & 1pm Sun. 🚫

DOMINATING THE Old Town Square are the magnificent multiple steeples of this historic church. The present Gothic church was started in 1365 and soon became associated with the reform movement in Bohemia. From the early 15th century until 1620 Týn was the main Hussite church in Prague. The Hussite king, George of Poděbrady, took Utraquist communion (see *Church of St Martin in the Wall p73*) here and had a gold chalice – the Utraquist symbol – mounted on the façade. After 1621 the chalice was melted down to become part of the statue of the Madonna that replaced it.

On the northern side of the church is a beautiful entrance portal (1390) decorated with scenes of Christ's passion. The dark interior has some notable features, including Gothic sculptures of *Calvary*, a pewter font (1414) and a 15th-century Gothic pulpit. The Danish astronomer Tycho Brahe (1546–1601) is buried here.

Golz-Kinský Palace ❾
PALÁC GOLZ-KINSKÝCH

Staroměstské náměstí 12. **Map** 3 C3.
📞 24 81 07 58. 🚇 Staroměstská.
Open 10am–6pm Tue–Sun. 📷 🚫

THIS LOVELY Rococo palace, designed by Kilian Ignaz Dientzenhofer, has a pretty pink and white stucco façade crowned with statues of the four elements by Ignaz Franz Platzer. It was bought from the Golz family in 1768 by Štěpán Kinský, an Imperial diplomat.

In 1948 Communist leader, Klement Gottwald, used the balcony to address a huge crowd of party members – a key event in the crisis that led up to his *coup d'état*. The National Gallery now uses the Golz-Kinský Palace for temporary art exhibitions.

Kinský arms on Golz-Kinský Palace

Jan Hus Monument ❿
POMNÍK JANA HUSA

Staroměstské náměstí. **Map** 3 B3.
🚇 Staroměstská.

AT ONE END of the Old Town Square stands the massive monument to the religious reformer and Czech hero, Jan Hus (see pp26–7). Hus was burnt at the stake after being pronounced a heretic by the Council of Constance in 1415. The monument by Ladislav Šaloun was unveiled in 1915 on the 500th anniversary of his death. It shows two groups of people, one of victorious Hussite warriors, the other of Protestants forced into exile 200 years later, and a young mother symbolizing national rebirth. The dominant figure of Hus emphasizes the moral authority of the man who gave up life rather than his beliefs.

Church of St Nicholas ⓫
KOSTEL SV. MIKULÁŠE

Staroměstské náměstí. **Map** 3 B3.
🚇 Staroměstská. **Open**
10am–noon Tue–Fri , also 2–4pm
Wed. 📷

THERE HAS BEEN a church on this site since the 12th century. It was the Old Town's parish church and meeting place until Týn Church was completed in the 14th century. After the Battle of the White Mountain in 1620 (see pp30–31) the church became part of a Benedictine monastery. The present church by Kilian Ignaz Dientzenhofer, was completed in 1735. Its dramatic white façade is studded with statues by Antonín Braun. When in

Defiant Hussites on the Jan Hus Monument in Old Town Square

Church of St Nicholas in the Old Town

1781 Emperor Joseph II closed all monasteries not engaged in socially useful activities, the church was stripped bare. In World War I the church was used by the troops of Prague's garrison. The colonel in charge took the opportunity to restore the church with the help of artists who might otherwise have been sent to the front. The magnificent dome has frescoes of the lives of St Nicholas and St Benedict by Kosmas Damian Asam. In the nave is a huge crown-shaped chandelier. At the end of the war, the church of St Nicholas was given to the Czechoslovak Hussite Church. Concerts are given now in the church during the summer.

Old Town Hall ⓬
STAROMĚSTSKÁ RADNICE

See pp72–3.

House at the Two Golden Bears ⓭
DŮM U DVOU ZLATÝCH MEDVĚDŮ

Kožná 1. **Map** 3 B4. Můstek.
Closed to the public.

IF YOU LEAVE the Old Town Square by the narrow Melantrichova Street, make a point of turning into the first alleyway on the left to see the portal of the house called "At the Two Golden Bears". The present Renaissance building was constructed from two earlier houses in 1567. The portal was added in 1590, when a wealthy merchant, Lorenc Štork, secured the services of court architect Bonifaz Wohlmut, who had designed the spire on the tower of St Vitus's Cathedral *(see pp100–3)*. His ornate portal with reliefs of two bears is one of the most beautiful Renaissance portals in Prague. Magnificent arcades, also dating from the 16th century, have been preserved in the inner courtyard. In 1885 Egon Erwin Kisch, known as the "Furious Reporter", was born here. He was a German-speaking Jewish writer and journalist, feared for the force of his left-wing rhetoric.

Church of St Gall ⓮
KOSTEL SV. HAVLA

Havelská. **Map** 3 C4. Můstek.
231 81 86. **Open** only for services. 12:15pm Mon–Fri, 7:30am Sun.

DATING FROM around 1280, this church was built to serve an autonomous German community in the area known as Gall's Town (Havelské Město). In the 14th century this was merged with the Old Town. In the 18th century the church was given a dramatic Baroque facelift by Giovanni Santini-Aichel, who created a bold façade decorated with statues of saints by Ferdinand Brokof. Rich interior furnishings include several paintings by the leading Baroque artist Karel Škréta, who is buried in the church. Prague's best-known market was once held here. Havelská Street still has stalls of flowers, vegetables, toys, and clothes.

One of nine statues on façade of St Gall's

Carved Renaissance portal of the House at the Two Golden Bears

Old Town Hall ⑫

STAROMĚSTSKÁ RADNICE

O NE OF THE most striking buildings in Prague is the Old Town Hall, established in 1338 after King John of Luxemburg agreed to set up a town council. Over the centuries a number of old houses were knocked together as the Old Town Hall expanded, and it now consists of a row of colourful Gothic and Renaissance buildings, most of which have been carefully restored after heavy damage inflicted by the Nazis in the 1945 Prague Uprising. The tower is 69.5 m (228 ft) high and offers a spectacular view of the city.

Old Council Hall
This 19th-century engraving features the well-preserved 15th-century ceiling.

Old Town Coat of Arms
Above the inscription, "Prague, Head of the Kingdom", is the coat of arms of the Old Town, which was adopted in 1784 for the whole city.

Temporary art exhibitions

EXECUTIONS IN THE OLD TOWN SQUARE

A bronze tablet below the Old Town Hall chapel records the names of the 27 Protestant leaders executed here by order of the Catholic Emperor Ferdinand on 21 June 1621. This was the humiliating aftermath of the Battle of the White Mountain *(see pp30–31)*. This defeat led to the emigration of Protestants unwilling to give up their faith, a Counter-Reformation drive and Germanization.

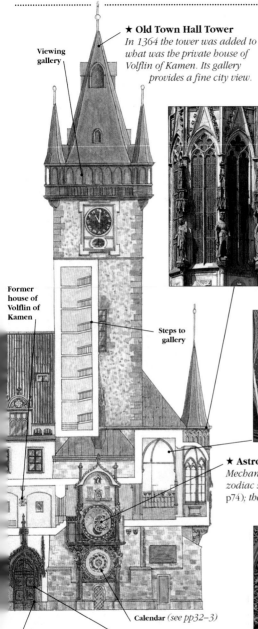

Viewing
gallery

★ **Old Town Hall Tower**
*In 1364 the tower was added to
what was the private house of
Volflin of Kamen. Its gallery
provides a fine city view.*

Former
house of
Volflin of
Kamen

Steps to
gallery

Entrance hall
decorated with
mosaics

Calendar *(see pp32–3)*

VISITORS' CHECKLIST

Staroměstské náměstí 1. **Map** 3
C3. 24 48 11 11.
Staroměstská (line A), Můstek (A
& B). 17. **Open** 9am–5:30pm
summer, (4:30pm winter) Tue–Sun.
Sections closed for renovation.
except for tower.

Oriel Chapel
*The original stained-glass
windows on the five-sided
chapel were destroyed in the
last days of World War II,
but were replaced in 1987.*

Oriel Chapel Ceiling
*The chapel, which was built
on the first floor of the tower
in 1381, has an ornate,
recently restored ceiling.*

★ **Astronomical Clock**
*Mechanical figures perform above the
zodiac signs in the upper section (see
p74); the lower section is a calendar.*

Gothic Door
*This late Gothic main
entrance to the Town
Hall and Tower was
carved by Matthias
Rejsek. The entrance
hall is filled with wall
mosaics after designs
by the Czech painter
Mikuláš Aleš.*

STAR FEATURES

★ **Astronomical Clock**

★ **Old Town Hall Tower**

Town Hall Clock

ORLOJ

Jan Táborský

THE TOWN HALL acquired its first clock at the beginning of the 15th century. In 1490, when it was rebuilt by a master clockmaker called Hanuš, the councillors are said to have been so anxious to prevent him from recreating his masterpiece elsewhere, that they blinded the poor man. Though it has been repaired many times since, the mechanism of the clock we see today was perfected by Jan Táborský between 1552 and 1572.

The Apostles

Vanity and Greed

Arabic numerals 1–24

Astronomical Clock with the sun in Libra

Death

Blue, representing the daylight hours

Calendar by Josef Mánes (see pp32–3)

The Turk, a symbol of lust

APOSTLES

THE CENTREPIECE of the show that draws a crowd of spectators every time the clock strikes the hour is the procession of

Vojtěch Sucharda's Apostles, sculpted after the last set was burnt in 1945

the 12 Apostles. First the figure of Death, the skeleton on the right of the clock, gives a pull on the rope that he holds in his right hand. In his left hand is an hourglass, which he raises and inverts. Two windows then open and the clockwork Apostles (or to be precise 11 of the Apostles plus St Paul) move slowly round, led by St Peter.

At the end of this part of the display, a cock crows and the clock chimes the hour. The other moving figures are a Turk, who shakes his head from side to side, Vanity, who looks at himself in a mirror and Greed, adapted from the original medieval stereotype of a Jewish moneylender.

ASTRONOMICAL CLOCK

THE CLOCKMAKER'S view of the universe had the Earth fixed firmly at the centre. The purpose of the clock was not to tell you the exact time but to imitate the supposed orbits of the sun and moon about the Earth. The hand with the sun, which points to the hour, in fact records three different kinds of time. The outer ring of medieval Arabic numerals measures Old Bohemian time, in which a day of 24 hours was reckoned from the setting of the sun. The ring of Roman numerals indicates time as we know it. The blue part of the dial represents the

visible part of the sky. This is divided into 12 parts. In so-called Babylonian time, the period of daylight was divided into 12 hours, which would vary in length from summer to winter.

The clock also shows the movement of the sun and moon through the 12 signs of the zodiac, which were of great importance in 16th-century Prague.

The figures of Death and the Turk

Church of St Martin in the Wall **❺**

KOSTEL SV. MARTINA VE ZDI

Martinská. **Map** 3 B5. ⟁ *Národní třída, Můstek.* 🚇 *6, 9, 18, 22.* **Closed** to the public.

THIS 12TH-CENTURY church became part of the newly erected town wall during the fortification of the Old Town in the 13th century, hence its name. It was the first church where blessed wine, usually reserved for the clergy, was offered to the congregation as well as bread. This was a basic tenet of belief of the moderate Hussites *(see pp26–7)*, the Utraquists, who took their name from the Latin *sub utraque specie*, "in both kinds". In 1787 the church was converted into workshops, but rebuilt in its original form in the early years of this century.

Náprstek Museum **❻**

NÁPRSTKOVO MUZEUM

Betlémské náměstí 1. **Map** 3 B4. 📞 *24 21 45 37.* ⟁ *Národní třída.* 🚇 *6, 9, 18, 22.* **Open** *9am–5:30pm Tue–Sun.* 📷

VOJTA NÁPRSTEK, art patron and philanthropist, created this museum as a tribute to modern industry following a decade of exile in America after the 1848 revolution *(see pp32–3)*. On his return in 1862, inspired by London's Victorian museums, he began his collection. He created the Czech Industrial Museum by joining five older buildings together, and in the process virtually destroyed the family brewery and home – an 18th-century house called At the Haláneks (U Halánků). His interests later turned to ethnography and the collection now consists of artefacts from Asian, African and Native American cultures. There are weapons, hunting implements and ritual objects from the Aztecs, Toltecs and Mayas. The collection of statues and masks is particularly interesting. The Náprstek Museum is now part of the National Museum.

Ceiling fresco by Václav Vavřinec Reiner in Church of St Giles

Church of St Giles **❼**

KOSTEL SV. JILJÍ

Husova. **Map** 3 B4. 📞 *24 22 02 35.* ⟁ *Národní třída.* 🚇 *6, 9, 18, 22.* **Open** for services only. ✝ *7am & 6:30pm Mon–Fri, 6:30pm Sat, 8:30am, 10:30am, noon, 6:30pm Sun.* 📷

DESPITE A beautiful Gothic portal on the southern side, the inside of this church is essentially Baroque. Founded in 1371 on the site of an old Romanesque church, it became a Hussite parish church in 1420. Following the Protestant defeat in 1620 *(see pp30–31)*, Ferdinand II presented the church to the Dominicans, who built a huge friary on its southern side. It has now been returned to the Dominicans, religious orders having been abolished under the Communists.

The vaults of the church are decorated with frescoes by the painter Václav Vavřinec Reiner, who is buried in the nave before the altar of St Vincent. The main fresco, a glorification of the Dominicans, shows St Dominic and his friars helping the pope defend the Catholic Church from non-believers.

Bethlehem Chapel **❽**

BETLÉMSKÁ KAPLE

Betlémské náměstí. **Map** 3 B4. ⟁ *Národní třída.* 🚇 *6, 9, 18, 22.* **Open** *9am–6pm daily.* 📷

THE PRESENT "chapel" is a faithful reconstruction of a hall built by the followers of the radical preacher Jan Milič z Kroměříže in 1391–4. The hall was used for preaching sermons in Czech. Between 1402 and 1413 Jan Hus *(see pp26–7)* preached in the Chapel, attracting a huge following. Strongly influenced by the teachings of the English religious reformer, John Wycliffe, Hus condemned the corrupt practices of the Church, arguing that the Scriptures should be the sole source of doctrine. After the Battle of the White Mountain in 1620 *(see pp30–31)*, when Protestant worship was outlawed, the building was handed over to the Jesuits, who completely rebuilt it with six naves. In 1786 it was almost demolished and an apartment house built on the site. After World War II the chapel was reconstructed following old illustrations.

16th-century illustration showing Jan Hus preaching in Bethlehem Chapel

Street-by-Street: Old Town (West)

THE NARROW STREETS near Charles Bridge follow
Prague's medieval street plan. For centuries Charles
Street (Karlova) was the main route across the Old
Town. The picturesque, twisting street is lined with
shops and houses displaying Renaissance and Baroque
façades. In the 17th century the Jesuits bought up a
vast area of land to the north of the street to house
the complex of the Clementinum university.

★ Clementinum
*This plaque records the
founding in 1783 of a state-
supervised seminary in place
of the old Jesuit university* ㉓

**Knights of the
Cross Square**
*From the façade of
the Church of the
Holy Saviour, black-
ened statues overlook
the small square* ㉕

Church of
St Francis

★ Smetana Museum
*A museum devoted to the life
and work of composer Bedřich
Smetana is housed in this Neo-
Renaissance building set on the
riverfront, which was once
an old waterworks* ㉔

ANENSKÁ

St Anne's Convent
was abolished in 1782.
Some of its buildings
are now used by the
National Theatre
(see pp156–7).

The Old Town Bridge Tower
dates from 1380. The Gothic sculptural
decoration on the eastern façade was
from Peter Parler's workshop. The
kingfisher was the favourite personal
symbol of Wenceslas IV (son of
Charles IV) in whose reign the tower
was completed (see p139).

Charles Street
*Among the many decorated houses
along the ancient street, be sure to
look out for this Art Nouveau
statue of the legendary Princess
Libuše (see p21) surrounded by
roses at No. 22/24* ㉑

Mariánské Square
The square used to be flooded so often, it was called "the puddle". The Art Nouveau sculptures on the balcony of the New Town Hall, built here in 1911, are by Stanislav Sucharda **20**

LOCATOR MAP
See Street Finder, map 3

Observatory tower

MARIÁNSKÉ NÁMĚSTÍ

Clam-Gallas Palace
One of Prague's grandest Baroque palaces and full of wonderful statuary, the Clam-Gallas is sadly in need of repair **19**

KARLOVA

LILIOVÁ

ŘETĚZOVÁ

HUSOVA

To Old Town Square

Church of St Giles
Much of the Baroque sculpture, like this angel on the altar (1738), is by František Weiss **17**

Palace of the Lords of Kunštát
George of Poděbrady lived here before he became King in 1458 **22**

Bethlehem Chapel
In this spacious chapel, rebuilt in the 1950s, Hus and other reformers preached to huge congregations **18**

0 metres   100
0 yards   100

KEY

– – – Suggested route

STAR SIGHTS

★ **Clementinum**

★ **Smetana Museum**

Clam-Gallas Palace ⓭
CLAM-GALLASŮV PALÁC

Husova 20. **Map** 3 B4. 📞 283 29 63. 📟 *Staroměstská.* **Closed** to the public during refurbishment.

SADLY THE INTERIOR of this magnificent Baroque palace has suffered somewhat since it has been used used to store the city archives. The palace, designed by Viennese court architect Johann Bernhard Fischer von Erlach, was built in 1713–30 for the Supreme Marshal of Bohemia, Jan Gallas de Campo. Its grand portals, each flanked by two pairs of muscular Hercules sculpted by Matthias Braun, give a tantalizing taste of what lies within. The main staircase is also decorated with Braun statues, set off by an illusionistic ceiling fresco,

Matthias Braun's statues on a portal of the Clam-Gallas Palace (c.1714)

The Triumph of Apollo by Carlo Carlone. The palace even has a theatre, where Beethoven performed some of his works.

Mariánské Square ⓴
MARIÁNSKÉ NÁMĚSTÍ

Map 3 B3. 📟 *Staroměstská, Můstek.*

TWO STATUES dominate the square from the corners of the forbidding Town Hall, built in 1912. One illustrates the story of the long-lived Rabbi Löw *(see p88)* finally being caught by the Angel of Death. The other is the Iron Man, a local ghost condemned to roam the Old Town after murdering his mistress. A niche in the garden wall of the Clam-Gallas Palace houses a statue of the River Vltava, depicted as a nymph pouring water from a jug. There is a story that an old soldier once made the nymph sole beneficiary of his will.

Charles Street ㉑
KARLOVA ULICE

Map 3 A4. 📟 *Staroměstská.*

A 19th-century sign on the House at the Golden Snake

DATING BACK to the 12th century, this narrow, winding street was part of the Royal Route *(see pp172–3)*, along which coronation processions passed on the way to Prague Castle. Many original Gothic and Renaissance houses remain, most converted into shops to attract the procession of tourists between Old Town Square and Charles Bridge.

The House at the Golden Snake (No. 18) is the oldest existing café in Prague. It was established here in 1714 by an Armenian, Deodatus Damajan, who handed out slanderous pamphlets from it. Look out for At the Golden Well (No. 3), which has a magnificent Baroque façade and stucco reliefs of saints including St Roch and St Sebastian, who are believed to offer protection against plagues.

Palace of the Lords of Kunštát ㉒
DŮM PÁNŮ Z KUNŠTÁTU

Řetězová 3. **Map** 3 B4. 📟 *Národní třída, Staroměstská.* 🚊 6, 9, 18, 22. **Open** May–Sep: 10am–6pm Tue–Sun. 🖼️ 📷

THE BASEMENT of the palace, dating from around 1200, contains three of the best-preserved Romanesque rooms in Prague. It was originally the ground floor, but over the years the surrounding ground level was raised by 3m (10 ft) to prevent flooding. In the 15th century the house was enlarged in Gothic style by its owners, the Lords of Kunštát and Poděbrady. The palace houses a historical exhibition devoted to Bohemia's only Hussite king, George of Poděbrady *(see pp26–7)*, who lived here for a time.

Clementinum ㉓
KLEMENTINUM

Křižovnické náměstí 4, Mariánské náměstí 5, Seminářská 1. **Map** 3 A4.
26 65 41. Staroměstská.
17, 18. **Library open** 8am–10pm Mon–Fri, 8am–7pm Sat. **Church of the Holy Saviour open** only for services. 2pm & 8pm Wed.

Former Jesuit Church of the Holy Saviour in the Clementinum

IN 1556 EMPEROR Ferdinand I invited the Jesuits to Prague to help bring the Czechs back into the Catholic fold. They established their headquarters in the former Dominican monastery of St Clement, hence the name Clementinum. This soon became an effective rival to the Carolinum *(see p65)*, the Utraquist university. Prague's first Jesuit church, the Church of the Holy Saviour (Kostel sv. Salvátora) was built here in 1601. Its façade, with seven large statues of saints by Jan Bendl (1659), is dramatically lit up at night.

Expelled in 1618, the Jesuits were back two years later more determined than ever to stamp out heresy. In 1622 the two universities were merged, resulting in the Jesuits gaining a virtual monopoly on higher education in Prague. They believed two-thirds of the population were secret heretics,

searched for books in Czech and then burnt them by the thousand. Between 1653 and 1723 the Clementinum expanded eastwards. Over 30 houses and three churches were pulled down to make way for the new complex.

When in 1773 the pope dissolved their order, the Jesuits had to leave Prague and education was secularized. The Clementinum became the Prague University library, today the National Library. Look out for any classical concerts performed in the beautiful Chapel of Mirrors (Zrcadlová kaple).

Smetana Museum ㉔
MUZEUM BEDŘICHA SMETANY

Novotného lávka 1. **Map** 3 A4.
726 53 71. Staroměstská.
17, 18. **Closed** until beginning of 1996.

ON A SPIT OF LAND beside the Vltava, a former Neo-Renaissance waterworks has been turned into a memorial to Bedřich Smetana, the father of Czech music. The museum contains documents, letters, scores and musical instruments detailing the composer's life and work. Smetana was a fervent patriot and his music helped inspire the Czech national revival. He went deaf towards the end of his life and never heard his famous cycle of symphonic poems, *Má Vlast* (My Country), being played.

Statue of Charles IV (1848) in Knights of the Cross Square

Knights of the Cross Square ㉕
KŘIŽOVNICKÉ NÁMĚSTÍ

Map 3 A4. Staroměstská.
17, 18. 135, 207. **Church of St Francis open** only for services.
9am Sun.

THIS SMALL SQUARE in front of the Old Town Bridge Tower offers wonderful views across the Vltava. On the northern side of the square stands the domed Church of St Francis (Kostel sv. Františka), once part of the monastery of the crusading Knights of the Cross with the Red Star. The eastern end is dominated by the façade of the Church of the Holy Saviour, part of the huge Clementinum complex. In the centre of the square stands a large bronze Neo-Gothic statue of Charles IV, erected to mark the 500th anniversary of his founding of the Carolinum *(see p65)*.

Sgraffitoed façade of the Smetana Museum

JEWISH QUARTER

JOSEFOV

IN THE MIDDLE AGES there were two distinct Jewish communities in Prague's Old Town: Jews from the west had settled around the Old-New Synagogue, Jews from the Byzantine Empire around the Old Shul (on the site of today's Spanish Synagogue). The two settlements gradually merged and were confined in an enclosed ghetto. For centuries Prague's Jews suffered from oppressive laws – in the 16th century they had to wear a yellow circle as a mark of shame. Christians

Art Nouveau detail on house in Kaprova

often accused them of starting fires and poisoning wells – any pretext for a pogrom. Discrimination was partially relaxed in 1784 by Joseph II, and the Jewish Quarter was named Josefov after him. In 1850 the area was officially incorporated as part of Prague. In the 1890s the city authorities decided to raze the ghetto slums because the area's complete lack of sanitation made it a health hazard. However, the Town Hall, a number of synagogues and the Old Jewish Cemetery were saved.

SIGHTS AT A GLANCE

Synagogues and Churches
Pinkas Synagogue ❹
Klausen Synagogue ❺
Old-New Synagogue
pp88–9 ❻
High Synagogue ❼
Maisel Synagogue ❾
Church of the Holy Ghost ❿
Spanish Synagogue ⓫
Church of St Simon
and St Jude ⓭
Church of St Castullus ⓮

Concert Hall
Rudolfinum ❶

Museums and Galleries
Museum of Decorative Arts ❷
St Agnes's Convent
pp92–3 ⓯

Historic Buildings
Jewish Town Hall ❽
Cubist Houses ⓬

Cemeteries
Old Jewish Cemetery
pp86–7 ❸

GETTING THERE

Staroměstská station on metro line A is close to all the major sights in the Jewish Quarter. The alternative is to take tram 17 or 18 to Náměstí Jana Palacha. For St Agnes's Convent, buses 126, 135 and 207 are convenient.

| 0 metres | 250 |
| 0 yards | 250 |

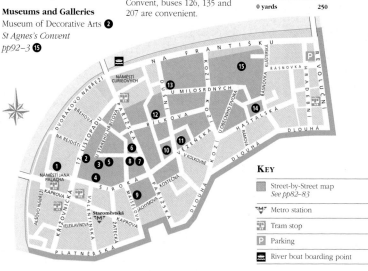

KEY

	Street-by-Street map *See pp82–83*
M	Metro station
	Tram stop
P	Parking
	River boat boarding point

◁ **Densely-packed gravestones in the Old Jewish Cemetery**

Street-by-Street: Jewish Quarter

T HOUGH THE OLD GHETTO has disappeared, much of the area's fascinating history is preserved in the synagogues around the Old Jewish Cemetery, while the newer streets are lined with many delightful Art Nouveau buildings. The old lanes to the east of the former ghetto lead to the quiet haven of St Agnes's Convent, beautifully restored as a branch of the National Gallery.

Cubist Houses
One of the new architectural styles used in the rebuilding of the old Jewish Quarter was based on the ideas of Cubism ⓬

★ Old Jewish Cemetery
Thousands of gravestones are crammed into the ancient cemetery ❸

★ Old-New Synagogue
The Gothic hall with its distinctive crenellated gable has been a house of prayer for over 700 years ❻

Klausen Synagogue
The exhibits of the State Jewish Museum include this alms box, dating from about 1800 ❺

High Synagogue
The interior has splendid Renaissance vaulting ❼

★ Museum of Decorative Arts
Stained glass panels on the staircase depict the crafts represented in the museum's wide-ranging collection ❷

Pinkas Synagogue
The walls are now a moving memorial to the Czech Jews killed in the Holocaust ❹

To Metro
Staroměstská

Jewish Town Hall
The 16th-century building still serves the Czech Jewish community ❽

Maisel Synagogue
The original synagogue was built as a tribute to Mayor Mordechai Maisel in 1591 ❾

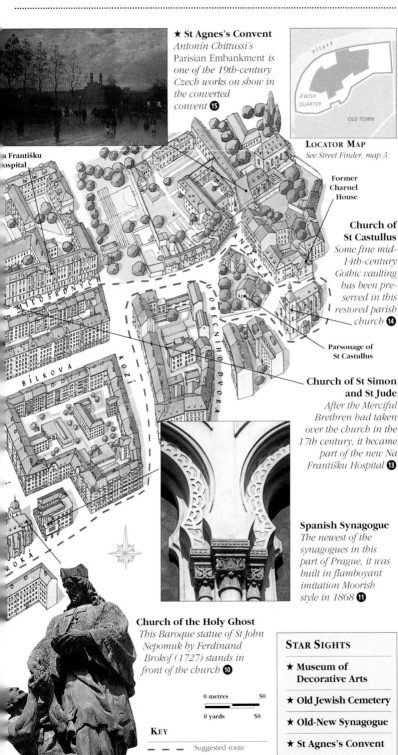

★ St Agnes's Convent
Antonín Chittussi's
Parisian Embankment *is
one of the 19th-century
Czech works on show in
the converted
convent* ⓯

LOCATOR MAP
See Street Finder, map 3

Na Františku
Hospital

Former
Charnel
House

**Church of
St Castullus**
*Some fine mid-
14th-century
Gothic vaulting
has been pre-
served in this
restored parish
church* ⓮

Parsonage of
St Castullus

**Church of St Simon
and St Jude**
*After the Merciful
Brethren had taken
over the church in the
17th century, it became
part of the new Na
Františku Hospital* ⓭

Spanish Synagogue
*The newest of the
synagogues in this
part of Prague, it was
built in flamboyant
imitation Moorish
style in 1868* ⓫

Church of the Holy Ghost
*This Baroque statue of St John
Nepomuk by Ferdinand
Brokof (1727) stands in
front of the church* ⓾

| 0 metres | 50 |
| 0 yards | 50 |

KEY

– – –   Suggested route

STAR SIGHTS

★ **Museum of
Decorative Arts**

★ **Old Jewish Cemetery**

★ **Old-New Synagogue**

★ **St Agnes's Convent**

Stage of the Dvořák Hall in the Rudolfinum

The glass collection is one of the largest in the world, but only a fraction of it is ever on display. Pride of place goes to the Bohemian glass, of which there are many fine Baroque and 19th- and 20th-century pieces. Medieval and Venetian Renaissance glass are also well represented.

Among the permanent exhibitions of other crafts, look out for the Meissen porcelain, the Gobelin tapestries and the intricate timepieces made by Erasmus Habermel, clockmaker to Rudolph II. The furniture collection has exquisitely carved escritoires and bureaux dating back to the Renaissance. On the mezzanine floor are halls for temporary exhibitions and an art library with over 100,000 publications.

Rudolfinum ❶

Alšovo Nábřeží. **Map** 3 A3.
🚇 *Staroměstská.* 🚋 17, 18.
🚌 135, 207. **Open** only for concerts & other cultural events. 🚫

Now the home of the Czech Philharmonic Orchestra, the Rudolfinum is one of the most impressive landmarks on the Old Town bank of the Vltava. Many of the major concerts of the Prague Spring music festival (see p50) are held here. There are several concert halls, the sumptuous Dvořák Hall ranking among the finest creations of 19th-century Czech architecture.

The Rudolfinum was built between 1876 and 1884 to a design by Josef Zítek and Josef Schulz and named in honour of Crown Prince Rudolph of Habsburg. Like the National Theatre (see pp156–7), it is an outstanding example of Czech Neo-Renaissance style. The curving balustrade is decorated with statues of distinguished Czech, Austrian and German composers and artists.

Also known as the House of Artists (Dům umělců), the building originally housed an art gallery and the Museum of Decorative Arts. It is still used

on occasions for temporary art exhibitions. Between 1918 and 1939, and for a brief period after World War II, the Rudolfinum was the seat of the Czechoslovak parliament.

Museum of Decorative Arts ❷
UMĚLECKOPRŮMYSLOVÉ MUZEUM

17. listopadu 2. **Map** 3 B3.
📞 24 81 12 41. 🚇 *Staroměstská.*
🚋 17, 18. 🚌 135, 207. **Open** 10am–6pm Tue–Sun. 📷 🚫

For some years after its foundation in 1885, the museum's collections were housed in the Rudolfinum. The present building, designed by Josef Schulz in French Neo-Renaissance style, was completed in 1901.

Old Jewish Cemetery ❸
STARÝ ŽIDOVSKÝ HŘBITOV

See pp86–7.

Pinkas Synagogue ❹
PINKASOVA SYNAGÓGA

Široká 3. **Map** 3 B3.
🚇 *Staroměstská.* 🚋 17, 18.
🚌 135, 207. **Open** 9:30am–5pm Sun–Fri. 📷 🚫 ♿

The synagogue was founded in 1479 by Rabbi Pinkas and enlarged in 1535 by Aaron Meshulam Horowitz, the rabbi's great-nephew. It has been rebuilt many times over the centuries. Excavations here have turned up several fascinating relics of life in the medieval ghetto, including a *mikva* or ritual bath. The core of the present building is a hall with

Names of Holocaust victims on Pinkas Synagogue wall

Gothic vaulting. The gallery for women was added in the early 17th century.

The synagogue now serves as a memorial to all the Jewish Czechoslovak citizens who were imprisoned in Terezín concentration camp and later deported to various Nazi extermination camps. The names of the 77,297 who did not return are inscribed on the synagogue walls.

Klausen Synagogue ❺
KLAUSOVÁ SYNAGÓGA

U starého hřbitova 1. **Map** 3 B3.
ˈMˈ *Staroměstská.* 🚋 *17, 18.*
🚌 *135, 207.* **Open** *9:30am–5pm Sun–Fri.* 📷 🚫

BEFORE THE FIRE of 1689, this site was occupied by a number of small Jewish schools and prayer houses known as *klausen*. The name was preserved in the Klausen Synagogue, built on the ruins and completed in 1694. The High Baroque structure has a fine barrel-vaulted interior with rich stucco decorations. It now houses Hebrew prints and manuscripts and an exhibition of Jewish traditions and customs, tracing the history of the Jews in Central Europe back to the early Middle Ages. Many exhibits relate to famous figures in the city's Jewish community including the 16th-century Rabbi Löw *(see p88),* who, according to legend, created an artificial man or *golem* out of clay.

19th-century Torah pointer in Klausen Synagogue

Adjoining the synagogue is a building which looks like a tiny medieval castle. It was built in 1906 as the ceremonial hall of the Jewish Burial Society. In 1944 an exhibition was put on here detailing the history of the Prague ghetto. The building now houses a permanent exhibition of children's drawings from the Terezín concentration camp.

18th-century silver-gilt Torah shield in the High Synagogue

Old-New Synagogue ❻
STARONOVÁ SYNAGÓGA

See pp88–9.

High Synagogue ❼
VYSOKÁ SYNAGÓGA

Červená 4. **Map** 3 B3.
ˈMˈ *Staroměstská.* 🚋 *17, 18.*
🚌 *135, 207.* **Open** *9:30am–6pm. Sun–Fri.* 📷 🚫

LIKE THE Jewish Town Hall, the building of the High Synagogue was financed by Mordechai Maisel, mayor of the Jewish Town, in the 1570s. Originally the two buildings formed a single complex and to facilitate communication with the Town Hall, the main hall of the synagogue was on the first floor. It was not until the 19th century that the two buildings were separated and the synagogue was provided with its own staircase and street entrance. You can still see the original Renaissance vaulting and stucco decoration.

The exhibition in the synagogue includes richly embroidered Torah mantles, curtains and other religious textiles. There are also silver ornaments,

such as shields and finials, used to decorate the Ark, where the Torah scrolls are kept. These date from the 16th to the 19th centuries.

Jewish Town Hall ❽
ŽIDOVSKÁ RADNICE

Maislova 18. **Map** 3 B3.
📞 *24 81 11 21.* ˈMˈ *Staroměstská.*
🚋 *17, 18.* 🚌 *135, 207.* **Closed** *to the public.*

THE CORE of this attractive pink and white building is the original Jewish Town Hall, built in 1570–77 by the immensely rich mayor, Mordechai Maisel. In 1763 it acquired a new appearance in the flowery style of the Late Baroque. The last alterations date from 1908, when the southern wing was enlarged.

On the roof stands a small wooden clock tower with a distinctive green steeple. The right to build the tower was originally granted to the Jewish community after their part in the defence of Charles Bridge against the Swedes in 1648 *(see pp30–31).* On one of the gables here is another clock. This one has Hebrew figures and, because Hebrew reads from right to left, hands that turn in an anti-clockwise direction. The Town Hall is now the seat of the Council of Jewish Religious Communities in the Czech Republic.

Façade and clock tower of the Jewish Town Hall

Old Jewish Cemetery ❸

STARÝ ŽIDOVSKÝ HŘBITOV

THIS REMARKABLE SITE was, for over 300 years, the only burial ground permitted to Jews. Founded in 1478, it was slightly enlarged over the years but still basically corresponds to its medieval size. Because of the lack of space people had to be buried on top of each other, up to 12 layers deep. Today you can see over 12,000 gravestones crammed into the tiny space, but an estimated 100,000 people are thought to have been buried here. The last burial was of Moses Beck in 1787.

View across the cemetery towards the western wall of the Klausen Synagogue

Jewish printers, Mordechai Zemach (d 1592) and his son Bezalel (d 1589), are buried under this square gravestone.

The Pinkas Synagogue is the second-oldest in Prague *(see p84)*.

David Gans' Tombstone
The tomb of the writer and astronomer (1541–1613) is decorated with the symbols of his name – a star of David and a goose (Gans in German).

The oldest tomb is that of the writer Rabbi Avigdor Kara (1439).

Rabbi David Oppenheim (1664–1736)
The chief rabbi of Prague owned the largest collection of old Hebrew manuscripts and prints in the city.

Klausen Synagogue *(see p85)*

The gravestone of Moses Beck

The Nephele Mound was where infants who died under a year old were buried.

STAR SIGHTS

★ **Tombstone of Rabbi Löw**

★ **Tombstone of Hendela Bassevi**

★ **14th-Century Tombstones**

★ **14th-Century Tombstones**
Embedded in the wall are fragments of Gothic tombstones brought here from an older Jewish cemetery discovered in 1866 in Vladislavova Street in the New Town.

VISITORS' CHECKLIST

U Starého hřbitova. **Map** 3 A2.
☎ 24 81 00 99 *(State Jewish
Museum)*. **Ⓜ** Staroměstská.
🚊 17, 18 to Staroměstská.
Open *Apr–Oct: 9:30am–5pm
Sun–Fri; Nov–Mar: 9:30am–
4:30pm Sun–Fri.* 🎫 *includes
entry into Pinkas, Klausen,
Maisel and High synagogues.*

Prague Burial Society
*Founded in 1564, the group carried out ritual
burials and performed charitable work in the
community. Members of the society wash their
hands after leaving the cemetery.*

**★ Tombstone of
Rabbi Löw**
*The most visited grave
in the cemetery is that
of Rabbi Löw (1520–
1609). Visitors place
hundreds of pebbles
and wishes on his
grave as a mark
of respect.*

**The Museum of
Decorative Arts
(see p84)**

**The Neo-
Romanesque
Ceremonial
Hall**

**Mordechai
Maisel**
(1528–1601) was
Mayor of Prague's
Jewish Town and a
philanthropist.

★ Tombstone of Hendela Bassevi
*The highly-decorated tomb (1628)
was built for the beautiful wife of
Prague's first Jewish nobleman.*

UNDERSTANDING THE GRAVESTONES

From the late 16th century
onwards, tombstones in
the Jewish cemetery were
decorated with symbols
denoting the background,
family name or profession
of the deceased person.

**Blessing
hands:
Cohen family**

**A pair of
scissors:
tailor**

**A stag:
Hirsch or
Zvi family**

**Grapes:
blessing or
abundance**

Old-New Synagogue ⑥

STARONOVÁ SYNAGOGA

Star of David in Červená Street

BUILT AROUND 1270, this is the oldest synagogue in Europe and one of the earliest Gothic buildings in Prague. The synagogue has survived fires, the slum clearances of the 19th century and many Jewish pogroms. Residents of the Jewish Quarter have often had to seek refuge within its walls and today it is still the religious centre for Prague's Jews. It was originally called the New Synagogue until another synagogue was built nearby – this was later destroyed.

The synagogue's eastern side

★ Jewish Standard
The historic banner of Prague's Jews is decorated with a Star of David and within it the hat that had to be worn by Jews in the 14th century.

The 14th-century stepped brick gable

These windows formed part of the 18th-century extensions built to allow women a view of the service.

Candlestick holder

RABBI LÖW AND THE GOLEM

The scholar and philosophical writer Rabbi Löw, director of the Talmudic school (which studied the Torah) in the late 16th century, was also thought to possess magical powers. He was supposed to have created a figure, the Golem, from clay and then brought it to life by placing a magic stone tablet in its mouth. The Golem went berserk and the Rabbi had to remove the tablet. He hid the creature among the Old-New Synagogue's rafters.

Rabbi Löw and the Golem

★ Five-rib Vaulting
Two massive octagonal pillars inside the hall support the five-rib vaults.

Right-hand Nave
The glow from the bronze chandeliers provides light for worshippers using the seats lining the walls.

VISITORS' CHECKLIST

Pařížská and Červená.
Map 3 B2. Ⓜ Staroměstská.
🚌 17, 18 to Staroměstská, 17 to Law Faculty (Právnická fakulta).
Open 9am–5pm Mon–Thu & Sun, 9am–3pm Fri. 📷 ⦸
✡ 8am Mon–Fri, 9am Sat (services in Czech).

The tympanum above the Ark is decorated with 13th-century leaf carvings.

★ **Rabbi Löw's Chair**
A star of David marks the chair of the Chief Rabbi, placed where the distinguished 16th-century scholar used to sit.

The cantor's platform and its lectern is surrounded by a wrought-iron Gothic grille.

Entrance to the Synagogue in Červená Street

The Ark
This shrine is the holiest place in the synagogue and holds the sacred scrolls of the Torah.

Entrance Portal
The tympanum above the door in the south vestibule is decorated with clusters of grapes and vine leaves growing on twisted branches.

STAR FEATURES

★ **Rabbi Löw's Chair**

★ **Five-rib Vaulting**

★ **Jewish Standard**

18th-century silver Torah crown in the Maisel Synagogue

Maisel Synagogue ⑨
MAISELOVA SYNAGÓGA

Maiselova 10. **Map** 3 B3.
🚇 *Staroměstská.* 🚊 17, 18.
🚌 135, 207. **Open** 9:30am–5pm
Sun–Fri. ⚡ ⊘ ♿

W HEN IT WAS FIRST built at
the end of the 16th
century, this was a private
house of prayer for the use of
mayor Mordechai Maisel and
his family. Maisel had made a
fortune lending money to
Emperor Rudolph II to
finance wars against the
Turks, and his synagogue was
the most richly decorated in
the city. The original building
was a victim of the fire that
devastated the Jewish Town
in 1689 and a new synagogue
was built in its place. Its
present crenellated, Gothic
appearance dates from the
beginning of this century.
  Since the 1960s the Maisel
Synagogue has housed a
fascinating collection of
Jewish silver and other
metalwork dating
from Renaissance
times to the 20th
century. It includes
many Torah crowns,
shields and finials.
Crowns and finials were
used to decorate the
rollers on which the text of
the Torah (the five books
of Moses) was kept. The
shields were hung over the
mantle that was draped over
the Torah and the pointers
were used to follow the text

so that it was not touched by
readers' hands. There are also
objects such as wedding
plates, lamps and candlesticks
made of pewter, brass and
ceramics. By a tragic irony,
nearly all these Jewish
treasures were brought to
Prague by the Nazis from
synagogues throughout
Bohemia and Moravia with
the intention of founding a
museum of a vanished people.

Church of the Holy Ghost ⑩
KOSTEL SV. DUCHA

Dušní, Široká. **Map** 3 B3.
🚇 *Staroměstská.* 🚊 17. 🚌 135,
207. **Open** only for services. 🕙 8am
Mon–Sat, 9:30am Sun. ⊘ ♿

T HIS CHURCH stands on the
narrow strip of Christian
soil which once separated the
two Jewish communities of
the Middle Ages – the Jews of
the eastern and western rites.
Built in the mid-14th century,
the single-naved Gothic church
was originally part of a convent
of Benedictine nuns. The
convent was destroyed in
1420 during the Hussite Wars
(see pp26–7) and not rebuilt.
  The church was badly
damaged in the Old Town
fire of 1689. The exterior
preserves the original Gothic
buttresses and high windows,
but the vault of the nave was
rebuilt in Baroque style after
the fire. The furnishings too

are mainly Baroque. The high
altar dates from 1760, and
there is an altar painting of
St Joseph by Jan Jiří Heintsch
(c1647–1712). In front of the
church stands a stone statue
of St John Nepomuk *(see p137)*
distributing alms (1727) by
the prolific sculptor of the
Czech Baroque Ferdinand
Maximilian Brokof. Inside the
church there are a few earlier
statues, including a 14th-
century *Pietà* (the heads of
the figures are later, dating
from 1628), a Late Gothic
statue of St Ann and busts of
St Wenceslas and St Adalbert
from the early 16th century.

Church of the Holy Ghost

Spanish Synagogue ⑪
ŠPANĚLSKÁ SYNAGÓGA

Vězeňská 1. **Map** 3 B2.
🚇 *Staroměstská.* 🚊 17.
Closed to the public.

P RAGUE's first synagogue,
known as the Old School
(Stará Škola), once stood
on this site, but no trace
of the earlier building
remains. In the 11th
century the Old
School was the
centre of the
community of
Jews of the
eastern rite, who
lived strictly apart
from the Jews of the
western rite, who were
concentrated round the
Old-New Synagogue.
  The present building
dates from the second half of
the 19th century. The exterior
and interior are both pseudo-
Moorish in appearance. The

**Motif of the Ten Commandments
on the Spanish Synagogue's façade**

rich stucco decorations on the walls and vaults are reminiscent of the Alhambra in Spain, hence the name of the synagogue. Only the exterior of the synagogue can be viewed; the building serves as the storehouse for the State Jewish Museum's collection of textiles.

Cubist Houses ⑫
KUBISTICKÉ DOMY

Elišky Krásnohorské, 10–14. **Map** 3 B2.
ᴹ Staroměstská. ⟦17⟧. **Closed** to the public.

THE REBUILDING of the old Jewish Quarter at the turn of the 20th century gave Prague's architects scope to experiment with many new styles. Most of the blocks in this area are covered with flowing Art Nouveau decoration, but on the corner of Bílkova and Elišky Krásno-horské there is a plain façade with a few simple repeated geometrical shapes. This is an example of Cubist architecture, a fashion that did not really catch on in the rest of Europe, but was very popular with the avant-garde in Bohemia and Austria before and after World War I. This block was built for a cooperative of teachers in 1919–21.

At No. 7 Elišky Krásnohorské you can see the influence of Cubism in the curiously flat-tened atlantes supporting the windows. Another interesting Cubist building is the House of the Black Mother of God in Celetná *(see pp172–3)*.

Church of St Simon and St Jude ⑬
KOSTEL SV. ŠIMONA A JUDY

U milosrdných. **Map** 3 B2.
ᴹ Staroměstská. ⟦17⟧. ⟦135, 207⟧. **Closed** to the public.

MEMBERS OF the Bohemian Brethren built this church with high Late Gothic windows in 1615–20. The Brethren, founded in the mid-15th century, agreed with the Utraquists *(see p75)* in directing the congregation to receive both bread and wine

Cubist-style atlantes framing a window in Elišky Krásnohorské Street

at Holy Communion. In other respects they were more conservative than other Protestant sects, continuing to practise celibacy and Catholic sacraments such as confession. After the Battle of the White Mountain *(see pp30–31)*, the Brethren were expelled from the Empire.

The church was then given to a Catholic order, the Brothers of Mercy, becoming part of a monastery and hospital. Tradition has it that the monastery's wooden steps were built from the scaffold on which 27 Czechs were executed in 1621 *(see p72)*. In the 18th century the city's first anatomy lecture hall was established here and the complex continues to serve as a hospital – the Na Františku. It has not been decided what use should be made of the church.

Detail of Baroque façade of Church of St Simon and St Jude

Church of St Castullus ⑭
KOSTEL SV. HAŠTALA

Haštalské náměstí. **Map** 3 C2. ⟦5, 14, 26⟧. ⟦135, 125, 207⟧. **Open** irregularly. ⟦5pm Sun⟧.

THIS PEACEFUL little corner of Prague takes its name – Haštal – from the parish church of St Castullus. One of the finest Gothic buildings in Prague, the church was erected on the site of an older Romanesque structure in the second quarter of the 14th century. Much of the church had to be rebuilt after the fire of 1689, but fortunately the double nave on the north side survived. It has beautiful slender pillars supporting a delicate ribbed vault.

The interior furnishings are mainly Baroque, though there are remains of wall paintings of about 1375 in the sacristy and a metal font decorated with figures dating from about 1550. Standing in the Gothic nave is an impressive sculptural group depicting *Calvary* (1716) from the workshop of Ferdinand Maximilian Brokof.

St Agnes's Convent ⑮
KLÁŠTER SV. ANEŽKY

See pp92–3.

St Agnes's Convent ⓯

KLÁŠTER SV. ANEŽKY

IN 1234 A CONVENT of the Poor Clares was founded here by Agnes, sister of King Wenceslas I. She was not canonized until 1989. The convent, one of the very first Gothic buildings in Bohemia, was abolished in 1782 and fell into disrepair. Following painstaking restoration in the 1960s, it has recovered much of its original appearance and is now used by the National Gallery to display a collection of 19th-century Czech art. The paintings include depictions of incidents from Czech myth and history, and Romantic landscapes.

Head of statue of St Agnes by Josef Myslbek

First floor

★ Josefina
This is one of the finest portraits by Czech artist Josef Mánes (1820–71).

★ Winter Evening in Town
Jakub Schikaneder (1855–1924) painted scenes of life in Prague. Many have a mysterious, melancholy quality, but this depiction of a woman and child trudging through the snow is lighter in tone.

Ground floor

★ George of Poděbrady and Matthias Corvinus
Mikuláš Aleš (1852–1913) painted many patriotic historical scenes. Corvinus, King of Hungary, was forced to sign a treaty with King George in 1469.

Steps to first-floor gallery

Terrace café

STAR EXHIBITS

- **★ Josefina by Josef Mánes**

- **★ George of Poděbrady and Matthias Corvinus by Mikuláš Aleš**

- **★ Winter Evening in Town by Jakub Schikaneder**

Cloister
The Gothic vaulting around the cloister of the convent dates from the 14th century.

GALLERY GUIDE

The permanent exhibition is housed on the first floor of the old convent in a long gallery and smaller rooms around the cloister. One displays a model and plans for the National Theatre (see pp156–7).

Steps down to cloister

Upper part of Church of the Holy Saviour

VISITORS' CHECKLIST

U milosrdných 17. **Map** 3 C2.
☎ 24 81 06 28. Ⓜ Náměstí Republiky, Staroměstská. 🚊 17 to Law Faculty (Právnická fakulta), 5, 14, 26 to Dlouhá třída. **Open** 10am–6pm Tue–Sun (last guided tour: 5pm).

The Engraver Vorlíček and his Family

This realistic group portrait is by Karel Purkyně (1834–68), son of the great physiologist Jan Purkyně (see p151).

Upper part of concert hall

Oldřich and Božena

František Ženíšek painted many episodes from Czech legend and history. Here Prince Oldřich, who lived in the 11th century, spots his future bride, the beautiful Božena, in a group of village girls.

Church of the Holy Saviour
This capital decorated with heads of five Bohemian queens is matched by one with five Přemyslid kings.

Chapel of St Mary Magdalene

Church of St Francis

Entrance to Convent from Anežská

KEY

▨	19th-century Czech Art
▨	Cloister
□	Churches
□	Concert hall
▨	Special exhibitions
▨	Non-exhibition space

PRAGUE CASTLE AND HRADČANY

PRAŽSKÝ HRAD A HRADČANY

Stained-glass window in St Vitus's Cathedral

THE HISTORY of Prague begins with the Castle, founded in the 9th century by Prince Bořivoj. Its commanding position high above the river Vltava soon made it the centre of the lands ruled by the Přemyslids. The buildings enclosed by the Castle walls included a palace, three churches and a monastery. In about 1320 a town called Hradčany was founded in part of the Castle's outer bailey. The Castle has been rebuilt many times, most notably in the reigns of Charles IV and Vladislav Jagiello. After a disastrous fire in 1541, the badly-damaged buildings were rebuilt in Renaissance style and the Castle enjoyed its cultural heyday under Rudolph II. Later Habsburgs resided in Vienna, using the Castle only occasionally. Since 1918 it has been the seat of the president of the Republic.

SIGHTS AT A GLANCE

Churches and Monasteries
St Vitus's Cathedral pp100–3 ❷
St George's Basilica ❺
Capuchin Monastery ⓲
The Loreto pp116–17 ⓳
Strahov Monastery pp120–21 ㉒

Palaces
Royal Palace pp104–5 ❹
Lobkowicz Palace ❽
Belvedere ⓫
Archbishop's Palace ⓭
Martinic Palace ⓯
Černín Palace ⓴

Historic Buildings
Powder Tower ❸
Dalibor Tower ❾

Museums and Galleries
Picture Gallery of Prague Castle ❶
St George's Convent pp106–9 ❻
Sternberg Palace pp112–15 ⓮
Schwarzenberg Palace ⓰

Historic Streets
Golden Lane ❼
New World ⓱
Pohořelec ㉑

Parks and Gardens
South Gardens ⓾
Royal Garden ⓬

KEY

▢	Street-by-Street map See pp96–7
🚊	Tram stop
P	Parking
—	Castle wall

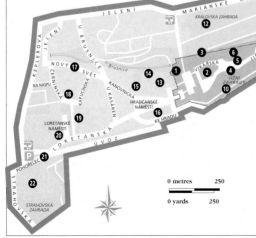

GETTING THERE

To avoid steep steps, take metro line A to Hradčanská (see Street Finder, map 2). Alternatively take the 22 tram to Pražský hrad (Prague Castle) or to Pohořelec. If you feel energetic, take the 12 or 22 tram to Malostranské náměstí in the Little Quarter, then walk up Nerudova or go to Malostranská metro and walk up Staré zámecké schody (Old Castle Steps).

◁ **The main entrance to Prague Castle**

Street-by-Street: Prague Castle

Despite PERIODIC FIRES and invasions, Prague Castle has retained churches, chapels, halls and towers from every period of its history, from the the Gothic splendour of St Vitus's Cathedral to the Renaissance additions of Rudolph II, the last Habsburg to use the Castle as his principal residence. The courtyards date from 1753–75 when the whole area was rebuilt in Late Baroque and Neo-Classical styles. The Castle became the seat of the Czechoslovak president in 1918 and Václav Havel, president of the Czech Republic, has an office here.

Powder Tower
Used in the past for storing gunpowder and as a bell foundry, the tower is now a museum ❸

Gothic reliquary of
St George's arm in
St Vitus's Cathedral

★ St Vitus's Cathedral
This relief decorates St Vitus's Golden Portal ❷

President's office

To Royal Garden

Picture Gallery of Prague Castle
Renaissance and Baroque paintings hang in the restored stables of the castle ❶

Second courtyard

Matthias Gate (1614)

First courtyard

To Hradčanské náměstí

Steps down to Little Quarter

Church of the Holy Rood

The Castle gates are crowned by copies of 18th-century statues of Fighting Giants by Ignaz Platzer.

South Gardens
18th-century statues decorate the gardens laid out in the old ramparts ❿

★ Golden Lane

The picturesque artisans' cottages along the inside of the castle wall were built in the late 16th century for the Castle's guards and gunners ⑦

LOCATOR MAP
See Street Finder, map 2

White Tower

Dalibor Tower
This grim tower takes its name from the first man to be imprisoned in it ⑨

Old Castle steps to Malostranská Metro

JIŘSKÁ

Lobkowicz Palace
The historical collection of the National Museum is housed here ⑧

★ St George's Convent

The convent houses early Bohemian art. This detail is from The Resurrection of Christ *by the 14th-century Master of the Třeboň Altar* ⑥

★ St George's Basilica

The vaulted chapel of the royal Bohemian martyr St Ludmilla is decorated with 16th-century paintings ⑤

KEY

– – – Suggested route

0 metres 60

0 yards 60

★ Royal Palace

The uniform exterior of the palace conceals many fine Gothic and Renaissance halls. Coats of arms cover the walls and ceiling of the Room of the New Land Rolls ④

STAR SIGHTS

★ **St Vitus's Cathedral**

★ **Royal Palace**

★ **St George's Basilica and Convent**

★ **Golden Lane**

Picture Gallery of Prague Castle ❶
OBRAZÁRNA PRAŽSKÉHO HRADU

Prague Castle, the first courtyard.
Map 2 D2. 🚋 *Malostranská,
Hradčanská.* 🚊 *22.* **Open** *9am–5pm
Tue–Sun.* 🖼 📷 ♿

THE GALLERY was created out of the old stables in 1965 to hold works of art collected since the reign of Rudolph II *(see pp28–9)*. Though most of the magnificent collection was looted by the Swedes in 1648, many interesting paintings remain. Paintings from the 16th–18th centuries form the bulk of the collection, but there are also sculptures, among them a copy of a bust of Rudolph by Adriaen de Vries. Highlights include Titian's *The Toilet of a Young Lady*, Rubens' *The Assembly of the Olympic Gods* and Guido Reni's *The Centaur Nessus Abducting Deianeira*. Master Theodoric, Paolo Veronese, Tintoretto and the Czech Baroque artists Jan Kupecký and Petr Brandl are among other artists represented. The National Gallery houses many of Rudolph's best paintings.

You can also see the remains of the Castle's first church, the 9th-century Church of our Lady, thought to have

been built by Prince Bořivoj, the first Přemyslid prince to be baptized a Christian *(see pp20–21)*. The historic site was discovered during the reconstruction of the stables.

St Vitus's Cathedral ❷
CHRÁM SV. VÍTA

See pp100–3.

Powder Tower ❸
PRAŠNÁ VĚŽ

Prague Castle, Vikářská. **Map** 2 D2.
🚋 *Malostranská, Hradčanská.*
🚊 *22.* **Open** *9am–5pm Tue–Sun.*
🖼 🚫 🍴

A TOWER WAS BUILT here in about 1496 by the King Vladislav II's architect Benedikt Ried as a cannon bastion overlooking the Stag Moat. The original was destroyed in the fire of 1541, but it was rebuilt as the home and workshop of gunsmith and bell founder Tomáš Jaroš. In 1549 he made Prague's largest bell, the 18-tonne Sigismund, for the bell tower of St Vitus's Cathedral.

During Rudolph II's reign (1576–1612), the tower became a laboratory for alchemists. It was here that adventurers such as Edward Kelley performed

View of the Powder Tower from across the Stag Moat

experiments that convinced the emperor they could transmute lead into gold.

In 1649, when the Swedish army was occupying the Castle, gunpowder exploded in the tower, causing serious damage. Nevertheless it continued to be used as a gunpowder store until 1754, when it was converted into flats for the sacristans of St Vitus's Cathedral. In the 1960s the building became a museum with exhibits relating to Jaroš's bell foundry and alchemy as practised in the reign of Rudolph II.

Royal Palace ❹
KRÁLOVSKÝ PALÁC

See pp104–5.

St George's Basilica ❺
BAZILIKA SV. JIŘÍ

Jiřské náměstí. **Map** 2 E2.
🚋 *Malostranská, Hradčanská.*
🚊 *22.* **Open** *9am–5pm (Nov–Mar: 4pm) Tue–Sun.* 🖼 🚫

FOUNDED by Prince Vratislav (915–21), the basilica predates St Vitus's Cathedral and is the best-preserved

Titian's *The Toilet of a Young Lady* in the Castle Picture Gallery

99

Romanesque church in Prague. It was enlarged in 973 when the adjoining St George's Convent was established here, and rebuilt following a fire in 1142. The massive twin towers and austere interior have been scrupulously restored to give a good idea of the church's original appearance. However, the rusty red façade was a 17th-century Baroque addition.

Buried in the church is St Ludmila, widow of the 9th-century ruler Prince Bořivoj (see pp20–21). She became Bohemia's first female Christian martyr when she was strangled as she knelt at prayer by Drahomíra, her daughter-in-law. Other members of the Přemyslid dynasty buried here include Vratislav. His simple tomb, made of painted wood, stands on the right-hand side of the nave at the foot of the curving steps that lead up to the choir. The Baroque grille opposite encloses the tomb of Boleslav II (973–99).

Façade and towers of St George's Basilica

St George's Convent ❻
KLÁŠTER SV. JIŘÍ

See pp106–9.

Golden Lane ❼
ZLATÁ ULIČKA

Map 2 E2. ᐧᐧ Malostranská, Hradčanská. 🚋 22.

NAMED AFTER the goldsmiths who lived here in the 17th century, this short, narrow street is one of the most picturesque in Prague. One side of the lane is lined with

One of the tiny houses in Golden Lane

tiny, brightly painted houses which were built right into the arches of the Castle walls. They were constructed in the late 1500s for Rudolph II's 24 Castle guards. A century later the goldsmiths moved in and modified the buildings. But by the 19th century the area had degenerated into a slum and was populated by Prague's poor and the criminal community. In the 1950s all the remaining tenants were moved and the area restored to something like its original state. Most of the houses were converted into shops selling books, Bohemian glass and other souvenirs for tourists, who flock to the narrow lane.

Golden Lane has been home to some well-known writers, including the Nobel prize-winning poet, Jaroslav Seifert, and Franz Kafka (see p68) who stayed at No. 22 with his sister for a few months in 1916–17.

Because of its name, legends have spread about the street being filled with alchemists huddled over their bubbling alembics trying to produce gold for Rudolph II. In fact the alchemists had laboratories in Vikářská, the lane between St Vitus's Cathedral and the Powder Tower.

Lobkowicz Palace ❽
LOBKOVICKÝ PALÁC

Jiřská 1. **Map** 2 E2. 📞 53 73 06, 53 73 64, 53 72 18. ᐧᐧ Hradčanská. 🚋 22. **Open** 9am–4:30pm Tue–Sun. 🎫 🚫 🏛

THIS IS ONE of the many new palaces that sprang up after the disastrous fire of 1541, when Hradčany was almost completely destroyed. The complex of buildings surrounding a central courtyard dates from 1570. Some of the original sgraffito on the façade has been preserved. Most of the present palace dates from Carlo Lurago's 17th-century reconstruction for the Lobkowicz family, who had bought the palace in 1627. The

Detail of 16th-century sgraffito on façade of Lobkowicz Palace

most splendid room is the 17th-century banqueting hall with mythological frescoes by Fabian Harovník, which is used for concerts and recitals.

In 1976 the palace became a museum with a permanent exhibition called Monuments of the Nation's Past. It traces Czech history from the first settlement of the Czech lands to the revolution of 1848 by means of documents, paintings, engravings, jewellery, glass, sculpture and weapons. Copies of the Czech Coronation Jewels, kept in St Vitus's Cathedral, are also on display.

St Vitus's Cathedral ❷
CHRÁM SV. VÍTA

W ORK BEGAN ON THIS, the city's most distinctive landmark, in
1344 on the orders of Charles IV. The first architect was the
French Matthew of Arras. After his death, Swabian Peter Parler
took over. His masons' lodge continued to work on the building
until the Hussite Wars. Finally completed by architects and artists
of the 19th and 20th centuries, the cathedral houses the crown
jewels and the tomb of "Good King" Wenceslas *(pp20–21)*.

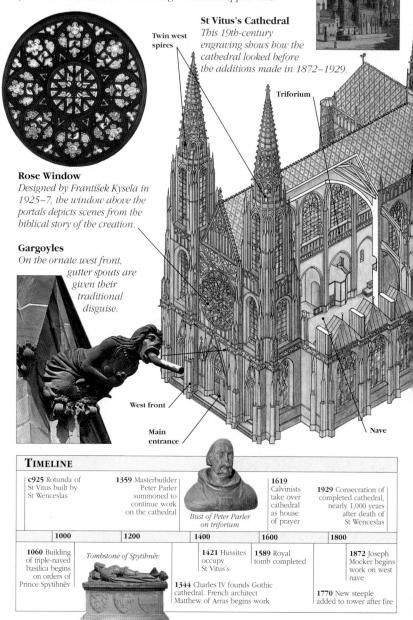

St Vitus's Cathedral
*This 19th-century
engraving shows how the
cathedral looked before
the additions made in 1872–1929.*

Twin west spires

Triforium

Rose Window
*Designed by František Kysela in
1925–7, the window above the
portals depicts scenes from the
biblical story of the creation.*

Gargoyles
*On the ornate west front,
gutter spouts are
given their
traditional
disguise.*

West front

Main entrance

Nave

TIMELINE

c925 Rotunda of St Vitus built by St Wenceslas

1359 Masterbuilder Peter Parler summoned to continue work on the cathedral

Bust of Peter Parler on triforium

1619 Calvinists take over cathedral as house of prayer

1929 Consecration of completed cathedral, nearly 1,000 years after death of St Wenceslas

1000	1200	1400	1600	1800

1060 Building of triple-naved basilica begins on orders of Prince Spytihněv

Tombstone of Spytihněv

1421 Hussites occupy St Vitus's

1589 Royal tomb completed

1872 Joseph Mocker begins work on west nave

1344 Charles IV founds Gothic cathedral. French architect Matthew of Arras begins work

1770 New steeple added to tower after fire

★ Flying Buttresses
The slender buttresses that sur-round the exterior of the nave and chancel, supporting the vaulted interior, are richly decorated like the rest of the cathedral.

The Renaissance bell tower is capped with a Baroque "helmet".

Chancel

VISITORS' CHECKLIST

Prague Castle, third courtyard.
Map 2 D2. Hradčanská,
Malostranská. 22 to
Prague Castle (Pražský hrad)
or to U Prašného mostu.
Cathedral open 9am–5pm
(Nov–Mar: 4pm) daily.
Steeple open
10am–4pm daily. **Closed** in
bad weather.

★ Chapel of St Wenceslas
The bronze ring on the chapel's north portal was thought to be the one to which St Wenceslas clung as he was murdered by his brother Boleslav (see pp20–21).

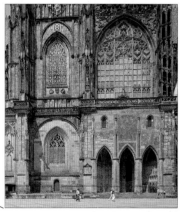

To Royal Palace
(See pp104–5)

The tomb of St Wenceslas is connected to an altar, decorated with semi-precious stones.

Gothic Vaulting
The skills of architect Peter Parler are never more clearly seen than in the delicate fans of ribbing that support the three Gothic arches of the Golden Portal.

★ Golden Portal
Until the 19th century this was the main cathedral entrance, and it is still used on special occasions. Above it is a mosaic of The Last Judgment *by 14th-century Venetian craftsmen.*

STAR FEATURES

★ **Chapel of St Wenceslas**

★ **Golden Portal**

★ **Flying Buttresses**

A Guided Tour of St Vitus's Cathedral

West door:
St Wenceslas'
murder

A WALK AROUND St Vitus's takes you back through a thousand years of history. Go in through the west portal to see some of the best elements of the modern, Neo-Gothic style and continue past a succession of side chapels to catch glimpses of religious artefacts such as saintly relics, and works of art from Renaissance paintings to modern statuary. Allow plenty of time to gaze at the richly decorated, jewel-studded St Wenceslas Chapel before leaving through the glorious 14th-century Golden Portal.

② Chancel
The chancel was built by Peter Parler from 1372. It is remarkable for the soaring height of its vault, counter-pointed by the intricacy of the webbed Gothic tracery.

Cathedral organ (1757)

New sacristy

① Alfons Mucha Window
The cathedral contains many superb examples of 20th-century Czech stained glass, notably St Cyril and St Methodius.

Main entrance (West Portal)

Thun Chapel

Chapel of St Ludmilla

THE FOUR ERAS OF ST VITUS'S

Excavations have revealed sections of the northern apse of St Wenceslas's original rotunda, and architectural and sculptural remains of the later basilica, beneath the existing cathedral. The western, Neo-Gothic end is a faithful completion of the 14th-century plan.

KEY

☐ Rotunda, 10th century

■ Basilica, 11th century

☐ Gothic cathedral, 14th century

☐ 19th- and 20th-century additions to cathedral

Leopold II is shown in a contemporary engraving being crowned King of Bohemia at the cathedral in September 1791. Mozart composed an opera, *La Clemenza di Tito*, in honour of the occasion.

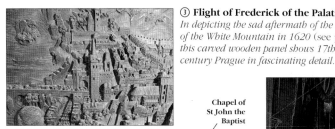

③ Flight of Frederick of the Palatinate
In depicting the sad aftermath of the Battle of the White Mountain in 1620 (see p31), this carved wooden panel shows 17th-century Prague in fascinating detail.

Chapel of St John the Baptist

Pulpit (1618)

Chapel of the Holy Relics

Chapel of the Holy Rood

Stairs to crypt

Golden Portal

Exit from crypt

④ Tomb of St John Nepomuk
Crafted from solid silver in 1736, this elaborate tomb honours the saint who became the focus of a Counter-Reformation cult (see p137).

⑤ Royal Oratory
The vault of the 15th-century Late-Gothic oratory is carved with branches instead of ribs.

⑥ Crypt
Steps lead down to the royal tombs, including those of Charles IV and his four wives, as well as vestiges of the early rotunda and basilica.

⑧ St Wenceslas Chapel
Gothic frescoes with scenes from the Bible and the life of the saint cover the walls, interspersed with a patchwork of polished gemstones and fine gilding. Every object is a work of art – this golden steeple held the wafers and wine for Holy Communion.

⑦ Royal Mausoleum
Ferdinand I died in 1564. His beloved wife and son, Maximilian II, are buried alongside him in the mausoleum.

KEY

– – – Tour route

Royal Palace ❹

KRÁLOVSKÝ PALÁC

FROM THE TIME Prague Castle was first fortified in the 11th century (see pp22–3), the palace was the seat of Bohemian princes. The building consists of three different architectural layers. A Romanesque palace built by Soběslav I around 1135 forms the cellars of the present building. Přemysl Otakar II and Charles IV then added their own palaces above this, while the top floor, built for Vladislav Jagiello, contains the massive Gothic Vladislav Hall. During the period of Habsburg rule the palace housed government offices, courts and the old Bohemian Diet (parliament). In 1924 it was extensively restored.

Riders' Staircase

These wide and gently sloping steps, with their Gothic rib vault, were used by knights on horseback to get to Vladislav Hall for indoor jousting competitions.

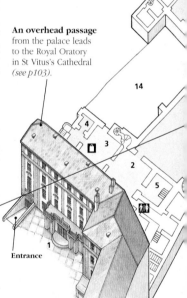

The Diet, the medieval parliament, was also the throne room. Destroyed by fire in 1541, it was rebuilt by Bonifaz Wohlmut in 1563.

An overhead passage from the palace leads to the Royal Oratory in St Vitus's Cathedral (see p103).

Entrance

Vladislav Hall

The 17th-century painting by Aegidius Sadeler shows that the Royal Court was very like a public market. The hall's magnificent rib vaulting was designed by Benedikt Ried in the 1490s.

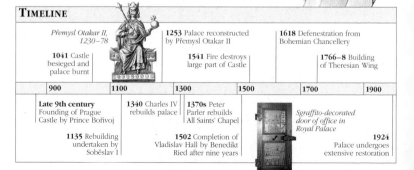

TIMELINE

Late 9th century Founding of Prague Castle by Prince Bořivoj

1041 Castle besieged and palace burnt

Přemysl Otakar II, 1230–78

1135 Rebuilding undertaken by Soběslav I

1253 Palace reconstructed by Přemysl Otakar II

1340 Charles IV rebuilds palace

1370s Peter Parler rebuilds All Saints' Chapel

1502 Completion of Vladislav Hall by Benedikt Ried after nine years

1541 Fire destroys large part of Castle

1618 Defenestration from Bohemian Chancellery

1766–8 Building of Theresian Wing

Sgraffito-decorated door of office in Royal Palace

1924 Palace undergoes extensive restoration

900	1100	1300	1500	1700	1900

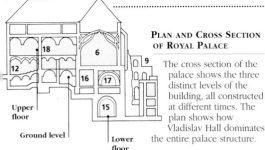

PLAN AND CROSS SECTION OF ROYAL PALACE

The cross section of the palace shows the three distinct levels of the building, all constructed at different times. The plan shows how Vladislav Hall dominates the entire palace structure.

Upper floor

Ground level

Lower floor

VISITORS' CHECKLIST

Prague Castle, third courtyard.
Map 2 D2. (*33 37 11 11.*
Hradčanská, up K Brusce, then through the Royal Garden; Malostranská, left up Klárov, then up Old Castle Steps. 22 to Prague Castle (Pražský hrad). **Open** 9am–5pm (Nov–Mar: 4pm) Tue–Sun (last adm: 1 hr before closing).*

All Saints' Chapel was built by Peter Parler for Charles IV. After the 1541 fire, its vault had to be rebuilt and it was redecorated in the Baroque style.

KEY TO ROYAL PALACE

☐ Romanesque and Early Gothic

☐ Late Gothic

☐ Rebuilt after 1541 fire

☐ Baroque and later

1 Eagle Fountain
2 Vestibule
3 Green Chamber
4 King's Bedchamber
5 Romanesque tower
6 Vladislav Hall
7 Bohemian Chancellery
8 Imperial Council Room steps
9 Terrace
10 All Saints' Chapel
11 Diet Hall
12 Riders' Staircase
13 Court of Appeal
14 Palace courtyard
15 Hall of the Romanesque palace
16 Old Land Rolls
17 Palace of Charles IV
18 New Land Rolls

The Theresian Way was built to house the office registers.

Bohemian Chancellery

This 17th-century Dutch-style stove decorates the former royal offices of the Habsburgs. The chancellery is the site of the 1618 defenestration.

DEFENESTRATION OF 1618

Painting by Václav Brožík, 1889

On 23 May, 1618, more than 100 Protestant nobles, led by Count Thurn, marched into the palace to protest against the succession to the throne of the intolerant Habsburg Archduke Ferdinand. The two Catholic Governors appointed by Ferdinand, Jaroslav Martinic and Vilém Slavata, were confronted and, after a row, the Protestants threw both the Governors and their secretary, Philipp Fabricius, out of the eastern window. Falling some 15 m (50 ft), they survived by landing in a dung heap. This event signalled the beginning of the Thirty Years' War. The Catholics attributed the survival of the Governors to the intervention of angels.

The New Land Rolls
These rooms are decorated with the crests of clerks who worked here from 1561 to 1774.

St George's Convent ❻

KLÁŠTER SV. JIŘÍ

THE FIRST CONVENT in Bohemia was founded here close to the Royal Palace in 973 by Prince Boleslav II. His sister Mlada was its first abbess. Rebuilt many times over the centuries, the convent was finally abolished in 1782 and converted into barracks. In 1962–74 it was reconstructed to house the National Gallery's Czech art of the Gothic, Renaissance and Baroque periods. It includes magnificent religious paintings from the 14th century, when Bohemia was one of the most cultured kingdoms in Europe.

★ St Elizabeth
Master Theodoric painted 127 such panels for the Chapel of the Holy Cross at Karlstein in 1360–65 (see p166). His art is remarkable for the realism in the faces of his saints.

Lower floor

★ Christ on the Mount of Olives
This coloured panel (c1350) is by the Master of the Vyšší Brod (Hohenfurth) Altar, and is one of a series of Scenes from the Life of Christ.

Stairs down from ground floor

GALLERY GUIDE

The exhibits are arranged in chronological order, beginning with sculpture and paintings of the 14th century, which means you must begin your tour on the lower floor. You have to follow a more or less fixed route, which takes you back up to the ground floor for later Gothic art, then up to the first floor to the Renaissance and Baroque collections.

Stairs to upper and lower floors

Ground floor

KEY

- ☐ 14th-century Czech art
- ☐ 15th-century Czech art
- ☐ 16th-century Czech art
- ☐ Rudolphian Mannerism (c1600)
- ☐ Czech art of the Baroque
- ☐ Chapel of St Anne
- ☐ St George's Basilica
- ☐ Special exhibitions
- ☐ Non-exhibition space

Entrance to Gallery from Jiřské náměstí

Assumption of the Virgin Mary
In 15th-century Bohemia the Church encouraged the cult of the Virgin. This painting (1450) by an unknown master used to hang in a chapel in Deštná in southern Bohemia.

★ **Tobias Restoring his Father's Sight**
Petr Brandl painted two versions of this touching story from the Apocrypha (c1705).

Upper floor

VISITORS' CHECKLIST

Prague Castle, Jiřské náměstí.
Map 2 E2. (53 52 40.
ᴹ Hradčanská or Malostranská,
then 10 mins walk up steep flight
of steps. 22 to Prague Castle
(Pražský hrad). **Open** 10am–6pm
Tue–Sun.

Stairs down to exit

Stairs from ground floor

Statue of Moor
This is one of a pair of Moorish warriors (1719) by Ferdinand Brokof, commissioned by the Morzin family (see p130) for their country seat in Kounice.

Maria Maximiliana of Sternberg
In this portrait by Karel Škréta (1610–74), the countess appears as a shepherdess, an artistic fashion that remained popular with the nobility of Europe for more than 100 years.

St George's Basilica
(see pp98–9)

Still Life with Watch
Johann-Adalbert Angermayer (1674–1740) filled his delicate still lifes with symbols of the transience and vanity of human life.

STAR EXHIBITS

★ **Christ on the Mount of Olives by the Master of the Vyšší Brod Altar**

★ **St Elizabeth by Master Theodoric**

★ **Tobias Restoring his Father's Sight by Petr Brandl**

Exploring the St George's Collection

T HIS WONDERFUL COLLECTION gives a fascinating insight into the art and sculpture of the two periods of Prague's history that are so conspicuous in the city's architecture – the Gothic from the age of Charles IV and the Baroque. The earlier period is represented by many naive, but expressive woodcarvings and panel paintings, while the Baroque has dramatic biblical paintings and statues of saints and angels in flamboyant poses. Some exhibits are occasionally on loan to museums in other parts of the country.

Wooden statue of *Suckling Madonna* from Konopiště (c1380)

14TH-CENTURY CZECH ART

B OHEMIA'S great period of political and economic power under the Emperor Charles IV was also a golden age for painting and sculpture. The first section of the gallery contains works by the two greatest painters of Charles's reign, the anonymous Master of the Vyšší Brod Altar and the only painter of the time whose name we know – Master Theodoric. The latter is justly famous for his panels of saints from Karlstein *(see p166)*. It is the humanity of his portraits of *St Elizabeth, St Jerome, St Matthew* and *St Vitus* that makes them so appealing. The influence of Theodoric is evident in the large *Votive Panel of Bishop*

Jan Očko of Vlašim, which shows Charles IV kneeling before the Virgin in heaven *(see p24)*. The Master of the Vyšší Brod Altar, who like Theodoric was active in the middle of the 14th century, painted a magnificent series of brilliantly coloured *Scenes from the Life of Christ*.

The wood carvings from various churches in Bohemia are mainly of Madonnas and the Crucifixion. Originally they would all have been painted and gilded, but few traces of their bright colours remain. There are also sights you may recognize from the streets of Prague, including the tympanum of the Gothic gateway to the Church of Our Lady of the Snows *(see p146)* and the statue of *St George Slaying the Dragon* that stands in the courtyard right outside St Vitus's Cathedral.

The ones in situ are copies; these are the originals, on display here for safekeeping.

On the ground floor make sure you go into the room containing the works of the Master of the Třeboň Altar to see his *Resurrection* and *The Madonna of Roudnice*.

15TH-CENTURY CZECH ART

A FTER 1400 Bohemia never recovered the prosperity of the preceding century and art, especially in the period of the Hussite Wars *(see pp26–7)*, was generally of lesser quality. Nevertheless look out for the delightful *Assumption of the Virgin Mary* from Deštná and the triptych from St George's Basilica with a central panel depicting the death of the Virgin. In the many grim and gory paintings of the Crucifixion in this section, notice the souls of the two thieves crucified with Christ. Angels carry the good thief's soul up to heaven, while demons drag the other's down to hell.

EARLY 16TH-CENTURY CZECH ART

L ATER WORKS in the gallery's collection of Gothic art show greater similarity with contemporary German and

Altarpiece of *The Holy Trinity* by Master of the Litoměřice Altar (c1515)

Stag Hunt (c1610) by Roelant Savery, artist at the court of Rudolph II

Italian paintings. The finest Bohemian painter of this period is the Master of the Litoměřice Altar, active at the beginning of the 16th century. His most impressive works are an altar triptych showing *The Holy Trinity* and *The Visitation of the Virgin Mary*. The last room in this section is devoted to reliefs by a woodcarver who signed his works with the initials I P. His style is that of the so-called Danube school and his figures are clearly influenced by Dürer. Dating from about 1520, the *Votive Altarpiece of Zlíchov* shows a kneeling knight with the Virgin Mary, St Andrew, Christ and Death.

RUDOLPHIAN MANNERISM (c1600)

MANNERISM is the rather disparaging term used to describe a style that evolved in Italy after the Renaissance. Many 16th-century painters and sculptors strove to outdo the exaggerated poses of Michelangelo's later works just for the sake of creating a startling effect. A typical example of this is *The Last Judgment* by Josef Heintz. A more successful exponent of this style was Bartholomaeus Spranger from Antwerp. He died in Prague in 1611 while in the employment of the Emperor Rudolph II *(see p28–9)*. With his passion for the unusual and the artificial, Rudolph loved Mannerist artists and invited many to work at his court in Prague.

Rudolph's great collection was dispersed when Prague Castle was looted in 1648, but the few works on show here give an idea of his tastes. The best are probably the paintings of the German-born Hans von Aachen and the sculptures of the Dutch-born Adriaen de Vries. Not all the works here are typically Mannerist. The landscapes of Roelant Savery, for example, show a genuine feeling for the beauty of the Bohemian forests gained during his stay in Prague (1604–12).

CZECH ART OF THE BAROQUE

THERE ARE many agreeable surprises in the collection of Baroque art. Of the paintings of religious subjects, the finest are undoubtedly those by Petr Brandl. The old men who feature in many of his works are beautifully painted. Particularly moving are *Tobias Restoring his Father's Sight* and *Simeon and the Infant Jesus*. Then there are several masterly portraits by the 17th-century Karel Škréta and by Jan Kupecký. On a smaller scale, look out for the delightful still lifes by the Swiss painter Johann Rudolf Bys and his pupil Johann-Adalbert Angermayer.

The sculptures are chiefly by the 18th-century artists whose works decorate so many of the city's Baroque churches: Ferdinand Brokof, Matthias Braun and Ignaz Platzer. Several of the more flamboyant saints and angels are in painted wood, an unexpected link with the early polychrome wood carvings of the Gothic period.

Hedvika Francesca Wussin by Jan Kupecký (1710)

Old prison in the Dalibor Tower

Dalibor Tower ⑨
DALIBORKA

Prague Castle, Zlatá ulička.
Map 2 E2. **Ⓜ** *Malostranská.* **🚋** 22.
Closed *for renovation.*

THIS 15TH-CENTURY tower with a conical roof was part of the fortifications built by King Vladislav Jagiello *(see p26–7)*. His coat of arms can be seen on the outer wall. The tower also served as a prison and is named after its first inmate, Dalibor of Kozojedy, a young knight sentenced to death for harbouring some outlawed serfs. While awaiting execution, he was kept in an underground dungeon, into which he had to be lowered through a hole in the floor.

According to legend, while in prison he learnt to play the violin. People sympathetic to his plight came to listen to his playing and provided him with food and drink, which they lowered on a rope from a window – prisoners were often left to starve to death. The story was used by Bedřich Smetana in his opera *Dalibor.* The tower ceased to serve as a prison in 1781. Visitors can see part of the old prison.

South Gardens ⑩
JIŽNÍ ZAHRADY

Prague Castle (access from Hradčanské náměstí). **Map** 2 D3.
Ⓜ *Malostranská, Hradčanská.*
🚋 22. **Open** May–Oct: 10am–6pm Tue–Sun. 📷

THE GARDENS occupy the long narrow band of land below the Castle overlooking the Little Quarter. Several small gardens have been linked to form what is now known as the South Gardens. The oldest, the Paradise Garden (Rajská zahrada), laid out in 1562, contains a circular pavilion built for Emperor Matthias in 1617. Its carved wooden ceiling shows the coloured emblems of the 39 countries of the Habsburg Empire. The Garden on the Ramparts (Zahrada Na valech) dates from the 19th century. It occupies a former vegetable patch and is famous as the site of the defenestration of 1618 *(see p105)*, when two Imperial governors were thrown from a first-floor window. Two obelisks were subsequently erected by Ferdinand II to mark the spots where they landed. Extensive modifications were carried out in the 1920s by Josip Plečnik, who built the Bull Staircase leading to the Paradise Garden and the observation terrace. Below the terrace, in the former Hartig Garden, is a Baroque music pavilion designed by Giovanni Battista Alliprandi. Beside it stand four statues of Classical gods by Antonín Braun.

Alliprandi's music pavilion in the South Gardens

Belvedere ⑪
BELVEDÉR

Prague Castle, Royal Garden. **Map** 2 E1.
Ⓜ *Malostranská, Hradčanská.*
🚋 22. **Open** only for exhibitions.

BUILT BY FERDINAND I for his beloved wife Anne, the Belvedere is one of the finest Italian Renaissance buildings north of the Alps. Also known as the Royal Summer Palace (Královský letohrádek), it is an arcaded summerhouse

The Belvedere, Emperor Ferdinand I's summer palace in the Royal Garden beside Prague Castle

Antonín Braun's statue of *The Allegory of Night* in front of the *sgraffito* decoration of the Ball Game Hall in the Royal Garden

The Royal Garden is the best-kept garden in Prague and a beautiful place for a stroll, especially in spring when thousands of tulips bloom in its immaculate beds. This is where tulips, bought from Turkey by Ferdinand I's ambassador, were first acclimatized to Europe before being taken to Holland.

At the entrance to the garden is the Lion Court where Rudolph II had his zoo (now a restaurant). As well as lions, Rudolph kept bears, leopards, panthers and many other wild animals. Some roamed free in the Stag Moat, which separates the garden from the Castle.

Archbishop's Palace ⑬
ARCIBISKUPSKÝ PALÁC

Hradčanské náměstí 16. **Map** 2 D3. 2451 12 64. **M** Malostranská, Hradčanská. 22. **Not open** to the public.

Ferdinand I bought this sumptuous palace in 1562 for the first Catholic Archbishop since the Hussite Wars (see pp26–7). It replaced the old Archbishop's Palace in the Little Quarter, which had been destroyed during the wars, and has remained the Archbishop's seat in Prague ever since. In the period after the Battle of the White Mountain (see p30–31), the presence of the Archbishop's Palace right beside the castle was a powerful symbol of Catholic domination of the city and the Czech lands. Its spectacular cream-coloured Rococo façade was designed by Johann Joseph Wirch in the 1760s for Archbishop Antonín Příchovský, whose coat of arms sits proudly above the earlier 17th-century portal.

Sternberg Palace ⑭
ŠTERNBERSKÝ PALÁC

See pp112–15.

with slender Ionic columns topped by a roof shaped like an inverted ship's hull clad in blue-green copper. The main architect was Paolo della Stella, who was also responsible for the ornate reliefs inside the arcade. Work began in 1538, but was interrupted by the great Castle fire of 1541. The Belvedere was eventually completed in 1564.

In the middle of the small geometrical garden in front of the palace stands the Singing Fountain. Dating from 1568, it owes its name to the musical sound the water makes as it hits the bronze bowl, though you have to place your head very close to appreciate the effect. The fountain was cast by Tomáš Jaroš, the famous bell founder, who lived and worked in the Powder Tower (see p98).

Many of the Belvedere's works of art were plundered by the occupying Swedish army in 1648. The statues stolen included Adriaen de Vries's 16th-century bronze of *Mercury and Psyche*, which is now in the Louvre in Paris. The Belvedere is now used as an art gallery.

Royal Garden ⑫
KRÁLOVSKÁ ZAHRADA

Prague Castle, U Prašného mostu. **Map** 2 D2. **M** Malostranská, Hradčanská. 22. **Open** May–Oct: 10am–6pm Tue–Sun.

The garden was created in 1535 for Ferdinand I. Its appearance has been altered over time, but nevertheless some excellent examples of 16th-century garden architecture have survived, notably the Belvedere and the Ball Game Hall (Míčovna), built by Bonifaz Wohlmut in 1569. The building is covered in beautiful, though much re-stored, Renaissance *sgraffito*, a form of decoration created by cutting a design through the wet top layer of plaster onto a contrasting undercoat. The Ball Game Hall was used primarily for playing a form of real tennis, but the game gradually went out of fashion and in 1723 the building was converted into stables.

Příchovský coat of arms

Sternberg Palace ⓮
ŠTERNBERSKÝ PALÁC

FRANZ JOSEF STERNBERG founded the Society of Patriotic Friends of the Arts in Bohemia in 1796. Fellow noblemen would lend their finest pictures and sculpture to the society, which had its headquarters in the early-18th-century Sternberg Palace. The collection became the property of the State just before World War II, and since 1949 the fine Baroque building has been used to house the National Gallery's collection of European art.

★ **Haymaking** (1565)
These three country maids are a foreground detail from the large canvas by Pieter Brueghel the Elder.

★ **Self-Portrait by Picasso**
This was painted in 1907, a period when the artist's work was strongly influenced by primitive sculpture and art.

First floor

Balzac by Rodin

Ground floor

Entrance to exhibition on ground floor

Garden room

Stairs to second floor

Ticket office

GALLERY GUIDE
The gallery is arranged on three floors around the central courtyard of the palace. The exhibition of French art and sculpture of the 19th and 20th centuries is on the ground floor and is reached from the courtyard. The stairs to the collections on the upper floors are opposite the ticket office at the main entrance. With a few exceptions, the earlier works are on the first floor, the later ones on the second.

Stairs to first floor

Passageway to Hradčanské náměstí

Self-Portrait by Henri "le Douanier" Rousseau
The only existing self-portrait by Rousseau (1890) has the same surreal quality as all his works. Note the Eiffel Tower in the background.

★ **Head of Christ**
*Painted by El Greco
in the 1590s, this
portrait emphasizes
the humanity of
Christ. At the same
time the curious
square halo framing
the head gives the
painting the qualities
of an ancient icon.*

Second floor

Dürer's *Feast of the Rosary*

★ **Adam and Eve** *(c1538)*
*The nudes in Lucas Cranach
the Elder's painting show the
spirit of the Renaissance,
tempered by Lutheran reform.*

Stairs down to
other floors
and exit

**Charles Bridge and
Hradčany** *(1935)*
*The Austrian-born
Oskar Kokoschka
painted several
views of Prague,
stamped with the
artist's colourful,
expressionist vision.*

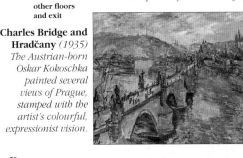

The Lamentation of Christ
*The frozen, sculptural
figures make this one of the
finest paintings by Lorenzo
Monaco (1408). The artist
lived most of his life in a
Florentine monastery.*

KEY

- ☐ Icons, Classical and ancient art
- ☐ German and Austrian art (1350–1600)
- ☐ Italian art (1300–1500)
- ☐ Flemish and Dutch art (1400–1700)
- ☐ Italian, French and Spanish art (1500–1820)
- ☐ 19th- and 20th-century French art
- ☐ 20th-century European art
- ☐ Special exhibitions
- ☐ Non-exhibition space

STAR EXHIBITS

★ **Adam and Eve
by Lucas Cranach**

★ **Haymaking
by Pieter Brueghel
the Elder**

★ **Head of Christ
by El Greco**

★ **Self-Portrait
by Picasso**

Exploring the Sternberg Collections

THE NATIONAL GALLERY'S collection of European art is small, but ranks among the best collections of comparable size. The greatest treasures are among the French art of the 19th and 20th centuries, where there are works by almost all the major painters from Manet to Matisse. The older European art of the 14th–18th centuries is a less comprehensive collection, but the Flemish and Dutch sections have some fine paintings. In 1994 or 1995 many of the works in the Sternberg Palace will be transferred to a new gallery of modern art in the Trade Fair Palace, between Letná Park and the Exhibition Ground.

St John the Baptist by Rodin

ICONS, CLASSICAL AND ANCIENT ART

A SMALL ROOM on the first floor contains an odd assortment of paintings that do not quite fit in with the rest of the collection. These include a *Portrait of a Young Woman* dating from the 2nd century AD, discovered during excavations at Fayoum in Egypt in the 19th century.

The majority of the exhibits, however, are icons of the Orthodox church. These come from a variety of Eastern European countries – some are Byzantine, some Italo-Greek and some Russian. The finest examples are two of the later 16th-century works, *The Lamentation of Christ* from Crete and *Christ's Entry Into Jerusalem* from Russia.

Christ's Entry into Jerusalem, a 16th-century Russian icon

GERMAN AND AUSTRIAN ART (1350–1600)

O NE OF THE most celebrated paintings in the Sternberg is Albrecht Dürer's *The Feast of the Rosary*. It has special significance for Prague since it was bought by Emperor Rudolph II. The two figures in front of the Virgin and Child are Maximilian I (Rudolph's great-great-grandfather) and Pope Julius II. There are works by several other important German painters of the Renaissance, including Hans Holbein the Elder and the Younger and Lucas Cranach the Elder. Cranach is represented by 13 works including a striking *Adam and Eve* and two panels, one showing St Christine, the other St Barbara and St Catherine. The panels are relics of a destroyed altarpiece that once stood in St Vitus's Cathedral.

ITALIAN ART (1300–1500)

W HEN YOU ENTER the rooms on the first floor, you are greeted by a splendid array of early diptychs, triptychs and other richly gilded panel paintings from the churches of Tuscany and northern Italy. Most came originally from the d'Este collection at Konopiště Castle (*see p167*). Of particularly high quality are the two triangular panels of saints by the 14th-century Sienese painter Pietro Lorenzetti and a moving *Lamentation of Christ* by Lorenzo Monaco.

FLEMISH AND DUTCH ART (1400–1700)

T HERE IS A RICH and varied collection of Flemish and Dutch art, ranging from rural scenes by Pieter Brueghel the Elder to portraits by Rubens and Rembrandt. Brueghel's huge canvas *Haymaking* ranks among the finest paintings in the Sternberg. It was originally one of a series of paintings of the months of the year. Four others in the set still exist – in Vienna and New York.

Other early works of interest include *St Luke Drawing the Virgin* by Jan Gossaert (c1515), one of the first paintings from the Netherlands to show the clear influence of the ideas of the Italian Renaissance.

The 17th-century collection has several major works, notably by Rubens, who in

The Feast of the Rosary by Dürer (1506)

Equestrienne (1927), one of a series of circus paintings by Marc Chagall

19TH- AND 20TH-CENTURY FRENCH ART

THIS IMPRESSIVE COLLECTION of some 120 paintings and 40 sculptures starts with the Romantic Delacroix and the realistic landscape artists, Corot and Courbet. However, most of the collection consists of the great French Impressionists and Post-Impressionists. Among the former look out for Monet's *Ladies in Flowers*, Renoir's *Lovers* and works by Sisley and Pissarro. There are also paintings by Manet, Seurat, Rousseau (*Self-Portrait*), Van Gogh (*Green Rye*), Toulouse-Lautrec, Utrillo, Degas, Dufy, Cézanne and Gauguin.

The rooms also contain sculptures and there are casts of several celebrated works by Auguste Rodin including *The Age of Bronze* and *Balzac*.

Highlights among the more recent paintings are the Cubist works of Picasso and Braque and the colourful *Equestrienne* by Chagall. Prague's important collection of Picassos has attracted the attention of art-thieves. Three were stolen recently, but were retrieved in Germany and returned to the gallery.

1639 sent two paintings to the Augustinians of the Church of St Thomas *(see p127)* in the Little Quarter. The originals were lent to the gallery in 1896 and replaced by copies. The violence and drama of *The Martyrdom of St Thomas* is in complete contrast to the spiritual calm of *St Augustine*. Another fine contemplative portrait is Rembrandt's *Scholar in His Study* of 1634.

ITALIAN, FRENCH AND SPANISH ART (1500–1820)

PAINTERS ARE GROUPED in a slightly arbitrary way in this part of the gallery, but there are several delightful surprises among the works on show. The Italian paintings include *St Jerome* by Tintoretto and *The Flagellation of Christ* and *Portrait of an Elderly Man* by Jacopo Bassano. There is also an expressive portrait by Bronzino of *Eleanor of Toledo*, wife of Cosimo de' Medici.

French art is represented chiefly by the 17th-century painters Simon Vouet (*The Suicide of Lucretia*), Sébastien

Bourdon and Charles Le Brun. Spanish painting is even less well represented, but two of the collection's finest works are a haunting *Head of Christ* by El Greco and a half-length portrait of the politician *Don Miguel de Lardizábal* by Goya.

Most unexpected of all the paintings in this section is a *View of the Thames* by Canaletto, showing Lambeth Palace and Westminster Bridge, painted in about 1746.

Eleanor of Toledo (1540s) by the Florentine Mannerist painter Agnolo Bronzino

20TH-CENTURY EUROPEAN ART

THE MODERN European art shown in the Sternberg Palace is only a fraction of the National Gallery's collection. Many more works will be displayed when the new gallery in the former Trade Fair Palace is opened. At present there are only a few dozen works displayed on the second floor of the Sternberg Palace, chiefly by Austrian, German and Russian artists. The best-known include Gustav Klimt, Egon Schiele, Oskar Kokoschka, Max Ernst and Edvard Munch. Be sure to see Kokoschka's *Charles Bridge and Hradčany*, and Klimt's *Virgin*.

The Loreto ⓳

LORETA

EVER SINCE ITS CONSTRUCTION in 1626, the Loreto has been an important place of pilgrimage. It was commissioned by Kateřina of Lobkowicz, a Czech aristocrat who was very keen to promote the legend of the Santa Casa of Loreto *(see opposite)*. The heart of the complex is a copy of the house believed to be the Virgin Mary's. The Santa Casa was enclosed by cloisters in 1661, and

Katerina Lobkowicz, founder of the Santa Casa

a Baroque façade 60 years later by Christoph and Kilian Ignaz Dientzenhofer. The grandiose design and miraculous stories about the Loreto were part of Ferdinand II's campaign to re-catholicize the Czechs *(see pp30–31)*.

Bell Tower
Enclosed in this large Baroque tower, is a set of 27 bells cast in 1694 by the Danish engineer Petr Naumann.

Chapel of St Joseph

Fountain decorated with a sculpture of the Resurrection

Chapel of St Francis Seraphim

Chapel of St Ann

Entrance from Loretánské náměstí

★ Loreto Treasury
This gold-plated, diamond-encrusted monstrance, for displaying the host, is one of the valuable liturgical items in the Loreto treasury, most of which originated in the 16th–18th centuries.

STAR SIGHTS

- ★ Loreto Treasury
- ★ Santa Casa
- ★ Church of the Nativity

Baroque Entrance
The balustrade above the Loreto's front entrance is decorated with statues of St Joseph and St John the Baptist by Ondřej Quitainer.

★ **Santa Casa**
Stucco figures of many of the Old Testament prophets and reliefs from the life of the Virgin Mary by Italian artists decorate the chapel.

VISITORS' CHECKLIST

Loretánské náměstí, Hradčany.
Map 1C3 [C] 24 51 07 89.
[T] 22 to Pohořelec. **Open**
9am–12:15pm, 1–4:30pm
Tue–Sun. [icons]

★ **Church of the Nativity**
Gruesome relics, including fully-clothed skeletons with death masks made of wax, line the walls of this 18th-century church. The frescoes are by Václav Vavřinec Reiner.

Chapel of the Holy Rood

17th-Century Cloister
Built originally as a shelter for the many pilgrims who visited the shrine, the cloister is covered with frescoes.

Chapel of St Anthony of Padua

Chapel of Our Lady of Sorrows

Fountain Sculpture
This copy of The Ascension of the Virgin Mary *is taken from Jan Brüderle's 1739 sandstone statue, now in the Lapidarium (see pp176–7).*

LEGEND OF THE SANTA CASA

The original house, said to be where the Archangel Gabriel told Mary about the future birth of Jesus, is in the small Italian town of Loreto. It was believed that angels transported the house from Nazareth to Loreto in 1278 following threats by infidels. After the Protestants' defeat in 1620 *(see pp30–31)*, Catholics promoted the legend, and 50 replicas of the Loreto were built in Bohemia and Moravia. This, the grandest, became the most important in Bohemia, and received many visitors.

The stuccoed Santa Casa

Martinic Palace ❶

MARTINICKÝ PALÁC

Hradčanské náměstí 8. **Map** 1 C2.
❏ 2451 09 27. **☗** *Malostranská,
Hradčanská.* **⊡** 22. **Closed** to the
public.

I N THE COURSE of the palace's
restoration in the early
1970s, workmen uncovered
the original 16th-century
façade decorated with ornate
cream and brown *sgraffito
(see p111).* It depicts Old
Testament scenes, including
the story of Joseph and
Potiphar's wife. More *sgraffito*
came to light in the courtyard,
showing the story of Samson
and the Labours of Hercules.

Martinic Palace was enlarged
by Jaroslav Bořita of Martinice,
who was one of the imperial
governors thrown from a
window of the Royal Palace
in 1618 *(see p105).*

According to an old legend,
between 11pm and midnight
the ghost of a fiery black dog
appears at the palace and
accompanies walkers as far as
the Loreto *(see pp116–17),*
where it disappears again.
Today the palace houses the
city architecture department.

Schwarzenberg Palace ❶

SCHWARZENBERSKÝ PALÁC

Hradčanské náměstí 2. **Map** 2 D3.
❏ 53 64 88. **☗** *Malostranská,
Hradčanská.* **⊡** 22. **Open** 10am –
6pm Tue –Sun. **☉** (free Tue). **✏**

F ROM A DISTANCE, the façade
of this grand Renaissance
palace appears to be clad in
projecting pyramid-shaped
stonework. On closer inspec-
tion, this turns out to be an
illusion created by *sgraffito*
patterns incised
on a flat wall.
Built originally for

the Lobkowicz family
by the Italian architect
Agostino Galli in 1545–
76, the gabled palace
is Florentine rather
than Bohemian in style.
It passed through
several hands before
the Schwarzenbergs, a
leading aristocratic
family in the Habsburg
Empire, bought it in
1719. Much of the
interior decoration has
survived, including
four painted ceilings
on the second floor
dating from about
1580. Since 1945 the
palace has housed the
Museum of Military
History, a collection of
arms, armour and uniforms
from the wars that have
plagued Bohemia from the
time of the first Slavs up to
1918. Look out for the section
illustrating the highly original
tactics adopted by the
Hussites in the 15th century.

Tycho Brahe, Rudolph II's astronomer

New World ❶

NOVÝ SVĚT

Map 1 B2. **⊡** 22.

N OW A CHARMING STREET of
small cottages, Nový Svět
(New World) used to be the
name of this area of Hradčany.
Developed in the mid-14th
century to provide houses for
the castle workers, the area
was twice destroyed by fire,
the last time being in 1541.
Most of the cottages date from
the 17th century. They have
been spruced up, but are
otherwise unspoilt and very
different in character from the

rest of Hradčany. In defiance
of their poverty, the inhabitants
chose golden house signs to
identify their modest houses –
you will see a Golden Pear,
a Grape, a Foot, a Bush and
an Acorn. Plaques identify
No. 1 as the former home of
Rudolph II's brilliant court
astronomer, Tycho Brahe, and
No. 25 as the 1857 birthplace
of the great Czech violinist
František Ondříček.

Capuchin Monastery ❶

KAPUCÍNSKÝ KLÁŠTER

Loretánské náměstí 6. **Map** 1 B3.
⊡ 22. **Closed** to the public except
the church.

B OHEMIA'S FIRST Capuchin
monastery was founded
here in 1600. It is connected
to the neighbouring Loreto
(see pp116–17) by an overhead roofed passage. Attached
to the monastery is the Church
of Our Lady Queen of Angels,
a single-naved building with
plain furnishings, typical of
the ascetic Capuchin order.

The church is famous for
its miraculous statue of the
Madonna and Child. Emperor
Rudolph II liked the statue so
much he asked the Capuchins
to give it to him to place in
his private chapel. The monks
agreed, but then the statue
somehow found its way back
to the church. Three times
Rudolph had the Madonna
brought back but each time

Schwarzenberg Palace, showing the loggia and the sgraffitoed façade

she returned to her original position. The Emperor eventually gave up, left her where she was and presented her with a gold crown and a robe. Each year at Christmas the church attracts crowds of visitors to see its delightful Baroque nativity scene of life-sized figures dressed in costumes from the period.

Church of the Capuchin Monastery

The Loreto ⑲
LORETA

See pp116–17.

Černín Palace ⑳
ČERNÍNSKÝ PALÁC

Loretánské náměstí 5. **Map** 1 B3.
📞 *24 18 11 11.* 🚊 *22.* **Closed** *to the public.*

B UILT IN 1668 for Count Černín of Chudenice, the Imperial Ambassador to Venice, the Černín Palace is 150 m (500 ft) long with a row of 30 massive Corinthian half-columns running the length of its upper storeys. The palace towers over the attractive, small, grassy square that lies between it and the Loreto.

The huge building suffered as a result of its prominent position on one of Prague's highest hills. It was looted by the French in 1742 and badly damaged in the Prussian bombardment of the city in 1757. In 1851 the impoverished Černín family sold the palace to the state and it became a

barracks. After the creation of Czecho-slovakia in 1918 the palace was restored to its original design and became the Ministry of Foreign Affairs. A few days after the Communist Coup in 1948 the Foreign Minister, Jan Masaryk, the popular son of Czechoslovakia's first President, Tomáš Masaryk, died as the result of a fall from a top-floor window of the Palace. He was the only non-Communist in the government that had just been formed. No-one really knows whether he was pushed or jumped, but he is still widely mourned.

Capital on Černín Palace

Pohořelec ㉑

Map 1 B3. 🚊 *22.*

F IRST SETTLED IN 1375, this is one of the oldest parts of Hradčany. The name is of more recent origin: Pohořelec means "place destroyed by fire", a fate the area has suffered three times in the course of its history – the last time being in 1741. It is now a large open square on a hill high over the city and part of the main access route to Prague Castle. In the centre stands a large monument to St John Nepomuk (1752) *(see p137)*, thought to be by Johann Anton Quitainer. The houses around the square are mainly Baroque and Rococo. In front of the Jan Kepler grammar school stands a monument to Kepler and his predecessor as astronomer at the court of Rudolph II, Tycho Brahe, who died in a house on the school site in 1601.

Strahov Monastery ㉒
STRAHOVSKÝ KLÁŠTER

See pp120–21.

Kučera Palace, a Rococo building in Pohořelec

Strahov Monastery ❷

STRAHOVSKÝ KLÁŠTER

W HEN IT WAS FOUNDED in 1140 by an austere religious order, the Pre-monstratensians, Strahov rivalled the seat of the Czech sovereign in size. Destroyed by fire in 1258, it was rebuilt in the Gothic style, with later Baroque additions. Its famous library, in the theological and philosophical halls, is over 800 years old and despite being ransacked by many invading armies, is one of the finest in Bohemia. Strahov also escaped Joseph II's 1783 dissolution of the monasteries by changing its library into a research institute. It is now a working monastery and museum.

The bust of St Norbert over entrance gate

Statue of St John
A Late-Gothic, painted statue of St John the Evangelist situated in the Theological Hall, has the saint's prayer book held in a small pouch.

Baroque tower

The Museum of National Literature is devoted to Czech literature.

Refectory

Entrance to main courtyard of the monastery

Baroque organ on which Mozart played

★ Church of Our Lady
The interior of this Baroque church is highly decorated. Above the arcades of the side naves, there are 12 paintings with scenes from the life of St Norbert, founder of the Premonstratensian order, by Jiří Neunhertz.

Entrance to Church of Our Lady

Church Façade
The elaborate statues, by Johann Anton Quitainer, were added to the western façade of the church when it was remodelled by the architect Anselmo Lurago in the 1750s.

STAR FEATURES

★ Church of Our Lady

★ Philosophical Hall

★ Theological Hall

View from Petřín Hill
A gate at the eastern end of the first courtyard leads to Petřín Hill, part of which was once the monastery's orchards.

VISITORS' CHECKLIST

Památník národního písemnictví (Museum of National Literature), Strahovské nádvoří 1, Strahovská. **Map** 1 B4. **[** *24 51 11 37.* **[** 22 to Pohořelec. ***Philosophical Hall & Theological Hall*** open *9am–5pm Tue–Sun.* ***Church of Our Lady closed*** for restoration.

★ Theological Hall
One of the 17th-century astronomical globes by William Blaeu that line the hall. The stucco and wall paintings relate to librarianship.

The façade of the Philosophical Hall is decorated with vases and a gilded medallion of Franz II by Ignaz Platzer.

ntrance libraries

★ Philosophical Hall
The ceiling fresco depicts the Struggle of Mankind to Know Real History by Franz Maulbertsch. It was built in 1782 to hold the Baroque bookcases and their valuable books from a dissolved monastery near Louka, in Moravia.

Strahov Gospel Book
This 9th-century volume, the oldest manuscript from the huge Strahov library, is on display in the entrance.

LITTLE QUARTER

MALÁ STRANA

THE LITTLE QUARTER is the part of Prague least affected by recent history. Hardly any new building has taken place here since the late 18th century and the quarter is rich in splendid Baroque palaces and old houses with attractive signs. Founded in 1257, it is built on the slopes below the Castle hill with magnificent views across the river to the Old Town.

Sign from At the Golden Horseshoe in Nerudova

The centre of the Little Quarter has always been Little Quarter Square (Malostranské náměstí), dominated by the Church of St Nicholas. The Grand Prior's millwheel at Kampa Island still turns, pilgrims still kneel before the Holy Infant of Prague in the Church of Our Lady Victorious, and music rings out from churches and palaces as it did when Mozart stayed here.

SIGHTS AT A GLANCE

Churches
Church of St Thomas **3**
Church of St Nicholas pp128–9 **5**
Church of Our Lady Victorious **9**
Church of Our Lady beneath the Chain **13**
Church of St Lawrence **21**

Parks and Gardens
Vrtba Garden **8**
Vojan Park **17**
Ledebour Garden **18**
Observation Tower **19**
Mirror Maze **20**
Observatory **22**
Petřín Park **24**
Funicular Railway **25**

Historic Monuments
Hunger Wall **23**

Historic Restaurants and Beer Halls
At St Thomas's **2**
At the Three Ostriches **15**

Historic Streets and Squares
Little Quarter Square **4**
Nerudova Street **6**
Italian Street **7**
Maltese Square **10**
Grand Priory Square **12**
Bridge Street **16**

Bridges and Islands
Kampa Island **11**
Charles Bridge pp136–9 **14**

Palaces
Wallenstein Palace and Garden **1**
Michna Palace **26**

KEY

	Street-by-Street map *See pp124–5*
	Street-by-Street map *See pp132–3*
M	Metro station
	Tram stop
	Funicular railway
	River boat boarding point
—	City wall

0 metres 250

0 yards 250

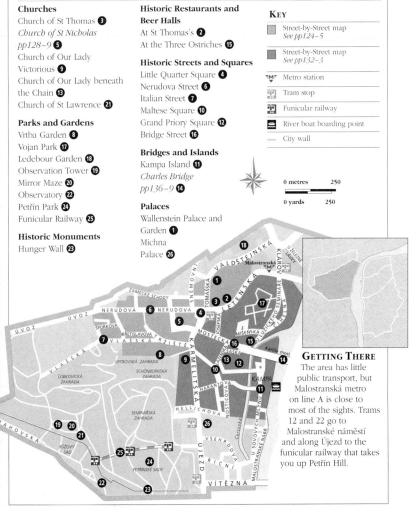

GETTING THERE

The area has little public transport, but Malostranská metro on line A is close to most of the sights. Trams 12 and 22 go to Malostranské náměstí and along Újezd to the funicular railway that takes you up Petřín Hill.

◁ **Charles Bridge and the Little Quarter Bridge Towers**

Street-by-Street: Around Little Quarter Square

THE LITTLE QUARTER, most of whose grand Baroque palaces now house embassies, has preserved much of its traditional character. The steep, narrow streets and steps have an air of romantic mystery and you will find fascinating buildings decorated with statues and house signs at every turn. Some smart new restaurants have been established in the old buildings.

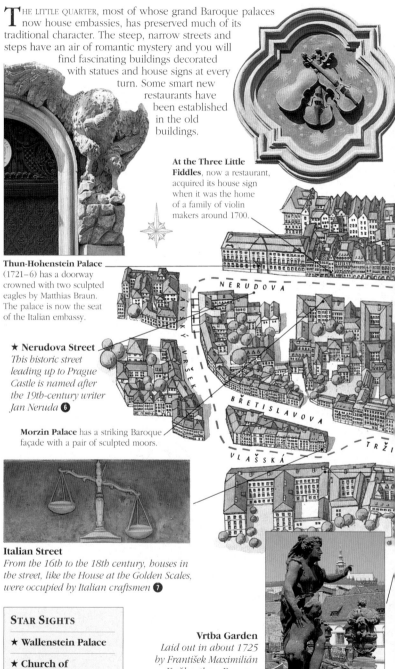

At the Three Little Fiddles, now a restaurant, acquired its house sign when it was the home of a family of violin makers around 1700.

Thun-Hohenstein Palace (1721–6) has a doorway crowned with two sculpted eagles by Matthias Braun. The palace is now the seat of the Italian embassy.

★ **Nerudova Street**
This historic street leading up to Prague Castle is named after the 19th-century writer Jan Neruda **6**

Morzin Palace has a striking Baroque façade with a pair of sculpted moors.

NERUDOVA

LÁNSKÝ VRŠEK

BŘETISLAVOVA

VLAŠSKÁ

TRŽI

Italian Street
From the 16th to the 18th century, houses in the street, like the House at the Golden Scales, were occupied by Italian craftsmen **7**

STAR SIGHTS

★ Wallenstein Palace

★ Church of St Nicholas

★ Nerudova Street

Vrtba Garden
Laid out in about 1725 by František Maximilián Kaňka, these Baroque terraces provide wonderful views over the rooftops of the Little Quarter **8**

★ Wallenstein Palace
On the main hall ceiling, Albrecht von Wallenstein, the great general of the 30 Years' War, appears as the god Mars **1**

Czech National Assembly

Plague Column

To Malostranská Metro

Wallenstein Gardens

LOCATOR MAP
See Street Finder, map 2

Little Quarter Town Hall

At St Thomas's
This traditional beer hall occupies the cellars of a medieval monastery brewery **2**

Church of St Thomas
A statue of St Augustine by Hieronymus Kohl (1684) decorates the church's dramatic Baroque façade **3**

Little Quarter Square
This 18th-century view shows the lower half of the square between the church of St Nicholas and the Town Hall **4**

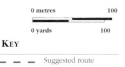

★ Church of St Nicholas
The cupola and bell tower of this Baroque church are the best-known landmarks of the Little Quarter **5**

Schönborn Palace, on Tržiště Square, is decorated with caryatids from the workshop of Matthias Braun.

0 metres	100
0 yards	100

KEY

– – – Suggested route

Wallenstein Palace and Garden ①

VALDŠTEJNSKÝ PALÁC

Valdštejnské náměstí 4. **Map** 2 E3.
ⓜ *Malostranská.* 🚋 *12, 22.*
***Riding school open** 9am–6pm
Tue–Sun.* 🚫 ♿ *from Valdštejnská.*
***Garden open** May–Sep: 9am–7pm
daily.* 📷 ♿ *from Valdštejnské
náměstí.*

THE FIRST LARGE secular building of the Baroque era in Prague, the palace stands as a monument to the fatal ambition of imperial military commander Albrecht von Wallenstein (1581–1634). His string of victories over the Protestants in the 30 Years' War (*see pp30–31*) made him indispensable to Emperor Ferdinand II. Already showered with titles, Wallenstein started to covet the crown of Bohemia for himself. In 1630 he was relieved of command, but was reinstated the following year. He then began to negotiate totally independently with the enemy and in 1634 was killed on the Emperor's orders by mercenaries.

Wallenstein

The main hall of Wallenstein Palace

Wallenstein's intention was to overshadow even Prague Castle with his palace, built between 1624 and 1630. To obtain a suitable site, he had to purchase 23 houses, three gardens and the municipal brick kiln. The magnificent main hall rises to a height of two storeys with a ceiling fresco of Wallenstein himself portrayed as Mars, the god of war, riding in a triumphal chariot. The architect, Andrea Spezza, and nearly all the artists employed in the decoration of the palace were Italians.

Today the palace is used for state functions, but there are sometimes public concerts. From Letenská you can enter the palace gardens. These are laid out as they were when Wallenstein dined in the huge *sala terrena* (garden pavilion) that looks out over a fountain and rows of bronze statues. These are copies of works by Adriaen de Vries that were stolen by the Swedes in 1648 (*see pp30–31*). There is also a large and grotesque structure of artificial stalactites and a pavilion with fine frescoes showing scenes from the legend of the Argonauts and the Golden Fleece. Wallenstein was a holder of the Order of the Golden Fleece, the highest order of chivalry of the Holy Roman Empire. At the far end of the garden from the palace is a large ornamental pond with a central statue. Behind the pond stands the old Riding School. This is now used to house exhibitions of modern art by the National Gallery.

Palace

Sala terrena

Copy of a bronze statue of Eros by Adriaen de Vries

Avenue of sculptures

Riding School

Valdštejnská Street entrance

The grotesquery is a curious imitation of the walls of a limestone cave, covered in stalactites.

Letenská Street entrance

Statue of Hercules

At St Thomas's ❷
U SV. TOMÁŠE

Letenská 12. **Map** 2 E3. 🕻 24 51 00 16. 🚇 Malostranská. 🚊 12, 22. **Open** 11:30am–11pm daily. 📷

NO OTHER BEER HALL in Prague can match the antiquity of At St Thomas's. Beer was first brewed here in 1352 by Augustinian monks. The brewery soon gained such renown that it was appointed sole purveyor of beer to Prague Castle. It remained in operation until 1951. Since then a special dark beer from the Braník brewery has been sold here. The basement of the old brewery has three beer halls, the most spectacular being the so-called "Cave", furnished in mock medieval style.

Church of St Thomas ❸
KOSTEL SV. TOMÁŠE

Letenská . **Map** 2 E3. 🕻 53 02 18. 🚇 Malostranská. 🚊 12, 22. **Open** only for services. 🕂 6pm Mon & Wed, 10am, 11:30am & 6pm Sun. 🚫 ♿

FOUNDED by Wenceslas II in 1285 as the monastery church of the Augustinians, the original Gothic church was completed in 1379. In the Hussite period (see pp26–7) this was one of the few churches to remain Catholic. As a result it suffered serious fire damage and had to be rebuilt. During the reign of Rudolph II (see pp28–9), St Thomas developed strong links with the Imperial court. Several prominent members of Rudolph's entourage were buried here, including court architect Ottavio Aostalli and the sculptor Adriaen de Vries.

In 1723 the church was struck by lightning and Kilian Ignaz Dientzenhofer was called in to rebuild it. The shape of the original church was preserved in spite of the Baroque reconstruction, but apart from the prominent spire, the church today betrays little of its Gothic origins.

The interior of the dome and the curving ceiling frescoes in the nave were painted by Dientzenhofer's collaborator Václav Vavřinec Reiner. Above the altar in elaborate frames are copies of paintings by Rubens – *The Martyrdom of St Thomas* and a picture of St Augustine. The originals are in the Sternberg Palace (see pp112–15).

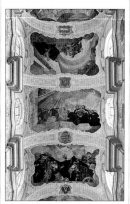

Baroque ceiling in the nave of the Church of St Thomas

Little Quarter Square ❹
MALOSTRANSKÉ NÁMĚSTÍ

Map 2 E3. 🚇 Malostranská. 🚊 12, 22.

THE SQUARE HAS BEEN the centre of life in the Little Quarter since its foundation in 1257. It had started life as a large marketplace in the outer bailey of Prague Castle. Buildings sprang up in the middle of the square dividing it in half – a gallows and pillory stood in its lower part.

Most of the houses around the square have a medieval core, but all were rebuilt in the Renaissance and Baroque periods. The centre of the square is dominated by the splendid Baroque church of St Nicholas. The large building beside it was a Jesuit college. Along the upper side of the square, facing the church, runs the vast Neo-Classical façade of Lichtenstein Palace. In front of it stands a column raised in honour of the Holy Trinity to mark the end of a plague epidemic in 1713.

Other important buildings include the Little Quarter Town Hall with its splendid Renaissance façade and the Sternberg Palace, built on the site of the outbreak of the fire of 1541, which destroyed most of the Little Quarter. Beside it stands the Smiřický Palace. Its turrets and hexagonal towers make it an unmistakable landmark on the northern side of the lower square. The Baroque Kaiserstein Palace is situated at the eastern side. On the façade is a bust of the great Czech soprano Emmy Destinn, who lived there between 1908 and 1914. She often sang with the famous Italian tenor Enrico Caruso.

Church of St Nicholas ❺
KOSTEL SV. MIKULÁŠE

See pp128–9.

Arcade in front of buildings on the west side of Little Quarter Square

Church of St Nicholas ⑤

KOSTEL SV. MIKULÁŠE

T HE CHURCH OF ST NICHOLAS divides and dominates the two
sections of Little Quarter Square. Building began in 1703,
and the last touches were put to the glorious frescoed nave
in 1761. It is the acknowledged masterpiece of father-and-
son architects Christoph and Kilian Ignaz Dientzenhofer,
Prague's greatest exponents of High Baroque *(see opposite)*,
although neither lived to see the completion of the
church. The statues, frescoes and paintings inside
the church are by leading artists of the day, and
include a fine *Crucifixion* of 1646 by Karel Škréta.
Extensive renovation in the 1950s reversed the damage
caused by 200 years of leaky cladding and condensation.

Altar Paintings
*The side chapels hold many
works of art. This painting
of St Michael is by
Francesco Solimena.*

★ Pulpit
*Dating from 1765,
the ornate pulpit is
by Richard and
Peter Prachner. It is
lavishly adorned
with golden cherubs.*

Baroque Organ
*A fresco of St Cecilia, patron
saint of music, watches over
the superb organ. Built in
1746, the instrument was
played by Mozart in 1787.*

**Entrance
from west
side of Little
Quarter Square**

**Chapel of
St Ann**

**Chapel of
St Catherine**

STAR FEATURES

★ Dome Fresco

★ Pulpit

★ Statues of the
  Church Fathers

Façade
*St Paul, by John Frederick Kohl, is
one of the statues that grace the
curving façade. It was completed in
1710 by Christoph Dientzenhofer,
who was influenced by Italian
architects Borromini and Guarini.*

The dome was completed by Kilian Ignaz Dientzenhofer in 1751, shortly before his death.

The belfry was the last part to be built. It was added in 1751–6 by Anselmo Lurago.

★ Dome Fresco
Franz Palko's fresco, The Celebration of the Holy Trinity *(1752–3), fills the 70 m (230 ft) high dome.*

High Altar
A copper statue of St Nicholas by Ignaz Platzer surmounts the high altar. Below it, the painting of St Joseph is by Johann Lukas Kracker, who also painted the nave fresco.

★ Statues of the Church Fathers
The great teachers by Ignaz Platzer stand at the four corners of the crossing. St Cyril dispatches the devil with his crozier.

Chapel of
Francis
avier

THE DIENTZENHOFER FAMILY
Christoph Dientzenhofer (1655–1722) came from a family of Bavarian master builders. His son Kilian Ignaz (1689–1751) was born in Prague and educated at the Jesuit Clementinum *(see p79).* They were responsible for the greatest treasures of Jesuit-influenced Prague Baroque architecture. The Church of St Nicholas, their last work, was completed by Kilian's son-in-law, Anselmo Lurago.

Kilian Ignaz Dientzenhofer

Nerudova Street **6**
NERUDOVA ULICE

Map 2 D3. **M** *Malostranská.*
🚊 *12, 22.*

A PICTURESQUE narrow street
leading up to Prague
Castle, Nerudova is named
after the poet and journalist
Jan Neruda, who wrote many
short stories set in this part of
Prague. He lived in the house
called At the Two Suns (No.
47) between 1845 and 1857.

Up until the introduction
of numbers in 1770, Prague's
houses were distinguished
by signs. Nerudova's houses
have a splendid selection of
heraldic beasts and emblems.
As you make your way up
Nerudova's steep slope, look
out in particular for the Red
Eagle (No. 6), the Three
Fiddles (No. 12), the Golden
Horseshoe (No. 34), the
Green Lobster (No. 43) and
the White Swan (No. 49). In
many of the houses there
are now cafés, wine bars
and beer halls.

There are also a number
of grand Baroque buildings
in the street, including the
Thun-Hohenstein Palace (No.
20, now the Italian embassy)
and the Morzin Palace (No. 5,
the Rumanian embassy). The
latter has a façade with two
massive statues of moors (a
pun on the name Morzin)
supporting the semicircular
balcony on the first floor.
Another impressive façade is
that of the Church of Our
Lady of Unceasing Succour,
the church of the Theatines,
an order founded during the
Counter-Reformation.

**Italian Street, heart of the former
colony of Italian craftsmen**

Italian Street **7**
VLAŠSKÁ ULICE

Map 1 C4. **M** *Malostranská.*
🚊 *12, 22.*

ITALIAN IMMIGRANTS started to
settle here in the 16th
century. Many were artists or
craftsmen employed to rebuild
and redecorate the Castle. If
you approach the street from
Petřín, on the left you will see
the former Italian Hospital, a
Baroque building with an
arcaded courtyard. Today it
maintains its traditional
allegiance as the cultural
section of the Italian embassy.

The grandest building in the
street is the former Lobkowicz
Palace, now the German
embassy. One of the finest
Baroque palaces in Prague, it
has a large oval hall on the
ground floor leading out onto
a magnificent garden. Look
out too for the pretty stucco
sign on the house called At
the Three Red Roses, dating
from the early 18th century.

Vrtba Garden **8**
VRTBOVSKÁ ZAHRADA

Karmelitská 25. **Map** 2 D4.
M *Malostranská.* 🚊 *12, 22.*
Closed for reconstruction. 📷

BEHIND VRTBA PALACE lies a
beautiful Baroque garden
with steep flights of steps and
balustraded terraces. From
the highest part of the garden
there are magnificent views
of Prague Castle and the Little
Quarter. The Vrtba Garden
was designed by František
Maximilián Kaňka in about
1720. The statues of Classical
gods and stone vases are the
work of Matthias Braun and
the paintings in the *sala
terrena* (garden pavilion) in
the lower part of the garden
are by Václav Vavřinec Reiner.

**View of the Little Quarter from
the terrace of the Vrtba Garden**

Church of Our
Lady Victorious **9**
KOSTEL PANNY MARIE VÍTĚZNÉ

Karmelitská. **Map** 2 E4. 📞 *53 07 52.*
🚊 *12, 22.* **Open** *8:30am–7pm
(Jul & Aug: 6pm) daily.* 📷

THE FIRST BAROQUE building
in Prague was the Church
of the Holy Trinity, built here
for the German Lutherans by
the Italian architect, Giovanni
Maria Filippi. It was finished
in 1613, but after the Battle of
the White Mountain *(see p31)*
the Catholic authorities gave
the church to the Carmelites,
who rebuilt it and renamed it
in honour of the victory. Little
has survived of the Lutheran

Sign of Jan Neruda's house, At the Two Suns, 47 Nerudova Street

church except the portal on the right of the present façade.

Most visitors, however, are not interested in the church's architecture. Enshrined on an elaborate marble altar in the right aisle is a glass case containing the Holy Infant of Prague (better-known by its Italian name – *il Bambino di Praga*). This wax effigy has an impressive record of miracle cures and is one of the most revered images in the Catholic world. It was brought from Spain by Polyxena of Lobkowicz, who presented it to the Carmelites in 1628.

Maltese Square ❿
MALTÉZSKÉ NÁMĚSTÍ

Map 2 E4. 🚋 *12, 22.*

THE SQUARE TAKES its name from the Priory of the Knights of Malta, which used to occupy this part of the Little Quarter. At the northern end stands a group of sculptures featuring St John the Baptist by Ferdinand Brokof – part of a fountain erected in 1715 to mark the end of a plague epidemic.

Most of the buildings were originally Renaissance houses belonging to prosperous townspeople, but in the 17th and 18th centuries the Little Quarter was taken over by the Catholic nobility and many were converted to flamboyant Baroque palaces. The largest, Nostitz Palace, stands on the southern side. Part of the palace now houses the Dutch embassy. It was built in the mid-17th century, then in about 1720 a balustrade was added with Classical vases and statues of emperors. In summer, concerts are given at the Palace. The Japanese embassy is housed in the Turba Palace (1767), an attractive pink Rococo building designed by Joseph Jäger.

Čertovka (the Devil's Stream) with Kampa Island on the right

Ferdinand Brokof's statue of John the Baptist in Maltese Square

Kampa Island ⓫
KAMPA

Map 2 F4. 🚋 *6, 9, 12, 22.*

KAMPA, AN ISLAND formed by a branch of the Vltava known as the Devil's Stream (Čertovka), is a delightfully peaceful corner of the Little Quarter. The stream got its name in the 19th century, allegedly after the diabolical temper of a lady who owned a house nearby in Maltese Square. For centuries the stream was used as a millrace and from Kampa you can see the remains of three old mills. The wheel of the Grand Prior's Mill has been totally restored. Beyond it, the stream disappears under a small bridge below the piers of Charles Bridge. From here it flows between rows of houses. Predictably, the area has become known as "the Venice of Prague", but instead of gondolas you will see canoes.

For most of the Middle Ages there were only gardens on Kampa, though the island was also used for washing clothes and bleaching linen. After the Little Quarter fire of 1541, rubble from the ruins was used to reinforce the banks, making building on Kampa safer. In the 17th century the island became well-known for its pottery markets. There are some enchanting houses from this period around Na Kampě Square. Most of the land from here to the southern tip of the island is a quiet park, created out of two old palace gardens.

Grand Priory Square ⓬
VELKOPŘEVORSKÉ NÁMĚSTÍ

Map 2 F4. Ⓜ *Malostranská.* 🚋 *12, 22.*

ON THE NORTHERN SIDE of this small leafy square stands the former seat of the Grand Prior of the Knights of Malta. In its present form the palace dates from the 1720s. The doorways, windows and decorative vases were made at the workshop of Matthias Braun. On the opposite side of the square is the Buquoy Palace, now the French embassy, a delightful Baroque building roughly contemporary with the Grand Prior's Palace.

The only incongruous features are a painting of John Lennon and graffiti exhorting the world to "give peace a chance". These have decorated the wall of the Grand Prior's garden since Lennon's death.

Street-by-Street: Little Quarter Riverside

O N EITHER SIDE of Bridge Street lies a delightful
half-hidden world of gently decaying squares,
picturesque palaces, churches and gardens.
When you have run the gauntlet of the trinket-
sellers on Charles Bridge, escape to Kampa
Island to enjoy a stroll in its informal park, the
views across the Vltava weir to the Old Town
and the flocks of swans
gliding along the river.

**The Church of
St Joseph** dates
from the late
17th century.
The painting
of *The Holy
Family* (1702)
on the gilded
high altar is
by the leading
Baroque artist
Petr Brandl.

**The House at the Golden
Unicorn** in Lázeňská Street
has a plaque commemorating
the fact that Beethoven
stayed here in 1796.

Bridge Street
*A major thoroughfare for
750 years, the narrow street
leads to Little Quarter Square* **16**

To Little
Quarter Square

**Grand Priory
Square**
*On the garden
wall of the Grand
Priory of the
Knights of Malta,
graffiti artists
have created a
mural in memory
of John Lennon* **12**

Church of Our Lady beneath the Chain
*Two massive towers survive from when
this was a fortified priory* **13**

**Church of Our Lady
Victorious**
*This Baroque church houses
the famous effigy, the Holy
Infant of Prague* **9**

Maltese Square
*Grand palaces surround the
oddly-shaped square. This
coat of arms decorates the
17th-century Nostitz Palace, a
popular venue for concerts* **10**

0 metres	100
0 yards	100

KEY

‒ ‒ ‒ Suggested route

Vojan Park
Quiet shady paths have been laid out under the apple trees of this former monastery garden **17**

At the Three Ostriches
A restaurant and hotel have kept the sign of a seller of ostrich plumes **15**

LOCATOR MAP
See Street Finder, map 2

U LUŽICKÉHO SEMINÁŘE

★ Charles Bridge
The approach to this magnificent 14th-century bridge, with its files of Baroque statues, passes under an arch below a Gothic tower **14**

Čertovka (the Devil's Stream)

The Grand Priory Mill has had its wheel meticulously restored, though it now turns very slowly in the sluggish water of the Čertovka, the former millrace.

NA KAMPĚ

Lichtenstein Palace

★ Kampa Island
This 19th-century painting by Soběslav Pinkas shows boys playing on Kampa. The island's park is still a popular place for children **11**

STAR SIGHTS

★ Charles Bridge

★ Kampa Island

Church of Our Lady beneath the Chain

KOSTEL PANNY MARIE POD ŘETĚZEM

Lázeňská. **Map** 2 E4. ☎ *53 32 32.* ⓜ *Malostranská.* 🚊 *12, 22.* **Open** *only for services.* ✝ *6:30pm (5pm in winter) Sat, 10am Sun.* 📷

THIS CHURCH, the oldest in the Little Quarter, was founded in the 12th century. King Vladislav II presented it to the Knights of St John, the crusading order which later became known as the Knights of Malta. It stood in the centre of the Knights' heavily fortified monastery that guarded the approach to the old Judith Bridge. The church's curious name refers to the chain used in the Middle Ages to close the monastery gatehouse.

A Gothic presbytery was added in the 13th century, but in the following century the original Romanesque church was demolished. A new portico was built with a pair of massive square towers, but work was then abandoned and the old nave became a courtyard between the towers and the church. This was given a Baroque facelift in 1640 by Carlo Lurago. The painting by Karel Škréta on the high altar shows the Virgin Mary and John the Baptist coming to the aid of the Knights of Malta in the famous naval victory over the Turks at Lepanto in 1571.

Charles Bridge ⓮

KARLŮV MOST

See pp136–9.

View along Bridge Street through the tower on Charles Bridge

At the Three Ostriches ⓯

U TŘÍ PŠTROSŮ

Dražického náměstí 12. **Map** 2 F3. ☎ *24 51 07 79.* ⓜ *Malostranská.* 🚊 *12, 22. See* **Where to Stay** *pp182–9,* **Restaurants** *pp198–209.*

MANY OF PRAGUE'S colourful house signs indicated the trade carried on in the premises. In 1597 Jan Fux, a merchant dealing in ostrich feathers, bought this house beside Charles Bridge. At the time ostrich plumes were very fashionable as decoration for hats among the courtiers and officers at Prague Castle. Fux even supplied feathers to foreign armies. So successful was his business, that in 1606 he had the house rebuilt and decorated with a large fresco of ostriches. He could afford to employ a respected artist to paint his sign rather than the usual journeymen.

The first floor of the house was added in 1657 and some beamed ceilings painted with vine motifs have been preserved from that time. In 1714 Prague's first coffee house opened here. The building is now an expensive hotel and restaurant.

Bridge Street ⓰

MOSTECKÁ ULICE

Map 2 E3. ⓜ *Malostranská.* 🚊 *12, 22.*

SINCE THE MIDDLE AGES this street has linked Charles Bridge with the Little Quarter Square. Crossing the bridge from the Old Town you can see the doorway of the old customs house built in 1591 in front of the Judith Tower. On the first floor of the tower there is a 13th-century relief of a king and a kneeling man.

Throughout the 13th and 14th centuries the area to the north of the street was the Court of the Bishop of Prague. This was destroyed during the Hussite Wars *(see pp26–7)*, but one of its Gothic towers is preserved in the courtyard of the house called At the Three Golden Bells. It can be seen from the higher of the two bridge towers. The street is lined with a mixture of Renaissance and Baroque

Fresco that gave At the Three Ostriches its name

houses. As you walk up to Little Quarter Square, look out for the house called the Black Eagle on the left. It has rich sculptural decoration and a splendid Baroque wrought-iron grille. Kaunic Palace, also on the left, was built in the 1770s. Its Rococo façade has striking stucco decoration and sculptures by Ignaz Platzer.

Vojan Park ⓱
VOJANOVY SADY

U lužického semináře. **Map** 2 F3.
M *Malostranská.* 12, 18, 22.
Open 9am–6pm daily.

A TRANQUIL SPOT hidden behind high white walls, the park dates back to the 17th century, when it was the garden of the Convent of Barefooted Carmelites. Two chapels erected by the Order have survived among the park's lawns and fruit trees. One is the Chapel of Elijah, who, because of his Old Testament associations with Mount Carmel, is regarded as the founder of the Order. His chapel takes the form of a stalagmite and stalactite cave. The other chapel, dedicated to St Theresa, was built in the 18th century as an expression of gratitude for the convent's preservation during the Prussian siege of Prague in 1757. In a niche to the left of the entrance to the park, there is an 18th-century statue of St John Nepomuk *(see p137)* by Ignaz Platzer. The saint is depicted standing on a fish – a reference to his martyrdom by drowning in the Vltava.

Ledebour Garden ⓲
LEDEBURSKÁ ZAHRADA

Valdštejnská. **Map** 2 F2.
M *Malostranská.* 12, 18, 22.
Closed for reconstruction, normally open May–Sep: 9am–7pm daily.

T HE STEEP SOUTHERN slope below Prague Castle was covered with vineyards and gardens during the Middle Ages. But in the 16th century, when nobles started building palaces here, they laid out

larger formal terraced gardens based on Italian Renaissance models. Most of these were then rebuilt during the 18th century and decorated with Baroque garden statuary and fountains. Three of the gardens – those belonging to the former Ledebour, Černín and Pálffy Palaces – have been linked together and are normally open to the public. At the moment, however, some of the crumbling old stone staircases are far from safe and the gardens are being completely restored.

The faded elegance of the gardens is enhanced by magnificent views of Prague from their terraces. The Ledebour Garden, designed in the early 18th century, has a fine *sala terrena* (garden pavilion) by Giovanni Battista Alliprandi. The Pálffy Garden was laid out in the mid-18th century with terraces (the second still has its original sundial) and loggias. The most beautiful of the three and architecturally the richest

18th-century statue of Hercules located in the Ledebour Garden

is the Kolowrat-Černín Garden, created in 1784 by Ignaz Palliardi. The highest terrace has a *sala terrena* decorated with statues and Classical urns. Below this there is a wonderful assortment of staircases, archways, balustrades, and the slightly battered remains of Classical statuary and old fountains.

Staircases and terraces at the foot of the Ledebour Garden

Charles Bridge (Little Quarter Side) ⓮

KARLŮV MOST

Prague's most familiar monument, now a haven for craft and trinket stalls, connects the Old Town with the Little Quarter. Although it is now pedestrianized, at one time it could take four carriages abreast. Today, due to wear and tear, many of the statues on the bridge are copies; the originals are kept in the Lapidarium of the National Museum *(see p162)*. The Gothic Old Town Bridge Tower *(see p139)* is one of the finest buildings of its kind in existence.

★ View from Little Quarter Bridge Tower
The tall pinnacled wedge tower, gives a superb view of the city of 100 spires. The shorter tower is the remains of Judith Bridge.

Little Quarter Bridge Tower

Tower entrance

St Adalbert, 1709
Adalbert, Bishop of Prague, founded the Church of St Lawrence (see p141) on Petřín Hill in 991. He is known to the Czechs as Vojtěch.

St Wenceslas, 1858

St Philip Benzi, 17

Steps to Saská Street

Judith Bridge Tower, 1188

Christ between St Cosmas and St Damian, 1709

St John de Matha, St Felix de Valois and the Blessed Ivan, 1714
These saints, sculpted by Ferdinand Brokof, founded the Trinitarian Order of mendicants to collect money to buy the freedom of Christians enslaved by the infidels (represented at the foot of the sculpture).

St Vitus, 1714
This engraving of the statue shows the 3rd-century martyr with the lions which were supposed to maul him, but licked him instead. St Vitus is the patron saint of dancers and often invoked against convulsive disorders.

STAR FEATURES

★ Little Quarter Bridge Tower and View

★ St John Nepomuk

★ St Luitgard

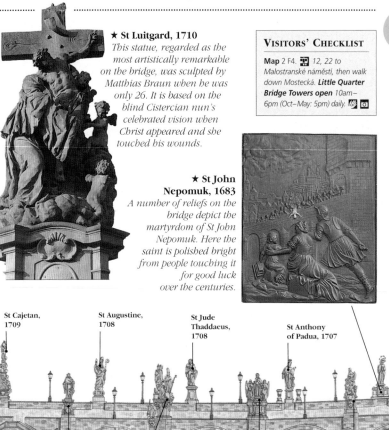

★ St Luitgard, 1710
This statue, regarded as the most artistically remarkable on the bridge, was sculpted by Matthias Braun when he was only 26. It is based on the blind Cistercian nun's celebrated vision when Christ appeared and she touched his wounds.

VISITORS' CHECKLIST

Map 2 F4. 12, 22 to Malostranské náměstí, then walk down Mostecká. **Little Quarter Bridge Towers open** 10am–6pm (Oct–May: 5pm) daily.

★ St John Nepomuk, 1683
A number of reliefs on the bridge depict the martyrdom of St John Nepomuk. Here the saint is polished bright from people touching it for good luck over the centuries.

St Cajetan, 1709

St Augustine, 1708

St Jude Thaddaeus, 1708

St Anthony of Padua, 1707

Steps to Kampa Island

St Nicholas Tolentino, 1708

St Francis of Assisi, with two angels, 1855

St Ludmilla, 1710

St Vincent Ferrer and St Procopius, 1712
This detail shows a rabbi saddened by St Vincent's success in converting many Jews to Christianity. St Procopius is one of Bohemia's four patron saints.

ST JOHN NEPOMUK

The cult of St John Nepomuk, canonized in 1729, was promoted by the Jesuits to rival the revered Jan Hus *(see p27)*. Jan Nepomucký, vicar-general of the Archdiocese of Prague, was arrested in 1393 by Wenceslas IV along with the archbishop and others who had displeased the king over the election of an abbot. The archbishop escaped, but John died under torture. The body was bound and thrown off Charles Bridge. Statues modelled on the one placed here in 1683 can be seen throughout central Europe, especially on bridges.

Charles Bridge (Old Town Side) ⓴

KARLŮV MOST

U NTIL 1741, CHARLES BRIDGE was the only crossing over the Vltava. It is 520 m (1,706 ft) long and is built of sandstone blocks, rumoured to be strengthened by mixing mortar with eggs. The bridge was commissioned by Charles IV in 1357 to replace the Judith Bridge and built by Peter Parler. The bridge's original decoration was a simple cross. The first statue – of St John Nepomuk – was added in 1683, inspired by Bernini's sculptures on Rome's Ponte Sant'Angelo.

★ 17th-Century Crucifixion

For 200 years, the wooden crucifix stood alone on the bridge. The gilded Christ dates from 1629 and the Hebrew words "Holy, Holy, Holy Lord", were paid for by a Jew as punishment for blasphemy.

St Francis Xavier, 1711

The Jesuit missionary is supported by three Moorish and two Oriental converts. The sculptor Brokof is seated on the saint's left.

St Norbert, St Wenceslas and St Sigismund, 1853

St Francis Borgia, 1710

St John the Baptist, 1857

St Cyril and St Methodius, 1938

St Christopher, 1857

St Ann, 1707

St Joseph, 1854

Thirty Years' War

In the last hours of this war, the Old Town was saved from the Swedish army. The truce was signed in the middle of the bridge in 1648.

STAR FEATURES

- ★ Old Town Bridge Tower
- ★ 17th-Century Crucifixion

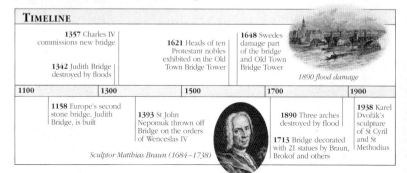

TIMELINE

1357 Charles IV commissions new bridge

1342 Judith Bridge destroyed by floods

1621 Heads of ten Protestant nobles exhibited on the Old Town Bridge Tower

1648 Swedes damage part of the bridge and Old Town Bridge Tower

1890 flood damage

1100	1300	1500	1700	1900

1158 Europe's second stone bridge, Judith Bridge, is built

1393 St John Nepomuk thrown off Bridge on the orders of Wenceslas IV

Sculptor Matthias Braun (1684–1738)

1890 Three arches destroyed by flood

1713 Bridge decorated with 21 statues by Braun, Brokof and others

1938 Karel Dvořák's sculpture of St Cyril and St Methodius

The Madonna, St Dominic and St Thomas, 1708

The Dominicans, (known in a Latin pun as Domini canes, *the dogs of God), are shown with the Madonna and their emblem, a dog.*

Madonna and St Bernard, 1709

Cherubs and symbols of the Passion, including the dice, the cock and the centurion's gauntlet, form part of the statue.

Old Town Bridge Tower

Tower entrance

Pietà, 1859

St Barbara, St Margaret and St Elizabeth, 1707

★ OLD TOWN BRIDGE TOWER

This magnificent Gothic tower, designed by Peter Parler, was built at the end of the 14th century. A fitting ornament to the new Charles Bridge, it was also an integral part of the Old Town's fortifications.

Pinnacled wedge spire

Roof viewing point

The viewing gallery is a rib-vaulted room, on the tower's first floor. It provides a wonderful view of Prague Castle and the Little Quarter.

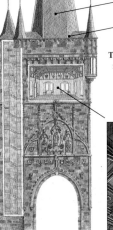

Bridge Tower sculptures by Peter Parler include St Vitus, the bridge's patron saint, Charles IV (left) and Wenceslas IV.

Observation Tower ⓳
ROZHLEDNA

Petřín. **Map** 1 C4. 🚋 22, then take funicular railway. 🚌 132, 143, 149, 217. **Open** 9:30am–5pm Tue–Sun.
📷 ◻

T HE MOST conspicuous landmark in Petřín Park is an imitation Eiffel Tower, built as one of the attractions of the Jubilee Exhibition of 1891. The octagonal Petřín tower is only 60 m (200 ft), about a quarter the height of the Eiffel Tower. The only way to the viewing platform at the top is to haul yourself up the 299 steps of its spiral staircase. You will be rewarded by magnificent views. On a clear day, you can see as far as Bohemia's highest peak, Sněžka in the Krkonoše (Giant) Mountains, 150 km (100 miles) to the northeast.

Mirror Maze ⓴
ZRCADLOVÉ BLUDIŠTĚ

Petřín. **Map** 1 C4. 📞 53 13 62. 🚋 22, then take funicular railway. 🚌 132, 143, 149, 217. **Open** Apr–Oct: 9:30am–5pm Tue–Sun.
📷 ◻ ♿

L IKE THE Observation Tower, the maze, which has walls lined with distorting mirrors, is a relic of the Exhibition of 1891. It is housed in a wooden pavilion built in the shape of the old Špička Gate, part of the old Gothic fortifications of Vyšehrad (see pp178–9). This

The 100-year-old Observation Tower overlooking the city

curious amusement house was transferred to Petřín at the end of the exhibition and has stood here ever since. When you have threaded your way through the maze and laughed at your reflection, your reward is to see the diorama of *The Defence of Prague against the Swedes*, on Charles Bridge in 1648.

Church of St Lawrence ㉑
KOSTEL SV. VAVŘINCE

Petřín. **Map** 1 C5. 🚋 22, then take funicular railway. 🚌 132, 143, 149, 217. **Closed** to the public.

A CCORDING TO LEGEND, the church was founded in the 10th century by the pious Prince Boleslav II and St Adalbert on the site of a former pagan shrine. The

sacristy ceiling is decorated with a painting of the legend. This dates from the 18th century when the diminutive Romanesque church was swallowed up by a large new Baroque structure with a lanterned cupola flanked by two onion-domed towers. The small Calvary Chapel (1735), just to the left of the entrance to the church, has a façade decorated with modern *sgraffito* that portrays *The Resurrection of Christ*. To the northeast of the church is the Chapel of the Holy Sepulchre, built in 1732, a replica of the tomb of Christ in Jerusalem.

Observatory ㉒
HVĚZDÁRNA

Petřín 205. **Map** 2 D5. 📞 24 51 07 09. 🚋 22, then take funicular railway. **Open** 6–8pm Mon–Fri, 10am–noon & 2–8pm Sat and Sun.
📷 ⌀ ♿ ground floor only.

One of the telescopes in the Observatory on Petřín Hill

S INCE 1930, PRAGUE'S amateur astronomers have been able to enjoy the facilities of this observatory on Petřín Hill. You can use its telescopes to view anything from the craters of the moon to unfamiliar distant galaxies. There is an exhibition of old astronomical instruments and special events for children are held on Saturdays and Sundays.

Hunger Wall ㉓
HLADOVÁ ZEĎ

Újezd, Petřín, Strahovská. **Map** 2 D5. 🚋 6, 9, 12, 22, then take funicular railway. 🚌 132, 143, 149, 217.

T HE FORTIFICATIONS built around the southern edge of the Little Quarter on the orders of Charles IV in

Diorama of *The Defence of Prague against the Swedes* in the Mirror Maze

1360–62 have been known for centuries as the Hunger Wall. Nearly 1,200 m (1,300 yards) of the wall have survived, complete with crenellated battlements and a platform for marksmen on its inner side. It runs from Újezd across Petřín Park to Strahov. The story behind the name is that Charles commissioned its construction with the aim of giving employment to the poor during a period of famine. It is true that a great famine did break out in Bohemia in the 1360s and the two events, the famine and the building of the wall, became permanently linked in the people's memory.

Petřín Park ㉔
PETŘÍNSKÉ SADY

Map 2 D5. 6, 9, 12, 22, then take funicular railway. See **Four Guided Walks** pp174–5.

To the west of the Little Quarter, the wooded slopes of Petřín hill rise above the city to a height of 318 m (960 ft). The name derives either from the Slavonic god Perun, to whom sacrifices were made on the hill or from the Latin name Mons Petrinus, meaning "rocky hill". A forest used to stretch from here as far as the White Mountain *(see p31)*. In the 12th century the southern side of the hill was planted with vineyards, but by the 18th century most of these had been transformed into gardens and orchards. The lower slopes are still covered with old apple and pear trees.

Today a path winds up the slopes of Petřín, offering magnificent panoramas of Prague. The park is especially popular in the spring when the fruit trees are in blossom and young lovers lay flowers on the monument to Karel Hynek Mácha, the most famous Czech Romantic poet, who died aged 26 in 1836.

Nebozízek, the station halfway up Petřín's funicular railway

Statue of Karel Hynek Mácha in Petřín Park

Funicular Railway ㉕
LANOVÁ DRÁHA

Újezd. **Map** 2 D5. 6, 9, 12, 22. **In operation** 5am–midnight daily.

Built to carry visitors to the 1891 Jubilee Exhibition up to the Observation Tower at the top of Petřín hill, the funicular was originally powered by water. In this form, it remained in operation until 1914, then between the wars was converted to electricity. In 1965 it had to be shut down because part of the hillside collapsed – coal had been mined here during the 19th century. Shoring up the slope and rebuilding the railway took 20 years, but since its reopening in 1985 it has proved a reliable way of getting up Petřín Hill. At the halfway station, Nebozízek, there is a restaurant *(see p202)* with fine views of the Castle and the city across the river.

Michna Palace ㉖
MICHNŮV PALÁC

Újezd 40. **Map** 2 E4. 24 51 06 07. 12, 22. **Open** 9am–5pm Tue–Sat, 10am–5pm Sun.

In about 1580 Ottavio Aostalli built a summer palace here for the Kinský family on the site of an old Dominican convent. In 1623 the building was bought by Pavel Michna of Vacínov, a supply officer in the Imperial Army, who had grown rich after the Battle of the White Mountain. He commissioned a new Baroque building that he hoped would rival the palace of his late commander, Wallenstein *(see p126)*.

In 1767 the Michna Palace was sold to the army and over the years it became a crumbling ruin. After 1918 it was bought by Sokol (a physical culture association) and converted into a gym and sports centre with a training ground in the old palace garden. The restored palace was renamed Tyrš House in honour of Sokol's founder. The ground floor now houses the Museum of Physical Culture and Sport.

Restored Baroque façade of the Michna Palace (Tyrš House)

NEW TOWN

NOVÉ MĚSTO

Art Nouveau
decoration on No. 12
Wenceslas Square

THE NEW TOWN, founded in 1348 by Charles IV, was carefully planned and laid out around three large central market-places: the Hay Market (Senovážné Square), the Cattle Market (Charles Square) and the Horse Market (Wenceslas Square). Twice as large as the Old Town, the area was mainly inhabited by tradesmen and craftsmen such as blacksmiths, wheelwrights and brewers. During the late 19th century, much of the New Town was demolished and completely redeveloped, giving it the appearance it has today.

SIGHTS AT A GLANCE

Churches and Monasteries
Church of Our Lady of the Snows **2**
Church of St Ignatius **8**
Church of St Cyril and St Methodius **11**
Church of St John on the Rock **13**
Slavonic Monastery **14**
Church of St Catherine **16**
Church of St Stephen **19**
Church of St Ursula **22**

Historic Buildings
Hotel Europa **4**
Jesuit College **9**
Faust House **12**
New Town Hall **20**

Theatres and Opera Houses
State Opera **6**
National Theatre pp156–7 **23**

Museums and Galleries
National Museum **5**
Dvořák Museum **18**

Historic Squares
Wenceslas Square **1**
Charles Square **10**

Historic Restaurants and Beer Halls
Slavonic House **7**
Chalice Restaurant **17**
U Fleků **21**

Parks and Gardens
Franciscan Garden **3**
Botanical Gardens **15**

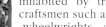

GETTING THERE

The entire area is well served by the metro with two main stations, Můstek and Muzeum in Wenceslas Square, and others at Karlovo náměstí and Národní třída. Tram routes from most parts of the city pass through Karlovo náměstí.

KEY

	Street-by-Street map *See pp144–5*
	Street-by-Street map *See pp150–51*
M	Metro station
	Tram stop
P	Parking
	River boat boarding point

◁ Art Nouveau sculptures on the Hlahol Choir Building (1905) on Masarykovo nábřeží

Street-by-Street: Wenceslas Square

HOTELS AND RESTAURANTS occupy many of the buildings around Wenceslas Square, though it remains an important commercial centre – the square began life as a medieval horse market. As you walk along, look up at the buildings, most of which date from the turn of this century, when the square was redeveloped. There are fine examples of the decorative styles used by Czech architects of the period. Many blocks have dark covered arcades leading to shops, clubs, theatres and cinemas.

Statue of St Lawrence at U Pinkasů

Koruna Palace (1914) is an ornate block of shops and offices. Its corner turret is topped with a crown (*koruna*).

To Powder Gate

NA PŘÍKOPĚ

U Pinkasů became one of Prague's most popular beer halls when it started serving Pilsner Urquell *(see pp196–7)* in 1843.

Můstek

Church of Our Lady of the Snows
The towering Gothic build-ing is only part of a vast church planned during the 14th century ❷

Můstek

Můs

VODIČKOVA

Lucerna Palace

Jungmann Square is named after Josef Jungmann (1773–1847), an influential scholar of language and lexicographer, and there is a statue of him in the middle. The Adria Palace (1925) used to be the Laterna Magika Theatre *(see p214)*, which was where Václav Havel's Civic Forum worked in the early days of the 1989 Velvet Revolution.

Franciscan Garden
An old monastery gar-den has been laid out as a small park with this fountain, rose-beds, trellises and a children's playground ❸

Wiehl House, named after its architect Antonín Wiehl, was completed in 1896. The five-storey building is in striking Neo-Renaissance style, with a loggia and colourful *sgraffito*. Mikuláš Aleš designed some of the Art Nouveau figures.

STAR SIGHTS

★ Wenceslas Square

★ Hotel Europa

★ National Museum

★ **Wenceslas Square**
The dominant features of the square are the equestrian statue of St Wenceslas (1912) and the National Museum behind it ❶

LOCATOR MAP
See Street Finder, maps 3, 4 & 6

The Monument to the Victims of Communism consists of just a few simple wreaths, photographs of victims, crosses and candles. Since the Velvet Revolution in 1989 an unofficial shrine has been maintained here in front of the St Wenceslas Monument.

The Assicurazioni Generali Building was where Franz Kafka *(see p68)* worked as an insurance clerk for 10 months in 1906–7.

★ **Hotel Europa**
Both the façade and the interior of the hotel (1906) preserve most of their original Art Nouveau features ❹

OBĚTEM KOMUNISMU

St Wenceslas Monument

State Opera
Meticulously refurbished in the 1980s, the interior retains the luxurious red plush, crystal chandeliers and gilded stucco of the original late-19th-century theatre ❻

VÁCLAVSKÉ NÁMĚSTÍ

OPLETALOVA

WILSONOVA

Muzeum

Muzeum

Fénix Palace

Former Federal Assembly

★ **National Museum**
The grand building with its monumental staircase was completed in 1890 as a symbol of national prestige ❺

| 0 metres | 100 |
| 0 yards | 100 |

KEY

– – – Suggested route

Wenceslas Monument in Wenceslas Square

Wenceslas Square ❶
VÁCLAVSKÉ NÁMĚSTÍ

Map 3 C5. ᴹ Můstek, Muzeum. 3, 9, 14, 24.

THE SQUARE HAS witnessed many key events in recent Czech history. It was here that the student Jan Palach burnt himself to death in 1969, and in November 1989 a protest rally in the square against police brutality led to the Velvet Revolution and the overthrow of Communism.

Wenceslas "Square" is something of a misnomer, for it is some 750 m (825 yd) long and only 60 m (65 yd) wide. Originally a horse market, today it is lined with hotels, restaurants, clubs and shops, reflecting the seamier side of Western consumerism. The huge equestrian statue of St Wenceslas that looks the length of the square from in front of the National Museum was erected in 1912. Cast in bronze, it is the work of Josef Myslbek, the leading Czech sculptor of the late 19th century. At the foot of the pedestal there are smaller statues of Czech patron saints. An improvised memorial near the statue commemorates the victims of the former regime.

Church of Our Lady of the Snows ❷
KOSTEL PANNY MARIE SNĚŽNÉ

Jungmannovo náměsti. **Map** 3 C5. 26 57 42. ᴹ Můstek. **Open** 7am–7:30pm daily.

CHARLES IV FOUNDED the church to mark the occasion of his coronation in 1347. The name refers to a 4th-century miracle in Rome, when the Virgin Mary appeared to the pope in a dream telling him to build a church to her on the spot where snow fell in August. Charles's church was to have been over 100 m (330 ft) long, but was never completed. The towering building we see today was just the presbytery of the projected church. Over 33 m (110 ft) high, it was finished in 1397. The church was originally part of a Carmelite monastery. On the northern side there is a gateway with a 14th-century pediment that used to decorate the entrance to the monastery graveyard.

In the early 15th century a steeple was added, but further building was halted by the Hussite Wars *(see pp26–7)*. The Hussite firebrand Jan Želivský preached at the church and was buried here after his execution in 1422. The church suffered considerable damage in the wars and in 1434 the steeple was destroyed. For a long time the church was left to decay. In 1603 Franciscans

restored the building. The intricate net vaulting of the ceiling dates from this period, the original roof having collapsed. Most of the interior decoration, apart from the 1450s pewter font, is Baroque. The monumental three-tiered altar, crowded with statues of saints, is crowned with a crucifix attached to one of the pins placed across the vaulting.

Franciscan Garden ❸
FRANTIŠKÁNSKÁ ZAHRADA

Jungmannovo náměsti 18. **Map** 3 C5. ᴹ Můstek. **Open** 6am–7pm daily.

ORIGINALLY the physic garden of a Franciscan monastery, the area was opened to the public in 1950 as a tranquil oasis close to Wenceslas Square. By the entrance is a Gothic portal leading down to a cellar restaurant – U františkánů (At the Franciscans). In the 1980s several of the beds were replanted with herbs, cultivated by the Franciscans in the 17th century.

Hotel Europa ❹
HOTEL EVROPA

Václavské náměsti 29. **Map** 4 D5. 24 22 81 18. ᴹ Můstek. 3, 9, 14, 24. See **Where to Stay** pp182–9, **Restaurants, Pubs and Cafés** pp198–205.

THOUGH A trifle shabby in places, the Europa Hotel is a wonderfully preserved reminder of the golden age

Art Nouveau decoration on façade of the Hotel Europa

Façade of the State Opera, formerly the New German Theatre

of hotels. It was built in highly decorated Art Nouveau style between 1903 and 1906. Not only has its splendid façade crowned with gilded nymphs survived, but many of the interiors on the ground floor have remained virtually intact, including all the original bars, large mirrors, panelling and light fittings.

National Museum **5**
NÁRODNÍ MUZEUM

Václavské náměstí 68. **Map** 6 E1.
(24 23 04 85. **M** Muzeum.
Open 9am–5pm Mon & Wed–Sun.
(free first Mon of month).

THE VAST Neo-Renaissance building that dominates one end of Wenceslas Square houses the museum. Designed by Josef Schulz as a triumphal affirmation of the Czech national revival, the museum was completed in 1890. The entrance is reached by a ramp decorated with allegorical statues. Seated by the door are History and Natural History.

Inside, the rich marbled decoration is impressive, but it completely overwhelms the rather antique and uninspiring collections. These are devoted principally to mineralogy, archaeology, anthropology, and natural history. The museum also has a Pantheon containing busts and statues of Czech scholars, artists and writers. It is decorated with many historical paintings by František Ženíšek, Václav Brožík and Vojtěch Hynais.

State Opera **6**
STÁTNÍ OPERA

Wilsonova 8. **Map** 4 E5.
(26 53 53. **M** Muzeum.
Open for performances only. See
Entertainment pp210–15.

THE FIRST THEATRE built here, the New Town Theatre, was pulled down in 1885 to make way for the present building. This was originally known as the New German Theatre, built to rival the Czechs' National Theatre (see pp156–7). A Neo-Classical frieze decorates the pediment above the columned loggia at the front of the theatre. The figures include Dionysus and Thalia, the muse of comedy. The interior is stuccoed and original paintings in the auditorium and on the curtain have been preserved. In 1945 the theatre became the city's main opera house, but access has become difficult because of the adjacent freeway.

Slavonic House **7**
SLOVANSKÝ DŮM

Na příkopě 22. **Map** 4 D4.
(24 21 30 91. **M** Můstek,
Náměstí Republiky. 5, 14, 26.
Open 10am–9pm daily.

SINCE 1945 this large Neo-Classical building has been a cultural and social centre. Before then, as the Café Continental, it had been an exclusive meeting place of Prague's Germans. It now has venues for cultural events and a number of restaurants and bars, including a large garden with an open-air restaurant. It owes its present name to the 1848 Slav Congress which was held nearby.

Main staircase of the National Museum

Art Nouveau in Prague

THE DECORATIVE STYLE known as Art Nouveau originated in Paris in the 1890s. It quickly became international as most of the major European cities quickly responded to its graceful, flowing forms. In Prague it was at its height in the first decade of the 20th century but died out during World War I, when it seemed frivolous and even decadent. There is a wealth of Art Nouveau in Prague, both in the fine and decorative arts and in architecture. In the New Town and the Jewish Quarter *(see pp80–93)*, entire streets were demolished at the turn of the century and built in the new style.

Façade detail,
10 Masaryk
Embankment

Praha House
This house was built in 1903 for the Prague Insurance Company. Its name is in gilt Art Nouveau letters at the top.

ARCHITECTURE

ART NOUVEAU made its first appearance in Prague at the Jubilee exhibition of 1891. Architecturally, the new style was a deliberate attempt to break with the 19th-century tradition of monumental buildings. In Art Nouveau the important aspect was ornament, either painted or sculpted, often in the form of a female figure, applied to a fairly plain surface. This technique was ideally suited to wrought iron and glass, popular at the turn of the century. These materials were light but strong. The effect of this, together with Art Nouveau decoration, created buildings of lasting beauty.

Hotel Central
Built by Alois Dryák and Bedřich Bendelmayer in 1900, the façade of this hotel has plaster-work shaped like tree branches.

Hlahol Choir Building, 1905
The architect Josef Fanta embellished this building with mosaics and sculptures by Karl Mottl and Josef Pekárek (see also p142).

Hotel Evropa
Finished in 1904, this grand Art Nouveau building is notable for its fine detailing inside and out.

Ornate
pilasters

Decorative
statues

Brass and
wrought-
iron
balustrade

Hlavní nádraží
Prague's main railway station was completed in 1901. With its huge interior glazed dome and elegant sculptural decoration, it shows many Art Nouveau features.

DECORATIVE AND FINE ARTS

MANY PAINTERS, sculptors and graphic artists were influenced by Art Nouveau. One of the most successful exponents of the style was the artist Alfons Mucha (1860–1939). He is celebrated chiefly for his posters. Yet he designed stained glass (see p102), furniture, jewellery, even postage stamps. It is perhaps here, in the decorative and applied arts, that Art Nouveau had its fullest expression in Prague. Artists adorned every type of object – doorknobs, curtain ornaments, vases and cutlery – with tentacle- and plant-like forms in imitation of the natural world from which they drew their inspiration.

Postage Stamp, 1918
A bold stamp design by Alfons Mucha marked the founding of the Czechoslovak Republic.

Poster for Sokol Movement
Mucha's colour lithograph for the sixth national meeting of the Sokol gymnastic movement (1912) is in Tyrš's Museum (Physical Culture and Sports).

Záboj and Slavoj
These mythical figures (invented by a forger of old legends) were carved by Josef Myslbek for Palacký Bridge in 1895. They are now in Vyšehrad.

Glass Vase
This iridescent green vase made of Bohemian glass has relief decoration of intertwined threads. It is in the Museum of Decorative Arts.

Curtain Ornament and Candlestick
The silver and silk ornament adorns the Mayor's room of the Municipal House. The candlestick by Emanuel Novák with fine leaf design is in the Museum of Decorative Arts.

WHERE TO SEE ART NOUVEAU IN PRAGUE

Detail of doorway, Široká 9, Jewish Quarter

ARCHITECTURE
Apartment Building, Na příkopě 7
Hanavský Pavilion *p161*
Hlahol Choir Building, Masarykovo nábřeží 10
Hlavní nádraží, Wilsonova
Hotel Central, Hybernská 10
  see also *p185*
Hotel Evropa *p146*
Industrial Palace *p162 and Four Guided Walks pp176–7*
Ministerstvo Hospodářství *p67*
Municipal House *p64*
Palacký Bridge (Palackého most)
Praha House, Národní třída 7
Wiehl House *p144*

PAINTING
St Agnes's Convent *pp92–3*

SCULPTURE
Jan Hus Monument *p70*
Vyšehrad Garden *p160 and Four Guided Walks pp178–9*
Vyšehrad Cemetery *p160 and Four Guided Walks pp178–9*
Zbraslav Monastery *p163*

DECORATIVE ARTS
Museum of Decorative Arts *p84*
Prague Museum *p161*

Street-by-Street: Charles Square

Detail of house in Charles Square

THE SOUTHERN PART of the New Town resounds to the rattle of trams, as many routes converge in this part of Prague. Fortunately, the park in Charles Square (Karlovo náměstí) offers a peaceful and welcome retreat. Many of the buildings around the Square belong to the University and the statues in the centre represent writers and scientists, reflecting the academic environment. There are several Baroque buildings and towards the river stands the historic 14th-century Slavonic Monastery.

The Czech Technical University was founded here in 1867 in a grand Neo-Renaissance building.

Church of St Wenceslas

To the river

★ Church of St Cyril and St Methodius
A plaque and a bullet-scarred wall are reminders of the siege of the church in 1942, when German troops mounted an assault on the Czech and Slovak agents who were hiding there ⓫

★ Charles Square
The centre of the square is a pleasant 19th-century park with lawns, formal flowerbeds, fountains and statues ❿

Church of St Cosmas and St Damian

Slavonic Monastery
In 1965 a pair of modern concrete spires by František Černý were added to the church of the 14th-century monastery ⓮

Church of St John on the Rock
This view of the organ and ceiling shows the dynamic Baroque design of Kilian Ignaz Dientzenhofer ⓭

Church of St Ignatius
The sun rays and gilded cherubs on the side altars are typical of the gaudy decoration in this Baroque church built for the Jesuits **8**

Eliška Krásnohorská was a 19th-century poet who wrote the libretti for Smetana's operas. A statue of her was put up here in 1931.

LOCATOR MAP
See Street Finder, map 5

A statue of Jan Purkyně (1787–1869), an eminent physiologist and pioneer of cell theory, was erected in 1961. It is the most recent of the many memorials in the square.

Jesuit College
Founded in the mid-17th century, this imposing building has been a hospital since the suppression of the Jesuits in 1773 (see pp30–31) **9**

18th-century Institute of Gentlewomen (now a hospital)

Faust House
In the 18th century this house was owned by Count Ferdinand Mladota of Solopysky. The chemical experiments he performed reinforced the associations that gave the building its name **12**

Botanical Gardens
Though part of the Charles University, the gardens are open to the public and are known for their profusion of rare plants. This is an agreeable place to relax **15**

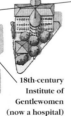

0 metres 100
0 yards 100

KEY
– – – Suggested route

Sculptures on the façade of St Ignatius by Tomasso Soldati

Church of St Ignatius ❽
KOSTEL SV. IGNÁCE

Karlovo náměstí. **Map** 5 C2.
🎫 29 44 31. ᴹ Karlovo náměstí.
🚋 3, 4, 6, 14, 18, 22, 24. **Open**
5am–noon (Sun: 6am–noon),
3pm–6:30pm daily. 📷

WITH ITS WEALTH of gilding and flamboyant stucco decoration, St Ignatius is typical of the Baroque churches built by the Jesuits to impress people with the power and glamour of their faith. The architects were the two men responsible for the adjoining Jesuit College, Carlo Lurago, who started work on the church in 1665, and Paul Ignaz Bayer, who added the tower in 1687. The painting on the high altar of *The Glory of St Ignatius* (St Ignatius Loyola, the founder of the Jesuit order) is by Jan Jiří Heinsch. The Jesuits continued to embellish the interior right up until the suppression of their order in 1773, adding stuccowork and statues of Jesuit and Czech saints.

Jesuit College ❾
JEZUITSKÁ KOLEJ

Karlovo náměstí 36. **Map** 5 B2.
ᴹ Karlovo náměstí. 🚋 3, 4, 6, 14,
16, 18, 22, 24. **Closed** to the public.

HALF THE EASTERN side of Charles Square is occupied by the former college of the Jesuit order in the New Town. As in other parts of Prague, the Jesuits were able to demolish huge swathes of the city to put up another bastion of their formidable education system. The college was built between 1656 and 1702 by Carlo Lurago and Paul Ignaz Bayer. The two sculptured portals are the work of Johann Georg Wirch who extended the building in 1770. After the suppression of the Jesuit order in 1773 the college was converted into a military hospital. It is now a teaching hospital and part of Charles University.

Charles Square ❿
KARLOVO NÁMĚSTÍ

Map 5 B2. ᴹ Karlovo náměstí.
🚋 3, 4, 6, 14, 16, 18, 22, 24.

SINCE THE MID-19TH CENTURY the square has been a park. Though surrounded by busy roads, it is a pleasant place to sit and read or watch people exercising their dachshunds.

The square began life as a vast cattle market, when Charles IV founded the New Town in 1348. Other goods sold in the square included firewood, coal and pickled herrings from barrels.

In the centre of the market Charles had a wooden tower built, where the coronation jewels were put on display once a year. In 1382 the tower was replaced by a chapel, from which, in 1437, concessions made to the Hussites by the pope at the Council of Basle were read out to the populace.

Church of St Cyril and St Methodius ⓫
KOSTEL SV. CYRILA A METODĚJE

Resslova. **Map** 5 B2. 🎫 29 55 95.
ᴹ Karlovo náměstí. 🚋 3, 4, 6, 14,
16, 18, 22, 24. **Open** 9–11am
Mon–Sat. 📷

THIS BAROQUE CHURCH, with a pilastered façade and a small central tower, was built in the 1730s. It was originally dedicated to St Charles Borromeo and served as the church of a community of retired priests, but both the priests' home and the church were closed in 1783.

In the 1930s the church was restored and given to the Czechoslovak Orthodox Church, hence its rededication to St Cyril and St Methodius, the 9th-century "Apostles to the Slavs" (*see pp20–21*). In May 1942 the parachutists who had assassinated Reinhard Heydrich, the Nazi governor of Czechoslovakia, hid in the crypt of the church along with members of the Czech Resistance. Surrounded by German troops, they took their own lives rather than surrender. Some of the bullet holes made by the German machine guns during the siege can still be seen – below the memorial plaque on the outer wall of the crypt.

Main altar in the Church of St Cyril and St Methodius

Faust House ⓬

FAUSTŮV DŮM

Karlovo náměstí 40, 41. **Map** 5 B3.
Ⓜ *Karlovo náměstí.* 🚊 *3, 14, 16.*
Closed to the public.

PRAGUE THRIVES on legends of alchemy and pacts with the devil, and this Baroque mansion has attracted many. There has been a house here since the 14th century when it belonged to Prince Václav of Opava, an alchemist and natural historian. In the 16th century it was owned by the alchemist Edward Kelley. The chemical experiments of Count Ferdinand Mladota of Solopysky, who owned the house in the mid-18th century, gave rise to its association with the legend of Faust.

Baroque façade of Faust House

Church of St John on the Rock ⓭

KOSTEL SV. JANA NA SKALCE

Vyšehradská 49. **Map** 5 B3.
📞 *29 38 50.* 🚊 *3, 4, 14, 18, 24.*
Open *for services only.* ✝ *6pm Mon & Thu, 7:30am Sun.* 🚫

ONE OF PRAGUE'S smaller Baroque churches, St John on the Rock is one of Kilian Ignaz Dientzenhofer's most daring designs. Its twin square towers are set at a sharp angle to the church's narrow façade and the interior is based on an octagonal floorplan. The church was completed in

1738, but the double staircase leading up to the west front was not added until the 1770s. On the high altar there is a wooden version of Jan Brokof's statue of St John Nepomuk *(see p137)* which stands on the Charles Bridge.

Slavonic Monastery ⓮

KLÁŠTER NA SLOVANECH

Vyšehradská. **Map** 5 B3. 📞 *29 38 50.* 🚊 *3, 4, 14, 18, 24.* **Open** *10am–5pm Tue–Sun.* 📷 ♿

BOTH THE MONASTERY and its church were almost razed to the ground in an American air raid in 1945. In the course of their reconstruction, the church was given a pair of strikingly modern reinforced concrete spires.

The monastery was founded in 1347 for the Croatian Benedictines, whose services were held in the Old Slavonic language, hence its name "Na Slovanech". In the course of Prague's tumultuous religious history it has since changed hands many times. In 1446 a Hussite order was formed here, then in 1635 the monastery was acquired by Spanish Benedictines. In the 18th century the complex was given a thorough Baroque treatment, but in 1880 it was taken over by some German Benedictines, who rebuilt almost everything in Neo-Gothic style. The monastery has managed to preserve some historically important 14th-century wall paintings in the cloister, though many of the paintings were damaged in the air raid of World War II.

Remains of 14th-century wall paintings in the Slavonic Monastery

Botanical Gardens ⓯

BOTANICKÁ ZAHRADA

Na slupi 18. **Map** 5 B3. 📞 *24 91 50 24.* 🚊 *18, 24.* 🚌 *148.* **Open** *Jan–Mar & Sep–Oct: 10am–5pm daily; Nov–Dec: 10am–4pm daily; April–Aug: 10am–6pm daily.* 📷 🚫 ♿

CHARLES IV founded Prague's first botanical garden in the 14th century. This is a much later institution. The university garden was founded in the Smíchov district in 1775, but in 1897 it was moved to its present site here in the New Town. The huge greenhouses date from 1938.

Special botanical exhibitions and shows of exotic birds and tropical fish are often held here. One star attraction of the gardens is the giant water lily, *Victoria cruziana*, whose huge leaves can support a small child. During the summer it produces dozens of flowers which only survive for a day.

Entrance to the university's Botanical Gardens

Octagonal steeple of St Catherine's

Church of
St Catherine 🔟

KOSTEL SV. KATEŘINY

Kateřinská. **Map** 5 C3. 🚊 *4, 6, 16, 22.* **Closed** *to the public.*

ST CATHERINE'S stands in the garden of a former convent, founded in 1354 by Charles IV to commemorate his victory at the Battle of San Felice in Italy in 1332. In 1420, during the Hussite revolution *(see pp26–7)*, the convent was demolished, but in the following century it was rebuilt as an Augustinian monastery. The monks remained here until 1787, when the monastery was shut down. Since 1822 it has been used as a hospital.

In 1737 a new Baroque church was built, but the slender steeple of the old Gothic church was retained. Its conspicuous octagonal shape has gained it the nickname of "the Prague minaret".

Chalice
Restaurant 🔟

RESTAURACE U KALICHA

Na bojišti 12. **Map** 6 D3. 🍴 *29 60 17.* ⓂP Pavlova. 🚊 *4, 6, 16, 22.* **Open** *11am–3pm, 5–11pm daily.* 📷 🚻 *See **Restaurants** pp198–205.*

THIS PILSNER URQUELL beer hall owes its fame to the novel *The Good Soldier Švejk* by Jaroslav Hašek. It was Švejk's favourite drinking

place and the establishment trades on the popularity of the best-loved character in 20th-century Czech literature. The staff dress in period costume from World War I, the era of this novel.

Dvořák Museum 🔟

MUZEUM ANTONÍNA DVOŘÁKA

Ke Karlovu 20. **Map** 6 D2. 🍴 *29 82 14.* ⓂP Pavlova. 🚌 *148.* **Open** *10am–5pm Tue–Sun.* 📷 🚫 🚻

ONE OF THE most enchanting secular buildings of the Prague Baroque, this red and ochre villa now houses the Antonín Dvořák Museum. On display are Dvořák scores and editions of his works, plus photographs and memorabilia of the great 19th-century Czech composer, including his piano, his viola and his desk.

The building is by the great Baroque architect Kilian Ignaz Dientzenhofer *(see p129)*. Just two storeys high with an elegant tiered mansard roof, the house was completed in 1720, for the Michnas of Vacínov and was originally known as the Michna Summer Palace. It later became known as Villa Amerika, after a nearby inn called Amerika. Between the two pavilions flanking the house is a fine iron

gateway, a replica of the Baroque original. In the 19th century villa and garden fell into decay. The garden statues and vases, from the workshop of Matthias Braun, date from about 1735. They are original but heavily restored, as is the interior of the palace. The ceiling and walls of the large room on the first floor, often used for recitals, are decorated with 18th-century frescoes by Jan Ferdinand Schor.

Church of
St Stephen 🔟

KOSTEL SV. ŠTĚPÁNA

Štěpánská. **Map** 5 C2. 🍴 *24 21 35 70.* 🚊 *4, 6, 16, 22.* **Open** *only for services.* ⛪ *5pm Mon–Fri, 8am & 11am Sun.* 🚫

FOUNDED BY CHARLES IV in 1351 as the parish church of the upper New Town, St Stephen's was finished in 1401 with the completion of the multi-spired steeple. In the late 17th century the Kornel Chapel was built on to the western side of church. It contains the tomb of the prolific Baroque sculptor Matthias Braun.

Most of the subsequent Baroque additions were removed when the church was scrupulously re-Gothicized in the 1870s by Josef Mocker. There are

The Michna Summer Palace, home of the Dvořák Museum

Renaissance painted ceiling in the New Town Hall

several fine Baroque paintings, however, including *The Baptism of Christ* by Karel Škréta at the end of the left hand aisle and a picture of St John Nepomuk *(see p137)* by Jan Jiři Heinsch to the left of the 15th-century pulpit. The church's greatest treasure is a Gothic panel painting of the Madonna, known as *Our Lady of St Stephen's*, which dates from 1472.

Gothic pulpit in St Stephen's

New Town Hall ⓴
NOVOMĚSTSKÁ RADNICE

Karlovo náměstí 23. **Map** 5 B1.
ꙮ *Karlovo náměstí.* 🚋 3, 4, 6, 14, 16, 18, 22, 24. **Closed** to the public.

IN 1960 A STATUE of Hussite preacher Jan Želivský was unveiled in front of the New Town Hall. It commemorates the first and bloodiest of the various defenestrations of Prague. On 30 July 1419 Želivský led a crowd of demonstrators to the Town Hall to demand the release of some prisoners. When they were refused, they stormed the building and threw the Catholic councillors out of

the windows. Those who managed to survive the fall were finished off with pikes.

The Town Hall already existed in the 14th century, but the oldest part of the present building is the Gothic tower, added in the mid-15th century. In the 16th century it acquired an arcaded courtyard. After the joining-up of the four towns of Prague in 1784 the Town Hall ceased to be the seat of the municipal administration and became a courthouse and a prison. It is now used for cultural and social events, and its splendid Gothic hall can be hired for wedding receptions.

U Fleků ⓴

Křemencova 11. **Map** 5 B1.
☎ 29 64 17. ꙮ *Národní třída, Karlovo náměstí.* 🚋 6, 9, 17, 18, 22.
See **Restaurants** pp198–205.

RECORDS INDICATE that beer was brewed on the site as early as 1459. This archetypal Prague beer hall has been fortunate in its owners, who have kept up the tradition of brewing as an art rather than just a means of making

money. In 1762 the brewery was purchased by a certain Jakub Flekovský, who gave it its name U Fleků (At the Fleks). The present brewery, the smallest in Prague, makes a special strong, dark beer, sold only on the premises. In summer you can drink at tables in the garden, while one of the vaulted rooms has a nightly cabaret.

Church of St Ursula ⓴
KOSTEL SV. VORŠILY

Národní 8. **Map** 3 A5. ꙮ *Národní třída.* 🚋 6, 9, 18, 22. **Open** only for services. 🕆 5pm daily, 10am Sun. 🚫

THE DELIGHTFUL Baroque church of St Ursula was built as part of an Ursuline convent founded in 1672. The original sculptures still decorate the façade and in front of the church stands a group of statues featuring St John Nepomuk (1747) by Ignaz Platzer the Elder. The light airy interior has a frescoed, stuccoed ceiling and on the various altars there are lively Baroque paintings. The main altar has one of St Ursula.

The adjoining convent has recently been returned to the Ursuline order and has now become a Catholic school. One part of the ground floor is still used for secular purposes – the Klášterní Vinárna (Convent Restaurant).

National Theatre ⓴
NÁRODNÍ DIVADLO

See pp156–7.

U Fleků, Prague's best-known beer hall

National Theatre ㉓

NÁRODNÍ DIVADLO

THIS GOLD-CRESTED THEATRE has always been an important symbol of the Czech cultural revival. Work started in 1868, funded largely by voluntary contributions. The original Neo-Renaissance design was by the Czech architect Josef Zítek. After its destruction by fire *(see opposite)*, Josef Schulz was given the job of rebuilding the theatre and all the best Czech artists of the period contributed towards its lavish and spectacular decoration. During the late 1970s and early 80s the theatre was restored and the New Stage was built by architect Karel Prager.

A bronze sculpture in the foyer

The theatre from Marksmen's Island

A bronze three-horse chariot, designed by Bohuslav Schnirch, carries the Goddess of Victory.

The New Stage auditorium

★ Auditorium
The elaborately-painted ceiling is adorned with allegorical figures representing the arts by František Ženíšek.

STAR FEATURES
★ Auditorium
★ Lobby Ceiling
★ Stage Curtain

The five arcades of the loggia are decorated with lunette paintings by Josef Tulka, entitled *Five Songs*.

★ Lobby Ceiling
This ceiling fresco is the final part of a triptych painted by František Ženíšek in 1878 depicting the Golden Age of Czech Art.

★ **Stage Curtain**
This sumptuous gold and red stage curtain, showing the origin of the theatre, is the work of Vojtěch Hynais..

VISITORS' CHECKLIST

Národní 2, Nové Město.
Map 3 A5. 24 91 34 37.
Národní třída, line B.
17, 22, 18 to Národní třída.
Auditorium open only when performances are taking place.

Façade Decoration
This standing figure on the attic of the western façade is one of many figures representing the Arts sculpted by Antonín Wagner in 1883.

The startling sky-blue roof covered with stars, is said to symbolize the summit all artists should aim for.

The President's Box
The former royal box, lined in red velvet, is decorated with famous historical figures from Czech history by Václav Brožík.

NATIONAL THEATRE FIRE

On 12 August, 1881, just days before the official opening, the National Theatre was completely gutted by fire. It was thought to have been started by metalworkers on the roof. But just six weeks later, enough money had been collected to rebuild the theatre. It was finally opened two years late in 1883 with a performance of Czech composer Bedřich Smetana's opera *Libuše (see p79).*

FURTHER AFIELD

VISITORS TO PRAGUE, finding the old centre packed with sights, tend to ignore the suburbs. It is true that once you start exploring away from the centre, the language can become more of a problem. However, it is well worth the effort, firstly to escape the crowds of tourists milling around the Castle and the Old Town Square, secondly to realize that Prague is a living city as well as a picturesque time capsule. Most of the museums and other sights in the first part of this section are easily reached by Metro, tram or even on foot. If you are prepared to venture a little further, do not miss the grand palace at Troja or the former monastery at Zbraslav, which houses the modern Czech sculpture collection of the National Gallery. The Day Trips (pp166–9) include visits to castles close to Prague and the historic spa towns of Marienbad and Karlsbad, which attracted the first tourists to Bohemia during the 19th century.

Vaulting in Church of St Barbara, Kutná Hora

SIGHTS AT A GLANCE

Museums and Galleries
Mozart Museum ❶
Prague Museum ❻
National Technical Museum ❽
Zbraslav Monastery ⓮

Monasteries
Břevnov Monastery ⓬

Historic Districts
Vyšehrad ❷
Žižkov ❹
Náměstí Míru ❺

Cemeteries
Olšany Cemeteries ❸

Historic Sites
White Mountain and Star Hunting Lodge ⓭

Historic Buildings
Troja Palace pp164–5 ❿

Parks and Gardens
Letná Park ❼
Exhibition Ground and Stromovka Park ❾
Zoo ⓫

KEY

Central Prague
Greater Prague
✈ Airport
Major road
Minor road

15 km = 10 miles

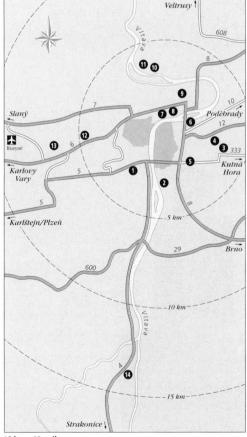

◁ **Part of the garden staircase at the 17th-century Troja Palace**

Bertramka, the villa that houses the Mozart Museum

Mozart Museum ①
BERTRAMKA

Mozartova 169. 🕿 *54 38 93.*
M̶ *Anděl.* 🚋 *4, 7, 9.* **Open**
9:30am – 6pm daily. 📷 🚫

THOUGH SLIGHTLY off the
beaten track, the museum
is well signposted because of
Prague's reverence for Mozart.
Bertramka is a 17th-century
farmhouse, enlarged in the
second half of the 18th century
to convert it into a comfortable
suburban villa. Mozart and his
wife Constanze stayed here
as the guests of the composer
František Dušek and his
wife Josefina in 1787, when
Mozart was working on *Don
Giovanni*. He composed the
overture to the opera in the

**Well-tended grave in the eastern
part of the Olšany Cemeteries**

garden pavilion just a few
hours before its premiere at
the Nostitz (now the Estates)
Theatre *(see p65)*. The house
contains a small exhibition
about Mozart and his various
visits to Prague.

Vyšehrad ②

Map 5 B5. **M̶** *Vyšehrad.* 🚋 *7, 18, 24.*

A ROCKY OUTCROP above the
Vltava, Vyšehrad means
"castle on the heights". It was
fortified in the 10th century
and, at times, used as the seat
of the Přemyslid princes in
preference to Prague Castle.
The area has great historical
and mythological significance
for the Czech people, and in
the 1870s it was chosen as the
site for a national cemetery.
This and Vyšehrad's other
important sights are described
in detail in a guided walk
(see pp178 – 9).

Olšany
Cemeteries ③
OLŠANSKÉ HŘBITOVY

Vinohradská, Jana Želivského. **M̶**
Želivského. 🕿 *67 31 06 52.* 🚋 *11,
16, 19, 26.* **Open** *9am – 7pm daily.*

AT THE NORTHWEST corner
of the main cemetery
stands the small Church of
St Roch (1682), protector
against the plague – the
first cemetery was founded
here in 1679 specifically for
the burial of plague victims.
In the course of the 19th
century, the old cemetery
was enlarged and new ones
developed on surrounding

land. These include a Russian
cemetery, distinguished by its
old-fashioned Orthodox church
(1924 – 5), and a Jewish one,
where the writer Franz Kafka
(see p68) is buried. The tombs
of famous Czechs include
those of painter Josef Mánes
(1820 – 71) who worked during
the height of the Czech Revival
movement *(see pp32 – 3)*, and
Josef Jungmann (1773 – 1847),
compiler of a five-volume
Czech-German dictionary.

Žižkov ④

M̶ *Jiřiho z Poděbrad, Želivského,
Flóra.* **National Monument.**
U památníku. 🚌 *133, 168, 207.*
Closed *to the public.*

Equestrian statue of Jan Žižka

THIS QUARTER of Prague was
the scene of a historic
victory for the Hussites *(see
pp26 – 7)* over Crusaders sent
by the Emperor Sigismund to
destroy them. On 14 July 1420
on Vítkov hill, a tiny force of
Hussites defeated an army of
several thousand well-armed
men. The determined, hymn-
singing Hussites were led by
the one-eyed Jan Žižka.
In 1877 the area around
Vítkov was renamed Žižkov in
honour of Žižka's victory, and
in 1950 a bronze equestrian
statue of Žižka by Bohumil
Kafka was erected on the hill.
About 9m (30 ft) high, this is
the largest equestrian statue
in the world. It stands in front
of the equally massive National
Monument (1927 – 32), built as
a symbol of the struggle for
independence of the Czechoslovak people. The Monument
later served as a mausoleum
for Klement Gottwald and
other Communist leaders.
Their remains have since
been removed, but the future
of the building is uncertain.

Relief by Josef Myslbek on portal of St Ludmilla in Náměstí Míru

An even more conspicuous landmark is a giant television transmitter, 260 m (850 ft) high. The locals have always been somewhat suspicious of the rays emanating from this great tube of reinforced concrete, built in 1984–8.

Náměstí Míru **❺**

Map 6 F2. **M** *Náměstí Miru.* **🚋** *4, 16, 22.* **🚌** *135, 148, 272.* **Church of St Ludmilla open** *only for services.*

THIS ATTRACTIVE SQUARE, with a well-kept central garden, is the focal point of the Vinohrady quarter. At the top of its sloping lawns stands the attractive, brick Neo-Gothic Church of St Ludmilla (1888– 93), designed by Josef Mocker, architect of the west end of St Vitus's Cathedral (*see pp100–3*). Its twin octagonal spires are 60 m (200 ft) high. On the tympanum of the main portal is a relief of Christ with St Wenceslas and St Ludmilla by the great 19th-century sculptor Josef Myslbek. Leading artists also contributed designs for the stained-glass windows and the church's colourful blue and gold interior.

The outside of the square is lined with attractive buildings, the most conspicuous being the Vinohrady Theatre, a spirited Art Nouveau building completed in 1907. The façade is crowned by two huge winged figures sculpted by Milan Havlíček, symbolizing Drama and Opera.

Prague Museum **❻**

MUZEUM HLAVNÍHO MĚSTA PRAHY

Křižíkova 1554. **Map** 4 F3. **C** *24 22 31 79.* **M** *Florenc.* **🚋** *3, 8, 24.* **Open** *10am–6pm Tue–Sun.*

THE COLLECTION records the history of Prague from primeval times to the 20th century. A new museum was built to house the exhibits in the 1890s. Its Neo-Renaissance façade is richly decorated with stucco and sculptures, and the interior walls are painted with historic views of the city. On display are examples of Prague china and furniture, relics of the ancient medieval guilds and paintings and engravings of Prague through the ages.

The most remarkable exhibit must be the model of Prague made of paper and wood by Antonín Langweil. Completed in 1834, it covers an area of 20 sq m (25 sq yards). The scale of the extraordinarily accurate model is 1:500.

Letná Park **❼**

LETENSKÉ SADY

Map 3 A1. **C** *32 57 92.* **M** *Malostranská, Hradčanská.* **🚋** *1, 8, 12, 18, 22, 25, 26.*

ACROSS THE RIVER from the Jewish Quarter, a large plateau overlooks the city. It was here that armies gathered before attacking Prague Castle. Since the mid-19th century it has been a wooded park.

On the terrace at the top of the granite steps that lead up from the embankment stands a curious monument – a giant metronome built in 1991. It was installed after the Velvet Revolution on the pedestal formerly occupied by the gigantic stone statue of Stalin leading the people, which was blown up in 1962. Nobody likes the metronome any more than they did Stalin and it may soon be replaced. A far more durable monument is the Hanavský Pavilion, a Neo-Baroque cast iron structure, built for the 1891 Exhibition. It was later dismantled and erected on its present site in the park, where it houses a popular restaurant and café.

View of the Vltava and bridges from Letná Park

National Technical Museum
NÁRODNÍ TECHNICKÉ MUZEUM

Kostelní 42. **[** *37 36 51.* **[** *1, 8, 25, 26.* **Open** *9am–5pm Tue –Sun.*

THOUGH IT TRIES to keep abreast of all scientific developments, the museum's strength is its collection of machines from the Industrial Revolution to the present day. This fascinating collection is one of the largest in Europe. The section that attracts the most visitors is the History of Transportation in the vast central hall. This is filled with old-fashioned locomotives and railway carriages, bicycles – including penny-farthings – veteran motorcars and motorcycles, with aeroplanes and a hot-air balloon suspended overhead.

The photography and cinematography section has several thousand exhibits and is well worth a visit, as is the collection of astronomical instruments. The section on clocks and other devices for measuring time is also popular, especially on the hour when everything starts to chime at once. In the basement of the building there is a huge reconstruction of a coal mine, with an interesting assortment of old tools, tracing the development of mining from the 15th to the 19th century.

Exhibition Ground and Stromovka Park 9
VÝSTAVIŠTĚ A STROMOVKA

[*1, 8, 25, 26.* **Exhibition Ground open** *10am–11pm daily.* **Stromovka Park open** *24hrs daily.* See **Four guided Walks** *p176–7.*

LAID OUT for the Jubilee of 1891, the Exhibition Ground has been used for trade fairs, sports and artistic events ever since. Under Communism it was called the Julius Fučik Park of Culture and Leisure (after a journalist executed by the Nazis). With its lively funfair, it is the obvious destination for a

The Industrial Palace, centrepiece of the 1891 Exhibition Ground

day out from central Prague with the children, and there are all kinds of temporary exhibitions, sporting events, spectacles and concerts staged there throughout the summer.

The large park to the west of the Exhibition Ground was the former royal hunting enclosure and deer park, which was first established in the late 16th century. The name Stromovka means "place of trees", a reminder that a large area of the park was once a flourishing tree nursery. Given over to the public in 1804, the park is still a pleasant wooded area and an ideal place for a walk.

Troja Palace 10
TROJSKÝ ZÁMEK

See pp164–5.

Zoo 11
ZOOLOGICKÁ ZAHRADA

U trojského zámku 3. **[** *66 41 04 80.* **M** *Holešovice, then* **[** *112.* **Open** *9am–6pm daily.*

ATTRACTIVELY SITUATED on a rocky slope overlooking the right bank of the Vltava, the zoo was founded in 1924.

It now covers an area of 64 hectares (160 acres) and there is a chair lift to take visitors to the upper part. To travel on the lift, you can use an ordinary metro/tram ticket.

The zoo's 2,500 animals represent 500 species, 50 of them extremely rare in the wild. It is best known for its breeding programme of Przewalski's horses, the only species of wild horse in the world. It has also enjoyed considerable success in breeding big cats, wolves, antelopes, giraffes, flamingoes, gorillas and orang-utans. Two new pavilions have recently opened – one for lions, tigers and other beasts of prey and one for elephants.

Red panda, relative of the famous giant panda, in Prague Zoo

Břevnov Monastery ⑫
BŘEVNOVSKÝ KLÁŠTER

Markétská. 🔔 *35 15 20.* 🚋 *8, 22.*
Open *10am–5pm daily.* 🎦 🚫

FROM THE surrounding sub-
urban housing, you would
never guess that Břevnov is
one of the oldest inhabited
parts of Prague. A flourishing
community grew up here
around the Benedictine abbey
founded in 993 by Prince
Boleslav II *(see p20)* and
Bishop Adalbert (Vojtěch) –
the first monastery in Bohemia.
An ancient well called Vojtěška
marks the spot where prince
and bishop are supposed to
have met and decided to
found the monastery.

The gateway, courtyard and
most of the present monastery
buildings are by the great
Baroque architects, father and
son, Christoph and Kilian
Ignaz Dientzenhofer *(see
p129)*. The monastery Church
of St Margaret is the work of
Christoph. Completed in 1715,
it is based on a floorplan
of overlapping ovals, as
ingenious as any of Bernini's
churches in Rome. In 1964
the crypt of the original 10th-
century church was discovered
below the choir and can now
be visited by the public. Of
the other buildings, the most
interesting is the abbey's
meeting hall, known as the
Theresian Hall, with a painted
ceiling dating from 1727.

White Mountain and Star Hunting Lodge ⑬
BÍLÁ HORA A HVĚZDA

🚋 *8, 22 (White Mountain), 18 (Star Hunting Lodge).* **White Mountain enclosure open** *24hrs daily.* **Star Hunting Lodge open** *10am–5pm Tue–Sun.* 🎦 🚫

THE BATTLE of the White
Mountain *(see p30–31)*,
fought on 8 November 1620,
had a very different impact
for the two main communities
of Prague. For the Protestants
it was a disaster that led to
300 years of Habsburg

Star Hunting Lodge

domination; for the Catholic
supporters of the Habsburgs
it was a triumph, so after the
battle they built a memorial
chapel on the hill. In the
early 18th century this was
converted into the grander
Church of Our Lady Victorious
and decorated by leading
Baroque artists, including
Václav Vavřinec Reiner.

In the 16th century the
woodland around the battle
site had been a royal game
park. The hunting lodge,
completed in 1556, survives
today. This fascinating building is shaped as a six-pointed
star – *hvězda* means star. The
lodge was restored in 1950
and converted into a museum
dedicated to the writer of
historical novels, Alois Jirásek
(1851–1930), and the painter,

Mikoláš Aleš (1852–1913).
Part of the museum also has
exhibits relating to the Battle
of the White Mountain.

Zbraslav Monastery ⑭
ZBRASLAVSKÝ KLÁŠTER

Zbraslav Ke Krňovu 🔔 *59 11 93.* 🚌 *129, 240, 241, 243, 255.* **Open** *Apr–Nov: 10am–6pm Tue–Sun.* 🎦 🚫 ♿

IN 1279 WENCESLAS II founded
a monastery to serve as the
burial place for the royal
family, though only he and
Wenceslas IV were ever
buried here. Destroyed during
the Hussite Wars *(see pp26–7)*,
the monastery was rebuilt in
1709–39, only to be abolished
in 1785 and made into a
factory. Earlier this century it
was restored and in 1941 was
given to the National Gallery
to house its collection of
modern Czech sculpture. The
works are displayed in the
gardens, courtyards and
cloisters as well as inside the
buildings. Pride of place is
given to the works of Josef
Václav Myslbek (1848–1929),
sculptor of the Wenceslas
Monument *(see p146)*, but look
out too for the works of Karel
Dvořák and Ladislav Šaloun,
and for the painted wood
carvings by Otto Gutfreund.

Zbraslav Monastery, home to the National Gallery's modern sculpture

Troja Palace ⑩

TROJSKÝ ZÁMEK

ONE OF THE MOST STRIKING summer palaces in Prague, Troja was built in the late 17th century by Jean-Baptiste Mathey for Count Sternberg, a member of a leading Bohemian aristocratic family. Situated at the foot of the Vltava Heights, the exterior of the palace was modelled on a Classical Italian villa, while its garden was laid out in formal French style. The magnificent interior took over 20 years to complete and is full of extravagant frescoes expressing the Sternberg family's loyalty to the Habsburg dynasty. Troja has recently been restored and houses a small collection of 19th-century art.

Terracotta urn on the garden balustrade

Defeat of the Turks
This turbaned figure, tumbling from the Grand Hall ceiling, symbolizes Leopold I's triumph over the Turks.

Belvedere turret

Statue of Olympian God

Statues of sons of Mother Earth

Personification of Justice
Abraham Godyn's image of Justice gazes from the lower east wall of the Grand Hall.

★ Garden Staircase
The two sons of Mother Earth which adorn the sweeping oval staircase (1685–1703) are part of a group of sculptures by Johann Georg Heermann and his nephew Paul, depicting the struggle of the Olympian Gods with the Titans.

VISITORS' CHECKLIST

U trojského zámku 4, Prague 7.
84 07 61. 112 from
Holešovice metro. summer
months only (see p55). **Open**
10am–5pm daily.

★ Grand Hall Fresco
*The frescoes in the Grand
Hall (1691–7), by Abraham
Godyn, depict the story of
the first Habsburg Emperor,
Rudolph I, and the many
victories of Leopold I over
the archenemy of
Christianity, the Sublime
Porte (Ottoman Empire).*

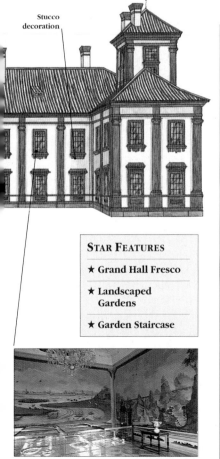

Stucco
decoration

★ LANDSCAPED GARDENS

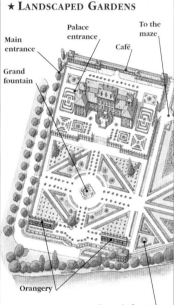

Palace
entrance

To the
maze

Main
entrance

Café

Grand
fountain

Orangery

Open-air theatre

STAR FEATURES

★ Grand Hall Fresco

★ Landscaped
Gardens

★ Garden Staircase

Sloping vineyards were levelled, hill-
sides excavated and terraces built to
fulfil the elaborate and grandiose plans
of French architect, Jean-Baptiste
Mathey, for the first Baroque French-
style formal gardens in Bohemia. The
palace and its geometric network of
paths, terracing, fountains, statuary and
beautiful terracotta vases, is best
viewed from the south of the garden
between the two orangeries. The
gardens have been carefully restored
according to Mathey's original plans.

Chinese Rooms
*Several rooms feature 18th-century murals
of Chinese scenes. This room makes a
perfect backdrop for a ceramics display.*

Day Trips from Prague

T HE SIGHTS THAT ATTRACT most visitors away from the city are Bohemia's picturesque medieval castles. Karlstein, for example, stands in splendid isolation above wooded valleys that have changed little since the Emperor Charles IV hunted there in the 14th century. We have chosen four castles, very varied in character. There are regular organized tours (see p219) to the major sights around Prague, to the historic mining town of Kutná Hora and, if you have more time to spare, to the famous spa towns of Karlsbad and Marienbad in western Bohemia.

St George and Dragon, Konopiště

SIGHTS AT A GLANCE

Castles	Historic Towns
Veltrusy ❶	Kutná Hora ❺
Karlstein ❷	Karlsbad ❻
Konopiště ❸	Marienbad ❼
Křivoklát ❹	

KEY

▨	Central Prague
▢	Greater Prague
✈	Airport
▭	Motorway
▬	Major road
▭	Minor road

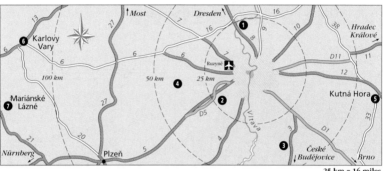

25 km = 16 miles

Veltrusy Château ❶
VELTRUSKÝ ZÁMEK

20 km (12 miles) north of Prague.
☎ 0205 243 87. 🚂 from Smichov to Kralupy nad Vltavou, then local bus.
Open May–Sep: 8am–noon & 1–5 pm Tue–Sun; Apr & Oct: 9am–noon & 1–4pm Tue–Sun. 🚫 🅿 ♿ (park only).

V ELTRUSY is a small town beside the Vltava, famous for the 18th-century château built by the aristocratic Chotek family. The building is in the shape of a cross, with a central dome and a grand staircase decorated with statues representing the months of the year and the four seasons.

The estate was laid out as an English-style landscaped deer park, covering an area of 300 hectares (750 acres). Near the entrance there is still an enclosure with a herd of deer. The Vltava flows along one side and dotted around the grounds are several summer houses. The Doric and Maria Theresa pavilions, the orangery and the grotto date from the late 18th century. The park is planted with some 100 kinds of tree, including rare and exotic species.

Karlstein Castle ❷
KARLŠTEJN

25 km (16 miles) southwest of Prague.
☎ 0301 213 66. 🚂 from Smichov to Karlštejn (1.5 km (1 mile) from castle). 🚌 from Anděl to Karlštejn (1 km (0.6 miles) from castle).
Open 9am–4pm (Nov–Mar: 3pm) daily. 🚫 🎦 compulsory. 🅿

T HE CASTLE WAS founded by Charles IV as a country retreat, a secure treasury for the imperial crown jewels and a symbolic expression of his divine right to rule the Holy Roman Empire. It stands on a limestone crag above the River Berounka. When you reach the castle after a long climb on

Karlstein Castle, built by Emperor Charles IV in the 14th century

foot from the village below, where the bus stops, what you see is largely a 19th-century reconstruction by Josef Mocker. The original building work (1348–67) was supervised by French master mason, Matthew of Arras, and after him by Peter Parler. Of the original interiors you can still see the audience hall and the bedchamber of Charles IV in the Royal Palace. On the third floor, the Emperor's quarters are below those of the Empress.

The central tower houses the Church of Our Lady, decorated with faded 14th-century wall paintings. A narrow passage leads to the tiny Chapel of St Catherine, Charles's private place of meditation. The walls are adorned with semiprecious stones set into the plaster.

The same extravagance was used in the Chapel of the Holy Rood in the Great Tower, with its gilded vaulting studded with glass stars. Charles IV housed the crown jewels and relics of the crucifixion here. Unfortunately it is no longer open to the public. It contained 127 panels painted by Master Theodoric (1357–65). These were damaged both by acts of vandalism and by the visitors' breath. Some restored panels can be seen at St George's Convent *(see pp106–9)*.

Konopiště Castle ❸

40 km (25 miles) southeast of Prague. (0301 213 66. 🚆 *from Hlavní nádraží to Benešov, then local bus.* **Open** *times subject to constant change. Phone for current information.* 🏛 ⊘

THOUGH IT DATES back to the 13th century, this moated castle is essentially a late 19th-century creation. In between, Konopiště had been rebuilt by Baroque architect František Kaňka and in front of the bridge across the moat is a splendid gate (1725) by Kaňka and sculptor Matthias Braun.

In 1887 Konopiště was bought by Archduke Franz Ferdinand, who later became heir to the Austrian throne. It was his assassination in 1914 in Sarajevo that triggered off World War I. His Czech wife,

View of the castle at Křivoklát, dominated by the Great Tower

Countess Sophie Chotek, was assassinated with him. To escape the Habsburg court's snobbish disapproval of his wife, Ferdinand spent much of his time at Konopiště. He amassed fine collections of arms, armour and Meissen porcelain, all on display in the richly furnished interiors. However, the abiding memory of the castle is of the hundreds of stags' heads lining the walls.

Hunting trophies at Konopiště

Křivoklát Castle ❹

45 km (28 miles) west of Prague. (0313 981 20. 🚆 *from Smíchov to Křivoklát (1 km (0.6 miles) from castle).* 🚌 *from Anděl.* **Open** *times subject to constant change. Phone for current information.* 🏛 ⊘

THIS CASTLE, like Karlstein, owes its appearance to the restoration work of Josef Mocker. It was originally a

hunting lodge belonging to the early Přemyslid princes and the seat of the royal master of hounds. In the 13th century King Wenceslas I built a stone castle here, which remained in the hands of Bohemia's kings and the Habsburg emperors until the 17th century.

Charles IV spent some of his childhood here and when he returned from France in 1334 with his first wife Blanche de Valois, she gave birth to their daughter Margaret in the castle. To amuse his queen and the young princess, Charles ordered the local villagers to trap nightingales and set them free in a wooded area just below the castle. Today you can still walk along the "Nightingale Path".

The royal palace is on the eastern side of the roughly triangular castle. This corner is dominated by the Great Tower, 42 m (130 ft) high. In places you can still see the 13th-century stonework, but most of the palace dates from the reign of Vladislav Jagiello. On the first floor there is a vaulted Gothic hall, reminiscent of the Vladislav Hall in the Royal Palace at Prague Castle *(see pp104–5)*. It has an oriel window and a beautiful loggia that was used by sentries. Also of interest is the chapel, which has a fine Gothic altar carving. Below the chapel lies the Augusta Prison, so-called because Bishop Jan Augusta of the Bohemian Brethren was imprisoned here for 16 years in the mid-16th century. The dungeon now houses a grim assortment of instruments of torture.

Kutná Hora ❺

70 km (45 miles) east of Prague.
🚇 *from Hlavní nádraží, Masarykovo nádraží or Holešovice.* 🚌 *from Florenc.*
Church of St Barbara open *10am–11pm (Oct–Mar: 9am–noon & 1–4pm) Tue–Sun.* 🅿 **Italian Court open** *9am–5pm (Oct–Mar: 10am–4pm) daily.* 🅿 **Hrádek open** *Apr–Oct: 9am–noon & 1–5pm daily.* 🅿 **Stone House open** *Apr–Oct: 9–11:30am & noon–5pm daily.* 🅿

T HE TOWN ORIGINATED as a small mining community in the second half of the 13th century. When rich deposits of silver were discovered, the king took over the licensing of the mines and Kutná Hora became the second most important town in Bohemia.

In the 14th century five to six tonnes of pure silver were extracted here each year, making the king the richest ruler in Central Europe. The Prague *groschen*, a silver coin that circulated all over Europe, was minted here in the Italian Court (Vlašský dvůr), so-called because Florentine experts were employed to set up the mint. Strongly fortified, it was also the ruler's seat when he visited the town. At the end of the 14th century a two-storey palace was built with reception halls and the Chapel of St Wenceslas and

St Ladislav, below which lay the royal treasury.

When the silver started to run out in the 16th century, the town began to lose its importance; the mint finally closed in 1727. The Italian Court later became the town hall. On the ground floor you can still see a row of forges. Since 1947 a mining museum has been housed in another ancient building, the Hrádek, which was originally a fort. A visit includes a 45-minute tour of a medieval mine. There is another museum in the Stone House (Kamenný dům), a much restored Gothic building of the late 15th century.

To the southwest of the town stands the great Church of St Barbara (who was the patron saint of miners), begun in 1380 by the workshop of Peter Parler, also the architect of St Vitus's Cathedral *(see pp100–3)*. The presbytery (1499) has a magnificent net vault and windows with intricate tracery. The slightly later nave vault is by royal architect Benedikt Ried. Look out too for the murals in the nave, many of which show scenes involving mining. The cathedral, with its three

The Italian Court, Kutná Hora's first mint

massive and tent-shaped spires rising above a forest of flying buttresses, is a wonderful example of Bohemian Gothic.

Karlsbad ❻

KARLOVY VARY

140 km (85 miles) west of Prague.
🚇 *from Masarykovo nádraží.*
🚌 *from Florenc.*

L EGEND HAS IT that Charles IV *(see pp24–5)* discovered one of the sources of mineral water that would make the town's fortune when one of his staghounds fell into a hot spring. In 1522 a medical description of the springs was published and by the end of the 16th century over 200 spa buildings had been built there. Today there are 12 hot mineral springs – *vary* means hot springs. The best-known is the Vřídlo (Sprudel), which rises to a height of 12 m (40 ft). At 72˚C, it is also the hottest. The water is good for digestive disorders, but you do not have to drink it; you can take the minerals in the form of salts.

The town is also known for its Karlovy Vary china and Moser glass, and for summer concerts and other cultural events. The race course is popular with the more sporting invalids taking the waters.

Outstanding among the local historic monuments is the Baroque parish church of

The three steeples of Kutná Hora's great Church of St Barbara

Mary Magdalene by Kilian Ignaz Dientzenhofer (1732–6). More modern churches built for foreign visitors include a Russian church (1896) and an Anglican one (1877). The 19th-century Mill Colonnade (Mlýnská kolonáda) is by Josef Zítek, architect of the National Theatre *(see p156–7)* in Prague. There have been many royal visitors over the centuries – from Peter the Great of Russia in 1711 to England's Edward VII in 1907.

Marienbad ❼

MARIÁNSKÉ LÁZNĚ

170 km (105 miles) west of Prague.
🚋 from Hlavní nádraží.
🚌 from Florenc.

THE ELEGANCE of Marienbad's hotels, parks and gardens has faded considerably since it was the playground of kings and princes at the turn of the century. The area's health-giving waters – *lázně* means bath (or spa) – have been known since the 16th century, but the spa was not founded until the beginning of the last century. The waters are used to treat all kinds of disorders; mud baths are also popular.

Most of the spa buildings date from the latter half of the 19th century. The great cast-iron colonnade with frescoes by Josef Vyletěl is still an impressive sight. In front of it is a "singing fountain", its jets of water now controlled by computer. Churches were provided for visitors of all

Bronze statue of a chamois at Jeleni skok (Stag's Leap), with a view across the valley to the Imperial Sanatorium, Karlsbad

denominations, including an Evangelical church (1857), an Anglican church (1879) and the Russian Orthodox church of St Vladimír (1902). Visitors can learn the history of the spa in the house called At the Golden Grape (U zlatého hroznu), where the German poet Johann Wolfgang von Goethe stayed in 1823. Musical visitors during the 19th century included the composers Weber,

Wagner and Bruckner, while writers such as Ibsen, Gogol, Mark Twain and Rudyard Kipling also found its treatments beneficial. King Edward VII came here frequently. In 1905 he agreed to open the golf course (Bohemia's first), even though he hated the game.

There are many pleasant walks in the countryside around Marienbad, especially in the protected Slavkov Forest.

The cast-iron colonnade at Marienbad, completed in 1889

FOUR GUIDED WALKS

PRAGUE OFFERS some good opportunities for walking. In the centre of the city, many streets are pedestrianized and the most important sights are confined to quite a small area *(see pp14–15)*. We have chosen four walks of varied character. The first passes through a main artery of the city, from the Powder Gate on the outskirts of the Old Town to St Vitus's Cathedral in Prague Castle. This is the Royal Coronation Route, followed for centuries by Bohemian kings. Away from the busy centre, the second and

House sign in Celetná Street
(See Royal Route Walk pp172–3)

third walks take in the peace and quiet of two of Prague's loveliest parks – Petřín and the Royal Enclosure. Petřín Park is rewarding for its spectacular views of the city. The Royal Enclosure is outside the centre in the old royal hunting park. The final part of this walk crosses a spur of the Vltava before ending at Troja Palace and the zoo. The final walk is in Vyšehrad – a peaceful, ancient fortress which is steeped in history and atmosphere. The views here of the Vltava and Prague Castle are unparalleled.

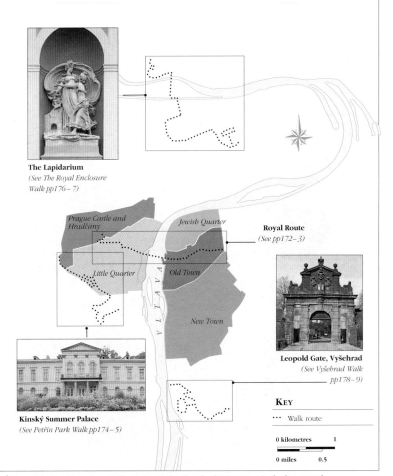

The Lapidarium
(See The Royal Enclosure Walk pp176–7)

Prague Castle and Hradčany

Jewish Quarter

Royal Route
(See pp172–3)

Little Quarter

Old Town

V L T A V A

New Town

Leopold Gate, Vyšehrad
(See Vyšehrad Walk pp178–9)

Kinský Summer Palace
(See Petřín Park Walk pp174–5)

KEY

••• Walk route

0 kilometres   1

0 miles   0.5

◁ **View of the New Town from Petřín Park with the Church of St Lawrence in the foreground**

A 90-Minute Walk along the Royal Route

THE ROYAL ROUTE ORIGINALLY linked two important royal seats; the Royal Court – situated on the site of the Municipal House and where the walk starts – and Prague Castle, where the walk finishes. The name of this walk derives from the coronation processions of the Bohemian kings and queens who passed along it. Today, these narrow streets offer a wealth of historical and architecturally interesting sights, shops and cafés, making the walk one of Prague's most enjoyable. For more details on the Old Town, the Little Quarter and Hradčany turn to pages 60–79; 122–41 and 94–121 respectively.

Figural *sgraffito* covers the façade of the Renaissance House at the Minute

History of the Royal Route

The first major coronation procession to travel along this route was for George of Poděbrady (*see p26*) in 1458. The next large procession took place in 1743, when Maria Theresa was crowned with great pomp – three Turkish pavilions were erected just outside the Powder Gate. September 1791 saw the coronation of Leopold II. This procession was led by cavalry, followed by mounted drummers, trumpeters and soldiers and Bohemian lords. Some 80 carriages came next, carrying princes and bishops. The most splendid were each drawn by six pairs of horses, flanked by servants with red coats and white leather trousers, and carried the ladies-in-waiting.

The distinct Baroque façade of the House at the Golden Well in Karlova Street ⑪

The last great coronation procession along the Royal Route – for Ferdinand V – was in 1836 with over 3,391 horses and four camels.

From the Powder Gate to Old Town Square

At Náměstí Republiky turn towards the Municipal House (*see p64*) and walk under the Gothic Powder Gate ① (*see p64*). Here, at the city gates, the monarch and a large retinue of church dignitaries, aristocrats, and foreign ambassadors were warmly welcomed by leading city representatives. The gate leads into one of Prague's oldest streets, Celetná (*see p65*). It was here the Jewish community and the crafts guilds, carrying their insignia, greeted their king.

The street is lined with Baroque and Rococo houses with unusual house signs. Behind the façades are Gothic buildings. At house No. 36 is the Mint ②. This moved

here after the mint at Kutná Hora (*see p168*) was occupied by Catholic troops in the Hussite Wars (*see pp26–7*). It minted coins from 1420 to 1784. Further along is the Cubist House at the Black Madonna ③ and the taverns, At the Spider ④ and At the Vulture ⑤, where revellers could watch processions through the windows.

House at the Black Madonna ③

At the end of Celetná Street is the Old Town Square ⑥ (*see pp66–9*). Here, the processions halted beside Týn Church ⑦ (*see p70*) for pledges of loyalty from the university. Keep to the left of the square, past No. 20, At the Unicorn ⑧. This is where Smetana began a music school in 1848. Proceed to the Old Town Hall ⑨ (*see pp72–4*).

Here, the municipal guard and a band waited for the royal procession and city dignitaries cheered from the temporary balcony around the hall.

Along Karlova Street and across Charles Bridge

Walk past the sgraffitoed façade of the House at the Minute and into Malé náměstí ⑩, where merchants waited with members of the various religious orders. Turn left down gallery-filled Karlova

months later he died. Walk under the Old Town Bridge Tower ⑫ and over Charles Bridge ⑬ and then under the Little Quarter Towers ⑭ *(see pp136–9)*.

The Little Quarter

The walk now follows Mostecká Street. On entering the Little Quarter the mayor handed the city keys to the king and the artillery fired a salute. At the end of this street is Little Quarter Square ⑮ *(see p124)* and the Baroque church, St Nicholas's ⑯ *(see pp128–9)*.

Sculpture of Moor by Ferdinand Brokof on Morzin Palace

sharp right and walk up the Castle ramp which leads you to Hradčanské Square. The route ends at the Castle's Matthias Gate *(see p48)* ⑲. The procession ended with the coronation held at St Vitus's Cathedral.

The Old Town from Charles Bridge ⑬

Street. Beyond Husova Street is an attractive Baroque house, At the Golden Well ⑪. Further on is the 16th-century Clementinum *(see p79)*, where the clergy stood. You then pass into Knights of the Cross Square *(see p79)*. When Leopold II's procession passed through here the clouds lifted, which was considered to be a good omen. But only a few

The procession passed the church to the sound of its bells ringing.

Leave this picturesque square by Nerudova Street ⑰ *(see p130)*. Poet and writer Jan Neruda, who immortalized hundreds of Little Quarter characters in books like *Mala Strana Tales*, grew up and worked at No. 47 ⑱. At the end of this street you turn

KEY

••• Walk route

Good viewing point

M Metro station

Tram stop

Castle wall

| 0 metres | 300 |
| 0 yards | 300 |

TIPS FOR WALKERS

Starting point: Náměstí Republiky.
Length: 2.4 km (1.5 miles).
Getting there: Line B goes to Náměstí Republiky metro station. At Hradčany you can get tram 22 back into town.
Stopping-off points: Rest beneath the sunshades of the outdoor cafés on Old Town Square in the summer. Karlova Street has one of the most popular cafés in Prague, At the Golden Snake (U Zlatého hada). There are also cafés in the lower part of Malostranské Square.

Coronation procession passing through the Knights of the Cross Square

A Two-Hour Walk through Petřín Park

PART OF THE CHARM of this walk around this large and peaceful hillside park are the many spectacular views over the different areas of Prague. The Little Quarter, Hradčany and the Old Town all take on a totally different aspect when viewed from above. The tree-covered gardens are dotted with châteaux, pavilions and statues and crisscrossed by winding paths leading you to secret and unexpected corners. For more on the sights of Petřín Hill see pages 140–41.

One of the gateways in the Hunger Wall ⑤

A 17th-century statue of Hercules that stands in the lower lake ②

Kinský Square to Hunger Wall

The walk starts at náměstí Kinských in Smíchov. Enter Kinský Garden through a large enclosed gateway. This English-style garden was founded in 1827 and named after the wealthy Kinský family, supporters of Czech culture in the 19th century.

Take the wide asphalt path on your left to the Kinský Summer Palace ①. This 1830s pseudo-classical building was designed by Jindřich Koch and its façade features Ionic columns terminating in a triangular tympanum. Inside the building is a large hall of columns with a triple-branched staircase beautifully-decorated with statues. The Ethnographical Museum is housed here; however, it is closed at present for reconstruction.

Next to the museum is a 1913 statue of the actress Hana Kvapilová.

About 50 m (150 ft) above the palace is the lower lake ② with a Baroque sandstone statue of Hercules. Walk left around the lake and continue up the hill to the Church of St Michael ③, on your left. This 18th-century wooden folk church was moved here from a village in the Ukraine.

Follow the path up the hill for about 20 m (60 ft), then go to the top of the steps to a wide asphalt path known as the Observation Path for its beautiful views of the city. Turn right and further on your left is the upper lake ④ with a 1950s bronze statue of a seal at its centre. Keep following the Observation Path; ahead of you stands a Neo-Gothic gate. This allows you to pass through the city's old Baroque fortifications.

Hunger Wall to Observation Tower

Continue along the path to the Hunger Wall ⑤ (see pp140–41). This was a major part of the Little Quarter's fortifications; the wall still runs from Újezd

Church of St Michael ③

Street across Petřín Hill and up to Strahov Monastery. Passing through the gate in the wall brings you to Petřín Park. Take the wide path to the left of the wall and walk up the hill beside the wall until you cross the bridge which spans the funicular railway *(see p141)*. Below on your right you can see the

Sunbathers on Petřín Hill

Nebozízek restaurant *(see p202)* famed for its views. On either side of the path are small sandstone rockeries. Most are entrances to reservoirs, built in the 18th and 19th centuries, to bring water to Strahov Monastery; others are left over from the unsuccessful attempts at mining the area. Walk up to the summit of the hill. On your right is the Mirror Maze ⑥ *(see p140)*. Facing the maze is the 12th-century St Lawrence's Church ⑦ *(see pp140–41)*, renovated in 1740 in the Baroque style.

KEY

••• Walk route

Good viewing point

Tram stop

Funicular railway

Hunger Wall

0 metres   300

0 yards   300

Observation Tower to Strahov Monastery

A little further on stands the Observation Tower ⑧ *(see p140)*. This steel replica of the Eiffel Tower in Paris is 60 m (200 ft) high. Opposite the tower is the main gate of the Hunger Wall. Pass through, turn left and follow the path to the Rose Garden ⑨.

The garden was planted by the city of Prague in 1932, and features a number of attractive sculptures. When you look down to the far end of the garden you can see The Observatory *(see p140)*. This was rebuilt from a municipal building in 1928 by the Czech Astronomical Society and was then modernized in the 1970s. It now houses a huge telescope and is open in the evenings to the public.

Returning to the Observation Tower, follow the wall on the left, passing some chapels of the Stations of the Cross dating from 1834. Then pass through a gap in the Hunger Wall, turn right, and walk past a charming Baroque house. About 50 m (150 ft) beyond this, you pass through another gap in the Hunger Wall on your right. Turn left into a large orchard above Strahov Monastery ⑩ *(see pp120–21)* for spectacular views of Prague. Continue onto a wide path which leads slightly downwards along the wall, through the orchard and past tennis courts to the

Sgraffitoed façade of the Calvary Chapel next to the Church of St Lawrence ⑦

Strahov Monastery courtyard. You can catch tram 22 from here, or linger in the peaceful monastery grounds. If you feel energetic you can walk back down the hill.

TIPS FOR WALKERS

Starting point: náměstí Kinských in Smíchov.
Length: 2.7 km (1.7 miles). The walk includes steep hills.
Getting there: The nearest metro station to the starting point is Anděl. Trams 6, 9 and 12 take you to Kinský Square.
Stopping-off points: There is a restaurant, Nebozízek, half way up Petřín Hill and during the summer a few snack bars are open at the summit of the Hill near the Observation Tower.

Hradčany and the Little Quarter from the summit of Petřín Hill

A 90-Minute Walk in the Royal Enclosure

THE ROYAL ENCLOSURE, more popularly called Stromovka, is one of the largest parks in Prague. It was created around 1266 during the reign of Přemysl Otakar II, who fenced the area in and built a small hunting château in the grounds. In 1804 it was opened to the public and became Prague's most popular recreational area. The large park of Troja Palace and the zoological garden are on the opposite river bank.

The Exhibition Ground
(Výstaviště)
From U Výstaviště ① pass through the gate to the old Exhibition Ground. This was created for the 1891 Jubilee Exhibition. Since the late 19th century it has been used for exhibitions and entertainment.

The large Lapidarium of the National Museum ② is on your right. This Neo-Renaissance exhibition pavilion was rebuilt in 1907 in the Art Nouveau style, and decorated with reliefs of figures from Czech history. Many architectural monuments and sculptures from the 11th to the 19th centuries are also housed here.

Facing you is the Industrial Palace ③, a vast Neo-Renaissance building constructed of iron. It is now only open for concerts and events. Walk to the right of the building and you will come to Křižík's Fountain ④. This was restored in 1991 in honour of the Czechoslovakia Exhibition. It

The Art Nouveau Lapidarium ②

A bust on the Academy of Fine Arts ⑥

was designed by the great inventor František Křižík (1847–1941), who established Prague's first public electric lighting system. From May to September the fountain is illuminated at night by computer-controlled lights which synchronize with the music (*see p51*).

Behind the fountain there is a permanent fairground. On the left of the Industrial Palace is a circular building which houses Marold's Panorama ⑤. This was painted by Luděk Marold in 1898 and depicts the Battle of Lipany. As you walk back to the Exhibition Ground entrance, you pass the Academy of Fine Arts ⑥, decorated with 18 busts of artists. On leaving the Exhibition Ground, turn

The summer palace created from a medieval Hunting Château ⑩

0 metres   300
0 yards   300

KEY

••• Walk route

☀ Good viewing point

🚊 Tram stop

═ Railway line

sharp right. Following the outer edge of the Ground you will pass the Planetarium ⑦ on your left; walk straight ahead, then take the road down the slope until you can turn left into a wide avenue of chestnut trees.

The Royal Enclosure
Continue for some way along the avenue until you reach a simple building among trees, on your left. Behind this is the Rudolph Water Tunnel ⑧, a grand monument of the age

The grand façade of Troja Palace *(see pp164–5)* ⑭

of Rudolph II *(see pp28–9)*, which is still in partial use. Hewn into rock, the aqueduct is over 1,000 m (3,000 ft) long. It was built in 1584 to carry water from the Vltava to Rudolph's newly constructed lakes in the Royal Park.

Continue along the path until you reach the derelict Royal Hall ⑨. Built in the late 17th century, it was converted into a restaurant, then rebuilt in 1855 in Neo-Gothic style.

Beyond the Royal Hall, at the bend in the main path, take a steep left fork up through woods to the former Hunting Château ⑩. This medieval building was built for the Bohemian kings who used the park as a hunting reserve. The Château was then later enlarged, and in 1805 was changed again by Jiří Fischer into a Neo-Gothic summer palace. Until 1918, this was a residence of the Governor of Bohemia. Today it is used to house the extensive library of newspapers and magazines of the National Museum.

Statue of lovers in the 16th-century gardens of the Enclosure ⑪

Retrace your steps to the main path, walk ahead and take the first small path on the right into a late-16th-century formal garden with a modern statue of lovers ⑪.

Return to the main path and turn right. At the fork, take the path which bends to the right along the railway embankment. Continue for a short way then turn left under the railway line to a canal ⑫.

Walk over the bridge, turn left along the canal, then right across the island. Cross the Vltava ⑬ and turn left into Povltavská Street where a wall marks the boundary of Troja Park. Carry along to the south entrance of the gardens of Troja Palace ⑭ *(see pp164–5)*, and then wander through them up to the palace itself.

TIPS FOR WALKERS

Starting point: U Výstaviště in Holešovice.
Length: 5 km (3 miles). The walk goes up a very steep incline to the former Hunting Château.
Getting there: Trams 5, 12 and 17 run to the starting point. The nearest metro stations are Vltavská or Nádraží Holešovice on line C, ten minutes walk away. At the end of the walk you can get on bus No. 112 at Troja to Nádraží Holešovice metro station.
Stopping-off points: There are a number of restaurants and kiosks in the Exhibition Ground. All the gardens are tranquil spots in which to rest. If you feel like a boat trip down the Vltava, there are often trips starting from the bridge over the canal to Palacký Bridge (see p55).

Disused entrance to the Rudolph Water Tunnel ⑧

A 60-Minute Walk in Vyšehrad

ACCORDING TO ANCIENT LEGEND, Vyšehrad was the first seat of Czech royalty. It was from this spot that Princess Libuše is said to have prophesied the future glory of the city of Prague *(see pp20–21)*. However, archaeological research indicates that the first castle on Vyšehrad was not built until the 10th century. The fortress suffered a turbulent history and was rebuilt many times. Today, it is above all a peaceful place with parks and unrivalled views of the Vltava valley and Prague. The fascinating cemetery is the last resting place of many famous Czech writers, actors, artists and musicians.

Decorative sculpture on the Baroque Leopold Gate ⑤

The ruin of Libuše's Baths on the cliff face of Vyšehrad Rock ⑩

V Pevnosti

From Vyšehrad metro ① make your way up the steps facing the metro exit to the complex of the Palace of Culture ② straight ahead. Walk west along its large granite terrace, go down the incline and straight ahead into the quiet street Na Bučance. Turn right at the end, cross the road and you find yourself on V Pevnosti, facing the brick walls of the original Vyšehrad Citadel. Ahead of you is the west entrance to the fortress, the mid-17th-century Tábor Gate ③. Past this gate on the right are the ruins of the 14th-century fortifications built by Charles IV. Further on are the ruins of the original Gothic gate, Špička ④. Pass that and you get to the sculpture-adorned Leopold Gate ⑤, one of the most impressive parts of these 17th-century fortifications. It adjoins the brick walls ⑥ that were widened during the French occupation of 1742.

K rotundě to Soběslavova Street

Turn right out of the gate and just before St Martin's Rotunda, turn left into K rotundě. A few metres on your right, almost concealed behind high walls, is the New Deanery, now the Vyšehrad Museum ⑦. This is used to house archaeological remains found around Vyšehrad. Situated at the corner of K rotundě and Soběslavova streets is the Canon's House ⑧.

Turn left down Soběslavova to see the excavations of the foundations of the Basilica of St Lawrence ⑨. This was built by Vratislav II in the late 11th century, but was destroyed by the Hussites *(see pp26–7)* in 1420. At the basilica turn left on to the fortified walls for a stunning view of Prague.

KEY

•••	Walk route
⚜	Good viewing point
Ⓜ	Metro station
🚋	Tram stop
—	Castle wall

0 metres	200
0 yards	200

18th-century engraving by I G Ringle, showing Vyšehrad and the Vltava

Vyšehrad Rock

The wooded outcrop of rock on which Vyšehrad was built drops in the west to form a steep rock wall to the river – a vital defensive position. On the summit of the rock are the Gothic ruins of the so-called Libuše's Baths ⑩. This was a defence bastion of the medieval castle. Further on your left is a grassy patch where the remains of a 14th-century Gothic palace ⑪ have been found.

The elaborate memorial to the composer Antonín Dvořák in Vyšehrad Cemetery ⑭

Vyšehrad Park

The western part of Vyšehrad has been transformed into a park. Standing on the lawn south of the Church of St Peter and St Paul are four groups of statues ⑫ by the 19th-century sculptor Josef Myslbek. The works represent figures from early Czech history – including the legendary Přemysl and Libuše (see pp20–21). The statues were originally on Palacký Bridge, but were damaged during the US bombardment of February 1945. After being restored, they were taken to Vyšehrad Park. The park was the site of a Romanesque palace, which was connected by a bridge to the neighbouring church. Another palace was built here in the reign of Charles IV (see pp24–5).

The Church of St Peter and St Paul

This twin-spired church ⑬ totally dominates Vyšehrad. It was founded in the latter half of the 11th century by Prince Vratislav II and was enlarged in 1129. In the mid-13th century it burned down and was replaced by an Early Gothic church. Since then it has been redecorated and restored many times in a variety of styles. In 1885, it was finally rebuilt in Neo-Gothic style, the twin steeples being added in 1902. Note the early-12th-century stone coffin, thought to be of St Longinus, and a mid-14th-century Gothic panel painting *Our Lady of the Rains* on the altar in the third chapel on the right.

Statue of Přemysl and Princess Libuše by Josef Myslbek in Vyšehrad Park ⑫

Vyšehrad Cemetery and the Pantheon

The cemetery ⑭ was founded in 1869 as the burial place for some of the country's most famous figures, such as Bedřich Smetana (see p79). Access is through a gate to the right of the church. On the east side of the cemetery is the Slavín (Pantheon) – a great tomb built in 1890 for the most honoured personalities of the Czech nation, including the sculptor Josef Myslbek.

Leave the cemetery by the same gate and walk back down K rotundě. On your left is the Devil's Column ⑮, said to be left by the devil after losing a wager with a priest. At the end of this street is St Martin's Rotunda (see p44) ⑯. This is a small Romanesque church built at the end of the 11th century and restored in 1878. Turn left, walk downhill through the Cihelná (Brick) Gate ⑰, which was built in 1741, and down Vratislavova Street to the Výtoň tram stop on the Vltava Embankment.

The Neo-Gothic Church of St Peter and St Paul ⑬

TIPS FOR WALKERS

Starting point: Vyšehrad metro station, line C.
Length: 1.5 km (1 mile).
Getting there: The walk starts from Vyšehrad metro station and ends at No. 17 tram which takes you back to the city centre.
Stopping-off points: The park in front of the church of St Peter and St Paul is a lovely place to relax. There is a café opposite the Basilica of St Lawrence.

TRAVELLERS' NEEDS

WHERE TO STAY

SINCE THE "VELVET REVOLUTION" of 1989, Prague has become one of the most visited cities in Europe. Despite investment in new hotels, helped by huge injections of foreign capital, the city is struggling to meet the demand for accommodation. Many old hotels have been rebuilt; others have just re-vamped the reception area, and the impression quickly fades as you climb the stairs. Most of the renovated hotels are as smart as any in Europe – and often just as expensive. Unfortunately there is little for the budget traveller. The few cheap hotels tend to be old-fashioned places in the centre of the city or smaller, pension-type hotels in the suburbs. We have inspected over 100 hotels in every price bracket and on pages 187–9 recommend 30 that offer good value. The chart on page 186 will help you select a hotel. A cheap alternative is to stay in a flat or a room in a private home, which is usually booked by an agency *(see p184)*. Hostels and campsites offer other budget options *(see p185)*.

Doorman at the exclusive Palace hotel *(see p189)*

The elegant Ungelt hotel *(see p187)*

WHERE TO LOOK

AS PRAGUE is such a small city, it is best to stay near the centre close to all the main sights, restaurants and shops. Most hotels are found around Wenceslas Square. Here you are at the hub of everything, and the prices of some (but not all) of the hotels reflect this. Another popular area is the nearby Náměstí Republiky, but the best area is around Old Town Square, a few minutes' walk from Charles Bridge. Hotels here include large, international establishments, old-fashioned Czech places, and some small, much more exclusive hotels.

To the south, in the New Town, there are a few cheaper hotels only a few metro stops from Old Town Square. But the area is less picturesque and some of the streets suffer from heavy volumes of traffic.

For a view of the river Vltava, stay in the Jewish Quarter, although most hotels here are new and expensive. There are also a few botels (floating hotels) moored along the embankments away from the city centre. They are a bit cheaper, but the small cabins are very cramped and uncomfortable, and most of the boats would benefit from some renovation.

Over Charles Bridge, in the Little Quarter, you will find a handful of interesting hotels in delightful surroundings, but there are far fewer by Prague Castle in Hradčany. Further north of this area, there are some large and particularly unappealing hotels. The city's suburbs too, have a number of rather nondescript places a few of these being new. These have some good facilities, but are often as expensive as their equivalents in the centre with the added inconvenience of travelling time and cost – the metro stops at midnight and taxis can become expensive.

HOW TO BOOK

TRYING TO BOOK hotels in Prague in advance can be frustrating. Most middle-range hotels have a contracted room allocation with a tour operator. If no other rooms are available, the hotel will ask you to call a week or two before you travel, by which time they will know if the rooms have been filled by tour groups. This may be nerve-racking for those who prefer to book in advance. It is important to receive written confirmation of your booking by letter or

Pool-side bar at the luxury Praha Penta *(see p189)*

fax. This can save trouble on arrival. Phone and fax communication with the Czech Republic has improved over the last few years, but the response from hotels can still be slow. If you would like to let someone else make the arrangements, a number of UK tour operators specialize in Prague *(see p184)*.

FACILITIES

FOLLOWING the refurbishment programme, most rooms now have en suite WC and shower or bath, telephone and TV, which may also offer video and satellite channels. Many hotels offer a reasonably-priced laundry service, and the larger hotels usually have 24-hour room service and mini bars. Guests are expected to vacate rooms by midday, but most hotels are happy to keep luggage safe if you are leaving later. Foreign-owned hotels sometimes import managers, but the Czech staff generally speak good English so you should encounter few communication problems.

DISCOUNT RATES

THE PRICE STRUCTURE for hotels in Prague is fairly flexible, but unfortunately not to the tourist's advantage. Rooms are usually twice as expensive for foreigners as for nationals, whether booked independently or through a tour operator. The only way to get a cheap rate is to turn up at the hotel and negotiate. The popular seasons are Christmas and New Year, and between Easter and October, when rooms are often hard to find.

HIDDEN EXTRAS

MOST HOTELS include tax (currently at 23%) and service charges in their tariff, but do check these details when you book. Telephone charges can be a shock when you receive your bill so be aware of the mark-up rate. A number of telephone boxes in the city take international phone cards and credit cards; they will cost you much less *(see p224)*. Some expensive

The Paříž is a national monument *(see p189)*

hotels charge an extra fee for breakfast, others include a continental breakfast, but hot dishes cost extra. Buffet-style continental breakfasts are popular, and usually offer fresh fruit, cereals, yogurt, muesli, cold meat and cheese, and juice, jugs of coffee and tea.

Tipping is not yet common and is only expected in some of the more expensive hotels.

As in most countries, single travellers receive no favours.

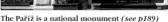

The ultra-modern Atrium hotel dominates the area *(see p189)*

There are few single rooms, particularly in newer hotels, and a supplement is charged for single occupancy of a double room; expect to pay about 80% of the standard rate.

DISABLED TRAVELLERS

WHEELCHAIR accessibility to hotels on pages 187–9 represents each hotel's own assessment. For information on accommodation for the disabled, write to the Czech Association of Persons with Disabilities *(see p226)*, or contact the Embassy of the Czech Republic in your country.

TRAVELLING WITH CHILDREN

CHILDREN are accommodated by most hotels, either in family rooms or with extra beds, but Prague is not geared to their needs. Hotel breakfasts offer plenty of choice, and although all the fresh milk is pasteurized, hotels also provide long life milk. Few places offer high-chairs or baby-sitters. It is worth asking if there are discounts, or if children can stay free in parents' rooms.

DIRECTORY

UK AGENCIES

British Airways Holidays
Astral Towers,
Betts Way,
Crawley, Middlesex
RH10 2XA.
☎ 01293 615353.

Čedok Tours
49 Southwark Street,
London SE1 1RU.
☎ 0171-378 6009.

Cresta Holidays
Cresta House, 32 Victoria
Street, Altrincham,
Cheshire WA14 1ET.
☎ 0161-927 7000.

Crystal Holidays
Eurobreak, Crystal House,
The Courtyard, Arlington
Road, Surbiton, Surrey
KT6 6BW.
☎ 0181-390 9900.

Czech Tourist Centre
30 Kensington Palace
Gardens, London W8 4QY.
☎ 0171-243 7981.

Hungarian Air Tours
Kent House, 87 Regent
Street, London W1R 7HF.
☎ 0171-437 9405.

JMB Music Travel Consultants
Rushwick', Worcester
WR2 5SN.
☎ 01905 425628.

Osprey Holidays
Broughton Market,
Edinburgh EH3 6NU.
☎ 0131-557 1555.

Page & Moy
136 & 140 London Road,
Leicester LE2 1EN.
☎ 01533 524433.

Peltours
Sovereign House, 11–19
Ballards Lane, Finchley,
London N3 1UX.
☎ 0181-346 9144.

Prospect Music and Art Tours
454–458 Chiswick High
Road, London W4 5TT.
☎ 0181-995 2151.

Sovereign Cities
Astral Towers, Betts Way,
Crawley, West Sussex
RH10 2GX.
☎ 01293 599000.

Thomson City Breaks
Ground Floor, Albert House,
Tindall Bridge, Edward
Street, Birmingham B1 2RA.
☎ 0121 252 3669.

Time Off
Chester Close, Chester
Street, London SW1X 7BQ.
☎ 0171-235 8070.

Travelscene
Travelscene House,
11–15 St Ann's Road,
Harrow, Middlesex
HA1 1AS.
☎ 0181-427 4445.

AGENCIES FOR FLATS AND ROOMS IN PRIVATE HOMES

IN UK

Canterbury Travel
248 Streatfield Road,
Kenton, Harrow,
Middlesex HA3 9BY.
☎ 0181-206 0411.

The Czechbook
Jopes Mill, Trebrownbridge,
Nr. Liskard, Cornwall
PL14 3PX.
☎ 01503 240629.

Intra Travel
44 Maple Street,
London W1P 5GD.
☎ 0171-323 3305.

Regent Holidays
15 John Street,
Bristol BS1 1DE.
☎ 01272 211711.

Rosemary and Francis Villas
Chester Close,
London SW1X 7BQ.
☎ 0171-235 8825.

IN PRAGUE

ADOS
☎ 73 33 51.
FAX 74 65 20.
24-hour service.

American Express Travel Service
Václavské náměstí 56.
Map 3 C5.
☎ 24 22 98 99.
FAX 24 22 77 08.

Autotourist Travel Agency
Londýnská 62. **Map** 6 F4.
☎ 24 91 18 30 Ex 202.
FAX 24 22 27 52.

AVE Ltd
Hlavní nádraží (main
station). **Map** 4 E5.
☎ 24 22 32 26. Offices
also at Ruzyne airport &
Holešovice railway station.

Balnea Travel Agency
Národní 28. **Map** 3 B5.
FAX 24 21 42 11.

CBT Travel Agency Ltd
Staroměstské náměstí 17.
Map 3 B3.
☎ 24 22 46 46.
FAX 24 22 47 24.

Čedok
Napříkopě 18. **Map** 4 D4.
☎ 231 69 78.
FAX 23 24 81.
One of several branches
(see p219).

Contrans Ltd
Spálená 31. **Map** 3 B5.
☎ 24 91 28 28.
FAX 29 76 00.

Pragoscan Travel Agency
Mikulandská 10. **Map** 3 B5.
☎ 24 91 04 75.
FAX 24 91 96 12.

Pragotur
Za Poříčskov Branov 7.
Map 4 D3.
☎ 24 81 61 20.
FAX 24 81 61 72.

Prague Bed and Breakfast Association
R. Luxemburgové
Kroftova 3, Prague 5.
☎ 54 93 44.
FAX 54 78 06.

Prague Information Service (PIS)
Na příkopě 20. **Map** 3 C4.
☎ 26 40 23.
Staroměstské
náměstí 22. **Map** 3 B3.
☎ 24 21 28 44.
Hlavní nádraží (main
station). **Map** 4 E5.

Prague Suites
8 Melantrichova. **Map** 3 B4.
☎ 24 22 99 61.
FAX 26 61 79.
Price includes transport to
& from the airport.

SCS Ltd
Botičská 4, Prague 2.
☎ 29 76 98.
FAX 29 99 52.

Top Tour
Rybná 3. **Map** 3 C2.
☎ 232 10 77.
FAX 24 81 14 00.
Registration charge.

Travel Agency of České Dráhy
Na příkopě 31,
Passage Sevastopol.
Map 3 C4.
☎ 24 22 36 00.
Offices also in Hlavní
nádraží (main station) &
Holešovice station.

HOSTELS

CKM Youth Agency
Žitná 12, Nové Město.
Map 5 C1.
☎ 24 91 57 67.

Juniorhotel
Žitná 12, Nové Město.
Map 4 E5.
☎ 24 91 57 67.
FAX 236 38 77.

CAMPING

Aritma Džbán
Nad lávkou 3, Vokovice.
☎ 36 85 51.
Open all year.

Kotva Braník
U ledáren 55, Braník.
☎ 46 13 97.
FAX 46 61 10.
Open Apr–Oct.

Troja
Trojská 157, Troja.
☎ 66 41 60 36.
Open mid-Apr–Sep.

DISABLED TRAVELLERS

Federation for Disabled Persons in the Czech Republic
Karlínské náměstí 12,
Prague 8.

Embassy of the Czech Republic
26 Kensington Palace
Gardens, London
W8 4QY.
☎ 071-243 1115.
FAX 727 96 54.

Pension Páv, in a quiet street of a historic neighbourhood *(see p188)*

PRIVATE ROOMS AND SELF-CATERING APARTMENTS

OVER THE PAST five years, the number of private rooms to rent in Prague has grown enormously. Although cheap and popular, they may be some distance from the centre. Private rooms in homes start at about Kč600 per person per night, usually with breakfast. There are also self-contained apartments – a fairly central one-bedroom apartment costs about Kč2,200 per night. Most agencies that offer private rooms also rent out apartments *(see Directory opposite)*.

To book a room or apartment, tell the agency exactly what you want, for how many, when and in which area. The agency will suggest places. Find out the exact location and the nearest metro before

accepting; if you are in Prague, see it yourself. Make sure you receive written or faxed confirmation of a booking to take with you. On arrival in Prague, pay the agency in cash; they give you a voucher to take to the room or apartment (sometimes you can pay the owner directly). If the agency requires advance payment by banker's draft or Eurocheque, go direct to the accommodation with your receipt. Agencies may ask for a deposit on bookings from abroad, or charge a registration fee payable in Prague.

HOSTELS

THERE AREN'T many hostels in Prague, but the CKM Youth Agency in the New Town provides up-to-date information on availability. The official IYHF hostel is the Juniorhotel, also in the New Town. It offers basic but clean, cheap accommodation, with reductions for members.

CAMPING

MOST CAMPSITES in or near Prague are closed from November to the start of April. They are very cheap with basic facilities, but are well served by transport. The largest site is at Troja *(see pp164–5)*, 3 km (1.5 miles) north of the centre. Aritma Džbán, 4 km (2.5 miles) west, is open all year for tents, and Kotva Braník is 6 km (4 miles) south of the city on the banks of the Vltava. For details contact the PIS *(see Directory opposite)*.

The smartly refurbished City Hotel Moran *(see p188)*

Choosing a Hotel

THE HOTELS LISTED on the following pages have all been inspected and assessed. This chart shows some of the factors which may affect your hotel choice. For more information on each hotel see pages 187–9. The hotels are listed by area and appear alphabetically within their price categories.

	Price	Number of Rooms	Large Rooms	Business Facilities	Children's Facilities	Recommended Restaurant	Close to Shops and Restaurants	Quiet Location	24-Hour Room Service
Old Town (see p187)									
Axa	Ⓚ	134		■					
Central	Ⓚ	65					●	▥	
Atlantic	ⓀⓀ	60					●		
Harmony	ⓀⓀ	60		■			●		
Meteor	ⓀⓀ	80					●		
Praha Penta	ⓀⓀⓀⓀ	309	●	■	●		●		
Ungelt	ⓀⓀⓀⓀ	10	●	■			●	▥	●
Jewish Quarter (see p187)									
Intercontinental	ⓀⓀⓀⓀⓀ	395	●	■			●		●
President	ⓀⓀⓀⓀⓀ	97		■			●		
Little Quarter (see p187)									
Kampa	Ⓚ	85	●				●	▥	
U Páva	ⓀⓀⓀ	11	●	■			●	▥	
U Tří pštrosu	ⓀⓀⓀ	18	●			▥	●		
New Town (see p188)									
Evropa	Ⓚ	89	●	■			●	▥	
Luník	Ⓚ	35					●		
Adria	ⓀⓀ	66	●				●		●
Interhotel Ambassador and Zlatá Husa	ⓀⓀⓀ	172		■			●		
Pension Páv	ⓀⓀⓀ	8	●	■				▥	●
City Hotel Moran	ⓀⓀⓀⓀ	57						▥	
Esplanade	ⓀⓀⓀⓀ	64	●	■			●	▥	●
Paříž	ⓀⓀⓀⓀ	98	●	■	●		●		●
Jalta Praha	ⓀⓀⓀⓀⓀ	89	●	■	●		●		●
Palace	ⓀⓀⓀⓀⓀ	125	●	▥			●		●
Further Afield (see p189)									
Belvedere	Ⓚ	116		■			●		
Carol	Ⓚ	40	●	■	●				●
Esprit	Ⓚ	63	●					▥	
Atrium	ⓀⓀⓀ	788	●	■					●
Praha	ⓀⓀⓀ	124	●	■				▥	●
Diplomat Praha	ⓀⓀⓀⓀ	387	●	■	●				
Forum Praha	ⓀⓀⓀⓀⓀ	531	●	■					●

Price categories for a double room per night, including breakfast, tax and service:
Ⓚ Kč2–3,000
ⓀⓀ Kč3–4,000
ⓀⓀⓀ Kč4–5,000
ⓀⓀⓀⓀ Kč5–6,000
ⓀⓀⓀⓀⓀ over Kč6,000

CLOSE TO SHOPS AND RESTAURANTS
Within a 5-minute walk of good shops, bars, cafés and restaurants.

BUSINESS FACILITIES
(see p185).

CHILDREN'S FACILITIES
(see p185).

OLD TOWN

Axa

Na poříčí 40, 110 00 Praha 1.
Map 4 E3. 24 81 25 80.
FAX 232 21 72. *Rooms: 135.*
AE, MC, V.

This old-style hotel opposite the Harmony is slightly dispiriting, yet reasonably priced and central. The rather uninviting exterior opens into a clean, efficient entrance hall. All the rooms have been renovated. A large open-plan public restaurant and bar overlooks the road. It is light and airy, but lacks character. The one great bonus is the swimming pool in the basement, open to the public.

Central

Rybná 8, 110 00 Praha 1. **Map** 3 C2.
24 81 20 41. FAX 232 84 04.
Rooms: 65.
MC, V.

The chief advantage of the Central is its location. Situated in a quiet backstreet with a minimal outlook, it is an old-style hotel, with reasonable prices. The lobby and reception have had a cursory face-lift, but this fades as you climb the stairs. The bedrooms, though old-fashioned and a bit rickety, are neat and clean with a mix of old and new furniture. The small bathrooms are immaculate with towels and bathmats the size of postage stamps.

Atlantic

Na poříčí 9, 110 00 Praha 1.
Map 4 D3. 24 81 10 84.
FAX 24 81 23 78. *Rooms: 60.*
AE, DC, MC, V, JCB.

A few minutes walk from Náměstí Republiky along a busy road, this hotel is well placed for exploring the city. Reconstructed in 1988–9, it is neat and modern, if lacking in character, and the bedrooms are functional and comfortable enough, with most facilities. The restaurant overlooks the main road and at the back there is a bistro cum bar serving lighter snacks and drinks.

Harmony

Na poříčí 31, 110 00 Praha 1.
Map 4 E3. 232 00 16/232 07 20.
FAX 231 00 09. *Rooms: 60.*
AE, DC, MC, V.

Not far from the Atlantic, the Harmony is in pristine condition after complete reconstruction. A compact place, it is run by young, friendly staff. Two small restaurants, one with tables on the pavement, give a choice of Czech or international cuisine.

Meteor

Hybernská 6, 110 00 Praha 1.
Map 4 D3. 24 22 06 64. FAX 24 21 30 05. *Rooms: 80.*
AE, DC, MC, V.

Though part of the international Best Western group, the Meteor still has a cosy, old-fashioned feel. Some parts are slightly scruffy, but most of it has been well modernized and made comfortable. Many of the bedrooms are on the small side, as are the marble showers. In the cellar there is an attractive restaurant.

Praha Penta

V celnici, PO Box 726, 110 00 Praha 1.
Map 4 E3. 24 81 03 96. FAX 231 31 33. *Rooms: 309.*
AE, DC, V, JCB.

The gleaming glass front of this expensive new hotel takes over one corner of Náměstí Republiky. Young men in bright uniforms buzz around the guests, giving friendly and efficient service. The luxurious bedrooms include soft furnishings, plump bedcovers and fluffy bathrobes. There is a choice of restaurants, a beer hall and a very smart pool and health club.

Ungelt

Štupartská 1, 110 00 Praha 1. **Map** 3 C3. 24 81 13 30. FAX 231 95 05.
Rooms: 10.
AE, V.

Tucked away in a quiet street just behind the Old Town Square, this discreet, elegant hotel has an air of exclusivity. The accommodation is in suites, simply but stylishly fitted out with spacious, airy rooms and useful kitchenettes. Some of the rooms feature magnificent wooden ceilings. The restaurant is neat and simple with plain wooden chairs on a marble floor softened with rugs, and there is a shady terrace.

JEWISH QUARTER

Intercontinental

Náměstí Curieových 43/5, 110 00 Praha 1. **Map** 3 B2. 24 88 11 11.
FAX 24 81 00 71. *Rooms: 394.*
AE, MC, DC, V, JCB.

An imposing 1970s building set right on the bank of the Vltava, this hotel is catching up with the competition by adding health and fitness facilities and a swimming pool. There is nothing particularly Czech about the place, but it is a good example of a five-star international hotel. Many of the rooms have lovely views over the river, but although comfortable enough, they are hardly inspired, the best features being the chic grey marble bathrooms.

President

Náměstí Curieových 100, 116 88 Praha 1. **Map** 3 B2. 231 48 12.
FAX 231 82 47. *Rooms: 97.*
AE, DC, MC, V, JCB.

The central location more than compensates for the President's aesthetic shortcomings. Built over 20 years ago for trade unionists, it has been thoroughly refurbished internally and is comfortable, if slightly package-tour-like. The bustling centre of the hotel is its large, airy reception area with lots of sofas, rugs and some bright original paintings. There is a choice of two restaurants, one Czech and one "international", and a roof terrace where, drink in hand, you can enjoy the view across the Vltava to Prague castle.

LITTLE QUARTER

Kampa

Všehrdova 16, 118 00 Praha 1.
Map 2 E5. 24 51 04 09.
FAX 24 51 03 77. *Rooms: 85.*
AE, DC, MC, V.

Built originally as an armoury at the beginning of the 17th century, the Kampa opened recently as a hotel after a complete renovation. Five minutes from Charles Bridge, it is tucked away in a peaceful side street, surrounded by trees and gardens. In the large reception hall, a bar and restaurant are combined under a huge Baroque vaulted ceiling. The effect is far from cosy, and the whole hotel has a slightly institutional feel but it is excellent value. The decor and furnishings are simple and the bedrooms are immaculately clean and neat with whitewashed walls, plain curtains and dark wooden furniture.

U Páva

U lužického semináře 32, 110 00 Praha 1. **Map** 2 F3. 24 51 09 22 / 53 22 51. FAX 53 33 79. *Rooms: 11.*
AE, MC, V.

U Páva translated means "At The Peacock". It is only a few minutes walk from Charles Bridge through a pretty, quiet part of the Little Quarter. The hotel is smart and stylish. The historical features of the house have been enhanced by traditional dark wooden furniture, crystal chandeliers and attractive rugs. Lots of personal touches give it an original and individual feel and the bedrooms, similarly furnished, are both spacious and comfortable.

U Tří pštrosů

Dražického náměstí 12, 118 00 Praha 1. **Map** 2 F3. █ 24 51 07 79. ▣ 24 51 07 83. *Rooms: 18.* ▦ ▣ ▦ ▦ ▦ ▣ ▦ ▦ *AE, V, MC.* ▦ ▦ ▦

Just beside Charles Bridge, the hotel "At The Three Ostriches" began life as the home of Jan Fux, a dealer in ostrich feathers (*see p134*). It is one of the best known hotel/ restaurants in Prague. Family run, the place has a special, intimate atmosphere and refuses to get involved with tour operators. The restaurant has an excellent reputation, so book ahead. The bedrooms have recently been refurbished and are extremely spacious and comfortable, being decorated in keeping with the style of the place.

NEW TOWN

Evropa

Václavské náměstí 25, 110 00 Praha 1. **Map** 4 D5. █ 24 22 81 17. ▣ 24 22 45 44. *Rooms: 89.* ▦ *30.* ▣ ▦ ▦ ▦ ▦ ▦ ▦ *AE, DC, MC, V.* ▦

The Evropa's flamboyant exterior outshines all its neighbours in Wenceslas Square. It is the most beautiful hotel in Prague with superb Art Nouveau decoration. The wonderful old dining room boasts some stunning glasswork and the hotel's café/bar is the most famous in Prague (*see p146*). As one of the few hotels that has not yet been renovated, it remains reasonably priced. Yet the bedrooms are rather disappointing. Each one varies enormously in size, style and facilities; the best are those on the first and second floors, with French windows and high ceilings. But even these bedrooms are not really grand – the furniture is a mish-mash of pieces dating from the 1970s and earlier, and the bathrooms, where they exist, are pretty basic.

Luník

Londýnská 50, 120 00 Praha 2. **Map** 6 E2. █ 25 27 01. ▣ 25 66 17. *Rooms: 35.* ▦ ▣ ▦ ▦ ▦ ▣ ▦

Located in a quiet street lined with trees, the Luník is 15 minutes' walk or two metro stops from Wenceslas Square, but well worth it for the price. The hotel reopened recently after undergoing a total reconstruction and is in immaculate condition. There is simple but smart decor throughout with whitewashed walls and good quality wooden furnishings. Bedrooms are pristine, albeit rather small and functional, with few frills.

Adria

Václavské náměstí 26, 110 00 Praha 1. **Map** 4 D5. █ 24 21 65 43. ▣ 24 21 10 25. *Rooms: 66.* ▦ ▣ ▦ ▦ ▣ ▦ ▦ *AE, DC, MC, V, JCB.* ▦ ▦

After being completely rebuilt, the reopened Adria is bright and chic with a dazzling yellow awning above its entrance on Wenceslas Square. Electric doors slide back to admit you to the marble-tiled reception. Clever use of glass and mirrors make this seem bigger than it is and with plenty of gleaming brass the whole impression is light and up-beat. The bedrooms are also bright and cheery with yellow walls and smartly co-ordinated furnishings.

Interhotel Ambassador/ Zlatá Husa

Václavské náměstí 5–7, 110 00 Praha 1. **Map** 3 C5. █ 24 19 31 11/ 24 21 21 85. ▣ 24 22 61 67. *Rooms: 172.* ▦ ▣ ▦ ▦ ▦ ▦ ▦ ▣ ▦ ▦ ▦ ▦ ▦ *AE, DC, V.* ▦ ▦ ▦

Right in the centre of Wenceslas Square, these neighbouring hotels are now under the same ownership. The result is rather a muddle, but it does give you a choice of bars and restaurants, some of which stay open until midnight or later, without having to leave the building. The lounge and reception areas look scruffy and rather old-fashioned, but the other public rooms are reasonably comfortable. Although all the bedrooms are the same price, the standard varies enormously, so insist on a recently refurbished room.

Pension Páv

Křemencova 13, 110 00 Praha 1. **Map** 5 B1. █ 24 91 32 86. ▣ 24 91 05 74. *Rooms: 8.* ▦ ▦ ▦ ▦ ▦ ▦ ▦ ▦

Located in a fairly quiet street in a historic part of Prague, this hotel is a compact place with just a few rooms and apartments. These are simple but quite stylishly decorated, and all are of a good size. The pension has its own cosy bar and a reasonable restaurant; both are ideal for those evenings when you feel too exhausted to venture out.

City Hotel Moráň

Václavská 5, 120 00 Praha 2. **Map** 5 A3. █ 24 91 52 08. ▣ 29 75 33. ▦ 12 21 34. *Rooms: 57.* ▣ ▦ ▦ ▦ ▦ ▣ ▦ ▦ ▦ *AE, DC, MC, V, JCB.* ▦ ▦ ▦ ▦

Recently reopened, the City Hotel Moráň is another reconstruction made to meet the higher standards of today's visitors to Prague. It has been beautifully decorated in an understated style and features whitewashed walls with soft green carpets in some areas, smart sofas and chairs on pale marble floors in others, and the scent of fresh flowers wafting through the airy rooms. There is also a smart café/ restaurant and bar overlooking the street. Although the bedrooms vary in size, the standard of comfort is high throughout and each one is equipped with all the conveniences you would expect to find in a modernized hotel.

Esplanade

Washingtonova 19, 110 00 Praha 1. **Map** 4 E5. █ 24 21 17 15. ▣ 24 22 93 06. *Rooms: 64.* ▦ ▣ ▦ ▦ ▦ ▦ ▣ ▦ ▦ *AE, DC, MC, V, JCB.* ▦ ▦ ▦ ▦

This refined, almost stately hotel is run with old-fashioned service and courtesy. The location in a wide tree-lined street just off Wenceslas Square is marred by the view of a freeway, but you are not aware of this once inside. Built early this century, the hotel has high ceilings with some glorious Art Nouveau features. There are two restaurants: the rather bizarre one down in the basement has the advantage of staying open till 2am – extremely useful after operas or concerts and very unusual for Prague. The decoration of the rooms varies, but each is large and comfortable.

Paříž

U Obecního domu 1, 110 00 Praha 1. **Map** 4 D3. █ 24 22 21 51. ▣ 24 22 54 75. *Rooms: 98.* ▦ ▣ ▦ ▦ ▦ ▦ ▦ ▣ ▦ ▦ ▦ *AE, DC, MC, V, JCB.* ▦ ▦ ▦ ▦

This turn-of-the-century hotel just off Náměstí Republiky was built by the celebrated architect Jan Vejrych. A Neo-Gothic building with Art Nouveau elements, it was declared a historic monument in 1984 and displays examples of beautiful craftsmanship. The restaurant is particularly attractive, with superb doors and fine decoration on the ceiling. The rooms have been well modernized in international style – that is, fairly characterless but extremely comfortable – and everything is in pristine condition.

Jalta Praha

Václavské náměstí 45, 110 00 Praha 1.
Map 4 D5. ▐ *24 22 91 33.* FAX *24 21 38 66.* **Rooms:** *89.*

AE, DC, MC, V, JCB.

One of Prague's old-fashioned hotels, the Jalta Praha has a central position on Wenceslas Square. The reception is chillingly unadorned with just a small desk at one end. Other parts of the hotel, however, have undergone some reconstruction: the exterior has been renovated and the main restaurant redesigned. The bedrooms have also been refurbished. They are comfortable, good-sized rooms that are attractively decorated, with modern bathrooms attached.

Palace

Panská 12, 110 00 Praha 1. **Map** 4 D4. ▐ *24 09 31 11.* FAX *23 59 373.* TX *12 33 37.* **Rooms:** *125.*

A short walk from Wenceslas Square, located in a quiet side street, this is the most expensive hotel in Prague. It reopened in 1989 after a complete refurbishment. The unusual mixture of styles – modern, Art Nouveau and traditional – with lashings of brass, glass, mirrors and fake flowers, may not be to everyone's taste, and in places the decor does go a touch over the top, but the hotel succeeds in its aim to provide any luxury its guests may require.

FURTHER AFIELD

Belvedere

Milady Horákové 19, 170 00 Praha 7. ▐ *37 47 41.* FAX *37 03 55.* **Rooms:** *116.*

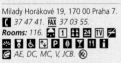

AE, DC, MC, V, JCB.

Just one metro stop north from Florenc, this area buzzes with activity – shops, restaurants, cafés. It has a life very much of its own, and shows you a more intimate side of Prague. The hotel is on a main corner and the bar/café opens onto the street. It is a friendly, relaxed place, which is why it is popular with groups. Although there is nothing special about the hotel and it can be slightly gloomy, it is clean, neat, reasonably central and moderately priced. The rooms are simple but comfortable, with good modern shower rooms.

Carol

Kurta Konráda 547 / 12, 190 Praha 9. ▐ *66 31 13 16.* FAX *684 42 76.* **Rooms:** *40.*

AE, DC, MC, V.

Another brand new hotel, opened in 1993, with a smart marble reception hall and efficient young staff. The hotel is Dutch owned, which perhaps explains why the simple, but chic restaurant and bar are open until 11pm and 3pm respectively. Bedrooms continue the somewhat minimalist decor, but are immaculate and comfortable. Like its neighbour the Esprit, its disadvantage is the distance from the centre.

Esprit

Lihovarská 1094–8, 190 00 Praha 9. ▐ *82 04 31.* FAX *684 59 17.* **Rooms:** *63.*

AE, MC, V.

The owners of this neat, modern hotel have converted the house next door, adding 10 bedrooms to its capacity. The breakfast-room/bar/restaurant is cheerfully decorated and kept pristine. The well-kept bedrooms are simple but smart with pine furniture, whitewashed walls and pale cotton duvet covers. The hotel's only drawback is its distance from the centre of Prague: a 10-minute walk from the last stop on the metro B line, and 5 minutes from a direct bus route in an area of uninspiring, dusty, residential suburbs. Beware of booking this hotel through a travel agent, as it will almost double the price.

Atrium

Pobřežní 1, 186 00 Praha 8.
Map 4 F2. ▐ *24 84 11 11.* FAX *24 81 18 96.* **Rooms:** *788.*

AE, DC, V, JCB.

The first atrium-type hotel to be built in the Czech Republic, this gleaming building stands out like a beacon of modernity against the background of the surrounding drab apartment buildings. French-owned and designed, it is the biggest hotel in the country, and despite the huge size, it does have a certain style. Sit in the airy, marble hall surrounded by plants and lulled by the sound of running water and watch the transparent lift capsules zoom up and down the atrium. The bedrooms are tastefully decorated with all the comforts you would expect to find in a large international hotel.

Praha

Sušiká 20, 166 35 Praha 6. ▐ *24 34 11 11.* FAX *24 31 12 18.* **Rooms:** *124.*

AE, DC, MC, V, JCB.

If you can't bear the noise of traffic or city smells 24 hours a day, then this large modern hotel surrounded by lovely gardens may be the place for you. Its disadvantages, apart from the price, are its distance from the centre. Way beyond the last metro stop on the B line, it is a good 15 minute walk to the nearest bus stop. But once you are there it has all the facilites you would expect of a big, modern hotel. It is less huge than it looks because all the bedrooms have a view towards the city and are a generous size. All that it offers in space, with acres of empty marble floors and small clusters of modern seating, it lacks in atmosphere. It is effeciently run and comfortable, if slightly clinical.

Diplomat Praha

Evropská 15, 160 00 Praha 6. ▐ *24 39 41 11.* FAX *34 17 31.* TX *12 32 80.* **Rooms:** *387.*

AE, DC, MC, V, JCB.

This hotel is located right at the end of metro line A, but is only 12 minutes from the city centre. It opened in 1990 and still looks and feels very new, with lots of shiny marble and brass, and huge open spaces. Very efficiently run by Austrians, the hotel offers excellent facilities including a nightclub, numerous restaurants, shops, and even a whirlpool in the health club. It is popular with tour operators, and very comfortable, but once inside, you could be anywhere in the world.

Forum Praha

Kongresová 1, 140 69 Praha 4. ▐ *61 19 12 18.* FAX *42 06 84.* TX *12 21 00.* **Rooms:** *531.*

AE, DC, V, JCB.

Beside the Vyšehrad metro stop, the Forum is only a few minutes' ride to the city centre. Built in 1988 as a modern high-rise filled with glass, brass and marble, it features an impressive sports and health centre and a beautiful indoor swimming pool with stunning views over the city. Sit in the lounge on roomy leather sofas and watch the water cascade from the marble fountain, or choose to eat in either the French or Czech restaurants or the snack bar. The bedrooms are a good size, well decorated and comfortable; the bathrooms are immaculate.

For key to symbols *see p185*

RESTAURANTS, CAFÉS AND PUBS

RESTAURANTS in Prague, just like the economy, seem to be getting better. For 40 years state-licensed eating and drinking establishments had little incentive to experiment or improve. But attitudes are rapidly changing. Fuelled by the booming tourist industry, new restaurants are opening constantly, many of them foreign-owned, offering the discerning eater an ever-increasing choice. The restaurants described in this

The Good Soldier Švejk at U Kalicha *(see p154)*

section reflect the change, though many only serve a limited range of standard Western dishes as well as staple Czech meals. *Choosing a Restaurant* on pages 198–9 summarizes the key features of the restaurants and cafés, listed by area. Full listings can be found on pages 200–4 and information on pubs, beer halls and bars appears on page 205. Compared to Western prices, eating out in Prague is still cheap.

TIPS ON EATING OUT

BECAUSE OF the huge influx of tourists, eating out has changed in character. The traditional lunch hour is still taken very early – between 11am and 1pm, and for most Czechs the normal time for the evening meal is around 7pm. However, many of the restaurants stay open late and it is possible to get a meal at any time from 10am until 2am. Until recently, these late hours were almost unheard of.

During spring and summer, the large numbers of visitors tend to put a strain on many of Prague's more popular restaurants. To be certain of a table, especially in the very well-known restaurants, book two or three days in advance. Although most restaurants are

in the city centre, quite a few are off the normal tourist track, away from Wenceslas and Old Town Squares, and worth the extra journey. Prices also tend to be lower the further you go from the centre.

PLACES TO EAT

THE IMPORTANCE of a stylish yet comfortable setting, and food which is inspired rather than just prepared, is slowly beginning to trickle down to Prague's better and more innovative restaurants. The places which follow this maxim are generally the best.

One of the simplest places to eat is the sausage stand, a utilitarian establishment, very common in Central Europe. It offers Czech sausages, which can either be eaten standing

Vinárna v Zátiší *(see p201)*

at the counter or taken away cold. For a late-night meal your best bet is often a snack bar *(bufet)*. But beware, even if a snack bar boasts a 24-hour sign, it may sometimes close before midnight.

For greater comfort, head for a café *(kavárna)*. Cafés range from loud, busy main street locations to quieter bookstore establishments. All have fully stocked bars and serve a variety of food from simple pastries and sandwiches to full-blown meals. Opening hours differ widely, but many open early in the morning and are good for a quick, if not quite a Western-style, breakfast.

A restaurant may be called a *restaurace* or a *vinárna* (one that sells wine). The best are those geared to non-Czech clientele. While usually cheap by Western standards, they are pricier than Czech places, but in return offer better service and higher quality food.

Plain Czech food is normally available at the local beer hall or pub *(pivnice)*, though the emphasis there is normally on drinking rather than eating.

Diners enjoying their meal at U Kalicha *(see p203)*

Tourists eating at the outdoor cafés in the Old Town Square

READING THE MENU

NEVER JUDGE a restaurant by the standard of its menu translations – mistakes are common in every class of restaurant. Many menus still list the weight of meat served (a relic of wartime rationing). Bear in mind that most main courses come with potatoes, rice or dumplings. Salads and other side dishes must be ordered separately. *(See pp194–5 for What to Eat in Prague.)*

Sign at U Zelené Žáby *(see p200)*

THINGS TO BEWARE OF

IN EXPENSIVE RESTAURANTS the waiter may bring nuts to your table. Yes, they are for you to eat, but at a price equal to, or higher than, an appetizer. You will not insult

Stained-glass window at Florianův Dvůr *(see p202)*

anybody by telling the waiter to take them away. The same applies to appetizers brought round by the waiter.

It's advisable not to order a meal on a waiter's suggestion. The chances are it will be the most expensive dish in the house, and if you have not seen the menu the price may be even higher still.

Check your bill carefully, because extra charges are often added – this is quite a common practice in Prague. However, legitimate extra costs do exist. Cover charges range from Kč10–25 and such basic items as milk, ketchup, bread and butter might be charged for. Finally, a 23% tax, normally included in the menu, is occasionally added to the total bill.

ETIQUETTE

YOU DON'T HAVE to wait to be seated in snack bars and smaller eateries. It is also quite normal for others to join your table if there is any room. No restaurant has an official dress code, but people tend to dress up when dining in up-market restaurants.

PAYMENT AND TIPPING

THE AVERAGE PRICE for a full meal in the centre of Prague is about Kč200. The waiter may write your order on a piece of paper and then leave it on your table for the person who comes around

when you are ready to pay. Levels of service vary – it can be very slow – but generally a 10% tip is appropriate. Add the tip to the bill, do not leave the money on the table.

More and more restaurants now accept major credit cards, but always ask before the meal to make sure. Traveller's cheques and Euro-cheques are rarely accepted.

VEGETARIANS

VEGETARIANS are not well catered for in Prague. In the past, fresh vegetables were rare in winter. But they are becoming more common throughout the year, although variable in quality. Even when a dish is described as meatless, it's always worth double checking. Vegans and those with special dietary needs will have a difficult time eating.

DISABLED

RESTAURANTS do not cater specifically for the disabled. The staff will almost always try and help, but Prague's ubiquitous stairs and basements will defeat all but the most determined.

USING THE LISTINGS
Key to symbols in the listings on pp200–4.

🍽	fixed-price menu
V	vegetarian dishes
Y	formal dress
♫	live music
⊞	outdoor tables
🍷	good wine list
★	highly recommended
🗀	credit cards accepted:
AE	American Express
DC	Diners Club
MC	Mastercard/Access
V	Visa
JCB	Japanese Credit Bureau

Price categories for a three-course meal including a half-bottle of house wine, tax and service:
Ⓚ under Kč175
ⓀⓀ Kč175–300
ⓀⓀⓀ Kč300–500
ⓀⓀⓀⓀ over Kč500

Prague's Best: Restaurants and Cafés

T HE VARIETY AND NUMBER of places to eat and drink in Prague has increased considerably in recent years. But despite a massive influx of discerning diners, some of the restaurants may disappoint visitors with their uninspired cuisine. The following restaurants, chosen from the listings on pages 200–4, will guide you to sample tasty, interesting meals while relaxing in venues which not only provide a pleasant atmosphere, but also offer reasonably priced, good quality food.

U Tří pštrosů
High-quality and traditional Czech dishes are found at this exclusive restaurant. (See p202.)

Peklo
The 12th-century beer cellars and delicious Italian fare make this well worth a visit. (See p201.)

Prague Castle and Hradčany

Little Quarter

Nebozízek
The spectacular view over Prague from this café terrace ensures the popularity of this establishment. (See p202.)

Café Savoy
A small, but delicious, selection of snacks can be enjoyed at this classy café. (See p201.)

U Malířů
This converted 16th-century house has an excellent reputation for its exquisite French dishes, in an atmosphere of discreet luxury. The murals and painted ceilings add to the romantic mood. (See p202.)

U Golema
This unusual modern representation of the mythological Golem stands in the entrance to this restaurant, where substantial meat-based dishes at reasonable prices are the main attraction. (See p201.)

U Červeného kola
Steaks and mouth-watering desserts are a speciality in this quiet restaurant, tucked away in a side street near St Agnes's Convent. (See p201.)

Jewish Quarter

Old Town

New Town

0 metres 300
0 yards 300

Hotel Evropa
A wide range of high-quality international dishes and snacks are served in this beautiful turn-of-the-century hotel, well-known for its elegant Art Nouveau interior decoration. (See p202.)

Pod Křídlem
International and Czech fare, a resident pianist and late-night opening make this a popular spot with tourists and affluent locals alike. (See p203.)

Opera Grill
French nouvelle cuisine is served in an intimate and exclusive atmosphere. (See p200.)

What to Eat in Prague

CZECH COOKERY IS VERY SIMILAR to Austrian – lots of meat (usually pork or beef) served with dumplings, potatoes or rice, in a sauce. Meat, poultry, fish, cabbage and potatoes are all prepared simply and without strong spices; meat tends to be fried, roasted, or oven-baked in stock. On special occasions, game is usually the main course: venison, boar steaks or quails. Standard dishes tend to be served in copious quantities, and main courses are virtually meals in themselves. The most common dish is pork served with dumplings and sauerkraut (vepřové, knedlíky a zelí). Dumplings are traditionally served with most hot dishes and gravy. Vegetable portions can be small, although there has been a slight increase in the consumption of fresh vegetables in recent years. Salads are variable in quality. Hot soups are the traditional start to a meal, and range from broth with liver dumplings to cabbage soup with sausage.

"Stuffed eggs" are a popular appetizer

Žitný chléb (rye bread)

Rohlík (finger roll)

Pletená houska (knot roll)

Chléb and Pečivo (breads)
An assortment of breads is served with most meals.

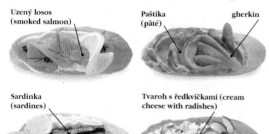

Uzený losos (smoked salmon)

Paštika (pâté)

gherkin

Sardinka (sardines)

Tvaroh s ředkvičkami (cream cheese with radishes)

Chlebíčky
These open sandwiches arranged on sliced baguette (French bread) can be found in any Lahůdky (delicatessen) and Bufet (snack bar) in Prague. They are popularly served to guests in Czech homes. Ham, fish, salami, roast beef, egg and cheeses are used, often with mayonnaise or garnished with a gherkin (nakládaná okurka). Unfortunately western-style fast food is encroaching on this snack's popularity.

Klobásy (grilled sausages)

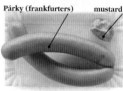
Párky (frankfurters)   mustard

Klobásy and Párky
Klobásy are grilled sausages; párky are boiled frankfurters (hot dogs). Both are sold with mustard (hořčice) from street stalls and in special sausage shops.

Plněná šunka
An appetizer of stuffed ham, filled with a mix of whipped cream and coarsely grated horseradish, which gives it a kick.

Polévka
Simple vegetable soups – pea, potato, cauliflower, cabbage or tomato – are popular starters.

Hovězí polévka s játrovými knedlíčky
Liver dumplings in beef broth is a warming soup for all seasons.

Pečená kachna
Roast duck with bacon dumplings (špekové knedlíky) and red sauerkraut is a popular main course.

Uzené
Smoked pork is mostly served with slices of potato dumplings (bramborové knedlíky) and white sauerkraut.

Vepřový řízek
Breaded and fried pork steak (schnitzel) is usually accompanied by hot potatoes or a cold potato salad. It often has a salad garnish and a slice of lemon.

Houskové knedlíky (sliced bread dumplings)

Brusinky (cranberries)

Hovězí (beef)

Svíčková na smetaně
Pot-roasted fillet of beef (svíčková) is served in a rich, creamy, slightly sweet vegetable sauce (na smetaně) and is garnished with either cranberries or a dollop of whipped cream.

Salát
In winter, salads are often pickled; in summer, they are simply-dressed mixtures of tomato, lettuce, cucumbers and peppers.

Jablkový strudel
Thin apple slices are wrapped in a light pastry case. Other strudel fillings include cherries or cream cheese.

Ovocné knedlíky
Fruit dumplings, in this case švestkové (plum), are served with melted butter, icing sugar and ground poppy seeds.

Vdolek
This round yeast pastry is served with redcurrant or plum jam and whipped cream.

Palačinky
Crêpe pancakes can be filled with ice cream and/or stewed fruit or jam, and coated in sugar, chocolate or almonds.

What to Drink in Prague

'Golden Tiger' beer mat

CZECH BEERS ARE FAMOUS around the world, but nowhere are they drunk with such appreciation as in Prague. The Czechs take their beer (*pivo*) seriously and are very proud of it. Pilsner and its various relations originate in Bohemia. It is generally agreed that the best Pilsners are produced close to the original source – and all the top producers are not far from Prague. Beers can be bought in cans, in bottles, and best of all, on draught. Canned beer is made mostly for export, and no connoisseur would ever drink it. The Czech Republic also produces considerable quantities of wine, both red and white, mainly in Southern Moravia. Little of it is bottled for export. Mineral water can be found in most restaurants; Mattoni and Dobrá voda (meaning good water) are the two most widely available brands.

Gambrinus, legendary King of Beer, and trademark of a popular brand of Pilsner

PILSNER AND BUDWEISER

THE BEST-KNOWN CZECH BEER is Pilsner. Clear and golden, with a strong flavour of hops, Pilsner is made by the lager method: top-fermented and slowly matured at low temperatures. The word "Pilsner" (which is now a generic term for similar lagers brewed all over the world) is derived from Plzeň (in German, Pilsen), a town 80 km (50 miles) southwest of Prague, where this type of beer was first made in 1842. The brewery that developed the beer still makes Plzňské pivo as well as the slightly stronger Plzňský prazdroj (original source), which is better known by its German name Pilsner Urquell. A slightly sweeter beer, Budweiser Budvar (which is no relation to the American beer of the same name), is brewed 150 km (100 miles) south of Prague in the town of České Budějovice (in German, Budweis).

Budweiser logo

Traditional copper brew-kettles in Plzeň

This higher percentage refers to the original gravity, not the alcohol content

e 0,5 l
Světlé means light / Alcohol content

Pilsner Urquell logo

Reading a Beer Label
The most prominent figure on the label (usually 10% or 12%) does not refer to the alcohol content. It is a Czech measure of original gravity, indicating the density of malt and other sugars used in the brew. The percentage of alcohol by volume is usually given in smaller type. The label also states whether it is a dark or a light beer.

BEER AND BEER HALLS

Staropramen

Plzeňské

Velkopopovický kozel

Budweiser Budvar

Plzňský prazdroj (Pilsner Urquell)

THE REAL PLACE TO ENJOY Czech beer is a pub or beer hall (*pivnice*). Each pub is supplied by a single brewery (*pivovar*), so only one brand of beer is available, but several different types are on offer. The major brands include Plzeňské and Gambrinus from Plzeň, Staropramen from Prague, and Velkopopovické from Velké Popovice, south of Prague. The usual drink is draught light beer (*světlé*), but a number of beer halls, including U Fleků (*see p155*) and U Kalicha (*see p154*) also serve special strong dark lagers (ask for *tmavé*). Another type you may encounter is *kozel*, a strong light beer like a German *bock*.

A half litre of beer (just under a pint) is called a *velké* (large), and a third of a litre (larger than a half pint) is called a *malé* (small). The waiters bring beers and snacks to your table and mark everything you eat and drink on a tab. In some pubs (*see p205*) there is a tacit assumption that all the customers want to go on drinking until closing time, so don't be surprised if more beers arrive without your ordering them. If you don't want them, just say no. The bill is totted up when you leave.

Beer gardens, such as U Fleků, serve "dark" lagers on draught

WINES

Rulandské, white and red

CZECH WINE PRODUCERS have not yet emulated the success of other East European wine-makers. The main wine-growing region is in Moravia, where most of the best wine is produced for local consumption. Some wine is also made in Bohemia, around Mělník, just north of Prague. The whites, made mostly from Riesling and Müller-Thurgau grapes, tend to be oversweet, though Rulandské is an acceptable dry white. The reds are slightly better, the main choices being Frankovka and Vavřinecké. In the autumn, a semi-fermented young white wine called *burčák* is sold and drunk across the capital; despite its sweet, juice-like taste, it is surprisingly intoxicating.

CZECH SPIRITS AND LIQUEURS

IN EVERY RESTAURANT and pub you'll find Becherovka, a bitter-sweet, yellow herbal drink served both as an aperitif and a liqueur. It can also be diluted with tonic. Other local drinks include Borovička, a juniper-flavoured spirit, and plum brandy or Slivovice. The latter is clear and strong and rather an acquired taste. Imported spirits are expensive and cocktails rare.

Becherovka

Choosing a Restaurant or Café

THE RESTAURANTS listed have been selected for their good value or exceptional food. This chart highlights some of the main factors which may influence your choice of places to eat, such as fixed-price menus, tables outside, late opening and Czech specialities. The entries appear alphabetically within the price category, and any special features are indicated. For more details about each restaurant, see pages 200–4, and refer to page 205 for further information about bars and beer halls.

	Price	FIXED-PRICE MENU	ATTRACTIVE SETTING	TABLES OUTSIDE	CZECH SPECIALITIES	SEAFOOD SPECIALITIES	LATE OPENING	LIVE MUSIC AT NIGHT
OLD TOWN *(see pp200–1)*								
Hogo Fogo	Ⓚ		●				●	
U Zelené žáby	Ⓚ						■	
Café Nouveau ★	ⓀⓀ			■			■	●
Na Poříčí	ⓀⓀ				●			
Na Příkopě	ⓀⓀ				●			
Pivnice Skořepka	ⓀⓀ				●			
Red, Hot and Blues	ⓀⓀ			■			●	■
U Černé Dory	ⓀⓀ				●		●	
U Zlate uličky	ⓀⓀ	●					●	
Café Four	ⓀⓀⓀ							
Opera Grill	ⓀⓀⓀⓀ	●		●			●	
Parnas	ⓀⓀⓀⓀ	●						
Vinárna v Zátiší	ⓀⓀⓀⓀ	●						
JEWISH QUARTER *(see p201)*								
Mikulka's Pizzeria	ⓀⓀ							
Valentin	ⓀⓀ	●						
Shalom	ⓀⓀⓀ	●	■					
U Golema	ⓀⓀⓀ	●	■		■	●		
U Červeného kola	ⓀⓀⓀⓀ	●	■					
U Staré Synagogy	ⓀⓀⓀ	●			■		■	
PRAGUE CASTLE AND HRADČANY *(see p201)*								
Peklo	ⓀⓀⓀⓀ	●					●	
U Labutí	ⓀⓀⓀⓀ			■		■		
LITTLE QUARTER *(see pp201–2)*								
Café Savoy	ⓀⓀ	●					●	
U Schnellů	ⓀⓀ							
David	ⓀⓀⓀ	●						
Italia	ⓀⓀⓀ							
Nebozízek	ⓀⓀⓀ	●	■					
U Sv. Tomáše	ⓀⓀⓀ	●	■					■
Florianův Dvůr	ⓀⓀⓀⓀ	●				■	●	
U Malířů	ⓀⓀⓀⓀ	●						
U Modré kachničky ★	ⓀⓀⓀⓀ	●						
U Tří pštrosů	ⓀⓀⓀⓀ	●		●				
Valdštejnská hospoda	ⓀⓀⓀⓀ	●		●				

Price categories
These have been calculated to represent the cost of an average three-course meal for one, including half a bottle of house wine, and all unavoidable extra charges such as cover, service and tax:
Ⓚ under Kč175
ⓀⓀ Kč175–300
ⓀⓀⓀ Kč300–500
ⓀⓀⓀⓀ over Kč500.

★ Means highly recommended.

FIXED-PRICE MENU
A restaurant which offers a set menu: usually three or four courses without wine or coffee, for a fixed price.

ATTRACTIVE SETTING
A restaurant with an unusual or historic interior, or with a beautiful view.

TABLES OUTSIDE
A restaurant where you can dine out-of-doors during the warmer months.

CZECH SPECIALITIES
A good selection of traditional dishes.

LATE OPENING
Last orders taken at or after 11:30pm.

		Fixed-Price Menu	Attractive Setting	Tables Outside	Czech Specialities	Seafood Specialities	Late Opening	Live Music at Night
NEW TOWN *(see pp202–3)*								
Hotel Evropa Café	Ⓚ		■				■	
Kmotra	Ⓚ					●		
Kavárna Velryba	Ⓚ							
Vltava	Ⓚ		■	●	●			
FX Café	ⓀⓀ							
Na Rybárně	ⓀⓀ	●			■	●		
Pod Křídlem	ⓀⓀⓀ				■			●
U Čížků	ⓀⓀⓀ		■		■			
U Kalicha	ⓀⓀⓀ				■			●
Hotel Evropa	ⓀⓀⓀⓀ	●	■		■			
Premiera	ⓀⓀⓀⓀ	●	■			●	■	●
FURTHER AFIELD *(see pp203–4)*								
Akropolis	Ⓚ		■					
The Globe Bookstore Café	Ⓚ		■				■	
Na Slamníku	Ⓚ			■			■	
U Koleje	Ⓚ							
U Tří hrochů	Ⓚ			●				
Elite	ⓀⓀ		■		■			
Quido	ⓀⓀ							
U Mikuláše Dačického	ⓀⓀ		■				■	
U Cedru ★	ⓀⓀⓀ		■					
U Sloupu	ⓀⓀⓀ	●			■			
U Zlatého rožně	ⓀⓀⓀ		■			●	■	
Zlatý Drak	ⓀⓀⓀ							
Principe	ⓀⓀⓀⓀ		■					
Schwaigerovy Sady	ⓀⓀⓀ	●		●				●

OLD TOWN

Hogo Fogo

Salvátorská 4. **Map** 3 B3. 【 *231 70 23.* **Open** *10:30am–midnight Sat–Thu, noon–1am Fri.* Ⓥ Ⓔ AE,DC, V. ⓚ

Despite its prime location near the Old Town Square, this restaurant and bar is surprisingly unpopular with tourists. Instead, it is populated by young, beautiful, professional Czechs and those foreigners in the know. The three large, airy rooms with their white walls, decorated with figurines, offer a relaxed setting in which to sit and read, drink or eat. There is a good selection of pasta dishes and vegetarian food – look out for the tasty fried cheese – all at very reasonable prices.

U Zelené žáby
AT THE GREEN FROG

U radnice 8. **Map** 3 B3. 【 *24 22 81 33.* **Open** *10am–midnight Mon–Thu, noon–midnight Fri & Sat.* ⛏ ⓚ

The oldest recorded *vinárna* (wine bar serving food) in Prague, this is supposedly where, 400 years ago, the city's executioners came after a day's work. In the subdued interior, this is not hard to imagine. But attentive service, a convenient location and intimate atmosphere make this a popular place to eat as well as drink. The roast beef platter served with fried bread and tartare sauce is renowned. Other popular dishes are cheese plates, and a mixed ham and cheese plate.

Café Nouveau

Náměstí Republiky 5. **Map** 4 D3. **Open** *11am– midnight daily.* 🎵 ★ ⓚⓚ

This grand and imposing room is located on the ground floor of the Municipal House (*see p64*). Under new management, the café offers a variety of well-prepared and simple dishes including sandwiches and fresh salads, and every night there is live jazz. It's worth visiting for the sumptuous interior alone.

Na Poříčí

Na poříčí 20. **Map** 4 E3. 【 *24 81 13 63.* **Open** *11am–11pm Mon–Sat, noon–11pm Sun.* Ⓔ V, DC, AE, MC. ⓚⓚ

Choose your setting in this large restaurant. It is part pub, part wine bar, and part elegant restaurant, with papered walls adorned with framed prints. The menu offers traditional Czech meals, poultry and fish, plus an attempt at more

original cuisine (lobster and brandy soup). Being one of the few good, inexpensive restaurants in the neighbourhood, it tends to be very busy at lunchtime.

Na Příkopě

Na příkopě 17. **Map** 3 C4. 【 *24 21 06 61.* **Open** *11am–11pm daily.* ⓚⓚ

The prices here are surprisingly reasonable for the central location. It was once a typical southern Bohemian pub, yet when the menu changed, the decor remained, with forest-green walls and carpeting, and butcher-block tables and chairs. The traditional Czech cooking is ideal for a quick daytime meal.

Pivnice Skořepka

Skořepka 1. **Map** 3 B4. 【 *24 21 47 15.* **Open** *11:30am–11pm Mon–Sat, noon–11pm Sun.* ⓚⓚ

This high-ceilinged, wood-panelled restaurant serves numerous Czech dishes, but most people go to eat the large pork knees – joints like those at a Tudor banquet. Served with mustard and horseradish, they make a memorable meal. Those who wish to eat less meat can choose a good chicken cutlet stuffed with ham and blue cheese. Wash it all down with light or dark beer.

Red, Hot and Blues

Jakubská 12. **Map** 3 C3. 【 *231 46 39.* **Open** *9am–11pm daily.* Ⓥ 🎵 🍴 Ⓔ AE, MC, V. ⓚⓚⓚ

Located in what were the king's stables 500 years ago, this place draws a crowd largely from the expatriate community who come for the good, home-town New Orleans and Creole cooking: chilli, chowder, burgers with all the trimmings, and étouffé. Seafood, salads and chicken are also prepared with imagination and there is a weekend brunch American-style. Live jazz or blues each night and happy hour specials are additional attractions. For live music (cover added), plan to stay past 7:30pm.

U Černé Dory
AT BLACK DORA'S

Masná 8. **Map** 3 C3. 【 *231 77 42.* **Open** *11:30am–midnight daily.* Ⓔ AE, DC, MC, V. ⓚⓚⓚ

Beef, chicken and more traditional Czech meals fill the menu in this slightly upmarket, chic designer restaurant. Tucked away on a small side street, the place escapes the normal tourist crowds while providing all the amenities of its more crowded competitors.

U Zlaté uličky
BY GOLDEN LANE

Masná 9. **Map** 3 C3. 【 *232 08 84.* **Open** *10am–midnight daily.* ⓚⓚ

Figurines line the window of this restaurant. Yugoslavian cuisine, specializing in veal, is the main fare, but there are pork and steak dishes too. The *palačinka* (fluffy whipped crêpe filled with cream and covered with chocolate sauce) is probably the best in town. A bar completes the cosy restaurant.

Café Four

Corner of Revoluční and Soukenická. **Map** 4 D2. 【 *231 25 24.* **Open** *9am–11pm daily.* Ⓔ AE, DC, MC, V. ⓚⓚⓚ

Many different teas and coffees are available at this café, and the setting, just off the beaten track, makes it a pleasant, chic place to escape from the bustle of central Prague. The food is standard, but reasonably priced.

Opera Grill

Karoliny Světlé 35. **Map** 3 A4. 【 *26 55 08.* **Open** *7pm–2am daily.* 🍴🍽 Ⓣ 🎵 Ⓔ AE, DC, V. ⓚⓚⓚⓚ

Years ago, this intimate restaurant was considered one of Prague's elite dining spots. With only seven tables, surrounded by armchairs, a pianist playing softly, and a serene, candle-lit elegance, it is easy to imagine that you are in a private dining room. The menu features international dishes: rack of lamb, pasta, salmon, chicken and steak. The prices do not reflect the exclusive ambience, nor do all the clientele dress formally. This is a dining experience to be tried before it becomes too exclusive.

Parnas
PARNASSUS

Smetanovo nábřeží 2. **Map** 3 A5. 【 *24 22 76 14/24 22 92 48.* **Open** *noon–3pm, 6–11pm daily.* Ⓣ Ⓔ AE, MC, V. ⓚⓚⓚⓚ

This Art Deco masterpiece has more going for it than inlaid wood walls and marble floors. Right by the river, it has a postcard view of Prague Castle. The menu is the same as Vinárna v Zátiší (*see p201*), with the same owners. A few Czech dishes are on offer, but the fare is mostly international, and includes items such as Beef Wellington and Norwegian salmon. Each dish is delightfully prepared, if rather uninspiring, so don't expect any surprises beyond the high standard of service. On Sundays there is an all-you-can-eat buffet brunch.

Vinárna v Zátiší
IN SECLUSION

Liliová 1, Betlémské náměstí.
Map 3 B4. 24 22 89 77.
Open noon–3pm, 5.30–11pm daily.
AE, MC, V.

Located near both Charles Bridge and the Old Town Square, Vinárna v Zátiší was Prague's first Western-owned and run restaurant. The British owner concentrated on quality of both food and service, and it rapidly became the hub of the foreign business community. Today, the place is crowded as word has spread about the tasty Beef Wellington and Norwegian salmon. White walls and colourful prints create a relaxing ambience. Buffet lunch is served on Sundays.

Mikulka's Pizzeria

Benediktská 16. **Map** 4 D3.
231 57 27. **Open** 11:30am–11:30pm daily. AE, V.

The first real pizzeria in Prague after the revolution, Mikulka's established its reputation early and has worked hard to retain it. Pizzas and huge bowls of pasta keep the restaurant full. At first it was only popular with the foreign community, so it is a tribute to the quality of the food and low prices that you now meet as many Czechs here as foreigners. Finding space can be difficult, but the wait is never long.

Valentin

Valentinská 9. **Map** 3 B3. 26 02 94.
Open 10am–10pm daily.

This modern restaurant calls itself a "day bar". While there is a complete selection of alcohol, most people come for the food or just coffee. The ultra-modern interior features black and white triangles, from the tiled floor, to the wood on the walls, to the lights. As well as chicken breasts with mushrooms and cream, and pepper steak, there are several vegetarian options.

Shalom

Maiselova 18. **Map** 3 B3.
24 81 09 29. **Open** noon–4pm, 6–9pm Sun–Fri.

Prague's only kosher restaurant is located in the old Jewish Town Hall community centre. It is a grand room with beautifully moulded ceilings and walls and crystal chandeliers. Set menus are available for lunch and dinner (drinks are extra) with three entrées

to choose from, usually meat (roast beef), chicken, and fish (trout with almonds). On Jewish holidays the restaurant hosts special functions. Book well ahead for dinner.

U Golema
AT THE GOLEM

Maiselova 8. **Map** 3 B3. 232 81 65.
Open 11am–10pm Mon–Fri.
AE, DC, MC, V, JCB, EC.

Named after Rabbi Löw's creation, the myth of the Golem (see p88), this restaurant caters mainly for tourists, although the non-English speaking staff would seem to indicate otherwise. Fish, poultry and Czech specialities are served in two small, cosy rooms, or one larger, more traditional dining room. There are fixed-price menus.

U Červeného kola
AT THE RED WHEEL

Anežská 2. **Map** 3 C2. 24 81 11 18.
Open 11am–3pm, 5–11pm daily.
AE, DC, MC, V, JCB.

Though hard to find, this elegant restaurant, behind the cloister of St Agnes's (see pp92–3), is worth the search. Red carpets and upholstered seats provide the setting for finely laid tables and antique clocks. Steaks predominate – the speciality is with garlic. A few chicken and fish dishes complete the offerings. There is a also garden room.

U Staré Synagogy
AT THE OLD SYNAGOGUE

Pařížská 17. **Map** 3 B3.
231 85 52/231 20 42. **Open**
11:30am–midnight daily.
AE, DC, MC, V, JCB.

Reconstructed after the Velvet Revolution, this place looks new, though the intention was to create an old, elegant eatery. The good service and food make it ideal for dinner. The menu is traditional Czech. The svíčková (beef in cream sauce) and goulash are delicious. There are fixed-price lunch menus.

Peklo
HELL

Strahovské nádvoří 1. **Map** 1 B4.
53 02 15/53 32 77. **Open**
7pm–4am daily. AE, V.

In the catacombs below Strahov Monastery (see pp120–21), Peklo is among Prague's most unusual

restaurants. The two caves which it occupies are filled with antique chairs and tables. Italian and Czech dishes are on offer, but as the ownership is Italian, pasta or steak are better choices than pork.

U Labutí
AT THE SWANS

Hradčanské náměstí 11. **Map** 1 C3.
53 69 62. **Open** noon–3pm & 7–11pm daily.

This establishment, which prides itself on being more of a club than a restaurant, offers a comfortable setting with antique tables and chairs. The cuisine is traditional Czech, with international dishes, including steak and chicken.

Café Savoy

Vítězná 1. **Map** 2 E5. 53 97 96.
Open 9am–11pm daily.
AE, V.

This popular café is stunningly decorated with restored murals. The attentive waiters and mellow music make it comfortably classy, if a little pricey. Although the food selection is small, the hors d'oeuvres alone are worth the trip.

U Schnellů
AT THE SCHNELL'S

Tomášská 2. **Map** 2 E3.
53 20 04/855 51 79.
Open 11am–11pm daily.

Attentive staff and delicious food make this restaurant worth a visit. Entrées are reasonably priced, the Pilsner Urquell beer is well chilled, and the nearby St Thomas's Church provides an attractive backdrop.

David

Tržiště 21. **Map** 2 D3.
53 93 25. **Open** noon–3pm, 6–11pm daily. AE, V.

Based near the American embassy, David caters for diplomats and business people. The modern art and classical music create a sophisticated atmosphere. The sliced, grilled lamb shank is a house speciality, and the chicken with fruit sauce is another favourite.

Italia

Nerudova 17. **Map** 2 D3. 53 03 86.
Open 9am–11pm daily.

Pizza, pasta, Italian desserts and coffees are served here in a bright, clean environment. Although it is nothing spectacular, it is a nice place to drop into after a day spent exploring the Castle or Little Quarter.

For key to symbols see p191

Nebozízek
LITTLE AUGER

Petřínské sady 411. **Map** 2 D5.
[53 79 05. **Open** 11am–6pm,
7–11pm daily. 🔲 🍴 AE, DC, MC, V,
JCB. Ⓚ Ⓚ Ⓚ

The view of Prague from this
restaurant, which takes its name
from the winding path up Petřín
Hill (*see p141*), is fantastic. In
spring and summer the outdoor
patio is very popular. Inside, the
place is cosy and elegant. The
menu is wide-ranging, offering
seafood, Chinese and Czech
dishes, steaks and more. To be
certain of a table, make your
reservation four days in advance.

U Sv. Tomáše
AT ST THOMAS'S

Letenská 12. **Map** 2 F3. [53 16 32.
Open 11:30am–11pm daily. 🎵 🔲
🍴 AE. Ⓚ Ⓚ Ⓚ (*See p125.*)

This combination of beer hall and
restaurant falls between a traditional
Czech eatery and a tropical haven.
An enclosed outdoor patio and
live music at night help to create a
festive atmosphere. Grilled meats
are the speciality. It is a real find.

Florianův Dvůr
FLORIAN'S YARD

Újezd 16. **Map** 2 E5. [53 05 02.
Open noon–midnight daily. 🍴 AE,
DC, JCB, MC, V. Ⓚ Ⓚ Ⓚ Ⓚ

The soft pastel interior of this fish
and seafood restaurant, with its
new Art Deco motifs and modern
stained-glass windows, would not
look out of place in New York or
Paris. The nouvelle cuisine-sized
portions of fish (and a little game)
might leave some hungry, but the
taste and freshness of these dishes
never disappoint. Some claim the
toilets shake to the vibrations of
the nearby Club Borát (*see p215*).

U Malířů
AT THE PAINTER'S

Maltézské náměstí 11. **Map** 2 E4.
[24 51 02 69. **Open** 7pm–
midnight daily. 🍴 🍴 AE, JCB, DC,
MC, V, JCB. Ⓚ Ⓚ Ⓚ Ⓚ

Notorious as the Czech Republic's
most expensive restaurant, U Malířů
is also the only authentic French
gastronomic restaurant in the
country. The French chef Daniel
Mutel uses only the freshest
ingredients, brought in twice a
week from France, to concoct such
original dishes as roasted young
pigeon in puff pastry and rack of
lamb. There are also traditional
French delicacies, including duck
liver pâté, and the restaurant will
happily prepare a dish for those

with special requirements. Bread is
baked on the premises, and home-
made sorbets are another speciality.
The restaurant was founded in 1543
and the beautiful ceilings were first
painted many centuries ago. All in
all, the ambience is romantic,
historical and beautiful with Gothic
windows and elegant table settings.

U Modré kachničky
AT THE BLUE DUCKLING

Nebovidská 6. **Map** 2 E4.
[53 97 51. **Open** noon–4pm,
6:30–11:30pm daily. ★
🍴 AE, DC, V. Ⓚ Ⓚ Ⓚ Ⓚ

On a quiet street in the Little
Quarter, this restaurant reflects the
intimate, romantic and charming
nature of this part of town. Hand-
painted walls boast Prague's best
display of modern Art Nouveau.
The restaurant has three rooms,
each with its own fabulous mural,
and each more stunning than the
last. Beautiful wooden antiques
combine with framed prints to add
an eclectic feel. The fare is strictly
game and meat, and vegetarian
diners will be disappointed, but
those who love duck, boar, veal,
venison and salmon are guaranteed
to enjoy the fresh, succulent
flavours and generous portions.

U Tří pštrosů
AT THE THREE OSTRICHES

Dražického náměstí 12. **Map** 2 E3.
[24 51 07 79. **Open** noon–3pm,
6–11pm daily. 🍴 DC, JCB. Ⓚ Ⓚ Ⓚ Ⓚ

Plants and flowers adorn the walls
of the two small, elegant dining
rooms on the ground floor of the
hotel of the same name (*see p134
& p188*). Situated at the base of
Charles Bridge, it boasts a good
selection of Czech and international
fare, although its pricey offerings
appear to be predominantly Czech
and central European, with carp,
goulash and various beef dishes
available.

Valdštejnská hospoda
WALDSTEIN INN

Tomášská 16. **Map** 2 E3. [53 61 95.
Open 11:30am–11:30pm daily.
🍴 AE, V. Ⓚ Ⓚ Ⓚ

A favourite with the staff of the
British embassy, this was once a
typical local pub, but it has been
re-vamped to highlight some of
the original architectural features
of the 15th-century building. The
present-day finery combines with
the older vaulted ceilings and
exposed stonework to create an
old-world atmosphere in which
you can enjoy all the traditional
Czech favourites as well as an
assortment of international dishes.

Hotel Evropa Café
HOTEL EUROPA CAFE

Václavské náměstí 25. **Map** 4 D5.
[24 22 81 17. **Open** 7am–midnight
daily. 🍴 AE, DC, MC, JCB. Ⓚ
(*See p146.*)

With its large windows facing onto
Wenceslas Square, this is a good
place to enjoy a cup of coffee and
a bite to eat while watching people
stroll by. The café is part of the
larger Hotel Evropa restaurant, a
grand old structure that has seen
better days. The price of a snack
or drink reflect its tourist clientele.

Kmotra
GODMOTHER

V jirchářích 12. **Map** 5 B1. [24 91
58 09. **Open** 11am–1am daily. Ⓚ

This basement pizzeria became an
overnight success by following a
simple recipe: large, tasty pizzas
at cheap prices. Czech students,
travellers, couples and business
people all rub elbows within the
whitewashed, vaulted rooms.

Kavárna Velryba
CAFE WHALE

Opatovická 24. **Map** 5 B1. [24 91
23 91. **Open** 11am–2am daily. Ⓚ

This subterranean café-cum-
restaurant is a trendy hangout for
Prague's young. It has a lively,
comfortable atmosphere as well as
good cheap food. A new addition
are the televisions on the walls. The
food is basic, including chicken
breast sandwiches, beefburgers,
fried mushrooms, lentil dishes and
decent salads. It tends to get very
smoky and the front door is likely
to be locked when it gets too
crowded inside, but the place
boasts the largest whisky selection
in Prague. Though the café is open
late, the kitchen closes at 11pm.

Vltava

Rašínovo nábřeží. **Map** 5 A2.
[29 49 64. **Open** 11am–10pm
daily. 🔲 Ⓚ

Located on the bank of the Vltava
river, the outdoor patio of this
restaurant provides a wonderful
setting during the warmer months
to view Prague Castle and watch
the tour boat activity on the river.
When it is too cold to sit outside,
the small restaurant is cosy and
warm. It is ostensibly a fish
restaurant (the speciality being
whole trout baked with garlic) and
there is a wonderful fish soup, but
the menu covers a great deal of
ground and also includes Chinese
food, chicken, pork and steak.

FX Café

Bělehradská 120. **Map** 6 E2.
[25 69 98. **Open** 11:30am–5am
daily. **V** (K)(K)

This small, vegetarian café is
popular with Czechs and foreigners.
It is connected to the nightclub
Radost FX (see p215) and people
tend to stop and eat before and
after clubbing. As a result, getting
a table can be difficult, especially
during the evenings. The menu
includes salads, fresh soup,
sandwiches (including marinated
tofu and humous in pitta bread),
vegetarian pizzas, nachos and
delicious home-made pastries.

Na Rybárně
FISH RESTAURANT

Gorazdova 17. **Map** 5 A3. [29 97
95. **Open** noon–midnight daily.
(S) AE, DC, MC, JCB. (K)(K)

The nautical decor makes it clear
that this restaurant specializes in
fish. In the front room a dramatic
mural of surging sea covers one
wall. The garlic soup is so strong
that it should only be eaten with
friends. Grilled or fried carp and
trout are offered, and if you order
the latter, the waiter brings a tray
of fish to your table so you can
choose the size of your meal.
Steaks and Chinese food are also
available. President Václav Havel
used to live right around the
corner, and this restaurant is still
one of his favourite haunts.

Pod Křídlem
UNDER THE WING

Voršilská 10. **Map** 3 B5. [24 91 23 77/
24 95 17 41. **Open** 11:30am–2am
daily. 🎵 (S) AE, DC, MC, V, JCB.
(K)(K)(K)

Shiny, bright and white, this seems
more like an international bistro
than an ethnic eatery. But the
decor and pianist create an entirely
enjoyable atmosphere. Try the
roast duck or pork dumplings and
sauerkraut. Open until 2am, unusual
in Prague, this bistro is a popular
venue after an evening at the
National Theatre (see pp156–7) –
only a few minutes' walk away.

U Čížků

Karlovo náměstí 34. **Map** 5 B2.
[29 88 91. **Open** noon–3:30pm,
5–10pm daily. (S) AE, MC, V.
(K)(K)(K)

Designed in the style of a typical
Bohemian farmhouse, and serving
the most traditional Czech foods,
U Čížků provides an opportunity
to get a taste of Czech cuisine and
culture at the same time. Try the
red cabbage soup with sausage, or

if you're very hungry, go for the
assortment dish with two kinds of
pork, duck, sausage, two types of
dumplings and two varieties of
sauerkraut. Combined with its low
prices, all the above features make
the restaurant popular with large
tour groups, so book early.

U Kalicha
AT THE CHALICE

Na bojišti 12–14. **Map** 6 D2.
[29 07 01/29 19 45. **Open** 11am–
3pm, 5–11pm daily. **V** 🎵 (S) AE,
DC, V, JCB. (K)(K)(K) (see p154)

From selections like beefsteak à la
Lieutenant Lukáš to cartooned walls,
practically everything in here will
make you feel part of the famous
Czech novel *The Good Soldier
Švejk*, the theme on which the
restaurant is based. Traditional
Czech cuisine is available at
inflated prices, and the in-house
souvenir shop, selling everything
from Švejk T-shirts and beer steins
to postcards discourages the
locals from coming in.

Hotel Evropa
HOTEL EUROPA

Václavské náměstí 25. **Map** 4 D5.
[24 22 81 17. **Open** 11am–3pm,
6–11:30pm daily. 🍴 (K)(K)(K)(K)
(See p146.)

The gorgeous Art Nouveau dining
room in this hotel provides a turn-
of-the-century dining experience.
When you walk in, you are struck
by the large marble mantelpiece
with built-in clock at the far end
of the room and the stained-glass
image of Prague Castle above. The
inlaid, panelled-wood walls are
gilded, and large intricate mirrors
enhance the decorative effect. The
two fixed-price menus offer
traditional Czech fare, including
goulash, duck, and *svíčková*, (beef
in cream sauce), and "international"
dishes such as steak, pork and
chicken. Both menus include an
aperitif, appetizers, soup, main
course and dessert.

Premiera

V jirchářích 6. **Map** 5 B1.
[24 91 56 72. **Open** 6pm–midnight.
🍴 🎵 (S) AE, MC, V. (K)(K)(K)(K)

Antique, Art Deco furniture, modern
art and a pianist combine to give
this seafood restaurant an elegant,
yet casual ambience. There are à
la carte options as well as three
set menus at different prices. This
is the only restaurant in Prague
where you can be served with
swordfish and shark. The salmon
with capers is delicious, as is the
entire menu, from the tasty prawn
rice appetizer to a fine lobster
entrée wrapped in beef.

Akropolis

Kubelíkova 27. [27 21 84. **Open**
noon–11pm daily. **V** (K)

This trendy café is popular with
young Czech intellectuals. Despite
the name, there are no classical
Greek features. Instead, there is a
canoe hanging from the ceiling,
and there are some enclosed sand
paintings. The reasonably diverse
menu portions are better than in
similar places. Try the soup, then
choose from, among other items,
fried cheese, Chinese stir fry or
chicken. Tap beer and wine are
on offer, as is absinthe.

The Globe
Bookstore Café

Janovského 14. **Open** 10am–midnight
daily. (K)

Cheap, good food, a great library
of English-language books and a
charming atmosphere keep the
expatriates coming back to this
café. The limited menu consists
mainly of sandwiches, bagels,
pasta and Greek salads, but the
comfortable armchairs and latest
editions of English-language
magazines make it very popular.

Na Slamníku
ON THE STRAW MATTRESS

Wolkerova 12. [32 85 66.
Open 3pm–midnight daily. (K)

The preparation and presentation
of the food here is simple, in
keeping with the decor and
atmosphere of a typical 300-year-
old Czech pub. Apart from the
pool table in the back "salon", it
has remained untouched, and the
Czech treats like pan-fried pork
are the tasty staples. One of the
best deals in town.

U Koleje
AT THE COLLEGE

Slavíkova 24. [627 41 63.
Open 11am–11pm daily. (K)

Floral tablecloths and low lamps
hanging over each table give this
former pub a cheerful but quiet,
intimate feel. Named after a student
dormitory, the restaurant features
a menu that is not as international
as its clientele. Yet for unpretentious
cooking at reasonable prices U
Koleje has few equals. The daily
soup specials are always good, and
for a treat try the spicy pork rolled
in a potato pancake. The menu is
geared towards meat-eaters, but a
few fish dishes are also offered.

U Tří hrochů
AT THE THREE RHINOS

Bubenečská 8. **(** 32 52 56.
Open 11:30am–10pm Mon–Fri,
5–10pm Sat & Sun. **V** 🏧 ⓚ

Though the atmosphere isn't great,
this restaurant offers courteous,
service and pizzas with a good
choice of toppings. It is mainly
frequented by locals, and its close
proximity to Prague's main
launderette makes it an excellent
place to visit between cycles.
Lentil and bean salads are on
offer, and bread lovers should not
miss the delicious home-made
cheese rolls, served piping hot
straight from the oven.

Elite

Korunni 1. **Map** 6 F2. **(** 25 46 32.
Open 11am–11pm daily. ⓚⓚ

Don't let the size of this restaurant
put you off. At one time, it used to
be the municipal house for its
district, but in the cavernous main
room you can now find the most
affordable – and the best – pizzas
and pasta. The winter-green walls,
and cartoon-like paintings do not
seem to be the most obvious
setting for Italian food, but the
good cooking defies the decor.
Czech cuisine is also available, as
is a large selection of ice cream.
For a more intimate experience,
ask to be given a table on the
mezzanine floor, where you can
marvel at the intricate century-old
moulding and not feel as if you
are dining in an aeroplane hangar.

Quido

Kubelíkova 22. **(** 27 09 50.
Open 11:30am–11pm daily.
🏧 AE, V. ⓚⓚ

The rustic wooden tables, hanging
plants and tasteful reproduction
paintings adorning the walls lend
this superb restaurant a pleasant,
country-kitchen atmosphere. The
wide choice of menu offers a
range of traditional Czech
specialities as well as many other
dishes. From steak stuffed with
blue cheese and olives smothered
in garlic butter, to chicken fillets
cooked with ham and mushrooms
in soy sauce, the portions are
ample and taste delicious.

U Mikuláše Dačického

Viktora Huga 2. **(** 54 93 12.
Open noon–1am Mon–Fri,
6pm–1am Sat. ⓚⓚ

As a token of appreciation, this
restaurant was decorated by set-
designers from the Barandov film
studios during the 1930s. They
chose a medieval motif, which

provides a courtly ambience.
Dark-stained panelled walls, large
wooden tables, chairs upholstered
in red leather, and murals depicting
noblemen, knights and a host of
courtesans feasting, make the
restaurant a unique place to eat in.
The food portions are large, and
although the menu is similar to
that found in other restaurants, the
food is prepared with more care.
The house speciality is a shish
kebab which consists of mixed
meats and vegetables, and while
some rave about the fish dishes,
they can vary in quality.

U Cedru
AT THE CEDAR

Na hutich 13. **(** 312 29 74.
Open 11am–11pm daily. **V** ★
🏧 AE, DC, MC, V, JCB. ⓚⓚⓚ

Although it is situated out of the
centre of town, this restaurant is
easily accessible by metro, and it
is well worth the trip. *Humous*
(chickpea dip), *felafel* (chickpea
balls), *baba ganuj* (aubergine dip),
stuffed vine leaves and other
staple Lebanese favourites are
served. Most people who eat here
do not even order a main course:
they find that a large selection of
appetizers (all served with pitta
bread) is usually more than
enough. The high quality of the
food and its consistent freshness
have turned the place into a hot
spot for the foreign community.
The restaurant is small, with a
decor that does not in any way
reflect the ethnic nature of its
menu, and, as it fills up quickly,
reservations are strongly
recommended.

U Sloupu
AT THE PILLAR

Lucemburská 11. **(** 27 14 57.
Open 11am–3pm, 5–11pm daily.
🍴 🏧 AE. ⓚⓚⓚ

Located on a quiet street outside
the city centre, this dignified
restaurant serves traditional Czech
meals in a modern Art Deco-style
environment. While favourites such
as fried carp and *svíčková* (beef
with a cream sauce) are all
available à la carte, there is also a
fixed-price menu, and this is
recommended for those who are
unfamiliar with Czech fare.

U Zlatého rožně
AT THE GOLDEN SPIT

Československé armády 22.
(24 31 11 61. **Open** 11am–12pm
daily. 🏧 AE, V, MC. ⓚⓚⓚ

Although this is billed as an
Icelandic fish restaurant, U Zlatého
rožně offers food from many
different culinary traditions, which

include Chinese and Czech fare,
steaks, chicken and a range of
international dishes. From a tasty
Chinese chicken and shrimp dish
to delicious plaice in cheese sauce,
all the food is both unusual and
imaginative. The decor in this
exclusive new restaurant, to be
found in the centre of ambassador-
land, is original, consisting of an
eclectic mixture of objects,
including a giant stuffed Scottish
salmon and, by contrast, an
attractive Art Deco screen.

Zlatý Drak
GOLDEN DRAGON

Anglická 6. **Map** 6 E2.
(24 21 81 54. **Open** 11:30am–3pm,
6–10pm daily. **V** 🏧 AE, DC, MC, V.
ⓚⓚⓚ

Unlike other Chinese restaurants
in Prague, Zlatý Drak underplays
the Chinese theme, and its glossy
atmosphere is enhanced by large
wall mirrors. This is the best
Chinese restaurant to be found in
town, although the portions are so
small that you might decide to
order an additional main course.
The dishes range from tofu to
duck, and there is also a variety of
vegetarian options on offer.

Principe

Anglická 23. **Map** 6 E2.
(25 96 14. **Open** noon–3pm,
6–10pm daily. 🍷 🏧 AE.
ⓚⓚⓚ

A chef from Florence, together
with freshly imported Italian
ingredients, combine to make this
authentic restaurant a number one
spot for the foreign business
community, despite prices that are
substantially higher than in other
restaurants. The calming, pastel-
coloured interior is a perfect
setting for many delicious Italian
favourites, ranging from spaghetti
al pesto to lasagne, along with
many fine Italian wines.

Schwaigerovy Sady
SCHWAIGEROV GARDENS

Schwaigerova 3. **(** 32 00 05.
Open 7am–10pm daily. 🍴 🍷
🏧 AE, DC, MC, V. ⓚⓚⓚ

Traditional French cuisine and an
extensive menu are on offer in this
impressive restaurant, where steak,
lobster and chicken are authenti-
cally prepared by the French
chefs. The speciality of the house
is rabbit Flemish-style, which is
cooked in black beer, accompanied
by potatoes and apple compote.
Although the interior is fancy, the
atmosphere is relaxed. There are
daily fixed-price menus.

Pubs, Beer Halls and Bars

PUBS IN PRAGUE ARE EITHER drinking pubs, which usually serve food as well; traditional beer halls, large enterprises dedicated to the mass consumption of beer; or pubs where people go mainly to eat. *Hostinec* and *hospoda* indicate a pub with food, whereas a *pivnice* serves only beer, but over time the distinctions have faded. Bars usually serve beer as well as wine and spirits. Most of them open at 10 or 11am and close at 10pm. Don't wait to be seated – just look for a free chair. If you sit at an empty table, don't be surprised if others join you. A waiter will bring more beer as you finish, until you say otherwise. Remember that imported spirits can be expensive.

TRADITIONAL PUBS AND BEER HALLS

THERE ARE a variety of drinking establishments in Prague, to suit all tastes. Recommended for the brave, **U Zlatého tygra** is *the* loud Czech literati pub, wall-to-wall with (mostly male) regulars. **U Fleků** has brewed its unique dark beer, Flekovské, since 1499. For authenticity, and Budvar, try **U Medvídků**, which is not too far away from the National Theatre (*see pp156–7*) and Old Town Square, or **Krušovická pivnice**, an airy local pub serving some food. The scaffolding-clad **U Vejvodů** looks the worse for four centuries' wear, but the interior is new and it also boasts a non-smoking room. The **Hospoda u Goldexu** shares its kitchen with a restaurant, so the food is good. Although this is seldom visited by out-of-towners, it is very popular with ex-pats. In the Castle area, **U Kocoura** most resembles a traditional pub, serving Prazdroj beer and fried cheese, while **Vinárna U Čerta** is more upmarket. A spacious former chapel, **U Betlémské kaple** serves a selection of wholesome Czech food and cold beer from Velké Popovické. The homely **U Králova dvora**, off the Celetná thoroughfare, also offers plenty of seating.

THEME BARS

A RECENT NOVELTY is the theme bar with a foreign atmosphere. The would-be English **John Bull Pub** is pleasant and affordable. The food, big on dumplings and meat, tastes better washed down with a pint of John Bull bitter. With the Municipal House concert hall a block away (*see p214*), it is a good pre-concert venue. The secret of **Jo's Bar** is a US clientele and good Mexican food. The margaritas are excellent and Sunday brunch very popular. Check the back room if it's crowded elsewhere. The **Nike Sports Bar** is for sports enthusiasts. TVs show the latest action, there is a shoe shop, and the salads, burgers and snacks are good.

CAFÉ SOCIETY

THE CITY IS also embedded in café society, ranging from old-fashioned smoky joints to cafés within bookstores, boutiques and billiard halls. Some are restaurants, others focus on drinking (see listings), but all serve alcohol. **Lávka** has the finest setting in the city. Situated at the foot of Charles Bridge, it offers a spectacular view of the Castle. Despite the menu, it is more a place to see and be seen, like **Dolce Vita**, where Prague's models meet. In contrast, **U Zeleného Čaje** is a Zen-like tea house with more than 80 varieties of tea. At night, head for the **Bunkr Café**, which buzzes with trendy clubbers.

DIRECTORY

Bunkr Café
Ve smečkách 30.
Map 6 D1.

Dolce Vita
Široká 15.
Map 3 B3.
(232 91 92.

Jo's Bar
Malostranské náměstí 7.
Map 2 E3.

John Bull Pub
Senovážné náměstí 8.
Map 4 E4.
(24 22 60 05.

Krušovická pivnice
Široká 20.
Map 3 B3.
(42 64 16.

Lávka
Novotného lávka 1.
Map 3 A4.
(24 21 47 97.

Nike Sports Bar
Ve smečkách 30.
Map 6 D1.
(24 19 62 55.

Hospoda u Goldexu
Vinohradská 25.
Map 6 E1.
(24 21 18 06.

U Betlémské kaple
Betlemské náměstí 2.
Map 3 B4.
(24 21 18 79.

U Fleků
Křemencova 11.
Map 5 B1.
(24 91 51 18.

U Kocoura
Nerudova 24. **Map** 2 D3.
(53 89 62.

U Králova dvora
U prašné 3. **Map** 4 D3.
(232 20 82/ 282 11 71/ 232 11 83.

U Medvídků
Na Perštýně 7. **Map** 3 B5.
(24 22 09 03.

U Pinkasů
Jungmannovo náměstí
15. **Map** 3 C5.
(24 22 29 65.

U Vejvodů
Jilská 4. **Map** 3 B4.
(24 21 05 91.

U Zeleného Čaje
Nerudova 19. **Map** 2 D3.
(53 26 83.

U Zlatého tygra
Husova 17. **Map** 3 B4.
(24 22 90 20.

Vinárna U Čerta
Nerudova 4. **Map** 2 D3.
(53 09 75.

SHOPS AND MARKETS

FOLLOWING THE TRANSITION to a market economy, and the breaking down of barriers between the West and East, the range of goods available in Prague's shops has increased enormously. A number of leading US and West European firms have established businesses in the city, and the quality of goods manufactured in the Czech Republic has improved considerably. Most of Prague's best shops are conveniently located in the city centre, especially in and around

Bohemian crystal

Wenceslas Square. Many of these areas have been pedestrianized, making for leisurely window-shopping, although they can get rather crowded. There are a number of department stores which sell an eclectic range of Czech and Western items. For a different shopping experience, the few traditional markets in the city offer everything from fresh fruit and vegetables to imported Russian caviar, toys, clothes, furniture, Czech crafts, electrical spare parts and even second-hand cars.

OPENING HOURS

MOST OF PRAGUE'S shops are open from 8am to 6pm Monday to Friday and until 1pm on Saturdays. However, they are often more flexible than that, as many shops rely almost entirely on tourists for their trade. The more expensive gift shops have adapted their opening hours to the needs of their Western customers and often do not open until 10am. They also close much later in the evening.

Food stores open earlier, most of them at 6am – reflecting the early working day of many locals – and close at around 7pm. Most shops also take a break for lunch, which can vary from any time between noon and 3pm. Department stores and the big shopping centres also open early but tend to close later, often around 8pm.

All the shops are at their most crowded on Saturdays and for stress-free shopping it's often better to wander around the shops during the week. Prague's markets are generally open early every morning weekday but have varied closing times.

One of the many antique shops in Bridge Street in the Little Quarter

HOW TO PAY

YOU WILL FIND that most staple goods, such as food, are much cheaper than comparable items in the West. However, with more multi-nationals, such as Benetton, moving into the city, prices are slowly starting to rise.

Never assume you can pay by credit card. The major ones (see p222) are often only accepted in the larger, more tourist-orientated shops and a very few department stores. Most shops will only accept payment in Czech crowns. Ignore any requests, polite or otherwise, to pay for your goods using Pounds Sterling, American Dollars or with German Marks, as

this is now illegal. The total price should always include Value Added Tax (this is 5 or 23% of the total price, depending on what is being sold), although all food is exempt from this. There is no tax-free shopping in Prague.

SALES AND BARGAINS

FOLLOWING THE examples of the newly arrived Western stores, sales are becoming more popular. As a result, it is now quite normal for clothes to be sold off cheaper at the end of each season. There is also an increasing number of post-Christmas sales in the shops found around Old Town Square, Wenceslas Square, Na příkopě and 28. října.

If you want fresh vegetables, fruit, meat or other perishable goods, buy them at the beginning of the day, when the best quality goods are still on sale. There is no point in

A set of Russian dolls available from one of the many street stalls

waiting till the end of the day in the hope of getting bargains, as is the case in Western shops that reduce prices to get rid of perishable items.

DEPARTMENT STORES

THE WIDEST selection of goods can be found in the large, modern department stores. There are about ten at present, although more are planned for the future.

The best-known and most frequently visited department store, **Kotva** (The Anchor), lies in the centre of the city. It was built in 1975 and its four storeys offer a wide range of Western goods, particularly fashion and electronics, with the bonus of an underground car park. But compared to many Western department stores, Kotva, along with its competitors, has a smaller selection of goods than you may be accustomed to – with the exception of food such as smoked meats, for example. Prices charged for some of the more luxurious items on sale, such as famous perfumes, can often be equivalent to the Western ones.

Another popular store is the American **K Mart**. This was built in 1975 and has a range of general consumer items. The city's oldest department store is **Bílá Labut'** (The White Swan) in Na poříčí. It was opened shortly before the occupation of Czechoslovakia in 1939 and was the first building in Prague to have an escalator. It has since been refurbished, and now

Two figurines decorate the façade of a chemist in the Old Town

specializes in furniture and interior accessories. **Dětský dům** (The Children's House) is a relatively small department store in Na příkopě, which, as the name suggests, sells almost anything that a child could want. **Krone** also supplies a good range of products at its small store.

In most supermarkets you are not allowed to go through the turnstiles unless you have a supermarket basket or trolley, and for these you need to queue behind each check-out counter. This system is to make sure the store does not become overcrowded.

MARKETS

PRAGUE'S MARKETS offer a vast range of goods in a friendly atmosphere where bargaining is all part of the fun. The largest market in the city, **Prague Market**, is in Holešovice. It was converted

from a former slaughter-house. The market now sells fresh fruit and vegetables, all kinds of poultry as well as fish, textiles, flowers, electronics and even second-hand cars and vehicle parts. These are all sold in several large halls and in outdoor stalls. The market is generally open from Monday to Friday, 6am to 5pm. In Havelská, right in the centre of the city, is the small **Havel Market**, which mainly sells fresh fruit and vegetables. **Vinohrady Market** has been recently reopened, following extensive modernization. Other well-known markets in Prague include **Prague Flea Market**, **Smíchov Market** and a small one in the street V kotcích. Remember that some of the goods sold at all these markets, especially the mass of clothes and shoes, can be of very poor quality.

STREET STALLS

HUNDREDS OF street stalls and wandering street vendors appear during the summer around Charles Bridge, the Old Castle Steps, Na příkopě and Old Town Square. Usually run by young Czechs, they sell a huge variety of goods. Most stalls have handmade items such as jewellery, pottery, carved wooden toys, puppets, Russian dolls, models of Prague's houses, and Czech crafts. Recently many have started to sell Communist and Soviet memorabilia such as medals, watches, caps and uniforms.

A second-hand bookshop in Karlova Street

What to Buy in Prague

THE INCREASINGLY LARGE selection of goods available in Prague's shops means that everyday items, such as food, books, camera film and toiletries are easily available, and you may find that imported clothing is a better buy here. Prague's more traditional products, such as Bohemian crystal, china, wooden toys and antiques make great souvenirs, and there are still some real bargains to be picked up. Increasingly popular are the more unusual goods which are sold by many of Prague's street vendors. These include Soviet army medals, Red Army uniforms, Russian dolls, wooden puppets, ceramics and a wide selection of jewellery. In general, prices are far lower than in the West.

GLASS AND CHINA

BOHEMIAN GLASS and china have always been ranked among the finest in the world. From huge, decorative vases to delicate glass figures, the vast selection of glass and china items for sale is daunting.

Crystal, glass, and china can be quite different depending on where they are made. Some of the best glass and china in Bohemia is produced at the Moser glassworks at Karlovy Vary and sold at the **Karlovy Vary China** shop and **Moser**. The large Crystalex glassworks at Nový Bor and Poděbrady produce some of the most highly-decorated glass, sold at **Crystal**. Other shops which sell a good selection of glass and china include **Bohemia Crystal, Dana-Bohemia, Glass-China** and **Glass**.

However, prices are starting to reflect the increasing popularity of a number of the rarer items and bargains are harder to find. Remember that many of the modern pieces are just as lovely and much cheaper. Because of the fragile nature of the goods, many shops will pack anything you buy there. But if you go for a more expensive piece, it is worth looking into insurance before you leave Prague.

ANTIQUE SHOPS

ANTIQUES IN PRAGUE have always been considered a good buy, as prices are still generally lower than in the West. Antique shops that are well worth a look at include; **At the Golden Cross**,

Vadamo Galerie Bohemia, Bohemia Aventis and **Galerie Lukas**. **Antique Clocks** sells exactly what it says and **Military Antiques** is a haven for all army fanatics. For goods over Kč1,000, check with the shop whether you will need a licence to export them. However, watch out for an increasing number of fakes appearing on the market.

TRADITIONAL CRAFTS

THE TRADITIONAL manufacture of high-quality and hand-crafted goods still survives. The variety of the products available in the shops – hand-woven carpets, wooden toys, table mats, beautifully-painted Easter eggs, baskets, figurines in folk costumes, and ceramics – are all based on Czech and Moravian folk crafts and then enriched with modern elements. You can buy them from many market stalls as well as a fair number of shops.

One of the best shops is **The Beautiful Room**, which has a very good selection of folk art and crafts. For beautifully-made figurines, it's worth visiting **Folk Figurines** in Železná Street, and for a huge choice of hand-carved toys, try **Folk Art Products**.

Other shops which sell arts and crafts include **Gifts** and **Albatros**. A number of street vendors – around Old Town Square, for instance – also sell a range of these goods as well as other handmade items which include jewellery, wooden ornaments and puppets.

BOOKS

THERE ARE numerous book-shops in Prague, but most books sold are in Czech. Foreign-language books are available, but only in specialist bookshops in the city centre.

One of the main bookshops is **Foreign Literature**. Here you'll find a range of English-language books (including Czech works which have been translated into English) as well as a fair number of German and French editions. Maps and guides to Prague in English can be bought at **Růžička's Bookshop**. Other specialist bookshops include **Orbis**, **Slavonic Book House**, **Arbes Bookshop**, **Melantrich**, **Fišer's Bookshop** and **Albatros**, which sells child-ren's books. Prague also has second-hand bookshops – look in Golden Lane and Karlova Street – which stock some English-language books, and they all offer hours of enjoyable browsing.

FOOD AND DELICATESSENS

PRAGUE'S SUPERMARKETS are well stocked with the basic foodstuffs (see p207). But for something special, there are a few delicatessens. **Pronto Supermarket** is a small shop with meat and fish counters. Specialist food shops, which sell smoked sausage, cheeses and other local delicacies, include **Delicacies**, **Jan Paukert** and **Milk Delicacies**, which sells dairy products. For freshly-baked bread visit the bakers around Wenceslas Square and Mostecká Street. **Bakery Bonal** sells a good selection of patisseries.

PHARMACIES

MOST PHARMACIES in Prague stock all modern medicines, but a prescription from a Czech doctor is needed to buy them. Check listings for addresses (see directory for 24-hour pharmacies). Toiletries can be bought at a drugstore.

DIRECTORY

DEPARTMENT STORES

Anchor
KOTVA
Náměstí Republiky 8.
Map 4 D3.
24 80 11 11.

Children's House
DĚTSKÝ DŮM
Na příkopě 15. **Map** 3 C4.
24 21 60 73.

K Mart
K MART
Národní 26. **Map** 3 B5.
24 22 79 71.

Krone
Václavské náměstí 21.
Map 4 D5.
24 23 04 77.

White Swan
BÍLÁ LABUŤ
Na poříčí 23.
Map 4 D3.
24 81 13 64.

MARKETS

Havel Market
Havelské náměstí.
Map 3 C4.

Prague Flea Market
PRAŽSKÁ BURZA
Výstavištěm (Exhibition Ground).

Prague Market
Bubenské nábřeží 306.
Prague 7.
80 05 92.

Smíchov Market
Náměstí 14. října 15.
Map 3 C4.
24 51 14 46.

Vinohrady Market
Vinohradská 50. **Map** 6 F1.
24 23 31 25.

GLASS AND CHINA

Bohemia Crystal
ČESKÝ KŘIŠTÁL
Národní 19. **Map** 3 B5.
26 44 36.
One of several branches.

Dana-Bohemia
GLASS, CHINA, CRYSTAL
Národní 43. **Map** 3 A5.
24 21 46 55.
One of several branches.

Crystal
Karlova 14.
Map 3 A4.
26 64 25.
One of several branches.

Glass
SKLO
Malé náměstí 8–9.
Map 3 B4.
24 22 84 59.

Glass-China
SKLO-PORCELÁN
Staroměstské náměstí 26–27.
Map 3 C3.
24 22 97 55.

Karlovy Vary China
KARLOVARSKÝ PORCELÁN
Pařížská 2.
Map 3 B2.
24 81 10 23.

Moser
Na příkopě 12.
Map 3 C4.
24 21 12 93/
24 21 12 94.

ANTIQUE SHOPS

Antique Clocks
STAROŽITNOSTI UHLÍŘ
Mikulandská 8.
Map 3 B5.
29 41 70.

At the Golden Cross
U ZLATÉHO KŘÍŽE
Uhelný trh 6.
Map 3 B5.
24 21 34 39.

Bohemia Aventis
Perlová 2.
Map 3 C5.
26 76 32.

Galerie Lukas
Národní 21.
Map 3 B5.
24 21 33 38.
One of several branches.

Military Antiques
Charvátova 11.
Map 3 C5.
24 22 74 34.
One of several branches.

Vadamo Galerie Bohemia
U ZLATÉHO KLASU
Na příkopě 23. **Map** 4 D4.
26 02 59.

GIFTS AND SOUVENIRS

Albatros
Na Perštýně 1.
Map 3 B5.
24 22 32 27.

Folk Figurines
Železná 16.
Map 3 C4.
24 22 65 90.

Folk Art Products
Karlova 23.
Map 3 A4.

Gifts
Národní 37.
Map 3 B5.
24 21 26 83.

The Beautiful Room
KRÁSNÁ JIZBA
Národní 36.
Map 3 B5.
26 56 83.

BOOKS

Albatros
Na Perštýně 1.
Map 3 B5.
24 22 32 27.

Arbes Bookshop
ARBESOVO KNIHKUPECTVÍ
Štefánikova 41.
Prague 5.
53 21 31/ 54 28 96 /
54 03 01.

Fišer's Bookshop
FIŠEROVO KNIHKUPECTVÍ
Kaprova 10.
Map 3 B3.
232 07 33.

Foreign Literature
ZAHRANIČNÍ LITERATURA
Na příkopě 27.
Map 4 D4.
26 28 37.

Melantrich
Václavské náměstí 33.
Map 4 D5.
24 22 72 58.

Orbis
Václavské náměstí 42.
Map 4 D5.
24 21 73 35.

Růžička's Bookshop
RŮŽIČKOVO KNIHKUPECTVÍ
Na příkopě 24.
Map 4 D4.
24 21 30 37.

Slavonic Book House
KNIHA SLOVANSKÝ DŮM
Na příkopě 31.
Map 4 D4.
24 22 82 04.

FOOD AND DELICATESSENS

Bakery Bonal
Václavské náměstí 57.
Map 4 D5.
24 21 49 36.

Delicacies
LAHŮDKY
Jungmannovo náměstí 19.
Map 3 C5.
24 09 86 32.

Delicatessen
LAHŮDKY DELIKATESY
Na příkopě 24.
Map 3 C4.
24 22 87 14.

Jan Paukert
Národní 17.
Map 3 B5.
24 23 00 31.

Milk Delicacies
Mostecká 19–21.
Map 2 E3.
53 36 89.

Pronto Supermarket
Rytířská 10.
Map 3 C4.

PHARMACIES

It is not usual for pharmacies to have individual names, so look out for **Léky** (drugs) or **Lékárna** (pharmacy).

Národní 35. **Map** 3 B5.
240 81 73.

Malé náměstí 13.
Map 3 B4.
24 23 00 86.

Na příkopě 7.
Map 3 C4.
24 21 02 29.

Václavské náměstí 64.
Map 3 C5.
24 21 65 75.

Lékárna na Starém Městě
Revoluční 19.
Map 4 D2.
23 31 42 26.

ENTERTAINMENT IN PRAGUE

S INCE THE VELVET REVOLUTION, Prague's entertainment programme has become increasingly varied. Whether you prefer opera to jazz or mini-golf to a football match, the city has plenty to offer. Movie buffs can choose from many of the latest Hollywood blockbusters, a lot of them in English with subtitles. For the adventurous, mime and fringe theatre are both thriving. Prague has a great musical tradition, which includes symphony orchestras, opera, musicals, jazz and folk music. Concerts are performed throughout the year, in venues which range from Baroque palaces to public parks and gardens. Even if you don't speak Czech, you can still enjoy the city's cultural offerings. Some plays can be seen in English, and for many types of entertainment, music, dance and sport, a knowledge of the language isn't necessary at all.

Street musicians entertaining the crowds

PRACTICAL INFORMATION

T HE BEST PLACE to look for information about what's on and where in Prague, is in the two English-language newspapers, *Prognosis* and *The Prague Post (see p219).* Both of the newspapers offer comprehensive details of the best entertainment and cultural events which will be of interest to an English-speaking audience. Those events that are in English or have translation facilities are marked. Other sources of information are the leaflets given out at the ticket agencies in the city like **Melantrich** or **PIS** *(see p211).* These are generally printed in Czech, English and German. You can also use the free booklets *Přehled* and *The Month in English* printed in English and available from any **PIS** office. For a comprehensive rundown of the week's events buy *PROgram*. This magazine has a small English section at the beginning, but is otherwise not very easy for non-Czech speakers to fully understand.

Theatre signs strung along Celetná Street

BOOKING TICKETS

T ICKETS CAN be bought in advance from the box office at most entertainment venues. You can also book tickets in advance by writing to, or ringing, the venue.
Remember that many of the city's box offices may not have any English speakers available. The more popular events tend to become heavily booked up in advance by tour groups – particularly during the summer – and by season-ticket holders. However, standby tickets are usually available about an hour before performances. If this isn't practical and you want to be sure of a ticket on a particular day, it is better to buy your tickets at one of the many booking agencies in the city. The drawback to using agencies

PUPPET THEATRE

Puppetry has a long tradition in Prague and is still strongly represented. The most famous puppet show in the city is held at the **Spejbl and Hurvínek Theatre** *(see p214).* The show revolves around Daddy Spejbl and his reprobate son Hurvínek. Other puppet theatres include the **National Marionette Theatre** *(see p214),* which uses all-string marionettes and the **Children's Theatre** *(see p214),* which has a show most days. The **Theatre in the Old Town** *(see p214)* and the **Children's Little Sun Club** *(see p214)* also put on puppet shows occasionally. Check listings magazines *(see p218).*

Theatre puppets

is that commission on these tickets can be high, sometimes doubling the original price. Your hotel receptionist may also be able to get you tickets.

TICKET PRICES

Ticket prices are still very cheap compared to Western prices, except for certain performances, most notably during the Prague Spring Festival (see p50). Prices range from around Kč20 for a small fringe production or puppet theatre to up to Kč600 for a performance of an inter-nationally-famous orchestra. Paying for your tickets by credit cards or Eurocheques is rarely, if ever, accepted by any entertainment venue.

TICKET TOUTS

There has been a recent spate of counterfeit tickets on sale, especially for the larger rock concerts. To be safe, always buy your tickets at reputable agencies or at the venue itself.

LATE-NIGHT TRANSPORT

Prague's metro (see p234) stops running shortly after midnight, while the normal bus and tram service ends around 11:30pm. Then the city's extensive night bus and tram service takes over. Timetables are displayed at each stop. Night trams and buses are regular and efficient and it is likely that there will

A view of the Rudolfinum auditorium (see p214)

Members of the Opera Mozart (see p214) performing Così Fan Tutte

be a tram or bus stop near your hotel. Taxis provide the most certain form of late-night transportation, but beware of unscrupulous drivers trying to overcharge you (see p237). Always try to walk a little way from the

Sparta Stadium (see p215)

theatre before you hail a cab, the fare will probably be a lot cheaper. Ask your hotel before you go out what the best transport options are.

MUSIC FESTIVALS

The most famous music festival of all is the Prague Spring Music Festival (see p50), held annually between May and June. Hundreds of international musicians come to Prague to take part in the celebrations. Other music festivals in the city include the Mozart Festival (see p51), which takes place during the summer months, and the International Jazz Festival (see p52), which is held during the autumn.

BOOKING AGENTS

Bohemia Ticket International
Salvátorská 6. **Map** 3 B3.
24 22 78 32.

CK Wolff
Na příkopě 24. **Map** 3 C4.
24 21 37 18/24 21 19 64.

IFB – Bohemia
Václavské náměstí 27.
Map 3 C5.
24 22 72 53.

Linda
Rytířská 31. **Map** 3 C4.

Lucerna
Štěpánská 61.
Map 5 C1.
24 22 55 85.

Melantrich
Václavské náměstí 38.
Map 4 D5.
24 21 50 18.

Pragotour
U Obecního domu.
Map 4 D3.
231 72 00.

Prague Information Service (PIS)
Staroměstské náměstí 22.
Map 3 C3.
24 21 28 44.
Na příkopě 20.
Map 3 C4.

Prague Tourist Centre
Rykiřská 12. **Map** 3 C4.
24 21 22 09.

Top Theatre Tickets
Celetná 13. **Map** 3 C3.
24 81 18 70.

Variety of Entertainment

Prague has always been known for its artistic heritage. Theatre has played an important role in the city's cultural development, and recently the range of entertainment has expanded considerably. Many new theatre groups have emerged, especially more experimental ones. In general, the theatre season runs from September to June. During the summer, open-air performances are given in Prague's gardens and parks. The city also has a strong musical tradition, including great musicians and performers such as Mozart, Smetana and Dvořák. For those who prefer to dance till dawn, relax to the sound of jazz or take in a movie, you'll find plenty to entertain you in this inexpensive city.

ENGLISH-LANGUAGE PERFORMANCES

Many theatres in Prague have started to stage a number of English-language productions – especially in the summer months. Even if the play is not performed in English, many theatre venues have installed simultaneous translation facilities. For more details, check in the listings magazines (see p219).

MAJOR THEATRES

Prague's first permanent theatre was built in 1738, but the city's theatrical tradition dates from the Baroque and Renaissance periods.

The **National Theatre** (see p156) is Prague's main venue for opera, ballet and plays. The neighbouring New Stage is another important venue. It is also the main stage for the multi-media **Laterna Magika** company, which is one of Prague's best-known theatre groups as well as being at the forefront of European improvisational theatre.

Other major theatres in the city include the "stone theatres". These gained importance during the 18th century and include the **Vinohrady Theatre**, the **Estates Theatre** (see p65) – one of the most respected in Prague – and the **Prague Municipal Theatre**, an acting company whose plays appear in turn at the **ABC Theatre**, the **K Theatre** and the **Rococo Studio of Drama**. The **Kolowrat Theatre** is based in the Kolowrat Palace.

FRINGE THEATRES

These originated during the 1960s and won renown for their fight against the status quo. The groups are still very innovative and largely experimental. They perform in small theatres, and many of Prague's best actors and actresses have developed their skills while working for some of these companies.

Fringe theatres include: the **Dramatic Club**, well known for its supporting ensemble; the **Ypsilon Studio**, with one of the finest acting companies in the city; the **Labyrinth Theatre**, which tends to stage many more modern works; the **Miraculous Theatre of the Baroque World**, which performs mainly historic plays; the large **Theatre Below Palmovka**, renowned for its mix of classical and modern plays and the **Theatre in Celetná**. One of Prague's most spectacular theatrical and music venues is **Křižík's Fountain** (see p176).

PANTOMIME, MIME AND "BLACK THEATRE"

Some of the most popular theatre entertainment in Prague is Black Theatre (where black-clad actors move objects against a dark stage without being seen), pantomime and mime. None of these three requires any understanding of Czech and all are strongly represented. One of the main venues for mime is **Boris Hybner's GAG Studio**, while the **Bomiel Pantomime** is

well worth a visit if you enjoy this form of theatre. **Jiří Srnec's Black Theatre** is one of the major venues for black theatre performance.

DANCE

In Prague, opera and ballet companies traditionally share the **National Theatre**, where the permanent ballet company is based. You can also watch ballet at the **Estates Theatre** and at the **Prague State Opera**. Musicals tend to be popular in Prague, and these are performed by some of the modern dance groups.

CLASSICAL MUSIC

The main concert venues for classical music are the **Rudolfinum** (see p84) and the Smetana Hall, found in the **Municipal House** (see p64). Other permanent concert halls include the **Atrium in Žižkov**, a converted chapel, the **Clementinum** and the imposing **Palace of Culture**. **Bertramka** is another venue with the added attraction of being the place where Mozart stayed when he was in Prague.

MUSIC IN CHURCHES AND PALACES

Concerts performed in the numerous churches and palaces around Prague are extremely popular. Many of these buildings are closed to the public, so this is the only chance to see inside them. Major churches include the **Church of St James** (see p65); the **Church of St Nicholas** (see p128) in the Little Quarter; the **Church of St Nicholas** (see p70) in the Old Town; the **Church of St Francis** in Knights of the Cross Square (see p79); **St Vitus's Cathedral** (see p100) and **St George's Basilica** (see p98). Among the palaces included are the **Wallenstein Palace** (see p126); the **Lobkowicz Palace** (see p99) and the **Sternberg Palace** (see p112). It's worth checking the listings magazines (p219) for the specific dates and times of concerts.

OPERA

DURING THE 20th century, opera has become very popular in Prague, and there are now two major opera companies in the city. One company performs solely in the **National Theatre** *(see pp156–7)* and the other in the **State Opera**. The latter presents all its performances in the language in which they were written, usually Italian, while the National Theatre has more Czech translations of the operas. The **Music Theatre in Karlin** puts on classical operettas and musicals only. More innovative pieces are staged by the **Lyra Pragensis**, while the **Mozart Opera** offers modern music programmes.

NIGHTCLUBS

EVEN THOUGH nightlife in Prague is not as extensive as in other European capitals, it is rapidly catching up. Since 1989 there have been great changes, so that now visitors have a wider choice of nightclubs, discos and cabaret.

The **Video Disco Club** is a popular venue and has been around for a relatively long time. The biggest club in the city is the **Lucerna Bar** which offers a varied programme, as does the **Bibita**. The **Carioca**, the **Little Horse** and the **Music Park** all have loud discos every night of the week. The **Eden-Palladium Dance Club** is the largest disco in Prague. At the **Tatran Bar** you will find live music and acts from 11pm to the early hours. The **Praga Variety** has a disco and revue programme and is one of Prague's more popular venues. The trendier clubs include **Radost FX**, **Barklub-Reggae**, **Obvodní Kulturní dům Vltavská** and **Euroclub**.

ROCK AND POP CLUBS

LOVERS OF ROCK MUSIC are well served in Prague. There are a large number of popular rock venues, generally small clubs and cafés, which host a variety of different groups. Prague's own rock bands play both their own compositions as well as cover versions of more famous numbers, many singing in English. Larger, more famous Western bands also play in Prague occasionally. One of the most popular rock venues is the **Bunker**, often the stage for foreign groups. The **Rock Café**, another popular venue, offers concerts which are followed by a disco.

Other venues include the **Futurum Rock Club**, open to the early hours; the **Junior Club na Chmelnici**, whose indie bands begin at 7:30pm, and the **U Zoufalců** club, which not only stages concerts but also exhibitions, films, lectures and discos. Other clubs where concerts are also followed by a disco include the **Repre Rock Club**, the **Uzi rock-bar** and the **Rock Club Borát**. For lovers of nostalgia, **Classic Club** plays an hour of 1960s classics.

JAZZ

THE ROOTS OF JAZZ in Prague can be traced not only to the American tradition but also to the pre-war heyday of Prague's famous jazz players, such as Jaroslav Ježek. Prague's many jazz clubs play all forms, from Dixieland to swing.

One of the leading and most popular jazz venues in the city is the **Jazz Club Reduta**, which has daily jazz concerts at around 9pm. The popular **Metropolitan Club** holds late-night concerts until 3 or 4am. At the **Agharta Jazz Centrum**, you can hear a high standard of playing while eating in its café. The **Café de Paris** has a regular Thursday night jazz slot, and the **120 Days Club** plays a mixture of jazz, blues, rock and folk. **Malostranská beseda** is the venue for more traditional jazz. For serious enthusiasts, the International Jazz Festival *(see p52)* during October attracts musicians from around the world.

ETHNIC MUSIC

A SMALL NUMBER of clubs and bars in Prague offer ethnic music. The **LA Klub** in the Slavonic House *(see p147)* plays all kinds of international music. The **House of Culture** hosts a variety of bands, while you can hear both African and Asian music at the **Club Exodus**, which serves food.

GAY AND LESBIAN VENUES

PRAGUE'S FEW gay venues tend to cater mainly for men; PROgram *(see p210)* will give you up-to-date listings. The **David Club**, the **America Club** and the **Mercury Club** all have discos. Other popular gay places include the wine bars **Barberina** and **At the Holans**, and the beer houses **Tom's Bar** and **At the Oak**.

CINEMAS

ALTHOUGH PRAGUE doesn't have all the latest Hollywood blockbusters, more than 80% of the films shown are recent US productions and a third of them have Czech subtitles. The listings magazines *(see p219)* show which films are on and in what language. Most major cinema screens are situated around Wenceslas Square, including the **Alfa**, **Hvězda**, **Lucerna** and **Blaník**; others are listed in the directory *(see p215)*. The **Illusion** and the **Ponrepo** cinemas show old films. For a cinema café, visit the **Jalta-DIF Centrum**.

SPORTING VENUES

IN CENTRAL PRAGUE, sports facilities are not extensive, so you may have to travel a little further out if you feel like some exercise.

Golf, mini-golf or tennis are on offer at the **Motol**, the **Exhibition Ground** *(see p162)* and **Štvanice Island**. Swimming pools are also further out, including two at **Divoká Šárka** and **Kobylisy**. There are natural lakes at **Lhotka** and **Šeberák** and a range of water sports are on offer at **Hostivař Reservoir** and **Imperial Meadow**.

The main spectator sports are soccer and ice hockey. Sparta Praha, the top soccer team, play at **Sparta Stadium** in Letná, while ice hockey matches are held in the sports hall at the Exhibition Ground.

DIRECTORY

THEATRES

Bomiel Pantomime
Lávka Theatre,
Novotného lávka 1.
Map 3 A4.
[24 21 47 97.

Boris Hybner's GAG Studio
STUDIO GAG BORISE HYBNERA
Národní 25.
Map 3 B5.
[24 22 90 95.

Children's Little Sun Club
DĚTSKÝ KLUB SLUNÍČKO
Vojtíškova 1783,
Prague 4.
[790 20 74.

Dramatic Club
ČINOHERNÍ KLUB
Ve Smečkách 26.
Map 6 D1.
[24 21 68 12.

Estates Theatre
STAVOVSKÉ DIVADLO
Ovocný trh.
Map 3 C3.
[24 22 85 03.

Jiří Srnec's Black Theatre
ČERNÉ DIVADLO JIŘÍHO SRNCE
Národní 40.
Map 3 B5.
[24 22 96 04.

Kolowrat Theatre
DIVADLO KOLOWRAT
(IN ESTATES THEATRE)
Ovocný trh.
Map 3 C3.

Křižík's Fountain
KŘIŽÍKOVA FONTÁNA
Výstaviště,
Prague 7.
[872 91 11.

Labyrinth Theatre
LABYRINT
Štefánikova 57, Prague 5.
[24 51 17 37.

Laterna Magika
Národní 4. **Map** 3 A5.
[24 91 41 29.

Miraculous Theatre of the Baroque World
ZÁZRAČNÉ DIVADLO BAROKNÍHO SVĚTA
Celetná 13.
Map 3 C3.

National Theatre
NÁRODNÍ DIVADLO
Národní 2.
Map 3 A5.
[24 91 34 37.

National Marionette Theatre
NÁRODNÍ DIVADLO MARIONET
Žatecká 1.
Map 3 B3.
[232 34 29.

Prague Municipal Theatre, ABC Theatre
MĚSTSKÁ DIVADLA PRAŽSKÁ DIVADLO ABC
Vodičkova 28.
Map 3 C5.
[24 21 25 85.

Prague Municipal Theatre, K Theatre
MĚSTSKÁ DIVADLA PRAŽSKÁ DIVADLO K
Jungmannova 1.
Map 3 C5.
[24 22 24 84.

Prague Municipal Theatre, Rococo Studio of Drama
MĚSTSKÁ DIVADLA PRAŽSKÁ ČINOHERNÍ STUDIO-ROKOKO
Václavské náměstí 38.
Map 4 D5.
[24 21 70 84.

Reduta Theatre
DIVADLO REDUTA
Národní 20.
Map 3 B5.
[24 91 22 46.

Spejbl and Hurvínek Theatre
DIVADLO SPEJBLA A HURVÍNKA
Římská 45.
Map 6 F2.
[312 12 41.

Theatre in Celetná
DIVADLO V CELETNÉ
Celetná 17.
Map 3 C3.
[24 81 27 62.

Theatre below Palmovka
DIVADLO POD PALMOVKOU
Zenklova 34,
Prague 8.
[66 31 17 08.

Theatre in the Old Town
DIVADLO NA STARÉM MĚSTĚ
Dlouhá 39. **Map** 3 C3.
[24 81 02 78.

Vinohrady Theatre
DIVADLO NA VINOHRADECH
Náměstí Míru 7.
Map 6 F2.
[25 24 52.

Ypsilon Studio
STUDIO YPSILON
Spálená 16.
Map 3 B5.
[29 22 55.

MUSIC VENUES

Atrium in Žižkov
ATRIUM NA ŽIŽKOVĚ
Čajkovského 12, Prague 3.
[627 04 53.

Bertramka
BERTRAMKA MUZEUM W A MOZARTA
Mozartova 169, Prague 5.
[54 38 93.

Church of St James
KOSTEL SV. JAKUBA
Malá štupartská.
Map 3 C3.

Church of St Nicholas (Old Town)
KOSTEL SV. MIKULÁŠE
Staroměstské náměstí.
Map 3 B3.

Church of St Nicholas
KOSTEL SV. MIKULÁŠE
Malostranské náměstí.
Map 2 E3.

Church of St Francis
KOSTEL SV. FRANTIŠKA
Křižovnické náměstí.
Map 3 A4.

Clementinum
ZRCADLOVÁ SÍŇ KLEMENTINA
Mariánské náměstí 10.
Map 3 B3.

Lobkowicz Palace
LOBKOVICKÝ PALÁC
Jiřská 1, Pražský hrad.
Map 2 E2.

Lyra Pragensis
Karlova 2.
Map 3 A4.
[26 55 13.

Mozart Opera
OPERA MOZART
Pohořelec 25.
Map 1 B3.
[232 34 29.

Music Theatre in Karlín
HUDEBNÍ DIVADLO V KARLÍNĚ
Křižíkova 10.
Map 4 F3.
[24 21 07 10.

Palace of Culture
PALÁC KULTURY
5. května 65, Prague 4.
[61 17 27 21.

Prague State Opera
STÁTNÍ OPERA PRAHA
Wilsonova třída.
Map 6 E1.
[26 53 53.

Rudolfinum
RUDOLFINUM – DVOŘÁKOVA SÍŇ
Alšovo nábřeží.
Map 3 A3.
[24 89 33 52.

St George's Basilica
BAZILIKA SV. JIŘÍ
Jiřské náměstí,
Pražský hrad.
Map 2 E2.

St Vitus's Cathedral
CHRÁM SV. VÍTA
Pražský hrad.
Map 2 D2.

Sternberg Palace
ŠTERNBERSKÝ PALAC
Hradčanské náměstí 15.
Map 1 C3.
[35 24 41.

Wallenstein Palace
VALDŠTEJNSKÝ PALÁC
Valdštejnské náměstí.
Map 2 E3.

NIGHTCLUBS

Barklub-Reggae
Hybernská 10.
Map 4 E3.
[26 35 46.

Bibita
V jámě 8.
Map 5 C1.
[24 22 71 70.

Carioca
Václavské náměstí 4.
Map 6 D1.
[24 21 92 24.

Eden-Palladium Dance Club
U Slavie 1.

Euroclub
Národní 25.
Map 3 B5.
℅ 242 126 18.

Little Horse
KONÍČEK
Staroměstské náměstí 200.
Map 3 C3.
℅ 235 89 27.

Lucerna Bar
Štěpánská 61.
Map 5 C1.
℅ 24 21 71 08.

Music Park
Francouská 2.

Obvodní Kulturní dům Vltavská
Bubenská 1.
℅ 87 96 83.

Praga Variety
VATIETĚ PRAGA
Vodičkova 30.
Map 3 C5.
℅ 24 22 20 99.

Radost FX
Bělehradská 120.
Map 6 E2.
℅ 25 12 10.

Tatran Bar
Juliš Hotel,
Václavské náměstí.
Map 4 D5.
℅ 24 21 70 92.

Video Disco Club
Ambassador Hotel,
Václavské náměstí 5–7.
Map 3 C5.
℅ 24 19 31 11.

ROCK AND POP CLUBS

Bunker
BUNKR
Lodecká 2.
Map 4 E2.
℅ 231 79 22.

Classic Club
Pařížská 4.
Map 3 B3

Futurum Rock Club
Zborovská 7.
Map 2 F5.
℅ 54 44 75.

Junior Club na Chmelnici
Koněvova 219.
℅ 82 85 98.

Rock Café
Národní 20.
Map 3 B5.
℅ 249 144 14.

Rock Club Borát
Újezd 18.
Map 2 E5.
℅ 53 63 62.

U Zoufalců
KLUB'U ZOUFALCŮ
Celetná 12.
Map 3 C3.

Uzi rock-bar
Legerova 44.
Map 6 D2.
℅ 24 91 32 01.

JAZZ CLUBS

Agharta Jazz Centrum
Krakovská 5.
Map 6 D1.
℅ 24 21 29 14.

Café de Paris
Hotel Pařiž,
U Obecního domu 1.
Map 4 D3.
℅ 24 22 21 51.

Jazz Club Reduta
Národní 20.
Map 3 B5.
℅ 249 122 46.

Malostranská Beseda
Malostranské náměstí 21.
Map 2 E3.
℅ 53 90 24.

Metropolitan Club
Jungmannova 14.
Map 3 C5.
℅ 24 21 60 25.

120 Days Club
120 DNI
Národní 11. **Map** 3 B5.
℅ 22 57 90.

ETHNIC MUSIC

Exodus Club
Národní 25. **Map** 3 B5.
℅ 26 20 85.

House of Culture
OBVODNÍ KULTURNÍ
DŮM VLTAVSKÁ
Bubenská 1.
℅ 87 96 83.

La Klub
Na příkopě 22.
Map 4 D4.

GAY AND LESBIAN CLUBS

America
Petřínská 5.
℅ 53 49 09.

At the Holans
U HOLANŮ
Londýnská 10.
Map 6 E2.
℅ 25 48 45.

At the Oak
U DUBU
Záhřebská 15.
Map 6 F3.

Barberina
Melantrichova 10.
Map 3 B4.
℅ 26 10 84.

David Club
Sokolovská 77.
Map 4 F2.
℅ 231 78 82.

Mercury Club
Kolínská 11,
Prague 2.

Tom's Bar
Pernerova 4.
℅ 232 11 70.

CINEMAS

Alfa
Václavské náměstí 28.
Map 3 C5.
℅ 26 30 63.

Blaník
Václavské náměstí 56.
Map 6 D1.
℅ 24 21 66 98.

Hvězda
Václavské náměstí 38.
Map 4 D5.
℅ 26 45 45.

Illusion
Vinohradská 48.
Map 6 F1.
℅ 25 02 60.

Jalta DIF-Centrum
Václavské náměstí 43.
Map 4 D5.
℅ 24 22 88 14.

Lucerna
Vodičkova 36.
Map 3 C5.
℅ 24 21 69 72.

Pasáž
Václavské náměstí 5.
Map 3 C5.
℅ 26 73 89.

Ponrepo
Národní 40.
Map 3 B5.

Praha
Václavské náměstí 17.
Map 4 D5.
℅ 26 20 35.

Sevastopol
Na příkopě 31.
Map 4 D4.
℅ 26 43 28.

64 U hradeb
Mostecká 21.
Map 2 E3.
℅ 53 50 06.

Světozor
Vodičkova 39.
Map 3 C5.
℅ 26 36 16.

SPORTING VENUES

Divoká Šárka
Prague 6.

Exhibition Ground
VÝSTAVIŠTĚ
Sports stadium,
Prague 7.

Hostivař Reservoir
Prague 10.

Imperial Meadow
CÍSAŘSKÁ LOUKA
Prague 5.

Kobylisy
Prague 8.

Lhotka
Prague 4.

Motol
V Úvalu 84,
Prague 5.

Šeberák
Prague 4.

Sparta Stadium
Milady Horákové,
Prague 7.

Štvanice Island
Ostrov Štvanice 1125,
Prague 7.

SURVIVAL
GUIDE

PRACTICAL INFORMATION

SINCE THE recent political upheavals, Prague has become far more open to visitors. The city has responded well to the enormous influx of tourists, and facilities such as hotels, banks, restaurants and information centres have improved considerably. Even so, a little forward planning is always worthwhile. Reading up about a sight, checking it is open and how best to get there, can save a lot of time

A Martin Tours sightseeing bus

and inconvenience. Prague's transport system is straightforward and most of the city's sights are within walking distance. In general, prices are still considerably lower than in the West, but a few of the more up-market restaurants and hotels are priced according to Western rather than Czech wallets. Despite a small increase in petty crime, especially pickpocketing, Prague is still safer than the majority of Western cities.

TOURIST INFORMATION

THERE ARE a number of tourist information offices ranging from specialized agencies to the state-owned **Čedok**. These can provide advice on anything from accommodation and travel to restaurants and guided tours. Many employ English speakers and print English language publications. The efficient **Prague Information Service (PIS)** is the city's best tourist information point. It has three offices in the city centre and it provides visitors with maps, advice, listings *(see pp210–11)* and other types of information in English, German and Czech. To help you find your way around the city, **Kiwi** has a large selection of maps and guides in English.

Čedok street sign

TIPS FOR TOURISTS

IN PRAGUE, there are enough English speakers to make booking a room, buying a ticket or ordering a meal relatively simple. A smattering of German may also help, as many Czechs have a working knowledge of the language.

One of the best times to visit Prague is during the summer, although it can be rather crowded. Other busy times of the year are Easter and major Catholic festivals *(see pp50–53)*. The main sights, such as the Old Town Square, are always packed during these periods, but the crowds give Prague a carnival atmosphere. Street entertainers, buskers and small street stalls spring up around the most popular attractions. If the crowds do get too much, just turn off into one of the smaller streets and you are almost guaranteed peace and quiet. Bring a light raincoat for the summer and some warm, woolly clothes for the rest of the year.

OPENING HOURS

THIS GUIDE lists the opening hours for the individual museums, galleries and churches. Most of the city's major sights can be seen throughout the year, but many of Prague's gardens and the castles outside the city are only open from 1 April to 31 October. Visiting hours are normally from 9am to 5pm, daily, but the final admission times can often be as much as an hour earlier. A number of major museums and castles are also closed every Monday, so be sure to check before visiting them. The National Museum is closed on Tuesdays

Entry tickets for some of Prague's major tourist sights

and the State Jewish Museum is closed on Friday afternoons and on Saturdays.

Opening hours of Prague's shops vary widely. Some businesses are open between 7am and 6pm, Monday to Friday, and 8am to noon on Saturdays. Some department stores *(see p208)* are open until 4pm on Saturdays and a few Sundays before Christmas.

The main office of the Prague Information Service in the street Na příkopě

A horse-drawn carriage in the Old Town Square

Prague does not have any standard late-night shopping, although many of the more expensive tourist shops stay open until around 10pm. Banks open from 8am to 4pm, Monday to Friday. Restaurants, cafés and bars all have varied opening hours (see pp188–9). Most of the city's bars open from 10am and as there are no licensing laws, often stay open until everyone leaves.

LISTINGS AND TICKETS

THERE ARE some 160 galleries and 40 museums scattered throughout the city, and to find out what's on it is best to look in a listings paper. The English-language newspapers *The Prague Post* and *Prognosis* give detailed listings of most events and exhibitions and are available from newsstands in the city centre. They also give tips for the visitor and informative articles on Prague, its politics and its people. The **PIS** has a free monthly English-language listings book.

The price of entry tickets for museums varies widely, from Kč2 to around Kč100. Most churches are free, with a collection box at the door. Tickets for entertainment events can be bought from the booking agencies in the city, or at the venue itself. Some of Prague's hotels can get you tickets, or try a large travel agent in the centre.

SIGHTSEEING TIPS

A GOOD WAY to see Prague is to take a sightseeing tour. Many firms offer trips around Prague's major sights as well as outings to castles such as Karlstein and Konopiště (see

pp166–7). Tours usually start from Náměstí Republiky (Republic Square) and from the upper part of Václavské náměstí (Wenceslas Square). These trips can be expensive but prices vary, so it is worth checking what's on offer before you make a booking. **Wittmann Tours** organizes trips around the Jewish Quarter and Terezín. For those on a tight budget, **PIS** offers some of the cheapest tours.

A trip on tram No. 91, run by the Museum of Municipal Mass Transport, is one of the cheapest and best city centre tours. It starts off at the Exhibition Ground (see pp176–7) and travels around the Old Town, the New Town and the Jewish Quarter. It runs from Easter to the end of October every weekend and public holiday. Tickets can be bought on board.

Sightseeing trips in horse-drawn carriages (fiacres) are run from the Old Town Square, and in summer, a "fun train" from Mostecká Street runs through some of the loveliest parts of Hradčany and the Little Quarter.

A street sign showing the services offered by Pragotur

Personal Security and Health

AT PRESENT PRAGUE suffers from a shortage of police officers. Because of their close identification with the former communist regime, they remain extremely unpopular with Czechs and tend to keep a low profile. This has led to a rise in the crime level. However, compared to many Western cities, Prague is relatively safe. If you should need emergency medical care in Prague, it will be given free. There are also a number of English-speaking services available, including health centres, dentists and US and British information centres.

A Prague police sign

ADVICE FOR VISITORS

PRAGUE IS A SAFE and un-threatening city to walk around. Violent crimes against tourists in the city centre are rare. The main crime problems that affect tourists are petty pilfering from cars, hotels and pockets; violence with robbery is very unusual. Using your common sense should help you to avoid Prague's only real plague – its pickpockets. The crowded summer months are a favourite time for these thieves. Always remember to keep your bag in sight and avoid carrying your passport, wallet and valuables in your back pocket or an open bag. Thieves do tend to operate around the popular sights, such as Charles Bridge, and many use diversionary tactics,

Municipal police badge

State police badge

one knocking into you while the other steals your belongings. It is very unlikely that anything stolen will ever be recovered. Never leave anything of value in your car. Car alarms have proved not to be a deterrent. Try and park your car in an underground car park, especially if you are driving a foreign make. Always take out adequate insurance before visiting Prague, as it is difficult to arrange once there. Report any thefts to the police for future insurance claims. Avoid getting drawn into a street card game known as shells. It is a classic con game.

Women may encounter a few stares and comments, but this is about as far as sexual harassment will go. However, one place to try and avoid at night if you are a woman

alone, is Wenceslas Square. Most men will assume you are one of the city's growing band of prostitutes. Prostitution is rife and has increased considerably since 1989. Although it is illegal, the police tend to turn a blind eye. A growing practice among many of the city's prostitutes is to drug their client's drink and then steal everything he has on him.

It is an unwritten law that you should carry your passport at all times and although you are unlikely to be asked to produce it, having it could save a lot of problems. Before you travel take photocopies of all essential documents as replacing them can be difficult and time-consuming.

THE POLICE AND SECURITY SERVICES

IN PRAGUE you will come across several kinds of policemen and women and members of various security services. Report any problems to a uniformed state police officer at a police station. The main stations are marked on the Street Finder maps (see pp238–45). The state police carry guns and can arrest a suspect. They patrol the streets on foot or drive green and white patrol cars. The municipal police are the other main security force, have greater powers, and are divided into different sections.

Traffic police ensure the smooth running of traffic and regulate parking, speeding and drink driving. Fines for illegal parking and speeding are huge. It is illegal to drive with any alcohol in your bloodstream. Occasionally the police have a clamp down on drink driving and if you are caught, the penalties are

A male state police officer

A municipal police officer

A female state police officer

A "black sheriff"

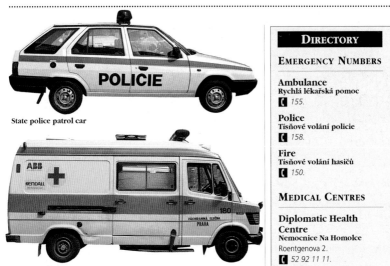

State police patrol car

Prague ambulance

DIRECTORY

EMERGENCY NUMBERS

Ambulance
Rychlá lékařská pomoc
(155.

Police
Tísňové volání policie
(158.

Fire
Tísňové volání hasičů
(150.

MEDICAL CENTRES

Diplomatic Health Centre
Nemocnice Na Homolce
Roentgenova 2.
(52 92 11 11.

Emergency Dental Care
První pomoc zubní
Vladislavova 22. **Map** 5 C1.
(24 22 76 63.

Fakultní Poliklinika
U nemocnice 2. **Map** 5 B3.
(24 96 11 11.

First Aid Centre
Služba první pomoci
Palackého 5. **Map** 3 C5.
(24 22 25 20.

24-hour Pharmacies
Štětánikova 6.
(53 70 39.
ᵀᴹᶠ Anděl.

GENERAL HELP

American Cultural Centre
Americké Kulturní středisko
Hybernská 7a. **Map** 4 D3.
(24 23 10 85.

British Cultural Centre
Britské kulturní oddělení
Národní 10. **Map** 3 B5.
(24 91 21 79.

Car Breakdown Service
Havarijní služba pro motoristy
(123.

Lost and Found
Ztráty a nálezy
Karoliny Světlé. **Map** 3 A5.
(24 23 50 85.

Road Accidents
Dopravní nehody
(42 41 41.

Samaritans
Linka důvěry
(29 79 00.

severe. The traffic police are also responsible for car clamping and collecting the fines *(see pp232–3)*. Finally, if you have a traffic accident, you must immediately ring **Road Accidents**. It is against the law to move anything before the police get there.

There are also a number of private security guards. These are often called "black sheriffs" (many of them actually wear black uniforms) and tend to guard banks and be used as security at football matches and so on. They are also armed but should only use their guns in self-defence. Many are also former members of the hated Communist secret service and most Czechs try to steer clear of them; it is strongly advised that you do too.

Pharmacy sign

HEALTH CARE

HEALTH CARE in Prague is divided into state and private care. If you need emergency treatment it will be provided free of charge. But all non-essential treatment has to be paid for there and then. So make sure you have adequate medical insurance before you arrive in Prague and a credit card or enough traveller's cheques to pay – don't forget the receipt for your insurance claim.

Your hotel should be able to put you in touch with a local doctor, but if you need more prompt service, Prague's emergency services are on call 24 hours a day and you can call an ambulance if necessary. Hospitals with casualty units are marked on the Street Finder maps *(see pp238–45)*.

There are also 24-hour pharmacies (lékárna) *(see p209)* and a **First Aid Centre** which gives advice and simple remedies. If you want to see an English-speaking doctor, visit **Fakultní Poliklinika** in the New Town, or else go to the **Diplomatic Health Centre** for foreigners at Na Homolce. You will need to take a passport and a means of immediate payment if you use these.

Those who have bad respiratory problems should be aware that between October and March, sulphur dioxide levels in Prague regularly exceed the World Health Organization's accepted levels – often by up to three times. With an increasing rate of car ownership and a lack of money for alternative fuels, this problem seems unlikely to decrease in the near future.

Money, Banks and Currency Exchange Offices

A bureau de change sign in Prague

TODAY PRAGUE is a relatively cheap city to visit. In the past few years, hundreds of banks and bureaux de change have been established, some staying open all night. For the lowest charges and, unfortunately, the longest queues, it is best to change money in a bank. Credit cards are becoming more accepted, but never assume that you can pay with them. Traveller's cheques can only be changed in banks.

BANKING

HUNDREDS OF private banks and bureaux de change have been opened in Prague since 1989. The large, modern banks – generally found outside the city centre – all open between 8am and 4pm Monday to Saturday. The banks may not close at lunch, but many exchange tills do. Lunch hour varies from around 12:30pm to 2:30pm. There are always long queues at the exchange tills so make sure you get there well before closing time. Bureaux de change are found in tiny shops throughout the city. However, despite offering much better exchange rates than the banks, their commission charges are huge, often as high as 12% compared to the bank's 1%. The main advantage of these exchange offices is their convenience. Many are open late every day, some offer a 24-hour service, and queues are rare.

Most of the larger hotels will also change foreign currency for you, but again commission rates may be very high. If you find you have some Czech currency left over from your stay, you can only reconvert your money if you have kept your transaction slips. Komerční bank, located on Na

Façade of the Československá Obchodní bank

příkopě, and the airport bank, will reconvert your extra crowns for a small commission. Finally, never change your money on the black market. As well as being illegal the rate is not any higher than banks or exchanges and it is likely you'll be given notes that are not legal tender.

An automatic teller machine for dispensing cash

CREDIT CARDS

PAYING BY credit card is becoming more popular. Even so, only the larger hotels, restaurants, international car hire agencies and a few of the more expensive tourist shops accept them as a matter of course. The majority of businesses in Prague do not recognize credit cards at all. Even if a shop or restaurant window sports a credit card sign, do not assume they will take them as payment – always ask before you have eaten your meal. The cards most often accepted are: American Express, VISA, Master Card and Access. Most banks will allow cash advances (up to your limit) on your card.

DIRECTORY

BANKS

Agrobanka
Opletalova 4. **Map** 4 D5.
☎ 24 22 92 39.
One of several branches.

Czech Bank
ČESKÁ BANKA
Spálená 51. **Map** 3 B5.
☎ 24 91 52 21.
One of several branches.

Investment Bank
INVESTIČNÍ BANKA
Senovážné náměstí 32.
Map 4 E4.
☎ 24 07 11 11.
One of several branches.

Czech Commercial Bank
ČESKÁ OBCHODNÍ BANKA
Na příkopě 14. **Map** 3 C4.
☎ 24 24 35 06.

Commercial Bank
KOMERČNI BANKA
Na příkopě 28. **Map** 3 C4.
☎ 24 02 11 11.
One of several branches.

Pragobanka
Vinohradská 230. **Map** 6 E1.
☎ 77 68 42.
One of several branches.

BUREAUX DE CHANGE

American Express
Václavské náměstí 56.
Map 3 C5.
☎ 24 22 46 06.
One of several branches.

City Exclusive
Václavské náměstí 47.
Map 3 C5.
☎ 26 56 87.
One of several branches.

Contrans
Spálená 31. **Map** 3 B5.
☎ 29 98 26
One of several branches.

Čekobanka Chequepoint
28. října 13.
Map 3 C5.
☎ 24 22 82 65 (24 hours).
One of several branches.

Exact Change
Václavské náměstí 21.
Map 3 C5.
☎ 24 21 44 14.
One of several branches.

CASH AND TRAVELLER'S CHEQUES

CURRENCY COMES in Czech crowns and hellers. There are 100 hellers to the crown. It is illegal to bring Czech crowns into the country or take more than a little out. Traveller's cheques are by far the safest alternative to carrying cash. It is best to take well-known brands – American Express, Thomas Cook, for example – although it is unlikely that the major banks will refuse any. Traveller's cheques are not accepted as currency by any shops or restaurants and must be changed at exchanges or banks. Keep receipts if you want to change crowns back to foreign notes. The American Express office (see p225) sells and cashes traveller's cheques. They don't charge commission for cashing their own cheques.

Banknotes
Czech banknotes come in the denominations Kč100, Kč200, Kč500 and Kč1,000. Future notes include Kč20, Kč50, Kč2,000 and Kč5,000.

Kč1,000 note

Kč500 note

Kč200 note

Kč100 note

Coins
Coins come in the following denominations: 10 and 20 hellers; Kč1, Kč2, Kč5, Kč10, Kč20 and Kč50. All the coins have the Czech emblem, a lion rampant, on one side.

10 hellers

20 hellers

1 crown (Kč1)

2 crowns (Kč2)

5 crowns (Kč5)

10 crowns (Kč10)

20 crowns (Kč20)

50 crowns (Kč50)

NEW CURRENCY

When Czechoslovakia split into two republics in 1992, the currency had to be changed. New notes and coins are being produced very slowly. Future denominations should include banknotes of Kč20, Kč50, Kč2,000 and Kč5,000 and a 50-heller coin.

The design of the Kč5,000-denomination banknote

Telephone and Postal Services

THE CZECH telephone and postal service, Telecom, is undergoing a major modernization programme. Modern digital phones are slowly replacing the older coin-operated ones, and the postal service is to become much more efficient. But there have been a few problems in the transition, and patience is often needed when using the phone.

The Main Post Office sign in Jindřišská Street

USING PUBLIC TELEPHONES

ALTHOUGH THERE are a large number of public phones on street corners and near metro stations, there is a high incidence of vandalism. Even when you do find a phone that works, the lines are often disconnected owing to the modernization programme. To make sure you have a working phone, it is better to use one in a post office.

International calls can be made more easily from a post office, a private phone or your hotel. At most major post offices you have to leave a deposit, make the call and then pay what you owe to the attendant. In hotels, you can usually get a direct line but commission charges on the call are often exorbitant. Remember also that international calls are extremely expensive, no matter what time of day you phone.

There is an increasing number of modern phonecard telephones in Prague. You can buy the cards *(Telefonní karta)* for these phones from most tabáks and newsstands.

The dialling tone is a short note followed by a long one; the ringing tone consists of long regular notes while the engaged signal has short and rapid notes. Remember that many people in Prague are still connected to a party line and that a number can remain engaged for a long time.

PROBLEM NUMBERS

IF YOU HAVE problems getting through to a number in Prague, it is very likely that the number has changed due to the gradual modernization of the phone system. To check, ring the directory and ask for an English speaker.

USING A COIN-OPERATED TELEPHONE

1 Lift the receiver and wait for the dialling tone.

2 Insert either a 1, 2 or 5 crown coin in the slot (the older orange phones only accept Kč1 coins).

3 The digital display shows how much credit is left. If you need to insert more money, the message *Vložte mince* appears.

4 When the words *Volte číslo* come up, dial the number then wait to be connected.

5 When you have finished speaking replace the receiver. Any coins that were unused are returned here. These phones do not give change.

Kč1   **Kč2**   **Kč5**

Coins that can be inserted in the newer coin-operated phones

USING A PHONECARD TELEPHONE

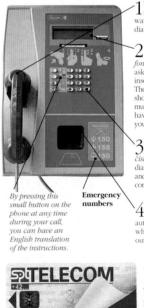

1 Lift the receiver and wait for the dialling tone.

2 The message *Vložte telefonní kartu*, asks you to insert your card. The display also shows you how much credit you have left on your phonecard.

3 When the words *Volte číslo* appear, dial the number and wait to be connected.

By pressing this small button on the phone at any time during your call, you can have an English translation of the instructions.

Emergency numbers

4 The card is ejected automatically when it runs out of credit.

100 telefonních jednotek

Telecom phonecards are available at 80, 100 and 150 units

POST OFFICES

THERE ARE A number of post offices in Prague *(see Street Finder on pp238–49)*. The best and largest one is the **Main Post Office** in Jindřišská just off Wenceslas Square. It has a huge variety of services and some, such as sending telegrams, operate for 24 hours a day. It also has a large phone room where you can make international calls. This service operates from 7am to 11pm.

The building can appear confusing as there are 53 windows, or counters, and no English signs. Usually, window 30 gives information about the services available at the other windows. These include buying stamps at windows 20 to 24; phonecards from window 20 and mailing your parcels from windows 10, 11

Post office sign

and 12. Window allocations do sometimes change. Make absolutely certain that you join the queue for the right window, as there will often be as many as twenty people standing in front of you.

USEFUL ADDRESSES

Main Post Office
Jindřišská 14. **Map** 4 D5.
📞 24 22 88 56.

American Express
Václavské náměstí 56.
Map 4 D5.
📞 24 22 46 06.

DHL
Běžecká 1.
📞 35 42 42.

REACHING THE RIGHT NUMBER

	Dial
• Internal (Czech) directory enquiries	121
• Prague directory enquiries and the operator	120
• International exchange and to make a collect call *(ask for an English-speaker)*	0132
• Prague from elsewhere in the Czech Republic	02
• International call followed by the country code	00
• Any problems	0135

• **In case of emergencies ring 158**

Tobacconist's, where you can also buy stamps and phonecards

SENDING A LETTER

THE POSTAL SERVICE, along with the phone service, is run under the auspices of Telecom. The service is fast, efficient and cheap, although prices for all the post office services are expected to increase slightly in the future.

There is no first or second class mail in the Czech Republic, but the majority of letters usually arrive at their destination within a few days.

If you want to send something more valuable through the post, use the registered mail service, which is reliable and efficient. Aerogrammes abroad do not exist.

Postcards or letters can be posted in the many orange post boxes scattered around Prague. Both take around five working days to arrive in England and about a week to get to America. Stamps can be bought from post offices, newsagents or tabáks – who will also tell you what stamps you need. All parcels and registered letters need to be handed in at a post office. For emergency parcels and packages, you can use an international courier service, such as **DHL**.

POSTE RESTANTE

POSTE RESTANTE letters are delivered to the Main Post Office in Jindřišská Street. Go to window 28 (open Monday to Friday 6:30am to 8pm and Saturday 6:30am to 1pm) with your passport or other official identification. The **American Express** office will also hold mail and parcels for up to a month for anyone who is a registered card holder.

Post letters in side flap

Old-style post box attached to a wall

Post your letters in the top flap

Collection times of the mail

One of the new-style post boxes

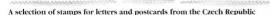

A selection of stamps for letters and postcards from the Czech Republic

Additional Information

Visitors resting around the Jan Hus Monument in the Old Town Square

DISABLED TRAVELLERS

FACILITIES FOR THE disabled are few and far between. Occasionally you will come across a ramp at the entrance to a building to allow the disabled easier access, but this is the exception rather than the rule. There are few organizations that campaign for the disabled and those that do are hampered by public inertia and a lack of money. But these attitudes are slowly changing and, although transport around the city is a major problem, groups do now exist who can help you with advice, sightseeing tours, accommodation and getting around the city. Two of the best organizations to contact are: the **Czech Association of Persons with Disabilities** and the **Federation of Persons with Disabilities**.

Czech Association of Persons with Disabilities
Karlínské náměstí 12.
Map 5 B2.
📞 24 21 59 15.

Union of the Disabled (Federation of Persons with Disabilities)
Konviktská 6. **Map** 3 A5.
📞 24 22 72 03.

International Student Identity Card

CUSTOMS REGULATIONS AND IMMIGRATION

A VALID PASSPORT is needed when entering the Czech Republic. British nationals must have a ten-year passport – a visitor's passport is not valid – but visas are not needed to enter. At present, New Zealand, Canadian, and Australian passport holders still need visas. These are valid for a month and can be obtained from your nearest Czech embassy or consulate before you travel. When you apply for your visa, your passport has to be valid for at least eight more months.

When you arrive at the airport, customs allowances per person are 2 litres (3.6 pints) of wine, 1 litre (1.8 pints) of spirits, 250 cigarettes or equivalent tobacco products. Goods under Kč3,000 in value can be imported duty-free.

You can take in as much foreign currency as you like. But if you want to reconvert Czech crowns into your own currency you have to produce legal cash-transaction slips. It is against the law to take any Czech currency worth above Kč100 out of the country. If you want to export authentic antiques you will have to obtain a special licence (see Shopping pp206–7).

STUDENT INFORMATION

IF YOU ARE ENTITLED to an International Student Identity Card (ISIC), it is worth getting one before travelling to Prague. Admission charges into most of Prague's major tourist sights are cheaper on production of a valid ISIC card. Students can also get cheaper coach travel, and while in the country, train travel. There are a couple of youth hostels in the centre of the city (see Where to Stay, pp182–9). For further up-to-date information about what is available visit the following organizations: **International Union of Students**, the **National Union of Students**, and the tour operator, **Universitas Tour**.

International Union of Students
Pařížská 25. **Map** 3 B3.
📞 24 81 04 38.

EMBASSIES AND CONSULATES

Australian High Commission
Uhland str. 181/3, 10632 Berlin.
📞 (30) 880 0880.
Open 9am–noon (2–5pm by appointment).

Canadian High Commission
Mickiewiczova 6. **Map** 2 F1.
📞 24 31 11 08. **Open** 8:30am–noon & 2–4pm, Mon–Fri.

New Zealand High Commission
Bundeskanzlerplatz 2/10, 5300 Bonn 1 Germany.
📞 228 22 80 70. **Open** 9am–1pm & 2–5:30pm Mon–Thu, 9am–1pm & 2–4pm Fri.

United Kingdom Embassy
Thunovská 14. **Map** 2 E3.
📞 24 51 04 39. **Open** 9am–noon & 12:30–5pm Mon–Fri.

United States Embassy
Tržiště 15. **Map** 2 E3.
📞 24 51 08 47. **Open** 8am–noon & 2:30–4pm Mon–Fri.

National Union of Students
17. listopadu.
Map 3 B2.
[📞] *24 81 04 38.*

Universitas Tours
Jednota Youth Hostel,
Opletalova 38. **Map** 4 D5.
[📞] *24 21 17 73.*

The two English-language newspapers published in Prague

NEWSPAPERS, TV, RADIO

PRAGUE HAS A number of
newspapers including two
weekly English-language
papers, *Prognosis* and *The
Prague Post*. Managed by
Americans, they are both well
produced and provide useful
tips for visitors to the city.
Up-to-date and informative
pieces on Prague, its people
and politics make these both
interesting reads.

Most of the newsstands that
are around Wenceslas Square
and other popular tourist spots
sell the main European papers
and the *International Herald
Tribune*. These are usually a
day old – with the exception

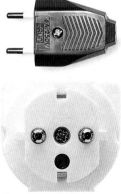

**A two-prong and a three-prong
plug adaptor for use in Prague**

of *The Guardian*, whose
European edition is actually
published in Germany.

There is a larger choice of
television in Prague than ever
before. Western films are
interspersed with well-made
nature programmes and classic
Czech films. The stations also
show a few soap operas, like
Dallas. CNN, the US news
channel, broadcasts weekdays
on CT3 from 11:30pm to
9:55am and 12:30pm to 4pm.
However, schedules are
liable to change.

You can listen to the BBC
World Service on 101.1FM,
but one of the most popular
radio stations is Europe II on
88.2MHz playing a blend of
mainstream pop. Club VOA
on 106.2FM has a similar mix
of music with English news.
Others include, Radio I on
91.9MHz, Radio Golem on
90.3MHz and Radio Bonton
on 99.7MHz. Reception can
be very bad outside the city.

CONVERSION CHART

Imperial to Metric
1 inch = 2.54 centimetres
1 foot = 30 centimetres
1 mile = 1.6 kilometres
1 ounce = 28 grams
1 pound = 454 grams
1 pint = 0.6 litre
1 gallon = 4.6 litres

Metric to Imperial
1 millimetre = 0.04 inch
1 centimetre = 0.4 inch
1 metre = 3 feet 3 inches
1 kilometre = 0.6 mile
1 gram = 0.04 ounce
1 kilogram = 2.2 pounds
1 litre = 1.8 pints

ELECTRICAL ADAPTORS

THE ELECTRICITY SUPPLY in
Prague is 220V AC and
two-pin plugs are used. For
British or US plugs, an adaptor
is needed. This will have to be
bought before leaving home.

PRAGUE TIME

PRAGUE IS ON Central
European time – Green-
wich Mean Time (GMT) plus
1 hour. From the end of March
until the end of September,
summer time is in effect –
this is GMT plus 2 hours.

RELIGIOUS SERVICES

Anglican
St. Clement's; Klimentská 18.
Map 4 D2.
[✝] *11am Sun.*

Baptist
Baptist Church of Prague;
Vinohradská 68. **Map** 6 F1.
[📞] *25 26 25.* [✝] *11am Sun.*

Hussite Church
Church of St. Nicholas;
Staroměstské náměstí.
Map 3 C3.
[✝] *5pm Wed, 12:30pm Sun.*

Interdenominational
International Church; Vrázova 4.
[📞] *311 53 91.*
[✝] *11:15am Sun, also Sunday
School & Bible study groups.*

Jewish
Old-New Synagogue *(see pp88–9).*
Jerusalem Synagogue;
Jeruzalémská 7. **Map** 4 E4.
[✡] *(in Czech) 8:45pm Sat,
sundown Fri.*

Methodist-Evangelical
Ječná 19. **Map** 5 C2.
[📞] *42 25 22 57.*
[✝] *7pm Tue–Sun, 9am Sun.*

Roman Catholic
Services are held in many
churches. Some are:
Dominican Priory; Husova 8.
Map 3 B4.
[📞] *24 21 84 39.*
[✝] *6:30pm daily, 8:30, 10:30am
& 6:30pm Sun.*

Church of St. Joseph; Josefská 4.
Map 2 E3.
[📞] *311 54 74.*
[✝] *10:30am Sun.*

A Roman Catholic service

GETTING TO PRAGUE

PRAGUE IS LOCATED at the heart of Europe and – apart from the Czech Republic's lack of motorways – has good transport connections with the rest of the continent. There are direct flights every day from most of Europe's major cities. However, there are no direct flights as yet from either Australia or the United States. International coach transport is efficient and cheap. But the

ČSA aircraft

journey is about 24 hours from London compared to an hour and a half by air. International rail transport is a popular method of travelling to Prague, but trains tend to get booked up early, especially in the summer. The main train station (Hlavní nádraží) is close to Wenceslas Square and the city centre and, except for the airport, the other major points of arrival to Prague are also fairly central.

AIR TRAVEL

THERE ARE 40 international airlines which now fly to Prague airport. If you are flying from the United States, **Delta Air** operate scheduled flights from the east coast of America. But these are not direct flights – there is a stopover in Frankfurt. There are no Australian or New Zealand carriers flying to Prague, although you can fly **British Airways** with a stop in London. Other airlines include **Air France**, **KLM**, **Air Canada** and **Czechoslovak Airlines (ČSA)**. It takes about one and a half hours to fly from London to Prague and about nine hours from the east coast of America – not including the stopover.

DISCOUNT FARES

BECAUSE OF the increasing popularity of Prague as a tourist destination, many new airlines are starting to fly to the city. Increased competition

has led to a significant drop in the price of flights.

Charter flights have been introduced by a few agents. They are set to become more popular and it is well worth investigating their availability. Remember that these can be subject to last-minute changes and cancellations. Check the ads in the travel sections of major papers for special fares.

APEX (advanced purchase) tickets can be good buys, but they have stringent conditions attached to them. These include having to book your ticket at least a month in advance and severe penalties if you cancel your flight.

If you ring well in advance, airlines will quote you the standard fare, but the price may be lowered nearer the time if seats remain unsold – this is rarely the case in the summer months. Students, senior citizens and regular business travellers may all be able to get discounts. Children under two (who do not occupy a separate seat) pay 10% of

Porters at Ruzyně

the adult fare. Remember fares are more expensive in July and August. If you do manage to get a cheaper deal, ensure that you will get a refund if your agent goes out of business.

AIRLINE OFFICES

Air Canada
Ruzyně Airport, Praha 6.
(643 39 43.

Air France
Václavské náměstí 10. **Map** 3 C5.
(24 22 71 64.

British Airways
Staroměstské náměstí 10. **Map** 3 C3.
(232 90 20.

Czechoslovak Airlines (ČSA)
Revoluční 1. **Map** 4 D2.
(24 21 01 32.

Delta Airlines
Národuí 32. **Map** 3 B5.
(24 23 93 09.

KLM
Václavské náměstí 37. **Map** 4 D5.
(24 22 86 78.

Lufthansa
Pařížská 28. **Map** 3 B3.
(24 81 10 07.

The recently modernized interior of Ruzyně Airport

Ruzyně Airport

Prague's only international airport, Ruzyně, is 15 km (9 miles) northwest of the city centre. Although small, the airport is modern, clean, efficient and functional. Built in 1936, it was modernized during the 1960s and now boasts all the facilities you would expect from an international airport: 24-hour exchange facilities; car rental offices; a small duty-free shop; restaurants; post office and a left-luggage office.

The airport was bought by Air France in 1992 and is presently undergoing further

Sign for passport control

modernization, including the addition of a business class lounge. Other changes include a newly opened catering facility. The quality of the food at the airport's restaurants and of the in-flight food on ČSA airlines has improved dramatically – a trained French chef has now been employed to oversee all the preparation of both the traditional Czech and international dishes.

Transport from the Airport to the City

The airport is linked to the city centre by a regular, efficient bus service run by ČSA. The buses leave from immediately outside the arrivals building. A timetable is available from the airport information office, listing hourly departures, but buses usually leave every half hour, departures often connecting with an incoming flight. You pay the driver on board in crowns and after a 30-minute journey arrive at the ČSA Vltava

Airport bus stop (letiště means airport)

The airport forecourt, where buses and taxis pull up

Two of the car rental agencies at Ruzyně airport

terminal in Revoluční Street (*see Street Finder, map 4*). There is also a public bus, No. 119, which is cheap, but takes longer to get to the city as it stops more frequently and terminates further from the centre at Dejvická metro station (*see the inside back cover*). You can also take a taxi; the rank is just in front of the terminal. It is more expensive, but ask at the information booth how much you should expect to pay to the city and use it as a guide.

Prague's European Air Connections

Prague, situated at the centre of Europe, has good flight connections to most major European cities. It can be reached in less than two and a half hours on direct flights from all the airports marked on the map.

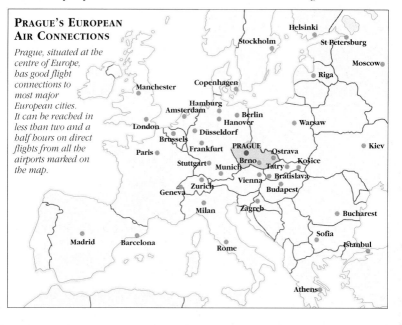

The spacious interior of Prague's main station, Hlavní nádraží

TRAVELLING BY TRAIN

PRAGUE IS CONNECTED by rail to all the major capitals of Europe. Rail travel can be an enjoyable, if rather slow, way to travel to and from Prague. International trains have dining cars and couchettes, and tickets are cheaper than air fares. The railways in the Czech Republic are run by the State (Česko-slovenské Stání Dráhy – ČSD).

The façade of Hlavní nádraží

There are information offices at stations, but they may not have English speakers. PIS and Čedok (see p219), will help you with timetables and prices. There are two types of train run by ČSD. The fastest ones are the *Rychlík* (express) trains. These stop at the major towns and you have to pay a small supplement to travel on them. The very slow trains are *Osobní* (passenger trains). These stop at every station and often travel as slowly as 30 km/h (20 mph). International trains are the fastest, but get delayed at borders.

Tickets can be bought at stations in advance or on the day, but trains tend to get booked up. If you do want to buy a ticket just before your train leaves, be warned that queues at ticket booths can be very long. When you buy your ticket, specify exactly where and when you want to go, whether you want a single or return and what class of ticket you want. First class carriages exist on all trains and guarantee you a seat. In the time-table, an 'R' in a box by a train number means you must have a seat reserved on that train. An 'R' without a box means a reservation is recommended. If you are caught in the wrong carriage, you have to pay an on-the-spot fine.

TRAIN STATIONS

THE BIGGEST and busiest railway station in Prague is Hlavní nádraží (see p34) (more popularly known as Wilsonova Station), which is only a five-minute walk from the city centre. In the 1970s, the original Art Nouveau structure was enlarged and a modern departure hall now dominates the whole terminal. The station is large, efficient and clean with a good-sized, inexpensive, 24-hr

left-luggage office in the base-ment. The nearby luggage lockers are convenient and very cheap but are often broken into. There are also food stalls, bureaux de change and a number of booking and information services in the departure hall.

The other rail stations in the city are Masarykovo nádraží – Prague's oldest terminal, the newly-built and modern Holešovice Station and the smallest, Smíchov Station.

TRAVELLING BY COACH

COACH CONNECTIONS from Prague to many of the major European cities can be infrequent and are often very booked up. However, many of these coach routes are much cheaper, and often faster, than the slower trains. The city's main bus terminal is Florenc, situated on the eastern edge of the New Town. The majority of long-haul, internal coach routes are still run by the large State bus company (Česko-slovenská stání automobilová doprava – ČSAD). During the summer months there are hundreds of coach trips to all the major coastal resorts in southern Europe. These get booked up quickly by Czechs, so buy your ticket in advance and be sure to reserve yourself a seat. International bus timetables are confusing; check with PIS (see p218) for more detailed information. Coach travel is cheap, but long-haul journeys can be uncomfortable and are slower than train or air.

A uniformed ČSD railway porter

Passengers boarding a long-haul coach

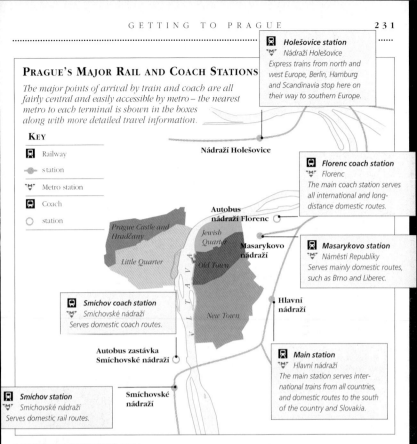

PRAGUE'S MAJOR RAIL AND COACH STATIONS

The major points of arrival by train and coach are all fairly central and easily accessible by metro – the nearest metro to each terminal is shown in the boxes along with more detailed travel information.

KEY

🚊 Railway
⊙ station
ᴹ Metro station
🚌 Coach
○ station

Holešovice station
ᴹ Nádraží Holešovice
Express trains from north and west Europe, Berlin, Hamburg and Scandinavia stop here on their way to southern Europe.

Florenc coach station
ᴹ Florenc
The main coach station serves all international and long-distance domestic routes.

Masarykovo station
ᴹ Náměstí Republiky
Serves mainly domestic routes, such as Brno and Liberec.

Main station
ᴹ Hlavní nádraží
The main station serves international trains from all countries, and domestic routes to the south of the country and Slovakia.

Smíchov coach station
ᴹ Smíchovské nádraží
Serves domestic coach routes.

Smíchov station
ᴹ Smíchovské nádraží
Serves domestic rail routes.

Nádraží Holešovice

Autobus nádraží Florenc

Masarykovo nádraží

Hlavní nádraží

Prague Castle and Hradčany

Jewish Quarter

Little Quarter

Old Town

New Town

Autobus zastávka Smíchovské nádraží

Smíchovské nádraží

VLTAVA

A Czech motorway sign

TRAVELLING BY CAR

TO DRIVE A CAR in the Czech Republic you must be at least 18. Most foreign driving licences are honoured; these include all Canadian, US and EC ones – New Zealand and Australian drivers should get an International Driving Licence. If you bring your own car to Prague, there are a few things which by law you must carry with you at all times. The documents needed are: a valid driver's licence, vehicle registration card, a hire certificate or, if you are borrowing the car, a letter signed by the owner and authorized by a recognized body, such as the AA or RAC, giving you permission to drive it and a Green Card (an international motoring certificate for insurance). Other items you have to carry at all times are a set of replacement bulbs, red warning triangles and a first-aid kit. You also have to display a national identification sticker. It is compulsory to wear seatbelts if fitted, and children under 12 are not allowed to travel in the front seat. When you are driving it is strictly forbidden to have any alcohol in your blood – penalties are severe if you are caught drink driving. There are few motorways in the Czech Republic, although there are good connections to Bratislava and Brno, and more major routes are currently under construction.

Road signs are clear and easy to follow. The speed limit on motorways is 110 km/h (68 mph); on dual and single carriageways 90 km/h (56 mph) and in urban areas 60 km/h (37 mph). The traffic police patrolling the roads are very vigilant, and any infringements are dealt with harshly – expensive cars from abroad are an obvious target (foreigners have to pay any fines immediately). There are also occasional road blocks to catch drunken drivers.

The popular, Czech-made Skoda car

GETTING AROUND PRAGUE

THE CENTRE OF PRAGUE is conveniently small and most of the sights can be reached comfortably on foot. But to cross the city quickly or visit a more remote sight, the public transport is efficient, clean and cheap. It is based on trams, buses and the underground (metro) system, all of which are run by the Prague Transport Corporation (Dopravní-podnik). Throughout this guide, the best method of transport

Walking around the city

is given for each sight. The metro and trams serve the city centre, while buses are used to reach the suburbs. The entire system is simple to use – only one ticket is needed for all three forms of transport. Bus, tram and metro routes are found on city maps, available at most city centre tabáks, bookshops and newsagents; or refer to the map on the inside back cover of this guide.

DRIVING A CAR

MOST VISITORS ARE better off not driving around the centre of Prague. The city's complex web of one-way streets, the large number of pedestrianized areas around the historic core of the city and a very severe shortage of parking spaces make driving very difficult. Prague's public

transport system is a much more efficient way of travelling around the city centre.

If you do decide to use a car, remember that on-the-spot fines for traffic violations are common, especially if you are caught driving in one of the city's restricted areas, such as Wenceslas Square. Prague's motorists have become less disciplined and caution is

often needed, You must drive on the right and the law states that both driver and front- and back-seat passengers should wear seat belts, if they are fitted. The speed limit in the city is 60 km/h (38 mph) unless a sign indicates otherwise. Traffic signs are similar

MIMO ZÁSOBOVÁNÍ
One-way traffic and No stopping except for supply lorries

PRAGUE ON FOOT

Pedestrian zone

Pedestrian crossing

Street or square name and Prague district

Street number   **City registration number**

Walking around Prague is the most enjoyable way to see the city. But it can also be rather hazardous: it is well known that the only drivers to stop for people at pedestrian crossings are foreigners. Some crossings are controlled by traffic lights, but be sure to cross only when the green man is flashing and even then, check the road carefully. Those crossings without lights are largely ignored by drivers. Remember that trams run in the centre of the road and go in both directions, which can be confusing. They also travel at high speeds, occasionally coming upon you unawares. With the uneven cobbled streets, steep hills and a mass of tram lines, flat comfortable shoes are strongly recommended.

Pedestrian traffic lights in Prague

to those in Western Europe. Cars can be useful for seeing sights outside the city. But car rental is expensive and public transport is almost as efficient getting out of the city as in it (see pp228–31).

PARKING

CAR PARKING SPACES in the city centre are scarce and the penalties for illegal parking, harsh. Many parking areas are restricted and the only places to park legally on the street are in front of the New Town Hall in Karlovo náměstí, in Na Florenci and at Hlavní station. Unfortunately, car theft is rife, and expensive Western cars are a favourite target. It is safer to park in an official – preferably under-ground – car park *(see the Street Finder pp244–9).* But these are expensive and tend to get full early on in the morning. Many parking spaces are reserved for office workers and disabled drivers. Parking at central hotels is limited, with only a few spaces allocated. It is better to park at one of the guarded car parks at the edge of the city and use public trans-port. Parking meters are rare in Prague but traffic wardens are not.

Parking sign

TOWING AND CLAMPING

Many Prague locals park on the pavement. But ignoring *No Parking* signs may well mean that you find your car has been towed away or clamped. Both the municipal and the private firms that patrol the city are vigilant and ruthless with illegally parked cars, especially with foreign cars. If your car has disappeared, ring 158 to find out if it has been towed away or stolen. To reclaim your towed-away car, you have to go to one of the parking lots (the police will tell you which one) and pay a hefty fine before the car is released. Wheel clamping is becoming very

Prague's colourful clamp, also known as the Denver Boot

popular. You must pay a fine of several hundred crowns at a police station (the ticket on your windscreen will tell you the address) and return to your car to wait for the clamp to be removed.

THE TRANSPORT SYSTEM

The best and quickest way to get around the city centre is by metro or tram. Prague's rush hours are between 6am and 8am and 3pm and 5pm, Monday to Friday. But more trains, trams and buses run at these times, so crowding is not a problem. Some bus routes to the suburbs only run during these peak hours. From 1 July to 31 August a summer timetable operates and the entire transport system is reduced. Fewer trains, trams and buses run but the service is still efficient and cheap. On-the-spot fines for not having a valid ticket have increased.

One of the many newsstands in Wenceslas Square

TICKETS

Paying on the transport system is based entirely on the honour system, with periodic checks by plain-clothes ticket inspectors who levy an on-the-spot and large fine if you don't have a valid ticket. There is one ticket for use on the entire system – bus, tram and metro. Buy the ticket before you travel and stamp or punch it yourself in the machines provided, otherwise you will be travelling illegally. Tickets are cheap and sold throughout the city. You can buy single ride tickets, from tabák stores and metro stations. There are automatic ticket machines in the metros *(see p234).* Under 10s travel free and 10- to 16-year-olds travel half price. You can also buy one-day and multi-day transport passes *(denní jízdenka).* These give you unlimited rides on buses, trams and metros for a period of one to five days. They are convenient as you do not have to validate them.

Prague's tourist tickets which allow unlimited travel for a specified period

Adult and child tickets for single journeys

Travelling by Metro

THE UNDERGROUND RAILWAY, known as the metro, is the quickest, most comfortable and widely used form of transport in Prague. Managed by the Prague Transport Corporation *(see p232)*, its construction began in 1967. It has three lines, A, B and C, three junctions and 41 stations. The straightforward layout and clear signs make finding your way around the system very easy.

The metro sign for Můstek metro station

FINDING YOUR WAY AROUND THE METRO

METRO ENTRANCES are not always easy to spot. Look for a sign displaying the 'M' within an upside-down triangle *(see right)*. The street entrance will normally lead you down a flight of steps. A high-pitched bleep (for the blind) at some entrances can also help to guide you. Once you have passed through the unmanned ticket barriers, continue down the fast-moving escalators to the trains. At the bottom of each escalator is a long central corridor with a platform on either side for trains travelling in either direction. Signs suspended from the ceiling indicate the direction of the trains *(see opposite page)*. The edges of the platforms are marked with a white, broken line which should not be crossed until the train stops. The metro doors open and close automatically, giving a recorded message when they are about to close. During the journey the name of the next station is announced in Czech.

Maps of the underground system can be found above each metro door. However, line B, which is bright yellow, can be hard to read. Before using this line, consult the map at the end of this book to see how many stops to travel.

Line A is the most useful for tourists, because it covers all the main areas of the city centre – Prague Castle, the Little Quarter, the Old Town and the New Town – as well as the main shopping area around Wenceslas Square.

Displayed above some seats are disabled signs. These seats should be given up for the elderly, disabled, and those with small children.

The spacious interior of Můstek metro station

AUTOMATIC TICKET MACHINES

You can buy transport tickets at designated ticket sellers *(see p233)* or at the automatic ticket machines in the metro. Machine tickets vary in design and colour, but are still valid on all forms of transport. Be sure you know which machine is for adults and which for children as you can't buy an adult's ticket from a child's ticket machine. Once stamped, the single-journey ticket is valid for an hour. The price of tickets increases regularly.

A child's and adult's ticket from ticket machines

1 The price of a child's or an adult's ticket is shown at the top left-hand corner of the machine. Check you are at the correct machine before you put any money in.

2 You must wait until the small green light comes on before putting your money in the machine.

3 Insert the correct amount of money into the slot for the type of ticket you require.

4 This indicates the fare for other travellers, such as dogs, pushchairs and large luggage.

5 Collect your ticket from this slot.

MAKING A JOURNEY BY METRO

1 The letters, each in a different colour, indicate the three metro lines. The number above the letter is the time it takes to get from one end of the line to the other.

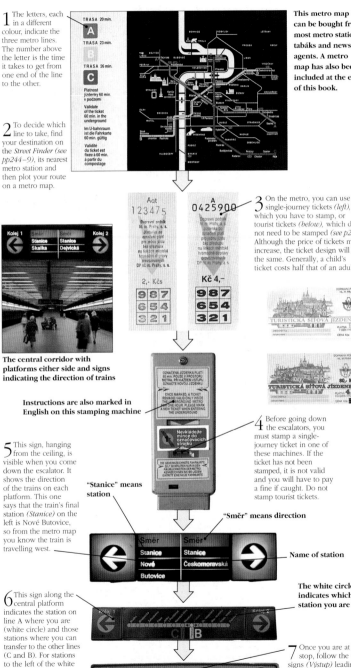

This metro map can be bought from most metro stations, tabáks and newsagents. A metro map has also been included at the end of this book.

2 To decide which line to take, find your destination on the *Street Finder (see pp244–9)*, its nearest metro station and then plot your route on a metro map.

The central corridor with platforms either side and signs indicating the direction of trains

3 On the metro, you can use single-journey tickets *(left)*, which you have to stamp, or tourist tickets *(below)*, which do not need to be stamped *(see p233)*. Although the price of tickets may increase, the ticket design will stay the same. Generally, a child's ticket costs half that of an adult's.

Instructions are also marked in English on this stamping machine

4 Before going down the escalators, you must stamp a single-journey ticket in one of these machines. If the ticket has not been stamped, it is not valid and you will have to pay a fine if caught. Do not stamp tourist tickets.

5 This sign, hanging from the ceiling, is visible when you come down the escalator. It shows the direction of the trains on each platform. This one says that the train's final station *(Stanice)* on the left is Nové Butovice, so from the metro map you know the train is travelling west.

"Stanice" means station

"Směr" means direction

Name of station

6 This sign along the central platform indicates the station on line A where you are (white circle) and those stations where you can transfer to the other lines (C and B). For stations to the left of the white circle follow the arrow to the left, and vice-versa for stations to the right.

The white circle indicates which station you are in

7 Once you are at your stop, follow the exit signs *(Výstup)* leading out of the metro system.

Travelling by Tram

Trams are Prague's oldest method of public transport. Horse-drawn trams appeared on the streets in 1879, but by 1891 the first electric tram was in operation. After the metro, the tram system is the fastest and most efficient way of getting around the city. Some lines only operate in the rush hour and there are a number of night trams, all of which pass by Lazarská in the New Town.

TRAM TICKETS

The tram system is run by the Prague Transport Corporation (see p230). Tram tickets are also valid for the metro and buses (see p233).

You have to buy your ticket before you board a tram. Once you have entered, you will see two or three small punching machines on metal poles just inside the door. Insert your ticket, then pull the lever towards you.

If you do not punch your ticket it is not valid and, if you are caught by a ticket inspector, you will have to pay an on-the-spot fine (see

p233). A single-journey ticket is valid for one journey only (see p233), however long.

At every tram stop there is a timetable – the stop underlined is where you are standing. All the stops below that line indicate where that tram is heading.

Trams run every 10 to 20 minutes. The doors open and close automatically and each stop is announced by a recorded message in Czech. After the metro closes, a small number of night trams run every 40 minutes or so. These trams (numbers 51 to 58) are marked by blue numbers at the tram stop.

Tram Signs
These are found at every tram stop and tell you which trams stop there, and in what direction each tram is going.

Tram logo

Name of the tram stop

The direction each tram is heading in

Numbers indicate which trams stop here

One of the traditional 1950s Tatra trams

USEFUL TRAM ROUTES

These three tram routes are the most useful for getting around the centre of Prague. They pass many of the major sights on both sides of the Vltava, so are also a cheap, pleasant way of sightseeing.

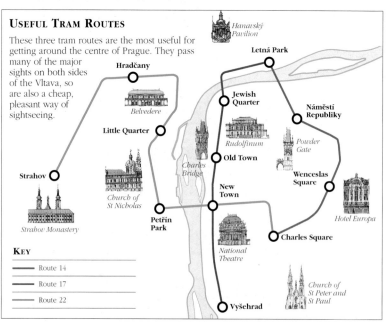

Hanavský Pavilion

Letná Park

Hradčany

Belvedere

Jewish Quarter

Náměstí Republiky

Little Quarter

Rudolfinum

Powder Gate

Strahov

Church of St Nicholas

Charles Bridge

Old Town

Wenceslas Square

Hotel Europa

Strahov Monastery

Petřín Park

New Town

National Theatre

Charles Square

Church of St Peter and St Paul

Vyšehrad

KEY

—— Route 14

—— Route 17

—— Route 22

Travelling by Bus

YOU ARE UNLIKELY to use a bus unless you want to visit the outer suburbs. By law, buses are not allowed in the city centre (they produce noxious fumes and the streets are too narrow), so they transport people from the suburbs to tram and metro stops outside the centre.

BUS TICKETS

A typical public bus in Prague

AS WITH THE TRAM, you must always buy a ticket before you board a bus. Tickets are available from all the usual agents *(see p233)*. Once

again, you must validate your ticket in the punching machine on the bus. If you buy a single-journey ticket, it is only valid for one journey. Each time you change bus, you will have to buy a new ticket, unless you have a tourist ticket *(see p233)*. The doors open and close automatically and the end of the boarding period is signalled by an irritating high-pitched signal. You are expected to give up your seat for the elderly and disabled.

Bus timetables are located at every stop. They have the

Bus stop logo

numbers of all the buses that stop there and the timetable for each route. Unlike in most other capitals, buses nearly always run on time. The frequency varies considerably. In the rush hour there may be 12 to 15 buses an hour, at other times as few as three.

Throughout the night there are 12 buses which go to the outer areas not served by the tram and metro system.

Travelling by Taxi

FOR VISITORS TO PRAGUE taxis are a useful but often frustrating form of transport. Until 1989 all taxis belonged to the Prague Transport Corporation but they are now all privately owned and run. Unfortunately there are more and more unscrupulous taxi drivers who are out to charge as much as they can get away with, so it's worth taking a few simple precautions.

TAXI FARES

One of the many taxi ranks in the centre of the town

AS SOON AS you enter a taxi there is a minimum charge. After that, by law the fare should increase at a set rate per kilometre. However, this set charge is rarely, if ever, adhered to and taxis can be a very expensive way of getting around the city. Taxi meters can be set at four different rates but for journeys in the city it should be set at one (the cheapest). However, rather than depend on the meters –

they are often rigged – it is a wise move to negotiate a fare you think is reasonable before you enter the cab. Vigorous bargaining can often bring the price down. Few taxi drivers speak more than the most rudimentary English, so communication can be difficult. Unless your Czech pronunciation is good, write down your destination for them in Czech. At night, charges will increase, some-times by 200 or even 300 per

Taxi receipts, if requested, are required to be given by law.

The distance travelled	Amount charged

An illuminated taxi sign

cent. Be sure surcharges are included in the figure you negotiate beforehand. If problems do arise at the end of the journey, ask for a receipt before you pay. This will normally deter drivers from trying to overcharge you. Avoid taxis around the main tourist sights, these can often be the worst offenders. Despite occasional problems, taxis are a safe form of transport and women should feel comfortable alone in them.

The meter displays your fare and surcharges.

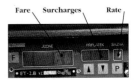

Fare   Surcharges   Rate

STREET FINDER

T HE MAP REFERENCES given for all the sights, hotels, restaurants, bars, shops and entertainment venues described in this book refer to the maps in this section. A complete index of street names and all the places of interest marked, can be found on the following pages. The key map (right) shows the area of Prague covered by the *Street Finder*. This map includes sightseeing areas, as well as districts for hotels, restaurants, pubs and entertainment venues.

In keeping with Czech maps, none of the street names in the index or on the Street Finder have the Czech word for street, *ulice*, included (though you may see it on the city's street signs). For instance, Celetná ulice appears as Celetná in both the index and the Street Finder. The numbers preceding some street names are dates. In our index we ignore the numbers, so that 17. listopadu (17 November), is listed under 'L'.

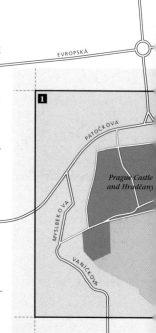

KEY TO STREET FINDER

	Major sight
	Places of interest
	Other building
"M"	Metro station
	Train station
	Coach station
	Tram stop
	Funicular railway
	River boat boarding point
	Taxi rank
P	Car park
	Tourist information office
	Hospital with casualty unit
	Police station
	Church
	Synagogue
	Post office
	Railway line
	One-way street
	City wall
	Pedestrian street

SCALE OF MAP PAGES

0 metres 200
0 yards 200
1:10,000

View of the Little Quarter, Hradčany and Prague Castle from the Old Town Bridge Tower

Aerial view of the
Baroque Church of
St Nicholas in the Old
Town Square, from the
tower at the top of the
Old Town Hall

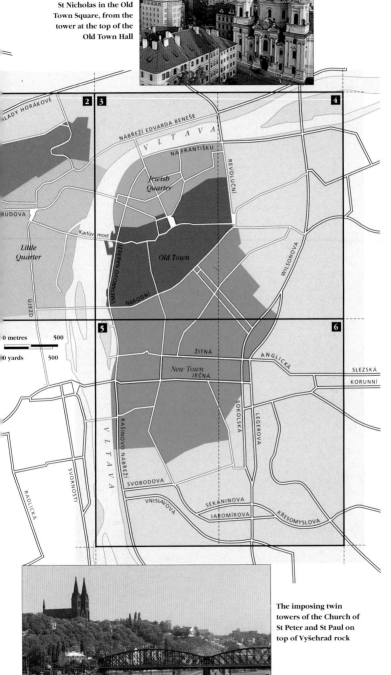

The imposing twin
towers of the Church of
St Peter and St Paul on
top of Vyšehrad rock

Street Finder Index

THE ORDER OF THE NAMES in the index is affected by the *háček*, the accent like an inverted circumflex (*háček* means "little hook"). In the Czech alphabet, **č**, **ř**, **š** and **ž** are treated as separate letters. Street names beginning with **ř**, for example, are listed after those beginning with **r** without an accent.

Churches, buildings, museums and monuments are marked on the Street Finder maps with their English and Czech names. In the index, both forms are listed. However, English names for streets and squares, such as Wenceslas Square, do not appear on the maps. Where they are listed in the index, the Czech name is given in brackets in the form that appears on the map.

USEFUL WORDS	
dům	house
hrad	castle
kostel	church
klášter	convent, monastery
most	bridge
nábřeží	embankment
nádraží	station
náměstí	square
sady	park
schody	steps
třída	avenue
ulice	street
ulička	lane
zahrada	garden

A

Albertov	5 C4
Alšovo nábřeží	3 A3
Americká	6 F3
Anenská	3 A4
Anenské náměstí	3 A4
Anežská	3 C2
Anglická	6 E2
Anny Letenské	6 F1
Apolinářská	5 C4
Archbishop's Palace	2 D3
Arcibiskupský palác	2 D3
At St Thomas's	2 E3
At the Three Ostriches	2 F3
autobusové nádraži Praha, Florenc	4 F3
autobusové zast. Hradčanská	2 D1

B

Badeniho	2 F1
Balbínova	6 E2
Bartolomějská	3 B5
Barvířská	4 E2
Bazilika sv. Jiří	2 E2
Bělehradská	6 E2
Belgická	6 F3
Bělohorská	1 A4
Belvedér	2 E1
Belvedere	2 E1
Benátská	5 B3
Benediktská	4 D3
Besední	2 E5
Bethlehem Chapel	3 B4
Betlémská	3 A5
Betlémská kaple	3 B4
Betlémské náměstí	3 B4
Bílkova	3 B2
Biskupská	4 E2
Biskupský dvůr	4 E2
Blanická	6 F2

Bolzanova	4 E4
Boršov	3 A4
Botanical Gardens	5 B3
Botanická zahrada	5 B3
Botič	6 D5
Botičská	5 B4
Boženy Němcové	6 D4
Bridge Street (Mostecká)	2 E3
Bruselská	6 E3
Brusnice	1 C2
Břehová	3 A2
Břetislavova	2 D3

C

Capuchin Monastery	1 B2
Carolinum	3 C4
Celetná	3 C3
Chaloupeckého	1 B5
Chalice Restaurant	6 D3
Charles Bridge (Karlův most)	2 F4
continues	3 A4
Charles Square (Karlovo náměstí)	5 B2
Charles Street (Karlova)	2 A4
continues	3 B4
Charvátova	3 B5
Chodecká	1 A5
Chotkova	2 E1
Chotkovy sady	2 F1
Chrám sv. Víta	2 D2
Church of Our Lady before Týn	3 C3
Church of Our Lady beneath the Chain	2 E4
Church of Our Lady of the Snows	3 C5
Church of Our Lady Victorious	2 D4
Church of St Castullus	3 C2

Church of St Catherine	5 C3
Church of St Cyril and St Methodius	5 B2
Church of St Gall	3 C4
Church of St Giles	3 B4
Church of St Ignatius	5 C2
Church of St James	3 C3
Church of St John on the Rock	5 B3
Church of St Lawrence	1 C5
Church of St Martin in the Wall	3 B5
Church of St Nicholas (Little Quarter)	2 D3
Church of St Nicholas (Old Town)	3 B3
Church of St Simon and St Jude	3 B2
Church of St Stephen	5 C2
Church of St Thomas	2 E3
Church of St Ursula	3 A5
Church of the Holy Ghost	3 B3
Cihelná	2 F3
Clam-Gallas Palace	3 B4
Clam-Gallasův palác	3 B4
Clementinum	3 A4
Cubist Houses	3 B2
Cukrovarnická	1 A1

Č

Čechův most	3 B2
Čelakovského sady	6 E1
continues	6 D1
Černá	5 B1
Černín Palace	1 B3
Černínská	1 B2
Černínský palác	1 B3
Čertovka	2 F4
Červená	3 B3

D

Dalibor Tower	2 E2
Daliborka	2 E2
Dělostřelecká	1 A1
Diskařská	1 A5
Dittrichova	5 A2
Divadelní	3 A5
Dlabačov	1 A4
Dlážděná	4 E4
Dlouhá	3 C3
Dražického	2 F3
Dražického náměstí	2 E3
Dřevná	5 A3
Dům pánů z Kunštátu	3 B4
Dům U Dvou zlatých medvědů	3 B4
Dušní	3 B2
Dvořák Museum	6 D2
Dvořákovo nábřeží	3 A2

E

Elišky Krásnohorské	3 B2
Estates Theatre	3 C4

F

Faust House	5 B3
Faustův dům	5 B3
Florenc (metro)	4 F3
Franciscan Garden	3 C5
Francouzská	6 F2
Františkánská zahrada	3 C5
Fügnerovo náměstí	6 D3
Funicular Railway	2 D5

G

Gogolova	2 F1
Golden Lane (Zlatá ulička	2 E2
Golz-Kinský Palace	3 C3

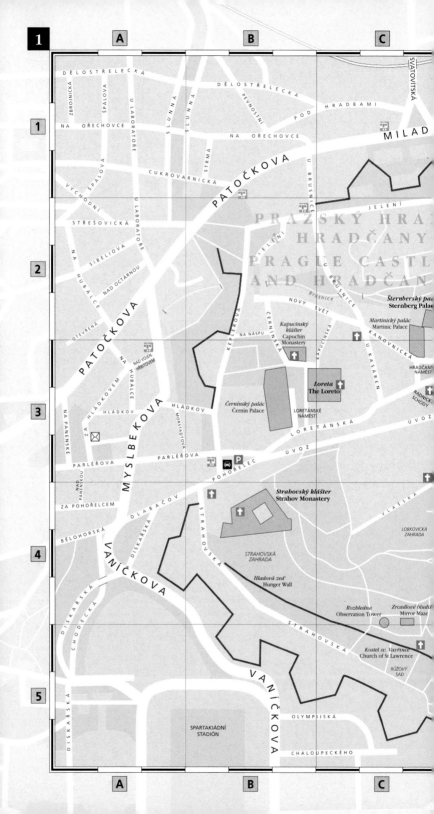

A   B   C

1

DĚLOSTŘELECKÁ

ZBROJNICKÁ
ŠPÁLOVA
U LABORATOŘE

SLUNNÁ
SLUNNÁ

DĚLOSTŘELECKÁ
PEVNOSTNÍ

POD HRADBAMI

SVATOVÍTSKÁ

NA   OŘECHOVCE

STRMÁ

NA   OŘECHOVCE

U BRUSNICE

MILAD

PATOČKOVA

VÝCHODNÍ
ŠPÁLOVA

CUKROVARNICKÁ

JELENÍ

STŘEŠOVICKÁ

U LABORATOŘE

JELENÍ

PRÁZSKÝ HRAD
HRADČANY
PRAGUE CASTLE
AND HRADČAN

2

NA   HUBALCE
ŠIBELIOVA
NAD OCTÁRNOU

OTEVŘENÁ

PATOČKOVA

Brusnice
BRUSNICE

NOVÝ SVĚT

Šternberský pa
Sternberg Palace

KEPLEROVA

NA NÁSPU

ČERNÍNSKÁ

*Kapucínský
klášter*
**Capuchin
Monastery**

KAPUCÍNSKÁ

U KASÁREN

Martinický palác
Martinic Palace

KANOVNICKÁ

HRADČANS'
NÁMĚSTÍ

3

NA PANENSKÉ

ZA HLÁDKOVEM

NA HUBALCE

NAD VOJEN
HŘBITOVEM

HLÁDKOV

HLÁDKOV
MORSTADTOVA

Černínský palác
Černin Palace

Loreta
The Loreto

LORETÁNSKÉ
NÁMĚSTÍ

RADNICK
SCHODY

PARLÉŘOVA

PARLÉŘOVA

POHOŘELEC

LORETÁNSKÁ

ÚVOZ

ÚVOZ

NAD
PANĚNSKOU

ZA POHOŘELCEM

DLABAČOV

BĚLOHORSKÁ

Strabovský klášter
Strahov Monastery

STRAHOVSKÁ

VLAŠSKÁ

LOBKOVICKÁ
ZAHRADA

4

DISKAŘSKÁ

VANÍČKOVA

STRAHOVSKÁ
ZAHRADA

Hladová zeď
Hunger Wall

Rozhledna
Observation Tower

Zrcadlové bludiš
Mirror Maze

STRAHOVSKÁ

DISKAŘSKÁ
CHODECKÁ

Kostel sv. Vavřince
Church of St Lawrence

*RŮŽOVÝ
SAD*

5

DISKAŘSKÁ

VANÍČKOVA

OLYMPIJSKÁ

SPARTAKIÁDNÍ
STADIÓN

CHALOUPECKÉHO

A   B   C

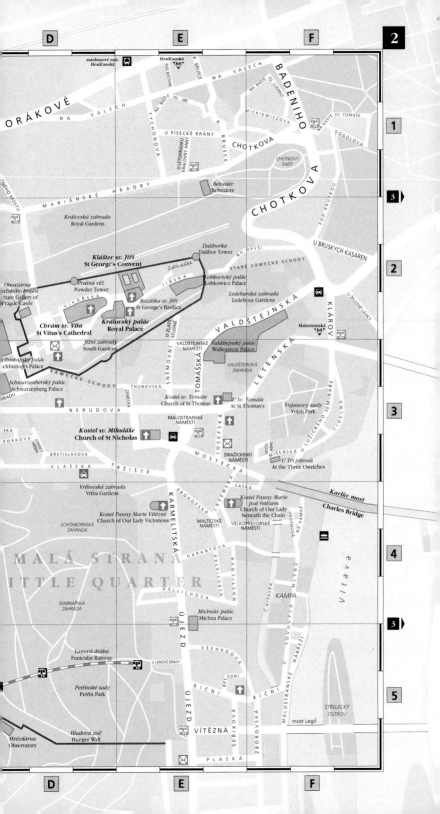

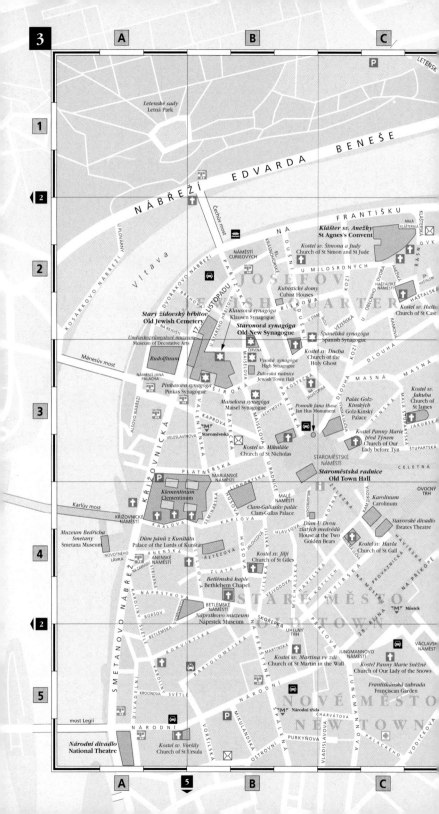

A   B   C

1

2

2

3

4

2

5

LETENSK

Letenské sady
Letná Park

NÁBŘEŽÍ   EDVARDA   BENEŠE

FRANTIŠKU

NA

Čechův most

NÁMĚSTÍ
CURIEOVYCH

PAŘÍŽSKÁ

EL.KRÁSNOHORSKÉ

DUŠNÍ

KOZÍ

MALÁ
KLÁŠTERSKÁ

Klášter sv. Anežky
St Agnes's Convent

Kostel sv. Šimona a Judy
Church of St Simon and St Jude

U MILOSRDNÝCH

RÁSNOVKA

KLÁŠTERSKÁ

JOSEFOV
JEWISH QUARTER

Vltava

DVOŘÁKOVO NÁBŘEŽÍ

17. LISTOPADU

U STARÉHO HŘBITOVA

U STARÉ ŠKOLY

BÍLKOVA

VĚZEŇSKÁ

U OBECNÍHO DVORA

HAŠTALSKÉ
NÁMĚSTÍ

ZA
HAŠTALEM

Kostel sv. Hašt
Church of St Cast

RÁMOVÁ

HAŠTALSKÁ

NA MIŠTRY

Kubistické domy
Cubist Houses

Klausová synagóga
Klausen Synagogue

KOSÁRKOVO NÁBŘEŽÍ

Starý židovský hřbitov
Old Jewish Cemetery

NA REJDIŠTI

Uměleckoprůmyslové muzeum
Museum of Decorative Arts

Staronová synagóga
Old-New Synagogue

ČERVENÁ

MAISELOVA

Vysoká synagóga
High Synagogue

Španělská synagóga
Spanish Synagogue

Kostel sv. Ducha
Church of the
Holy Ghost

DLOUHÁ

DLOUHÁ

MASNÁ

MASNÁ

Kostel sv.
Jakuba
Church of
St James

Mánesův most

Rudolfinum

NÁMĚSTÍ JANA
PALACHA

Pinkasová synagóga
Pinkas Synagogue

ŠIROKÁ

Maiselova synagóga
Maisel Synagogue

KOSTEČNÁ

PAŘÍŽSKÁ

NA

SAUTOVKA

JÁCHYMOVA

Židovská radnice
Jewish Town Hall

Pomník Jana Husa
Jan Hus Monument

Palác Golz-
Kinských
Golz-Kinský
Palace

MALÁ ŠTUPARTSKÁ

JAKUBSKÁ

ALŠOVO NÁBŘEŽÍ

VALENTINSKÁ

KAPROVA

MAISELOVA

STUPARTSKÁ

VELESLAVÍNOVA

Staroměstská

KŘIŽOVNICKÁ

U RADNICE

Kostel sv. Mikuláše
Church of St Nicholas

Kostel Panny Marie
před Týnem
Church of Our
Lady before Týn

STAROMĚSTSKÉ
NÁMĚSTÍ

CELETNÁ

Karlův most

P

PLATNÉŘSKÁ

MARIÁNSKÉ
NÁMĚSTÍ

LINHARTSKÁ

HUSOVA

MALÉ
NÁMĚSTÍ

Staroměstská radnice
Old Town Hall

OVOCNÝ
TRH

Klementinum
Clementinum

KARLOVA

KARLOVA

SEMINÁŘSKÁ

Clam-Gallasův palác
Clam-Gallas Palace

JILSKÁ

ŽELEZNÁ

ZLATNICKÁ

Karolinum
Carolinum

Stavovské divadlo
Estates Theatre

KŘIŽOVNICKÉ
NÁMĚSTÍ

Muzeum Bedřicha
Smetany
Smetana Museum

NOVOTNÉHO
LÁVKA

Dům pánů z Kunštátu
Palace of the Lords of Kunštát

ANENSKÁ

ŘETĚZOVÁ

JALOVCOVA

Dům U Dvou
zlatých medvědů
House at the Two
Golden Bears

Kostel sv. Havla
Church of St Gall

HAVÍŘSKÁ

NA PŘÍKOPĚ

PROVAZNICKÁ

ANENSKÉ
NÁMĚSTÍ

STŘÍBRNÁ

Kostel sv. Jiljí
Church of St Giles

SMETANOVO NÁBŘEŽÍ

ZLATÁ

VEJVODOVA

Betlémská kaple
Bethlehem Chapel

MICHALSKÁ

HAVELSKÁ

KOŽNÁ

KOTCE

RYTÍŘSKÁ

NA MŮSTKU

Müstek

NÁPRSTKOVA

BORŠOV

BETLÉMSKÉ
NÁMĚSTÍ

BETLÉMSKÁ

KONVIKTSKÁ

KAROLÍNY SVĚTLÉ

BARTOLOMĚJSKÁ

NÁPRSTKOVA

BETLÉMSKÉ
NÁMĚSTÍ

Náprstkovo muzeum
Náprstek Museum

SKOŘEPKA

PERŠTÝNE

UHELNÝ
TRH

PERLOVÁ

STARÉ MĚSTO
OLD TOWN

JUNGMANNOVO
NÁMĚSTÍ

VÁCLAVSKÉ
NÁMĚSTÍ

most Legií

DIVADELNÍ

KROCÍNOVA

SVĚTLÉ

OSTROVNÍ

PERŠTÝNE

MARTINSKÁ

Kostel sv. Martina ve zdi
Church of St Martin in the Wall

NÁRODNÍ

Kostel Panny Marie Sněžné
Church of Our Lady of the Snows

Františkánská zahrada
Franciscan Garden

JUNGMANNOVA

Národní třída

CHARVÁTOVA

NOVÉ MĚSTO
NEW TOWN

Národní divadlo
National Theatre

NÁRODNÍ

Kostel sv. Voršily
Church of St Ursula

VORŠILSKÁ

MIKULANDSKÁ

SPÁLENÁ

PURKYŇOVA

VLADISLAVOVA

PALACKÉHO

CHARVÁTOVA

VODIČKOVA

A   B   C

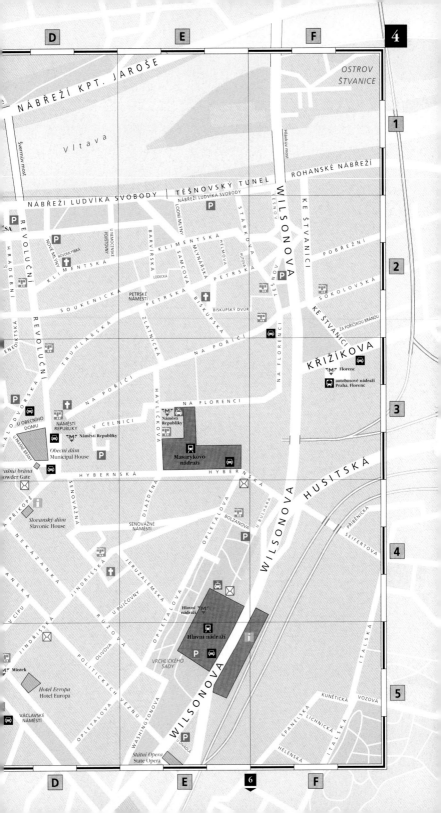

D   **E**   **F**   **4**

OSTROV
ŠTVANICE

NÁBŘEŽÍ KPT. JAROŠE

1

Švermův most

V l t a v a

ROHANSKÉ NÁBŘEŽÍ

TĚŠNOVSKÝ TUNEL

NÁBŘEŽÍ LUDVÍKA SVOBODY | NÁBŘEŽÍ LUDVÍKA SVOBODY

WILSONOVA

KE ŠTVANICI

2

REVOLUČNÍ

HRADEBNÍ

KLIMENTSKÁ

NOVÉ MLÝNY

U NEMOCNICE POŠTOVNY

NOVOMLÝNSKÁ

BARVÍŘSKÁ

KLIMENTSKÁ

SAMCOVA

MLYNÁŘSKÁ

HELMOVA

PETRSKÁ

STÁRKOVA

PUTOVÁ

POBŘEŽNÍ

LODECKÁ

SOUKENICKÁ

PETRSKÉ
NÁMĚSTÍ

PETRSKÁ

ZLATNICKÁ

BISKUPSKÁ

BISKUPSKÝ DVŮR

SOKOLOVSKÁ

KE ŠTVANICI

ZA PORÍČSKOU BRANOU

REVOLUČNÍ

TRUHLÁŘSKÁ

NA POŘÍČÍ

NA FLORENCI

TĚŠNOV

KŘIŽÍKOVA

3

M Florenc

autobusové nádraží
Praha, Florenc

KLADDVORSKÁ

U OBECNÍHO
DOMU

NÁMĚSTÍ
REPUBLIKY

Obecní dům
Municipal House

V CELNICI

HAVLÍČKOVA

NA FLORENCI

NÁMĚSTÍ
REPUBLIKY

M Náměstí Republiky

U PRAŠNÉ BRÁNY

prašná brána
Powder Gate

HYBERNSKÁ

Masarykovo-
nádraží

HYBERNSKÁ

WILSONOVA

HUSITSKÁ

PŘÍBĚNICKÁ

NA PŘÍKOPĚ

SENOVÁŽNÁ

Slovanský dům
Slavonic House

DLÁŽDĚNÁ

SENOVÁŽNÉ
NÁMĚSTÍ

OPLETALOVA

BOLZÁNOVA

U BULHARA

ŠEIFERTOVA

4

NEKÁZANKA

JINDŘIŠSKÁ

JERUZALÉMSKÁ

PANSKÁ

V CÍPU

U PŮJČOVNY

RŮŽOVÁ

OPLETALOVA

Hlavní
nádraží

M Hlavní
nádraží

JINDŘIŠSKÁ

OLIVOVA

POLITICKÝCH VĚZŇŮ

Hlavní nádraží

ITALSKÁ

Můstek

Hotel Evropa
Hotel Europa

VRCHLICKÉHO
SADY

5

VÁCLAVSKÉ
NÁMĚSTÍ

OPLETALOVA

WASHINGTONOVA

VÍTĚZNÁ

WILSONOVA

KUNĚTICKÁ

VOZOVÁ

ŠPANĚLSKÁ

LICHNICKÁ

ITALSKÁ

Státní Opera
State Opera

HELÉNSKÁ

D   **E**   **6**   **F**

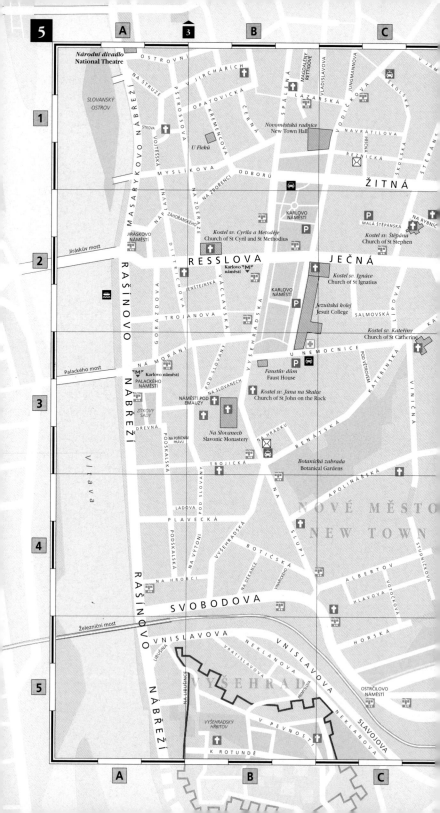

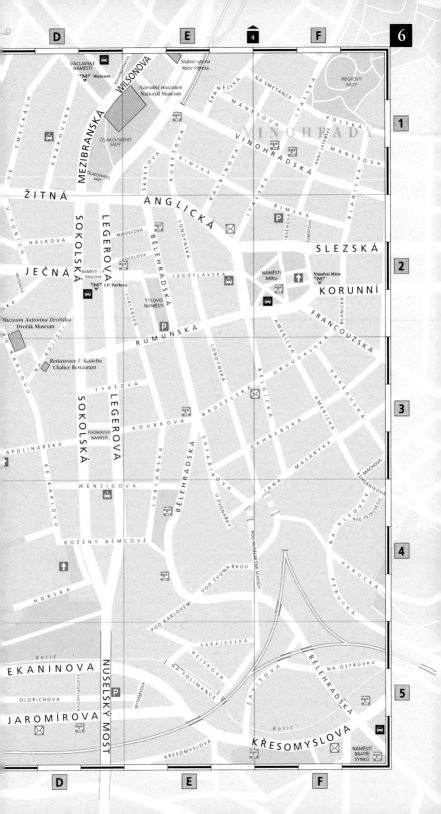

General Index

A

ABC Theatre 212, 214
Academy of Fine Arts 176
Adalbert, St 21, 22, 136, 140, 163
Adam and Eve (Cranach) 113, 114
Adria 186, 188
Adria Palace 144
Agencies (accommodation) 184
Agnes, St 23, 35, 44, 92
Air pollution 221
Air travel 228–9
Airport (Ruzyně) 228, 229
Akropolis 199, 203
Albatros 208, 209
Aleš, Mikuláš
    George of Poděbrady and
    Matthias Corvinus 92
    National Theatre murals 33
    Old Town Hall decorations 73
    Star Hunting Lodge museum 163
    Štorch house 62, 68
    U Rotta decorations 62
    Wiehl House 144
All Saints' Chapel (Royal Palace)
    104, 105
Allegory of Night (Braun) 111
Alliprandi, Giovanni Battista 110, 135
Altarpiece of the Holy Trinity (Master
    of the Litoměřice Altar) 108, 109
Amadeus (film) 63
American Cultural Centre 221
American Express 219, 222, 223, 225
Anchor 207, 209
Angermayer, Johann-Adalbert 109
    Still Life with Watch 107
Anglican Church 227
Ann, St 138
Anne, Empress 110
Anthony of Padua, St 69, 137
Antique Clocks 208, 209
Antiques 208, 209
    customs regulations 226
Aostalli, Ottavio 127, 141
Apartments (self-catering) 185
Arbes Bookshop 208, 209
Archbishop's Palace 48, 111
Arcibiskupský Palác 111
Arcimboldo, Giuseppe,
    Rudolph II 28
Art Nouveau 40, 148–9
Asam, Kosmas Damian 71
Assicurazioni Generali Building 145
Assumption of the Virgin Mary 106
At Black Dora's 200
At the Black Eagle 135
At the Black Madonna 63, 172
At the Black Sun 63
At the Blue Duckling 202
At the Cedar 204
At the Chalice 203
At the Fleks 155
At the Golden Cross 208, 209
At the Golden Grape (Marienbad) 169
At the Golden Horseshoe 123
At the Golden Snake 78
At the Golden Spit 204

At the Golden Unicorn
    (Little Quarter) 132
At the Golden Unicorn
    (Old Town) 68
At the Golden Scales 124
At the Golden Well 78, 172, 173
At the Golem 193, 198, 201
At the Green Frog 200
At the Haláneks 75
At the Minute 172, 173
At the Old Synagogue 201
At the Ox 69
At the Painter's 202
At the Pillar 204
At the Poor Wretch's 68
At the Red Fox 69
At the Red Wheel 201
At St Thomas's 125, 127, 202
At the Schnell's 201
At the Spider 172
At the Stone Bell 66
At the Stone Madonna 68
At the Stone Ram 68
At the Swans 201
At the Three Golden Bells 134
At the Three Little Fiddles 124
At the Three Ostriches 133, 134, 202
At the Three Red Roses 130
At the Three Rhinos 203
At the Two Golden Bears 29, 71
    Street-by-Street map 62
At the Two Suns 130
At the Unicorn 172
At the Vulture 172
Atlantic 186, 187
Atrium 182, 186, 189
Atrium in Žižkov 212, 214
Augusta, Bishop Jan 167
Augusta Prison (Křivoklát Castle) 167
Augustine, St 137
Augustinians 115, 127, 154
Austerlitz, Battle of (1805) 32
Australian High Commission 226
Aventis 209
Axa 186, 187

B

BBC World Service 227
Ball Game Hall 29, 111
Ballet 212
Balšánek, Antonín 64
Bambino di Praga 131
Banknotes 223
Banks 222
Baptist Church of Prague 227
Barbara, St 139
Baroque architecture 30–31, 44,
    45, 48–9
Baroque art 109
Bars 205, 219
Basle, Council of 152
Bassano, Jacopo 115
Bassevi, Hendela 87
Bayer, Paul Ignaz
    Church of St Ignatius 152
    Jesuit College 152

Bazilika sv. Jiří 98–9, 214
Beautiful Room 208, 209
Becherovka 197
Běchovice 52
Beck, Moses 86
Beer 196–7
Beer halls 127, 155, 190, 197, 205
Beethoven, Ludwig van 50, 78, 132
Belvedér 110–11
Belvedere 28, 29, 110–11
    Prague's Best 46, 48
Bendelmayer, Bedřich 148
Bendl, Jan 79
Benedictines 70, 90, 153, 163
Beneš, Edvard 19, 34
Benzi, St Philip 136
Bernard, St 139
Bernini, Gian Lorenzo 138, 163
Bertramka 31
    concerts 51, 212, 214
    Mozart Museum 160, 214
Bethlehem Chapel 75
    history 25, 26, 27
    Prague's Best 44
    Street-by-Street map 77
Betlémská kaple 75
Bibita 213, 214
Bílá Hora a Hvězda 163
Bílá Labut' 207, 209
"Black sheriffs" 220, 221
"Black Theatre" 212
Blaeu, William 121
Blanche de Valois 167
Boats, Vltava river trips 50
Bohemia Aventis 208
Bohemia Crystal 208, 209
Bohemia Glass 209
Bohemian Brethren 91
Bohemian Chancellery 105
Bohemian crystal 206, 208
Bohemian Diet 104
Boleslav I, Prince 17, 18, 20
Boleslav II, Prince 18, 20
    Břevnov Monastery 163
    Church of St Lawrence 140
    St George's Convent 106
    tomb of 99
Bomiel Pantomime 212, 214
Bookshops 207, 208, 209
Borgia, St Francis 138
Bořiat, Jaroslav 118
Borovička 197
Borromeo, St Charles 152
Borromini, Francesco 128
Bossi, CG 66
Botanical Gardens 153
    Prague's Best 49
    Street-by-Street map 149
Botanická zahrada 153
Botels (floating hotels) 182
Bourdon, Sébastien 115
Brahe, Tycho 29, 41, 118, 119
    tomb of 67, 70

E

Elbe (river) 54
Eleanor of Toledo (Bronzino) 115
Electrical adaptors 227
Elite 199, 204
Elizabeth, St 139
Elizabeth of Pomerania 42
Embassies 226
Embassy of the Czech Republic 184
Emergency telephone numbers 221
The Engraver Vorlíček and his Family
  (Purkyně) 93
Entertainment 210–15
Equestrienne (Chagall) 115
Ernst, Max 115
Eros (de Vries) 126
Esplanade 186, 189
Estates Theatre 65, 212, 214
  Street-by-Street map 63
Ethnographical Museum 174
Europa Hotel *see* Hotel Europa
Events (seasonal) 50–53
Evropa 186, 188
Exhibition Ground 162, 213
  Prague's Best 40
  Royal Enclosure walk 176–7

F

Fabricius, Philipp 105
Fakultní Poliklinika 221
Fanta, Josef 148
Faust House 153
  Street-by-Street map 149
Faustův Dům 153
Fauves 40
Feast of the Rosary (Dürer) 114
Federation of Persons with
  Disabilities 226
Felix de Valois, St 136
Fénix Palace 145
Ferdinand I, Emperor 19, 28, 79
  Archbishop's Palace 111
  Belvedere 110
  Loreto 116
  Mausoleum 103
  Prague Castle 95
  Royal Garden 111
Ferdinand II, Emperor 19, 30, 126
  Church of St Giles, 75
  defenestration (of 1618) 105, 110
Ferdinand III, Emperor 19
Ferdinand V, Emperor 19, 172
Ferrer, St Vincent 137
Festivals 50–53, 211
Fiala, Zdeněk 56
Fighting Giants (Platzer) 96
Filippi, Giovanni Maria 130
Films *see* Cinemas
Fire services 221
First Aid Centre 221
Fischer, Jiří 177
Fischer von Erlach, Johann
  Bernhard 65, 78
Fišerovo Knihkupectví 209
Fišer's Bookshop 208, 209
Fish Restaurant 203

Five Songs (Tulka) 156
Flats (agencies) 184
Flekovský, Jakub 155
Florian's Yard 202
Florianův Dvůr 191, 198, 202
Folk Art Products 208, 209
Folk Figurines (shop) 208, 209
Food and drink 194–7
  shops 208, 209
  see also Restaurants
Foreign Literature (shop) 208, 209
Forman, Miloš 63
Fountains
  Křižík 51, 176
  Singing 46, 48, 111
  Venus 46
Francis of Assisi, St 137
Francis Xavier, St 138
Franciscan Garden 146
  Street-by-Street map 144
Franciscans 65, 146
Frankovka 197
Františkánská zahrada 146
Franz II, Emperor 19, 121
Franz Ferdinand, Archduke 167
Franz Josef, Emperor 19, 32, 33
Franz Kafka Gallery 69
Franz Kafka Theatre 212, 214
Frederick of the Palatinate 30,
  72, 103
Fringe theatres 212
Fučík, Julius 162
Funicular railway 141
Fux, Jan 134
FX Café 199, 202

G

Galerie Lukas 209
Gall's Town 71
Gallas de Campo, Jan 78
Galli, Agostino 118
Gambrinus, King of Beer 196
Gans, David 86
Garden on the Ramparts 110
Gardens
  Prague's Best 46–9
  see also Parks and gardens
Gauguin, Paul 40, 115
George, St 96
George of Poděbrady 19, 26, 27
  Church of Our Lady before Týn 70
  Palace of the Lords of Kunštát 77
*George of Poděbrady and
  Matthias Corvinus* (Aleš) 92
Ghetto *see* Jewish Quarter
Gift shops 208–9
Gifts (shop) 208, 209
Glass
  Bohemian 41, 206, 208
  Museum of Decorative Arts 84
  shops 208, 209
Globe Bookstore Café 199, 203
Godmother (restaurant) 202
Godyn, Abraham
  Personification of Justice 164
  Troja Palace frescoes 165

Goethe, Johann Wolfgang von 169
Gogol, Maxim 169
Golden Age of Czech Art
  (Ženíšek) 156
Golden Dragon 204
Golden Horseshoe 130
Golden Lane 99
  Street-by-Street map 97
Golem 88
Golz-Kinský Palace 66, 70
  Prague's Best 47, 49
  Street-by-Street map 62
Good Soldier Švejk, The (Hašek) 33,
  154, 190
Gossaert, Jan 114
Gothic architecture 44
Gottwald, Klement 19, 34, 160
  proclaims Communist state 69, 70
Goya, Francisco de 115
Grand Priory of the
  Knights of Malta 131, 133
Grand Priory Mill 56
Grand Priory Square 131
  Street-by-Street map 132
El Greco, *Head of Christ* 113, 115
Green Lobster 130
The Guardian 227
Guarini, Guarino 128
Gutfreund, Otto 40, 163
  Commerce 40

H

Habermel, Erasmus 84
Habsburg dynasty 17, 18, 110
Hanavský Pavilion 56, 161
Hans von Aachen 109
Hanuš (clockmaker) 74
Harmony (hotel) 186, 187
Harovník, Fabian 99
Hartig Garden 110
Hašek, Jaroslav 154
Havel, Václav 19, 96
  Civic Forum 144
  Velvet Revolution 34, 35
Havel Market 207, 209
Havelské Město 71
Havlíček, Milan 161
Haydn, Josef 41
Haymaking (Breughel) 112, 114
Head of Christ (El Greco) 113, 115
Health care 220, 221
Hedvika Francesca Wussin
  (Kupecký) 109
Heermann, Johann Georg and Paul
  Troja Palace sculptures 164
Heger, Filip 67
Heger, František 67
Heinsch, Jan Jiří 90, 109, 152, 155
Heinsch, Josef 65
Hell (restaurant) 201
Henlein, Konrad 34
Hercules (Braun) 47, 78
Heydrich, Reinhard 34, 51, 152
High Synagogue 85
  Prague's Best 41, 45
  Street-by-Street map 82

Acknowledgments

DORLING KINDERSLEY wishes to thank the following people who contributed to the preparation of this book.

MAIN CONTRIBUTOR
Vladimír Soukup was born in Prague in 1949. He worked for the daily newpaper, *Evening Prague*, for 20 years, eventually becoming Deputy Chief Editor. He has written a wide range of popular guides to Prague.

ADDITIONAL CONTRIBUTORS
Ben Sullivan, Lynn Reich

ADDITIONAL EDITORS, RESEARCHERS AND DESIGNERS
Alistair Gunn, Elaine Harries, Charlie Hawkings, Jan Kaplan, Susannah Marriott, Robert Purnell, Helen Townsend, Daphne Trotter, Christopher Vinz.

ADDITIONAL PHOTOGRAPHY
DK Studio/Steve Gorton, Clive Streeter.

PICTURE CREDITS
Every effort has been made to trace the copyright holders and we apologize in advance for any unintentional omissions. We would be pleased to insert the appropriate acknowledgments in any subsequent edition of this publication.

t = top; tl = top left; tc = top centre; tr = top right; cla = centre left above; ca = centre above; cra = centre right above; cl = centre left; c = centre; cr = centre right; clb = centre left below; cb = centre below; crb = centre right below; bl = bottom left; b = bottom; bc = bottom centre; br = bottom right; d = detail.

Works of art on the pages detailed have been reproduced with the permission of the following copyright holders:

©ADAGP, Paris and DACS, London 1994: 115t; DACS 1994: 112tl, 113br.

Gustav Makarius Tauc (An der Aulenkaut 31, Wiesbaden, Germany) under commission of the Minorite Order in Rome: 35br.

The publishers are grateful to the following individuals, companies and picture libraries for permission to reproduce photographs or to photograph at their establishments:

ARCHEOLOGICKÝ ÚSTAV ČESKÉ AKADEMIE VĚD: 20t; ARCHIV FÜR KUNST UND GESCHICHTE, BERLIN: 17b, 18tl (d), 18tr, 18bc(d), 18br(d), 19tl(d), 19tc(d), 19tr(d), 19c(d), 19bc(d), 20clr, 20bl, 23cb(d), 29cla(d), 32t(d), 32bl, 34ca(d), 35ca(d), 35bl, 43tl, 50b(d), 105cr, 118t, Erich Lessing 28ca(d), 31bl(d), 88c, 89cb, 106c; ARCHÍV HLAVNIHO MESTA. PRAHY (CLAM-GALLASŮV PALÁC): 23cl, 24bl, 28bl, 28br, 30b, 33clb, 33bc, 72t, 136br, 137br(d), 138ca, 168c.

BILDARCHIV PREUSSISCHER KULTURBESITZ: 4t(d), 19bl(d), 29br, 34bc, 68tr, 104bl(d); BRIDGEMAN ART LIBRARY, London: Prado, Madrid 29t; Rosegarten Museum, Constance 26ca.

ČESKÁ TISKOVÁ KANCELÁŘ: 19br, 35cbr, 195cr; ČSA: 228t; JEAN-LOUP CHARMET: 18bl(d), 21c, 31br, 33t,

33bl, 33br(d), 34tr(d), 34bl, 62c, 69tc; COMSTOCK: Georg Gerster: 10; JOE CORNISH: 58–9, 60, 148br.

MARY EVANS PICTURE LIBRARY: 9, 59, 138cb, 181, 217.

GRAFOPRINT NEUBERT: 31clb, 38clb, 116c.

ROBERT HARDING PICTURE LIBRARY: Michael Jenner 128tl; Christopher Rennie 24ca, 103tr; Peter Scholey 30t, 129tl; HUTCHISON LIBRARY: Libuše Taylor 50c, 51b, 52t, 175tl, 197c.

Courtesy of ISIC, UK: 226c.

KANCELÁŘ PREZIDENTA REPUBLIKY: 20–1, 21tr, 21bl, 21br, 22c; KARLŠTEJN: 25tl; Vladimír Hyhlík 24–5, KAREL KESTNER: 35cbl; KLEMENTINUM: 23tl; Prokop Paul 22t; THE KOBAL COLLECTION: 35tl; DALIBOR KUSÁK: 164bl, 166–7 all, 16–9 all.

IVAN MALÝ: 210t, 211t; MUZEUM HLAVNÍHO MĚSTA PRAHY 32–3; MUZEUM POŠTOVNÍ ZNÁMKY: 149cl;

NÁRODNÍ FILMOVÝ ARCHIV: 34br; NÁRODNÍ GALERIE V PRAZE: 24br, 40b; Grafická sbírka 26t, 27bl, 31t, 67b, 69c, 100t, 102b, 121t, 125cb, 129br, 138b, 157cb, 173b, 178b; Klášter sv. Anežky 39tr, 83t, 92–3 all, 133b; Klášter sv. Jiří 16, 37br, 38t, 97br, 106–7 all except 106c, 108–9 all, Šternberský palác 38ca, 112–3 all, 114–5 all, Zbraslav 40b; NÁRODNÍ MUZEUM V PRAZE: Vlasta Dvořáková 20clb, 26–7, 26bl, 26bc, 26br, 27t, 27cl, 27cr, 27br, 29bl, 39cb, 75b, 72b, Jarmila Kutová 20c, 22bl, Dagmar Landová 28bc, 126c, Muzeum Antonína Dvořáka 39b, Muzeum Bedřicha Smetany 32ca, Prokop Paul 75b, Tyršovo muzeum; 34cb, 149bl; NÁRODNÍ TECHNICKÉ MUZEUM: Gabriel Urbánek 41t.

OBRAZÁRNA PRAŽSKÉHO HRADU: 98b; ÖSTERREICHISCHE NATIONALBIBLIOTHEK, WIEN: 25clb, 26cb.

PIVOVARSKÉ MUZEUM: 196rc, 196c; BOHUMÍR PROKŮPEK: 25bl, 30t, 120c, 121c, 121bl, 163b.

REX FEATURES LTD: Alfred 35tr, Richard Gardener 232t.

SCIENCE PHOTO LIBRARY: Geospace 11, 38crb; SOTHEBY'S/ THAMES AND HUDSON: 104c; STÁTNÍ ÚSTREDNÍ ARCHIV: 23b; STÁTNÍ ÚSTAV PAMÁTKOVÉ PÉČE: 23tc; STÁTNÍ ŽIDOVSKÉ MUZEUM: 39ca, 85t, 85c, 90t; SVATOVÍTSKÝ POKLAD, PRAŽSKÝ HRAD: 14t, 21tl, 24t, 24cb, 28t, 40tr.

UMĚLECKOPRÚMYSLOVÉ MUZEUM V PRAZE: 39tl, 40tl, 149c, 149br, Gabriel Urbánek 28clb, 41b; UNIVERZITA KARLOVA: 25tr.

PETER WILSON: 4b, 191t, 216–7, 238.

ZEFA: 33cra.

Front endpaper: all special or additional photography except (centre) JOE CORNISH.

Phrase Book

IN EMERGENCY

Help!	Pomoc!	*po-mots*
Stop!	Zastavte!	*za-stav-te*
Call a doctor!	Zavolejte doktora!	*za-vo-ley-te dok-to-ra!*
Call an ambulance!	Zavolejte sanitku!	*za-vo-ley-te sa-nit-ku!*
Call the police!	Zavolejte policii!	*za-vo-ley-te poli-tsi-yi!*
Call the fire brigade!	Zavolejte hasiče	*za-vol-ey-te ba-si-che*
Where is the telephone?	Kde je telefón?	*gde ye tele-fohn?*
the nearest hospital?	nejbližší nemocnice?	*ney-blish-ee ne-mots-nyitse?*

COMMUNICATION ESSENTIALS

Yes/No	Ano/Ne	*ano/ne*
Please	Prosím	*pro-seem*
Thank you	Děkuji vám	*dye-ku-ji vahm*
Excuse me	Prosím vás	*pro-seem vahs*
Hello	Dobrý den	*do-bree den*
Goodbye	Na shledanou	*na s-ble-da-no*
Good evening	Dobrý večer	*dob-ree vech-er*
morning	ráno	*rah-no*
afternoon	odpoledne	*od-po-led-ne*
evening	večer	*ve-cher*
yesterday	včera	*vche-ra*
today	dnes	*dnes*
tomorrow	zítra	*zeet-ra*
here	tady	*ta-di*
there	tam	*tam*
What?	Co?	*tso?*
When?	Kdy?	*gdi?*
Why?	Proč?	*proch?*
Where?	Kde?	*gde?*

USEFUL PHRASES

How are you?	Jak se máte?	*yak-se mah-te?*
Very well, thank you.	Velmi dobře děkuji.	*vel-mi dob-rzhe dye kuyi.*
Pleased to meet you.	Těší mě.	*tyesh-ee mye*
See you soon.	Uvidíme se brzy.	*u-vi-dyee-me-se-br-zi*
That's fine.	To je v pořádku.	*to ye vpo-rzhahdku*
Where is/are...?	Kde je/jsou ...?	*gde ye/jsou ...?*
How long does it take to get to..?	Jak dlouho to trvá se dostat do..?	*yak dlo ho to tr-va se do-stat do...?*
How do I get to..?	Jak se dostanu k ..?	*yak se do-sta-nu k ...?*
Do you speak English?	Mluvíte anglicky?	*mlu-vee-te an-glits-ki?*
I don't understand.	Nerozumím.	*ne-ro-zu-meem*
Could you speak more slowly?	Mohl(a)* byste mluvit trochu pomaleji?	*mohl- (a) bis-te mlu-vit tro-khu po-maley?*
Pardon?	Prosím?	*pro-seem?*
I'm lost.	Ztratil(a)* jsem se.	*stra-tyil (a) ysem se.*

USEFUL WORDS

big	velký	*vel-kee*
small	malý	*mal-ee*
hot	horký	*bor-kee*
cold	studený	*stu-den-ee*
good	dobrý	*dob-ree*
bad	špatný	*shpat-nee*
well	dobře	*dob-rzhe*
open	otevřeno	*ot-ev-rzhe-no*
closed	zavřeno	*zav-rzhe-no*
left	do leva	*do le-va*
right	do prava	*do pra-va*
straight on	rovně	*rov-nye*
near	blízko	*blee-sko*
far	daleko	*da-le-ko*
up	nahoru	*na-ho-ru*
down	dolů	*do-loo*
early	brzy	*br-zi*
late	pozdě	*poz-dye*
entrance	vchod	*vkhod*
exit	východ	*vee-khod*
toilets	toalety	*toa-leti*
free, unoccupied	volný	*vol-nee*
free, no charge	zdarma	*zdar-ma*

MAKING A TELEPHONE CALL

I'd like to place a long-distance call.	Chtěl(a)* bych volat meziměstsky.	*khtyel(a) bikh vo-lat me-zi-mye-stski*
I'd like to make a reverse-charge call.	Chtěl(a)* bych volat na účet volaného.	*khtyel(a) bikh volat na oo-chet volan-eh-ho*
I'll try again later.	Zkusím to později.	*skus-eem to poz-dyey*
Can I leave a message?	Mohu nechat zprávu?	*mo-bu ne-khat sprah-vu?*
Hold on.	Počkejte.	*poch-key-te*
Could you speak up a little, please?	Mohl(a)* byste mluvit hlasitěji?	*mo-bl (a) bis-te mluvit bla-si-tyey?*
local call	místní hovor	*meest-nyee bov-or*

SIGHTSEEING

art gallery	galerie	*ga-ler-riye*
bus stop	autobusová zastávka	*au-to-bus-o-vah za-stah-vka*
church	kostel	*kos-tel*
garden	zahrada	*za bra-da*
library	knihovna	*knyi-bov-na*
museum	muzeum	*muz-e-um*
railway station	nádraží	*nab-dra-zhee*
tourist information	turistické informace	*tooristi-iske in-for-ma-tse*
closed for the public holiday	státní svátek	*staht-nyee svab-tek*

SHOPPING

How much does this cost?	Co toto stojí?	*tso to-to sto-yee?*
I would like ...	Chtěl(a)* bych ...	*khtyel(a) bikh...*
Do you have ...?	Máte ...?	*maa-te ...?*
I'm just looking.	Jenom se dívám.	*ye-nom se dyee-vahm*
Do you take credit cards?	Berete kreditní karty?	*be-re-te kred-it nyee karti?*
What time do you open/close?	V kolik otevíráte/zavíráte?	*v ko-lik o-te-vee-rah-te/za vee rah-te?*
this one	tento	*ten-to*
that one	tamten	*tam-ten*
expensive	drahý	*dra-hee*
cheap	levný	*lev-nee*
size	velikost	*vel-ik-ost*
white	bílý	*bee-lee*
black	černý	*cher-nee*
red	červený	*cher-ven-ee*
yellow	žlutý	*zblu-tee*
green	zelený	*zel-en-ee*
blue	modrý	*mod-ree*
brown	hnědý	*bnyed-ee*

TYPES OF SHOP

antique shop	starožitnictví	*sta-ro zbit--nyits-tvee*
bank	banka	*banka*
bakery	pekárna	*pe-kabr-na*
bookstore	knihkupectví	*knib-kupets-tvee*
butcher	řeznictví	*rzbez-nyits-tvee*
camera shop	obchod s fotoaparaty	*op-kbot sfoto-aparabti*
chemist (prescriptions etc)	lékárna	*leh-kab-rna*
chemist (cosmetics, toiletries etc)	drogerie	*drog-erye*
delicatessen	lahůdky	*la-boo-dki*
department store	obchodní dům	*op-kbod-nyee doom*
grocery	potraviny	*pot-ra-vini*
glass	sklo	*sklo*
hairdresser (ladies)	kadeřnictví	*ka-derzb-nyits-tvee*
(mens)	holič	*bo-lich*
market	trh	*trkb*
newsstand	novinový stánek	*no-vi-novee stab-nek*
post office	pošta	*posb-ta*
supermarket	samoobsluha	*sa-mo-ob-slu-ba*
tobacconist	tabák	*ta-babk*
travel agency	cestovní kancelář	*tses-tov-nyi kantse-laarzb*

*Alternatives for a female speaker are shown in brackets.

STAYING IN A HOTEL

Do you have a vacant room?	Máte volný pokoj?	*mah-te vol-nee po-koy?*
double room	dvoulůžkový pokoj	*dvo-loozh-kovee po-koy*
with double bed	s dvojitou postelí	*sdvoy-to pos-telee*
twin room	pokoj s dvěma postelemi	*po-koy sdvye-ma pos-tel-emi*
room with a bath	pokoj s koupelnou	*po-koy s ko-pel-no*
porter	vrátný	*vraht-nee*
hall porter	nosič	*nos-ich*
key	klíč	*kleech*
I have a reservation.	Mám reservaci.	*mahm rez-ervatsi*

EATING OUT

Have you got a table for ...?	Máte stůl pro ...?	*mah-te stool pro ...?*
I'd like to reserve a table.	Chtěl(a)* bych rezervovat stůl.	*khtyel(a) bikh rez-er-vov-at stool*
breakfast	snídaně	*snyee-danye*
lunch	oběd	*ob-yed*
dinner	večeře	*vech e-rzhe*
The bill, please.	Prosím, účet.	*pro-seem oo-chet*
I am a vegetarian.	Jsem vegetarián(ka)*.	*ysem veghe-tariahn(ka)*
waitress!	slečno	*slech-no*
waiter!	pane vrchní!	*pane vrkh-nyee!*
fixed price menu	standardní menu	*stan-dard-nyee men-u*
dish of the day	nabídka dne	*nab-eed-ka dne*
starter	předkrm	*przhed-krm*
main course	hlavní jídlo	*hlav-nyee yeed-lo*
vegetables	zelenina	*zel-en-yin-a*
dessert	zákusek	*zah-kusek*
cover charge	poplatek	*pop-la-tek*
wine list	nápojový lístek	*nah-po-yo-vee lee-stek*
rare (steak)	krvavý	*kr-va-vee*
medium	středně udělaný	*strzhed-nye ud-yel-an-ee*
well done	dobře udělaný	*dobrzhe- ud-yel-an-ee*
glass	sklenice	*sklen-yitse*
bottle	láhev	*lah-hev*
knife	nůž	*noozh*
fork	vidlička	*vid-lich-ka*
spoon	lžíce	*lzhee-tse*

MENU DECODER

biftek	*bif-tek*	steak
bílé víno	*bee-leh vee-no*	white wine
bramborové knedlíky	*bram-bo-ro-veh kne-dleeki*	potato dumplings
brambory	*bram-bo-ri*	potatoes
chléb	*khlebb*	bread
cibule	*tsi-bu-le*	onion
citrónový džus	*tsi-tron-o-vee dzhuus*	lemon juice
cukr	*tsukr*	sugar
čaj	*chay*	tea
čerstvé ovoce	*cher-stveh-o-vo-ce*	fresh fruit
červené víno	*cher-ven-eh vee-no*	red wine
česnek	*ches-nek*	garlic
dort	*dort*	cake
fazole	*fa-zo-le*	beans
grilované	*gril-ov-a-neh*	grilled
houby	*ho-bi*	mushrooms
houska	*hous-ka*	roll
houskové knedlíky	*ho-sko-veh kne-dleeki*	bread dumplings
hovězí	*hov-ye-zee*	beef
hranolky	*hran-ol-ki*	chips
husa	*hu-sa*	goose
jablko	*ya-bl-ko*	apple
jahody	*ya-ho-di*	strawberries
jehněčí	*ye-hnye-chee*	lamb
kachna	*kakh-na*	duck
kapr	*ka-pr*	carp
káva	*kah-va*	coffee
krevety	*krev-et-i*	prawns
kuře	*ku-rzhe*	chicken
kyselé zelí	*kis-el-eh zel-ee*	sauerkraut
maso	*ma-so*	meat
máslo	*mah-slo*	butter
minerálka	*min-er-ahl-ka*	mineral water
šumivá/ nešumivá	*shum-i-vah/ ne-shum i-vah*	fizzy/ still

mléko	*mleh-ko*	milk
mořská jídla	*morzh-skah-yeed-la-*	seafood
ocet	*ots-et*	vinegar
okurka	*o-ku-rka*	cucumber
olej	*oley*	oil
párek	*paa-rek*	sausage/frankfurter
pečené	*petsh-en-eh*	baked
pečené	*pech-en-eh*	roast
pepř	*peprzh*	pepper
polévka	*pol-eh-vka*	soup
pomeranč	*po-me-ranch*	orange
pomerančový džús	*po-me-ran-ch-- o-vee dzhuus*	orange juice
pivo	*pi-vo*	beer
rajské	*rayskeh*	tomato
ryba	*rib-a*	fish
rýže	*ree-zhe*	rice
salát	*sal-at*	salad
sůl	*sool*	salt
sýr	*seer*	cheese
šunka	*shun-ka*	ham
vařená/ uzená	*varzh-enah u-zenah*	cooked smoked
telecí	*te-le-tsee*	veal
tuna	*tu-na*	tuna
vajíčko	*va-yee-chko*	egg
vařené	*varzh-en-eh*	boiled
vepřové	*vep-rzho-veh*	pork
voda	*vo-da*	water
vývar	*vee-var*	broth
zelí	*zel-ee*	cabbage
zelenina	*zel-enyina*	vegetables
zmrzlina	*zmrz-lin-a*	ice cream

NUMBERS

1	jedna	*yed-na*
2	dvě	*dvye*
3	tři	*trzhi*
4	čtyři	*chti-rzhi*
5	pět	*pyet*
6	šest	*shest*
7	sedm	*sedm*
8	osm	*osm*
9	devět	*dev-yet*
10	deset	*des-et*
11	jedenáct	*ye-de-nahtst*
12	dvanáct	*dva-nahtst*
13	třináct	*trzhi-nahtst*
14	čtrnáct	*chtr-nahtst*
15	patnáct	*pat-nahtst*
16	šestnáct	*shest-nahtst*
17	sedmnáct	*sedm-nahtst*
18	osmnáct	*osm-nahtst*
19	devatenáct	*de-va-te-nahtst*
20	dvacet	*dva-tset*
21	dvacet jedna	*dva-tset yed-na*
22	dvacet dva	*dva-tset dva*
23	dvacet tři	*dva-tset-trzhi*
24	dvacet čtyři	*dva-tset chti-rzhi*
25	dvacet pět	*dva-tset pyet*
30	třicet	*trzhi-tset*
40	čtyřicet	*chti-rzhi-tset*
50	padesát	*pa-de-saht*
60	šedesát	*she-de-saht*
70	sedmdesát	*sedm-de-saht*
80	osmdesát	*osm-de-saht*
90	devadesát	*de-va-de-saht*
100	sto	*sto*
1,000	tisíc	*tyi-seets*
2,000	dva tisíce	*dva tyi-see-tse*
5,000	pět tisíc	*pyet tyi-seets*
1,000,000	milión	*mi-li-ohn*

TIME

one minute	jedna minuta	*yed-na min-uta*
one hour	jedna hodina	*yed-na hod-yin-a*
half an hour	půl hodiny	*pool hod-yin-i*
day	den	*den*
week	týden	*tee-den*
Monday	pondělí	*pon-dye-lee*
Tuesday	úterý	*oo-ter-ee*
Wednesday	středa	*strzhe-da*
Thursday	čtvrtek	*chtvr-tek*
Friday	pátek	*pah-tek*
Saturday	sobota	*so-bo-ta*
Sunday	neděle	*ned-yel-e*

Alternatives for a female speaker are shown in brackets.

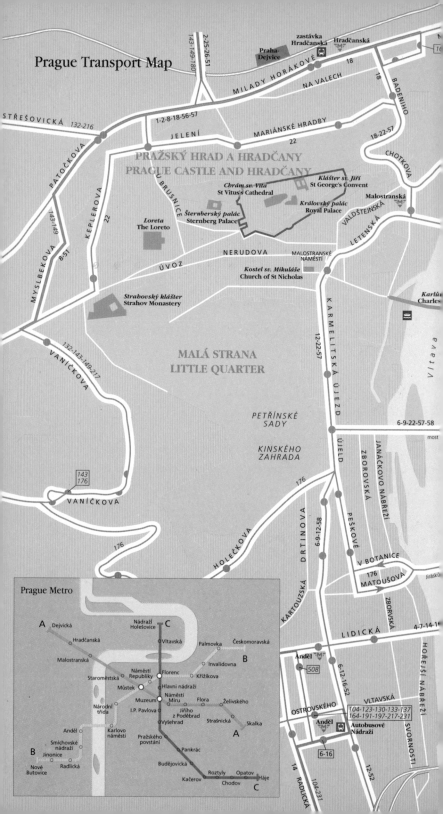